Vienna

THE ROUGH GUIDE

KU-295-967

There are more than one hundred Rough Guide titles
covering destinations from Amsterdam to Zimbabwe

Forthcoming titles include
Jamaica • New Zealand •
South Africa • Southwest USA

Rough Guide Reference Series
Classical Music • The Internet • Jazz • Opera• Rock Music • World Music

Rough Guide Phrasebooks
Czech • French • German • Greek • Hindi & Urdu • Indonesian • Italian
Mandarin Chinese • Mexican Spanish • Polish • Portuguese • Russian
Spanish • Thai • Turkish • Vietnamese

Rough Guides on the Internet
http://www.roughguides.com
http://www.hotwired.com/rough

Rough Guide Credits

Editor:	Samantha Cook
Series Editor:	Mark Ellingham
Editorial:	Martin Dunford, Jonathan Buckley, Jo Mead, Kate Berens, Amanda Tomlin, Ann-Marie Shaw, Paul Gray, Vivienne Heller, Sarah Dallas, Chris Schüler, Helena Smith, Kirk Marlow, Julia Kelly (UK); Andrew Rosenberg (US)
Online Editors:	Alan Spicer (UK); Geronimo Madrid (US)
Production:	Susanne Hillen, Andy Hilliard, Judy Pang, Link Hall, Nicola Williamson, Helen Ostick
Cartography:	Melissa Flack, David Callier, Maxine Burke
Finance:	John Fisher, Celia Crowley, Catherine Gillespie
Marketing & Publicity:	Richard Trillo, Simon Carloss, Niki Smith (UK); Jean-Marie Kelly, SoRelle Braun (US)
Administration:	Tania Hummel, Alexander Mark Rogers

Acknowledgements

At Rough Guides a very, very big thanks to Sam Cook for her enthusiasm beyond the call, also to Amanda Tomlin, Helen Ostick, David Callier, Melissa Flack, Andrew Rosenberg and Narrell Leffman; and to Susannah Walker for proofreading. Thanks, too, to Roman Wiche at the Austrian Youth Hostel Association; Marion Telsnig at the ANTO; Bettina for helping me out in several tight corners; Katya and her Berliners; Sara, Gordon, Val and Al for making it out there, ditto Kate, Josh and Stan, not to mention David (briefly); and Petr and Paula for weekends off.

The publishers and authors have done their best to ensure the accuracy and currency of all information in The Rough Guide to Vienna; however, they can accept no responsibility for any loss, injury, or inconvenience sustained by any traveller as a result of information or advice contained in the guide.

This edition published July 1997 by Rough Guides Ltd, 1 Mercer Street, London WC2H 9QJ.
Distributed by the Penguin Group:

Penguin Books Ltd, 27 Wrights Lane, London W8 5TZ.

Penguin Books USA Inc, 375 Hudson Street, New York 10014, USA.

Penguin Books Australia Ltd, 487 Maroondah Highway, PO Box 257, Ringwood, Victoria 3134, Australia.

Penguin Books Canada Ltd, 10 Alcorn Avenue, Toronto, Ontario, Canada M4V 1E4.

Penguin Books (NZ) Ltd, 182–190 Wairau Road, Auckland 10, New Zealand.

Printed in England by Clays Ltd, St Ives PLC

Typography and **original design** by Jonathan Dear and The Crowd Roars.

Illustrations throughout by Edward Briant.

© Rob Humphreys 1997.

368pp. Includes index.

A catalogue record for this book is available from the British Library.

ISBN 1-85828-244-6

Vienna

THE ROUGH GUIDE

Written and researched by
Rob Humphreys

THE ROUGH GUIDES

Help us update

We've gone to a lot of trouble to ensure that this first edition of the *Rough Guide to Vienna* is accurate and up-to-date. However, things inevitably change, and if you feel we've got it wrong or left something out, we'd like to know: any suggestions, comments or corrections would be much appreciated. We'll credit all contributions and send a copy of the next edition – or any other *Rough Guide* if you prefer – for the best correspondence.

Please mark letters "Rough Guide to Vienna" and send to:
Rough Guides, 1 Mercer St, London WC2H 9QJ or
Rough Guides, 375 Hudson St, 9th floor, New York, NY 10014.

E-mail should be sent to:
mail@roughguides.co.uk

Online updates about Rough Guide titles can be found on our website at http://www.roughguides.com

Rough Guides

Travel Guides • Phrasebooks • Music and Reference Guides

We set out to do something different when the first Rough Guide was published in 1982. Mark Ellingham, just out of University, was travelling in Greece. He brought along the popular guides of the day, but found they were all lacking in some way. They were either strong on ruins and museums but went on for pages without mentioning a beach or taverna. Or they were so conscious of the need to save money that they lost sight of Greece's cultural and historical significance. Also, none of the books told him anything about Greece's contemporary life – its politics, its culture, its people, and how they lived.

So with no job in prospect, Mark decided to write his own guidebook, one which aimed to provide practical information that was second to none, detailing the best beaches and the hottest clubs and restaurants, while also giving hard hitting accounts of every sight, both famous and obscure, and providing up-to-the-minute information on contemporary culture. It was a guide that encouraged independent travellers to find the best of Greece, and was a great success, getting shortlisted for the Thomas Cook travel guide award, and encouraging Mark, along with three friends, to expand the series.

The Rough Guide list grew rapidly and the letters flooded in, indicating a much broader readership than had been anticipated, but one which uniformly appreciated the Rough Guides' mix of practical detail and humour, irreverence and enthusiasm. Things haven't changed. The same four friends who began the series are still the caretakers of the Rough Guide mission today: to provide the most reliable, up-to-date and entertaining information to independent-minded travellers of all ages, on all budgets.

We now publish 100 titles and have offices in London and New York. The travel guides are written and researched by a dedicated team of more than 100 authors, based in Britain, Europe, the USA and Australia. We have also created a unique series of phrasebooks to accompany the travel series, along with the acclaimed series of music guides, and a best-selling pocket guide to the Internet and World Wide Web. We also publish comprehensive travel information on our two websites: http://www.hotwired.com/rough and http://www.roughguides.com

The Author

Rob Humphreys joined Rough Guides in 1989, having worked as a failed actor, taxi driver and male model. He has travelled extensively in central and eastern Europe, writing guides to Prague, the Czech and Slovak Republics, and St Petersburg, as well as London. He has lived in London since 1988.

Contents

List of Maps

MAP SYMBOLS

- - - -	Chapter division boundary	∴	Ruin
-∎-∎-	International boundary	✕	Airport
═══	Road	✚	Church
────	Railway	✡	Synagogue
~~	River/canal	✉	Post office
▓▓	Urban area	ⓘ	Information office
▒▒	Park	Ⓤ	U-Bahn
░░	Forest	Ⓢ	S-Bahn

Introduction

Most people visit Vienna with a vivid image of the city in their minds: a monumental vision of Habsburg palaces, trotting white horses, old ladies in fur coats and mountains of fat cream cakes. And they're unlikely to be disappointed in this city that positively feeds off imperial nostalgia – High Baroque churches and aristocratic piles pepper the old town or Innere Stadt, monumental projects from the late nineteenth century line the Ringstrasse, and postcards of the Emperor Franz-Josef and his beautiful wife Elisabeth still sell by the sackful. Just as compelling as the old Habsburg stand-bys are the wonderful Jugendstil and early modernist buildings, product of *fin-de-siècle* Vienna, when the city emerged as one of Europe's great cultural centres. This was the era of Freud, Klimt, Schiele and Schönberg, when the city's famous coffeehouses were filled with intellectuals from every corner of the empire. In a sense, this was Vienna's golden age, after which all has been in decline: with the end of the empire in 1918, the city was reduced from a metropolis of over two million, capital of a vast empire of fifty million, to one of barely more than one-and-a-half million, federal capital of a small country of just eight million souls.

Given the city's twentieth-century history, it's hardly surprising that the Viennese are as keen as anyone to continue plugging the good old days. This is a place, not unlike Berlin, which has had the misfortune of serving as a weather vane of European history. Modern anti-semitism as a politically viable force was invented here, in front of Hitler's very eyes, in the first decade of the century. It was the assassination of an arrogant Austrian archduke that started World War I, while the battles between Left and Right fought out in the streets of Vienna mirrored those in Berlin in the 1930s. The weekend Hitler enjoyed his greatest electoral victory in the Reichstag was the day the Austrians themselves invented Austro-fascism. In 1938, the country became the first victim of Nazi expansion, greeting the Führer with delirious enthusiasm. And after the war, for a decade, Vienna was divided, like Berlin, into French, American, British and Soviet sectors.

The visual scars from this turbulent history are few and far between – even Hitler's sinister Flacktürme are confined to the suburbs – but the destruction of the city's once enormous Jewish community is a wound that has proved harder to heal. Vienna's Jewish intellectuals and capitalists were the driving force behind much of the city's *fin-de-siècle* culture. Little surprise then, that the city has struggled since to live up to its glorious past achievements. After the war Vienna lost its cosmopolitan character and found itself stuck in a monocultural straightjacket. Since the end of the Cold War, however, this has begun to change, with a second wave of immigrants from the former provinces of the old empire. Whether Vienna will learn to accept its new, multicultural identity remains to be seen.

For all its problems, Vienna is still an inspiring city to visit, with one of the world's greatest art collections in the Kunsthistorisches Museum, world-class orchestras, and a superb architectural heritage. It's also an eminently civilized place, clean, safe (for the most part) and peopled by a courteous population who do their best to live up to their reputation for Gemütlichkeit or "cosiness". And despite its ageing population, it's also a city with a lively nightlife, of late opening Musikcafés and drinking holes. Even Vienna's traditional restaurants, long famous for quantity over quality, have discovered innovative methods of cooking and presentation, and are now supplemented by a wide range of ethnic restaurants.

When to go

Lying at the centre of Europe, Vienna experiences the extremes of temperature typical of a continental climate with hot summers and correspondingly cold winters. In terms of weather, therefore, late spring and early autumn are by far the best times to visit. There are other reasons, too, for avoiding July and August in particular, as this is when many of the city's theatres and concert halls close down. Sure, there's enough cultural activity to keep the tourists amused, but the Viennese tend to get the hell out. In contrast, Christmas and New Year are peak season in Vienna. Not only does the city look great in the snow – and you can be sure that the Viennese are very efficient about keeping the paths clear – but also the ball season, known as Fasching, gets underway, along with the glittering Christmas markets, and, of course, the world-famous New Year's Day concert.

Basics

Getting there from Britain and Ireland

The easiest way to get to get to Vienna from Britain is by plane. From London, it takes just over two hours (compared with around 24 hours by train), and there are daily direct flights from the capital throughout the year.

By plane

Both Austrian Airlines and British Airways run three or more daily **scheduled flights** from London to Vienna. Austrian Airlines fly out of Heathrow (Terminal 2), while British Airways fly from Heathrow (Terminal 1) and Gatwick (North Terminal). Lauda Air, founded as a charter company in 1979 by Austria's racing ace Niki Lauda, is now a scheduled airline, flying four times a week from Gatwick (North Terminal); it's also the only carrier flying direct from Manchester to Vienna. Though in general, fares vary slightly according to **season** – tending to be highest from April to October and in the two weeks

---

Airlines

Austrian Airlines ☎ 0171/434 7300
British Airways ☎ 0345/222111

Lauda Air ☎ 0171/630 5924

Discount Flight Agents

Campus Travel, 52 Grosvenor Gardens, London SW1W 0AG ☎ 0171/730 3402; 541 Bristol Rd, Selly Oak, Birmingham B29 6AU ☎ 0121/414 1848; 61 Ditchling Rd, Brighton BN1 4SD ☎ 01273/570226; 39 Queen's Rd, Clifton, Bristol BS8 1QE ☎ 0117/929 2494; 5 Emmanuel St, Cambridge CB1 1NE ☎ 01223/324283; 53 Forest Rd, Edinburgh EH1 2QP ☎ 0131/668 3303; 166 Deansgate, Manchester M3 3FE ☎ 0161/833 2046; 105–106 St Aldates, Oxford OX1 1DD ☎ 01865/242067; branches also in YHA shops and on university campuses all over Britain. *Student/youth travel specialist.*

Council Travel, 28a Poland St, London W1V 3DB ☎ 0171/437 7767. Flights and student discounts.

STA Travel, 86 Old Brompton Rd, London SW7 3LH; 117 Euston Rd, London NW1 2SX , 38 Store St London WC1 ☎ 0171/ 361 6161; 25 Queens Rd, Bristol BS8 1QE ☎ 0117/929 4399; 38 Sidney St, Cambridge CB2 3HX ☎ 01223/366966; 75 Deansgate, Manchester M3 2BW ☎ 0161/834 0668; 88 Vicar Lane, Leeds LS1 7JH ☎ 0113/244 9212; 36 George St, Oxford OX1 2OJ ☎ 01865/ 792800; and branches in Birmingham, Canterbury, Cardiff, Coventry, Durham, Glasgow, Loughborough, Nottingham, Warwick and Sheffield. *Student/youth travel specialist.*

Trailfinders, 42–50 Earls Court Rd, London W8 6FT ☎ 0171/937 5400; 194 Kensington High St, London W8 7RG ☎ 0171/938 3939; 58 Deansgate, Manchester M3 2FF ☎ 0161/839 6969; 254–284 Sauchiehall St, Glasgow G2 3EH ☎ 0141/353 2224; 22–24 The Priory, Queensway, Birmingham B4 6BS ☎ 0121/236 1234; 48 Corn St, Bristol BS1 1HQ ☎ 0117/929 9000.

Specialist Operators

Austrian Holidays, 5th Floor, 10 Wardour St, London W1 ☎0171/434 7399.
Austrian package tour specialist run by Austrian Airlines.

Habsburg Heritage Cultural Tours, 158 Rosendale Rd, London SE21 ☎0181/761 0444.
Highbrow cultural tours and independent packages.

Made to Measure, 43 East St, Chichester, West Sussex ☎01243/533333.
Luxury package tour specialist.

Martin Randal Travel, 10 Barley Mow Passage, London W4 ☎0181/994 6477.
Specialists in cultural tours at Christmas in Vienna.

Mondial Travel, 32 Links Rd, West Wycombe, BR4 0QW ☎0181/777 7000.
Specialists in flights and accommodation for central and eastern Europe.

Time Off, Chester Close, Chester St, London SW1 7BQ ☎0171/235 8070.
City breaks.

Travelscene, 11–15 St Ann's Rd, Harrow, Middlesex ☎0181/427 8800.
City breaks.

Worldwide Journeys, 243 Euston Rd, London NW1 ☎0171/388 0888.
City breaks.

around Christmas – all the above airlines offer **economy fares** year round for £200 or so. These tickets are non-changeable, non-refundable, valid for one month and must include a Saturday night in Vienna; you can book them up to the day before you travel (subject to availability).

Though none of the above airlines offers **Apex fares** for London to Vienna as a matter of course, they do pop up from time to time. It's always worth asking, as Apex tickets tend to be £20 or so cheaper. Depending on the specific conditions that apply, they must be bought 7 to 21 days in advance, and you may or may not be offered a 50 percent refund if you cancel before the deadline.

There are no charter flights to Vienna, but **discounted flights**, usually with one of the scheduled airlines, feature in most of the "bucket shop" adverts of the various London freebie magazines, *Time Out, The Evening Standard* and the quality Sunday papers. These can go for as little as £100 return and will certainly bring the price below £150. Note that airport tax will add another £15 or more on to all ticket prices quoted.

Packages and city breaks

Package holiday deals can be worth considering, saving you the hassle of finding accommodation when you arrive or phoning abroad yourself to try and organize it, though it's as well to check the whereabouts of your hotel before commiting yourself. Prices generally work out as equivalent to or less than if you organize every-

thing yourself – the one big disadvantage is that the hotels with the most character are rarely those on offer. Several tour operators can arrange simple flight and accommodation deals: for example, Austrian Holidays offers a city-break, with return flight from London and three nights' accommodation in a three-star hotel for around £300 to £350 depending on the season; Worldwide Journeys offers a similar package for as little as £200 to £230.

If you've more money to spend, it can be worth checking the **specialist agents**, who arrange much more than simply flight and accommodation. Your itinerary and activities will be more carefully mapped out, experienced guides will be on hand to help you get the most out of the sights, and you'll be saved the hassle of chasing after opera tickets and the like. For all this, of course, you pay a hefty all-inclusive price: Martin Randall Travel, for example, charge in excess of £1000 per person for their six-day Christmas package. A list of the main agents – and more specialized tour operators – can found in the box below.

Flights from Ireland

There are no direct flights from anywhere in Ireland to Vienna. The cheapest way of getting there is usually to fly via London, where you can pick up a connecting flight or package (see above). Discount agents such as USIT should be able to organize both legs of your trip.

Airlines in Ireland

Aer Lingus Dublin ☎01/844 4777; Belfast ☎0645/737747.

British Airways Dublin ☎1-800/626747; Belfast ☎0345/222111.

British Midland Dublin ☎01/283 8833; Belfast ☎0345/554554.

Jersey European Belfast ☎0990/676676

Ryanair Dublin ☎01/609 7800; Belfast ☎0541/569569.

Travel Agents and Tour Operators

Joe Walsh Tours, 8–11 Baggot St, Dublin ☎01/676 3053.
General budget fares agent.

Neenan Travel, 12 South Leinster St, Dublin 2 ☎01/676 5181.
European city breaks.

Student & Group Travel, 71 Dame St, Dublin 2 ☎01/677 7834.
Student specialists.

Thomas Cook, 11 Donegall Place, Belfast ☎01232/240833; 118 Grafton St, Dublin ☎01/677 1721.
Package holiday and flight agent, with occasional discount offers.

Travel Shop, 35 Belmont Rd, Belfast 4 ☎01232/471717.
General discount agent.

USIT, Fountain Centre, College St, Belfast BT1 6ET ☎01232/324073; 10–11 Market Parade, Patrick St, Cork ☎021/270900; 33 Ferryquay St, Derry ☎01504/371888; Aston Quay, Dublin 2 ☎01/679 8833; Victoria Place, Eyre Square, Galway ☎091/565177; Central Buildings, O'Connell St, Limerick ☎061/415064; 36–37 George's St, Waterford ☎051/872601.
Student and youth specialists for flights and trains.

There are numerous daily flights **from Dublin** operated by Ryanair, Aer Lingus and British Midland; the cheapest is Ryanair, which costs from around IR£60 return to Luton, Stansted or Gatwick. Aer Lingus fly to Stansted and Heathrow for around IR£70; British Midland offer IR£75 fares to Heathrow.

From Belfast, there are British Airways and British Midland flights to Heathrow for around £75. Jersey European fly from Belfast City to Gatwick, and from Belfast International to Stansted for the same price, though with all three airlines it's worth enquiring about any special deals they might have on offer.

All the above prices are for economy tickets, which are usually non-changeable, non-refundable, and assume you're prepared to travel midweek, and stay a Saturday night. Note Airport tax will add an extra £5 onto all prices quoted.

By train

From **London to Vienna** takes just under 22 hours by train, though if you go via the Channel Tunnel, you can cut the journey time by around six hours.

The routes

Trains leave London's Victoria Station daily at about 11am, arriving – via the **Ramsgate–Ostend** catamaran service – in Vienna's Westbahnhof the following morning at around 9.30am. At the moment, there's a direct train service from Ostend to Vienna from June to September, but in the winter months you must change at Brussels. However, the direct summer service may be discontinued, so check before you set off.

Although you can simply crash out on the seats, you won't get much sleep as the border guards and ticket inspectors wake you up at regular intervals. To travel in more comfort, it's best to book a **couchette** before you leave. Couchettes are mixed sex and allow little privacy but you do get the chance of an unbroken night and free rolls and coffee in the morning. For your very own compartment, you'll need to book a berth in a **sleeper** (and take a friend to share it with). Sleeper compartments are either two-berth or three-berth (the latter being slightly cheaper). If you're travelling alone, however, you will not be required to share with passengers of the opposite sex.

Travelling **Eurostar** from London to Brussels allows you to set off nearly four hours later from London Waterloo, and still catch the same Brussels–Vienna service. If you wish, you can cut a further couple of hours off the journey time by catching the train to Köln, and changing there in the evening for Vienna. This will get you into Vienna at the earlier time of 7.45am.

Tickets and passes

The **standard rail ticket** from London to Vienna is a whopping great £351 return, with an optional further £15 each way for a couchette. The ticket is available from London's Victoria Station and some travel agents, is valid for two months, and allows an unlimited number of stop-overs en route. All you have to do, however, is spend a weekend away during the course of your trip, and the price plummets to £249 return. Further reductions can sometimes be had from Wasteels, who sell **discounted tickets** on the Ramsgate–Ostend route, bringing the price right down to around £200 return. Everyone is eligible for these discounts, when available, and there are no restrictions.

At the moment, it's actually not that expensive to travel via **Eurostar**, who are desperate to get people to use their service, and currently offer a £59 London–Brussels return fare, which, when added to the Brussels–Vienna return fare, gives a grand total of £235. You can book right up to the last minute, subject to availability: the only snag is that you must travel mid-week and book your return journey on Eurostar. The ticket is non-changeable and non-refundable.

If you're under 26 and planning to visit Vienna as part of a more extensive trip round Europe, it may be worth buying an **InterRail pass** (currently £275 a month). InterRail passes are available from major train stations and some travel agents; the only restriction is that you must have been resident in Europe for at least six months. The pass entitles you to free travel on most European rail networks (including Austrian railways), as well as half-price discounts on British trains and on the Channel ferries.

By bus

The cheapest way to get to Vienna is by **bus**. There's a direct service run by Eurolines from London's Victoria Coach Station at least three times a week. The bus sets off at around 10.30am, arriving in Wien-Mitte/Landstrasse roughly 22 hours later. Tickets currently cost £71 single and £109 return, with a fare of £64 single and £99 return for those under 26. The tickets are valid for six months from the date of issue, but there are no stopoffs allowed on the journey. The trip is bearable (just about) and a bargain, but only really worth it if you absolutely can't find the extra cash for the flight.

By car

Though with two or more passengers it can work out relatively inexpensive, **driving to Vienna** is not the most relaxing option – unless you enjoy pounding along the motorway systems of Europe for the best part of a day and a night.

The quickest way of taking your car over to the continent is to drive to the **Channel Tunnel** near Folkestone, where Le Shuttle operates a 24hr service carrying cars, motorcycles, buses and their passengers to Calais. At peak times, services run every fifteen minutes, making advance bookings for the 35-minute journey unnecessary. However, if you simply turn up unannounced, you'll have to pay £169 return per carload, whereas if you give fixed dates for your travel, you can bring the price down to £99 return.

The alternative cross-Channel options for most travellers are the conventional **ferry and hovercraft** links between Dover and Calais or Boulogne, and Ramsgate and Dunkerque or Ostend. Fares vary enormously with the time of year, month and even day that you travel, and the size of your car. If you book in advance, the cheapest standard fare on the Dover–Calais run, for example, can be as little as £100 return for a carload (including passengers). However, turn up without a booking on an August weekend, and you'll pay more than twice that.

Once you've made it onto the continent, you've got something in the region of 1200km of driving ahead of you. Theoretically, you could make it in ten hours, but realistically it will take you at least sixteen hours of solid driving. The most direct route to Vienna from Ostend or Calais is via Brussels, Köln, Frankfurt, Nürnberg, Regensburg, Passau and Linz. It costs nothing to drive on motorways in Belgium and Germany, but Austria itself has recently introduced charges for travelling on an Autobahn. All cars using the motorway must display a sticker or Vignette (available at

Train Information

International Rail Centre	☎ 0171/834 2345
Eurostar	☎ 0345/881881
Wasteels	☎ 0171/834 7066

Bus Information

Eurolines	☎ 0990/808080

Cross-Channel Information

Hoverspeed	☎ 01304/240101
Dover–Calais and Folkestone–Boulogne	

Le Shuttle	☎ 0990/353535
Folkestone–Calais through the tunnel	
P&O European Ferries	☎ 0990/980980
Dover–Calais	
Holyman Sally Ferries	☎ 0990/595522
Ramsgate–Dunkirk and	
Ramsgate–Ostend	
Stena Line	☎ 01223/647047
Dover–Calais	

border crossings and petrol stations); the cheapest version costs öS70 (£4) and is valid for ten days.

If you're travelling by car, you'll need proof of ownership, or a letter from the owner giving you permission to drive the car. A British or other EU driving licence is fine; all other drivers must hold an International Driving Licence. You also need a red warning triangle in case you breakdown, a first-aid kit (both these are compulsory in Austria), and a "Green Card" for third party insurance cover at the very least. An even better idea is to sign up with one of the national motoring organizations like the AA or the RAC, who offer continental breakdown assistance, and in extreme circumstances will get you and your vehicle brought back home if necessary.

Insurance

Though not compulsory, **travel insurance** including medical cover is not a bad idea. Check before shelling out, however, that you are not already covered: many credit cards (particularly American Express) often have certain levels of medical or other insurance included, especially if you use them to pay for you use them to pay for your trip; in addition, if you have a good "all risks" home insurance policy it may well cover your possessions against loss or theft even when overseas, and many private medical schemes also cover you while abroad.

Most travel agents and tour operators will offer you travel insurance – those policies offered by Campus Travel or STA in the UK and USIT in Ireland are usually reasonable value. If you feel the cover is inadequate, or you want to compare prices, any insurance broker, bank or specialist travel insurance company should be able to help: call Columbus Travel Insurance (☎0171/375 0011) or Endsleigh Insurance (☎0171/436 4451). Two weeks' cover for a trip to Vienna should cost around £20.

Getting there from North America

The quickest and easiest way to get to Vienna from the US or Canada is by air. Austrian Airlines and Delta fly direct; many other airlines have flights to Vienna via other major European cities. A direct flight from the east coast of the States takes nine hours. Another option is to buy a cheap flight to London or Frankfurt and make your way overland from there (see p.5 for details of getting to Vienna from Britain).

Though in the account that follows we've quoted fares that are offered direct from the airlines, for cheaper flight options it's always worth contacting **discount travel agents** or **consolidators,** who buy up blocks of tickets from the airlines and sell them at a discount. There are no **courier** flights available from North America to Vienna.

The **high season** for flights is summer, June through mid-September, and the weeks around Christmas and New Year, when fares are at least $1000. Low season, when tickets can be as much as $400 cheaper, runs from the beginning of November to mid-March (excluding Christmas and New Year). The shoulder season, which sees a rise in cost from low season by about $200, runs from mid-March to the end of May and from mid-September to the end of October.

Flights from the USA

The cheapest options available from the airlines are **Apex fares**, which need to be bought 21 days in advance, and entail a stay from a week to thirty days. Austrian Airlines is your best bet, offering **non-stop daily flights** from New York and Atlanta to Vienna, and direct service from Washington DC and Chicago; fares start at $650 return in low season, rising to just over $1000 in summer. Delta's new non-stop service from New York costs around $50 more.

Numerous European-based airlines – Lufthansa, KLM, SwissAir, British Airways, CSA/Czechoslovak Airlines, Air France and Alitalia – fly from major US cities to Vienna stopping at their gateway cities (Frankfurt, Amsterdam, Zurich, London, Prague, Paris and Rome, respectively). The Apex fares on these airlines are all broadly similar, ranging from $650 return in winter to $1000 in summer. Lauda Air has one-stop flights three times weekly from Miami to Vienna through Munich, starting at $750 in low season.

Flights from the west coast are always routed through an eastern city (usually New York or Atlanta); figure on an extra $250 for the transatlantic leg of the journey. Austrian Airlines and Lufthansa each offer flights to Vienna from the west coast starting at $900 in winter, rising to $1250 during the high season; if you take Lufthansa, you will have to stop again in Frankfurt.

Flights from Canada

Though there are **no direct flights** from Canada to Austria, there are many competitively priced one-stop options. Flights take about eleven hours from Montréal, twelve from Toronto and fourteen from Vancouver. The best deals are usually on European carriers such as Air France, Lufthansa, KLM, or SwissAir, which fly from major Canadian cities to Vienna through Paris, Frankfurt,

Airlines

Air Canada Canada: ☎1-800/555-1212;
US: ☎1-800/776-3000

Air France US: ☎1-800/237-2747; Canada:
☎1-800/667-2747

Alitalia US: ☎1-800/223-5730; Canada:
☎1-800/361-8336

Austrian Airlines US & Canada: ☎1-800/843-
0002

British Airways US: ☎1-800/247-9297;
Canada: ☎1-800/668-1059

Canadian Airlines Canada: ☎1-800/665-1177;
US: ☎1-800/426-7000

CSA/Czechoslovak Airlines US: ☎1-800/223-
2365

Delta Airlines US & Canada: ☎1-800/241-
4141

KLM US: ☎1-800/374-7747; Canada:
☎1-800/361-5073

Lauda Air US: ☎1-800/645-3880; Canada:
☎1-800/563-5954

Lufthansa US: ☎1-800/645-3880; Canada:
☎1-800/563-5954

SwissAir US: ☎1-800/221-4750; Canada:
☎1-800/267-9477

Discount Travel Companies

Airhitch, 2641 Broadway, New York, NY 10025
☎1-800/326-2009.
Standby-seat broker: for a set price, they guarantee to get you on a flight as close to your preferred destination as possible, within a week.

Council Travel, 205 E 42nd St, New York,
NY 10017 ☎1-800/226-8624; branches in many other US cities.
Student/budget travel agency. A sister company, Council Charter ☎1-800/800-8222, specializes in charter flights.

International Student Exchange Flights,
5010 E Shea Blvd, Suite 104A, Scottsdale,
AZ 85254 ☎602/951-1177.
Student/youth fares, student IDs.

New Frontiers/Nouvelles Frontières, 12 E
33rd St, New York, NY 10016 ☎1-800/366-6387;
1001 Sherbrook East, Suite 720, Montréal, H2L
1L3 ☎514/526-8444; branches in LA, San

Francisco and Québec City.
French discount travel firm.

STA Travel, 10 Downing St, New York,
NY 10014 ☎1-800/777-0112; branches in the
Los Angeles, San Francisco and Boston areas.
Worldwide discount travel firm specializing in student/youth fares; also student IDs, travel insurance, car rental, rail passes, etc.

Travac Tours, 989 6th Ave, New York NY 10018
☎1-800/872-8800.
Consolidator and charter broker.

Travel CUTS, 243 College St, Toronto,
ON M5T 1P7 ☎1-800/667-2887; branches all over Canada.
Specialists in student fares, IDs and other travel services.

Worldtek Travel, 111 Water St, New Haven,
CT 06511 ☎1-800/243-1723.
Discount travel agency.

Amsterdam and Zurich respectively. Fares from Toronto or Montréal on any of these airlines range from CDN$980 to CDN$1300 depending on the season; from Vancouver, expect to add about CDN$300. You can fly on Air Canada or Canadian Airlines for as low as CDN$965 in winter, but you will have to switch planes and carriers in a European city, often in London to British Airways.

Packages and city breaks

If money is little object, it can be worth checking deals with **specialist agents**. Though in

many cases specialist tours don't include airfares, they do map your itinerary and activities, fix you up with experienced guides, and organize the purchase of opera tickets and the like.

Although we've given phone numbers of specialist operators in the box below, you're better off making tour reservations through your local travel agent. An agent will make all the phone calls, sort out the snafus and arrange flights, insurance and the like – all at no extra cost to you.

Specialist Tour Operators

Cross Culture ☎ 413/256-6303
City packages, with a nine-day Viennese waltz tour at around $2600, all inclusive.

Eastern Europe Tours ☎ 1-800/641-3456
Just as the name says. Most of the organized tours take in other countries as well as Austria; a three-night city package to Vienna starts around $300 double occupancy, airfare not included.

Europe Train Tours ☎ 1-800/551-2085
Bus tours of Austria, and packages centring around Vienna.

Fugazy International ☎ 1-800/828-4488
Group tours that include Vienna, or personalized packages to Vienna, with guided tours. The 15-day Vienna/Hungary tour is $3000, based on double occupany, all inclusive.

Great Composer Tours ☎ 1-800/228-SONG
Beethoven and Schubert "pilgrimages". Fairly costly, at $4200 for 10 days, including sightseeing trips, museum tours, accommodation and meals; airfare not included.

Herzerl Tours ☎ 1-800/684-8488
Food, wine-tasting, music and other cultural tours of Vienna and Austria. Week-long cooking tour, including airfare, accommodation, classes, some meals and various other sundries, is $2400.

Holiday Tours Ltd ☎ 1-800/234-2895
Art, architecture, cooking, horticulture and other special interest excursions in Vienna. Nine-day Schubert tour is $1800, all inclusive; Viennese cooking tours go for $2200.

Lotus Tours ☎ 1-800/675-0559
Arrangements for flights, accommodation, concert tickets, bike trips and the like. Flights start at $745, standard hotel rates are under $100 per night.

Rivers of Europe ☎ 1-800/999-0226
Christmas and New Year's specials in Vienna, featuring operas and river cruises; simple hotel and sightseeing packages; also, a four-day Musical Vienna package for around $500, no airfare included.

Smolka Tours Austria ☎ 1-800/722-0057
Specialists in Austrian group or independent travel, including culture and music-oriented itineraries.

Van Gogh Tours ☎ 1-800/435-6192
Nine-day guided bicycle tour called "The Trail of Mozart", through Vienna and other parts of the country. At $1250 for bike rentals, meals, and accommodation in three- and four-star hotels.

Rail passes

If you're planning on doing a decent amount of travelling in Europe, you may want to look into getting a **train pass** to get you into Austria. A regular **Eurail** pass can span from fifteen days (the two fares available are $365 for under-26s/$522 for first class) to three months $1028/1468). This covers seventeen countries: Austria, Belgium, Denmark, Finland, France, Germany, Greece, Hungary, Ireland (Rep.), Italy, Luxembourg, Netherlands, Norway, Portugal, Spain, Sweden and Switzerland. The option most likely to be worth your money is the **Flexipass** ($431/616), which gives you any ten days of train travel over a two-month period in any of the seventeen Eurail pass countries. Also available are the **Austrian Railpass**, for any three days unlimited train travel in a fifteen-day period ($98/145), and the **European East Pass**, for any five days in one month ($195) in Austria, Czech Republic, Hungary, Poland and Slovakia.

Rail Contacts in North America

CIT Tours, 342 Madison Ave, Suite 207, New York, NY 10173 ☎ 1-800/223-7987.

Rail Europe, 226 Westchester Ave, White Plains, NY 10604 ☎ 1-800/438-7245 in US; ☎ 1-800/361-7245 in Canada.

ScanTours, 3439 Wade St, Los Angeles, CA 90066 ☎ 1-800/223-7226.

Insurance

Before buying an insurance policy to travel in Austria, check that you're not already covered. **Canadian provincial health plans** typically provide some overseas medical coverage, although they are unlikely to pick up the full tab in the

American Express) often provide certain levels of medical or other insurance, and travel insurance may also be included if you use a major credit or charge card to pay for your trip. **Homeowners' or renters'** insurance often covers theft or loss of documents, money and valuables while overseas.

If you do need travel insurance, most travel agents will arrange it. The insurance companies in the box below can be called directly. The best **premiums** are usually to be had through student/youth travel agencies – ISIS policies, for example, cost $48–69 for fifteen days (depending on level of coverage), $80–105 for a month.

Most North American travel policies apply only to items lost, stolen or damaged while in the custody of an identifiable, responsible third party – hotel porter, airline, luggage consignment, etc. Even in these cases you will have to contact the local police within a certain time limit to have a complete report made out for your insurer to process the claim.

event of a mishap. Holders of official **student/teacher/youth cards** are entitled to accident coverage and hospital in-patient benefits. **Students** may also find that their student health coverage extends during the vacations and for one term beyond the date of last enrollment. Bank and credit cards (particularly

Getting there from Australasia

The only direct flights from Australasia to Vienna are with Lauda Air from Sydney; all others include either a transfer or stopover in the carrier's home city. Fares are steep, so if you're

on a budget, opt for a low-season fare to London, Amsterdam or Frankfurt, where you can shop around for cheap onward transport to Vienna. If you intend to take in other destinations in Austria or expand your trip into Europe there are several rail and bus passes that can be bought before you leave.

By plane

Air fares to Europe are seasonal: for most airlines low season runs from mid-January to the end of February, and October to the end of November; high season is mid-May to the end of August, and December to mid-January. There is no price variation during the week. Direct and connecting flights to Vienna are long – between 20 and 30 hours – and can be physically and mentally taxing, so you may consider a **stopover**.

Flights to Europe are generally cheaper via Asia than via the US. Fares from major eastern

Australian cities are all the same price ("common-rated"); flying from Perth and Darwin costs between $100–200 less via Asia, or A$200–400 more via Canada and the US. Fares from Christchurch and Wellington are between NZ$150–300 more than from Auckland.

Tickets purchased direct from the airlines tend to be expensive, with common-rated published fares (from the eastern cities/Auckland) listed at A$2399/NZ$2699 (low-season), rising to A$2999/NZ$3399 (high-season). Travel agents offer better deals and have the latest information on special offers such as free stopovers and fly-drive-accommodation packages. Flight Centres and STA (which also offer fare reductions for ISIC card holders and under 26s) generally offer the lowest fares.

Airlines

Alitalia Australia: ☎ 02/9247 9133; NZ: ☎ 09/379 4457
Three flights per week via Bangkok and a transfer in Rome, from major Australasian cities (code-share with Qantas).

Britannia Airways ☎ 02/9251 1299
Several flights per month to London, during their charter season, via Bangkok and Abu Dhabi, from major Australian cities and Auckland.

Garuda Indonesia Australia: ☎ 1800 800873; NZ: ☎ 09/366 1855
Several flights a week to London and Amsterdam with a transfer/stopover in Jakarta/Denpasar, from major Australasian cities.

Lauda Air Australia: ☎ 02/9367 3888; NZ: ☎ 09/303 1529
Twice weekly to Vienna via Sydney from major Australasian cities. Code share with Ansett/Air New Zealand.

Malaysian Airlines Australia: ☎ 13 2627; NZ: ☎ 09/373 2741
Twice weekly flights to Vienna wtih a transfer/stopover in Kuala Lumpur from major Australasian cities.

Philippine Airlines ☎ 02/9262 3333
Several flights a week to London and Frankfurt with transfer/stopover in Manila, from major Australian cities.

Singapore Airlines Australia: ☎ 13 1011; NZ: ☎ 09/379 3209
Several flights a week to Vienna with a transfer in Singapore, from major Australasian cities.

Discount Travel Agents

Anywhere Travel, 345 Anzac Parade, Kingsford, Sydney ☎ 02/9663 0411.

Brisbane Discount Travel, 260 Queen St, Brisbane ☎ 07/3229 9211.

Budget Travel, 16 Fort St, Auckland; other branches around the city ☎ 09/366 0061, toll-free 0800/808 040.

Destinations Unlimited, 3 Milford Rd, Milford, Auckland ☎ 09/373 4033.

Flight Centres Australia: Level 11, 33 Berry St, North Sydney ☎ 02/9241 2422; Bourke St, Melbourne ☎ 03/9650 2899; plus other branches nationwide. New Zealand: National Bank Towers, 205–225 Queen St, Auckland ☎ 09/309 6171; Shop 1M, National Mutual Arcade, 152 Hereford St, Christchurch ☎ 03/379 7145; 50–52 Willis St, Wellington ☎ 04/472 8101; other branches countrywide.

Northern Gateway, 22 Cavenagh St, Darwin ☎ 08/8941 1394.

STA Travel, Australia: 702–730 Harris St, Ultimo, Sydney ☎ 02/9212 1255, toll-free 1800/637 444; 256 Flinders St, Melbourne ☎ 03/9654 7266; other offices in state capitals and major universities. New Zealand: Travellers' Centre, 10 High St, Auckland ☎ 09/309 0458; 233 Cuba St, Wellington ☎ 04/385 0561; 90 Cashel St, Christchurch ☎ 03/379 9098; other offices in Dunedin, Palmerston North, Hamilton and major universities.

Thomas Cook, Australia: 321 Kent St, Sydney ☎ 02/9248 6100; 257 Collins St, Melbourne ☎ 03/9650 2442; branches in other state capitals local-call rate ☎ 131 771; New Zealand: 96–98 Anzac Ave, Auckland ☎ 09/379 3920.

Topdeck Travel, 65 Glenfell St, Adelaide ☎ 08/8232 7222.

Specialist Agents

Adventure World Australia: ☎ 1800/221 931;
NZ: ☎ 09/524 5118
Accommodation from $58 twin-share, with
full- and half-day sightseeing tours of Vienna
and surrounds; three-night accommodation–
concert packages from A$330 twin-share.

Australians Studying Abroad ☎ 03/9509 1955
or 1800/645 755
Twenty-day all-inclusive tour delving into the
art and culture of Vienna, plus Prague and
Budapest. From A$4100 twin-share, flight not
included.

CIT ☎ 02/9267 1255
Hotel–tour packages from A$165 for two
nights twin-share including half-day city
tour, five-day round-trip bus tours from
Vienna via Graz, Franz-Josefs-Hohe, Salzburg
and Melk from A$923 twin-share.

European Travel Office Australia: ☎ 03/9329
8844; NZ: ☎ 09/525 3074
Two-night accommodation–concert packages
from A$280 twin-share, half-day Vienna city
tours from A$50 and day boat trips on the
Danube from A$140. Also offer car rental.

To Vienna Lauda Air team up ("code-share")
with Ansett and Air New Zealand to provide a
direct service from major cities via Sydney for
around A$1899/2299–NZ$2299/2799. Through
European gateways the lowest fares are on
Britannia Airways to London and Amsterdam dur-
ing their limited charter season (Nov–March;
A$1290/NZ$1799–A$1799/NZ$2050), while you
can expect to pay around A$1500/NZ$1899–
A$1900/NZ$2400 on Philippine Airlines and
Garuda. Alternatively, Malaysia Airlines, Singapore
Airlines and Alitalia can take you there via a
transfer in their home cities for around
A$1999/NZ$2399–A$2399/NZ$2799.

Round the World (RTW) tickets that include
Vienna are Qantas's "Global Explorer" (A$2499/
3099; NZ$2399/2999) and Cathay-United's
"Globetrotter" (A$2349/$2899; NZ$2999/$3449);
both allow limited backtracking and six free
stopovers with additional stopovers at
A$100/NZ$110. Thai in conjunction with Cathay,
Air New Zealand and Varig offer unlimited
stopovers – except within the US and Canada –
for A$3199/NZ$3200. All fares are valid for one
year.

Specialist tours

If you're interested in Viennese architecture and
music there are a limited number of **specialist
agents** that offer good deals on concert–accommodation packages and city sightseeing tours, as
well as being able to book tours to other areas
of Austria from Vienna. Unfortunately there are no
pre-packaged tours that include airfares from
Australasia, but most specialist agents will also
be able to assist with flight arrangements.

By bus and rail

If you're planning to visit Vienna on part of a
longer European trip it may be worth looking into
a variety of **rail and bus passes**, many of which
have to be bought in your home country before
you leave. If you don't want to spend time in any
one place, Eurail and Eurail Youth passes offer
the best value at A$605/755 (youth/adult fares)
for fifteen days, A$870/1220 for one month and
A$1120/1670 for two months for unlimited trav-
el on consecutive days within a two-month period. A more flexible alternative, allowing stopoffs
along the way, are Eurail Flexipasses which are
valid for travel on non-consecutive days within
two months and cost A$640/900 for ten days
and A$860/1180 for fifteen days. If you just want
to explore Austria, the Austrian Railpass allows
unlimited travel for four days in ten for
A$155/230. If you prefer to travel by **bus** Eurobus
Passes cost around A$200/260 for two weeks,
A$280/370 for one month and A$370/500 for
two months. All passes are available from CIT,
123 Clarence St, Sydney (☎ 02/9299 4754), and
Thomas Cook World Rail (Australia: ☎ 1800/422
747; New Zealand: ☎ 09/263 7260).

Insurance

Comprehensive **travel insurance policies** are
generally put together by the airlines, major travel agents and some banks in conjunction with
insurance companies. All are fairly similar in pre-
mium and coverage, which includes medical
expenses, loss of personal property and travellers' cheques, cancellations and delays, as well
as most adventure sports. Ready Plan (Australia:

141–147 Walker St, Dandenong, Vic, toll free ☎1800 337 462; New Zealand: 10th Floor, 63 Albert St, Auckland) and Covermore (32 Walker St, North Sydney, toll free ☎1800 251 881) give the best-value coverage. A normal policy costs around A$190/NZ$220 for one month, A$270/NZ$320 for two months and A$330/NZ$400 for three months.

Red tape and visas

Citizens of EU countries (and of Iceland, Norway and Switzerland) need only a valid national identity card to enter Austria. Since Britain has no identity card, however, British citizens do have to take a passport. EU citizens can stay for as long as they want, but if they're planning on staying permanently, they should register with the local police. Citizens of the US, Canada, New Zealand and Australia require a passport, but no visa, and can stay up to three months.

Visa requirements do change, however, and it is always advisable to check the current situation before leaving home. A list of Austrian embassies abroad is given below; for a list of foreign embassies in Vienna, see p.309.

Customs

Customs and duty-free restrictions vary throughout Europe, with subtle variations even within the European Community. British and Irish travellers returning home directly from another EU country do not have to make a declaration to customs at their place of entry. In other words, British and Irish citizens can effectively take back as much duty-paid wine or beer as they can carry (the legal limits being 90 litres of wine or 110 of beer).

However, there are still restrictions on the volume of tax- or duty-free goods you can bring in or out of the country. In general, residents of EU countries travelling to other EU states are allowed a duty-free allowance of 200 cigarettes, one litre of spirits and five litres of wine; for non-EU residents the allowances are usually 200 cigarettes, one litre of spirits and 2.25 litres of wine.

Residents of the US and Canada can take up to 200 cigarettes and one litre of alcohol back home, as can Australian citizens, while New Zealanders must confine themselves to 200 cigarettes, 4.5 litres of beer or wine, and one litre of spirits. Again if in doubt consult the relevant – or your own – embassy.

Austrian Embassies Abroad

Australia
12 Talbot St, Forrest, Canberra ACT2603
☎02/6295 1533.

Britain
18 Belgrave Mews West, London SW1 8HU
☎0171/235 3731.

Canada
445 Wilbrod St, Ottawa, Ontario KIN 6M7
☎613/789-1444.

Ireland
15 Ailesbury Court, 93 Ailesbury Rd, Dublin 4
☎01/269 4577.

New Zealand
Consular General, 22 Garrett St, Wellington
☎04/801-9709

USA
3524 International Court NW, Washington, DC
20008 ☎202/895-6700.

Information and maps

There are branches of the Austrian National Tourist Office in most large foreign countries (a selection of addresses is given below). The staff are very helpful, but if you want more than general brochures and a map of the city, you'll need to be quite focused about your interests.

The main tourist information point **in Vienna** itself is at Kirntnerstrasse 38; it's run by the Vienna Tourist Board (*Wiener Tourismusverband*). The staff should be able to answer most enquiries, but it's a small office, so it's best to be specific about what you want. For more on the city's tourist offices and listings magazines, see *Introducing the City*, p.25.

Maps

The **maps** in this guide, together with the untold number of free city plans you'll pick up from tourist office and hotels, should be sufficient to help you find your way around. For something more durable, the best maps are by *Freytag & Berndt*, who produce a whole variety of plans of the city, marked with bus and tram routes. The 1:20,000 spiral bound *Buchplan Wien* map is the most comprehensive. Alternatively, *Falkplan* produce an attractive fold-out map, with a good large-scale section of the Innere Stadt.

To get hold of either of the above maps of Vienna in the UK, try *Stanfords*, 12–14 Long Acre, London WC2 (☎0171/836 1321). In the US, *Rand McNally* should be able to help (call ☎1-

800/333-0136 for the location of their nearest store and for mail-order details). In Australasia, the *Travel Bookshop*, 20 Bridge St, Sydney (☎02/9241 3554), are worth contacting, as are *Speciality Maps*, 58 Albert St, Aukland (☎09/307 2217). Otherwise, you can wait until you get to Vienna, where you can visit *Freytag & Berndt*'s own flagship store – see p.305 for details.

Vienna on the Net

Austrian National Tourist Board
www.austria-info.at
The national tourist board's web sit. Not much better than looking at the brochures, though it can give you the seating plan of the Staatsoper and various other venues in Vienna.

Vienna Tourist Board
wtv.magwien.gv.at
The local tourist board's web site. Good for finding out about the city's up and coming events.

Costs, money and banks

Although Vienna is by no means a budget destination, it is not quite as expensive as people often imagine. It's true to say that there are few bargain deals to be had, and even the cheapest coffee and cake at a traditional coffeehouse will cost you dear, but restaurants on the whole are moderately priced, as are rooms in the city's pensions and hotels. That said, if you have the money, Vienna has plenty of luxury shops, hotels and restaurants ready to relieve you of it.

Money

The **currency** in Austria is the Austrian Schilling or österreichische Schilling (abbreviated to öS within Austria, occasionally written as ATS or AS in English), which is divided into one hundred Groschen. Coins come in the denominations öS20, öS10, öS5 and öS1, plus 50 and 10 Groschen; notes as öS5000, öS1000, öS500, öS100, öS50 and öS20.

The Austrian economy is in a pretty healthy condition, despite what some Austrians would have you believe, and the Schilling is a relatively strong currency. Generally speaking, the **exchange rate** hovers between öS15 and öS20 to the pound sterling, and between öS10 and öS13 to the US dollar.

Average costs

Accommodation will be your biggest single expense, with the cheapest reasonable double rooms in a pension going for öS600–800 (£34–46/$54–73), though a few hostel-type places will undercut this. However, within that price range, you should be able to get somewhere pretty central and clean – all the details are on p.263.

After you've paid for your own room, count on a **minimum** of £20/$32 a day, which will buy you breakfast, a take-away lunch, a budget dinner and a beer or coffee, but not much else. Eating sit-down meals twice a day, visiting museums and drinking more beer and coffee (especially coffee) will mean allowing for more like £40/$64 a day; if you want to go to the opera or a nightclub, then you could easily double that figure.

Tipping is expected in the more upmarket hotels, taxis and in most cafés, bars and restaurants, usually up to the nearest öS5 or öS10 depending on how much you've spent and how good the service was. In more expensive restaurants, you'll find the bill arrives with a 15 percent service charge already tacked onto the total.

Travellers' cheques and credit cards

Travellers' cheques are the safest and easiest way to carry money. American Express and Thomas Cook are the most widely used – available for a small commission (usually one percent of the amount ordered) from any bank and some building societies, whether or not you have an account, and from branches of American Express and Thomas Cook.

Even if you have travellers' cheques, it's a good idea to take a **credit card** with a PIN number as well. You can pay with plastic in most hotels, shops and restaurants, though it's not as widely used as in the UK or the US. With Mastercard and Visa it is also possible to withdraw cash at certain Austrian banks in Vienna from the 24-hour cashpoint/automatic teller machines (ATMs); check with your bank before you leave home.

Changing money

The best place to change money is at a **bank**, which will tend to give you a more favourable

Exchange Booths and Banks

Banks (with 24hr automatic exchange machines)

Bank Austria, Stephansplatz 2.
Creditanstalt, Karntnerstrasse 7.
Die Erste Banke, Graben 21.

Exchange booths

Airport (daily 6.30am–11pm).
Westbahnhof (daily 7am–10pm).
Südbahnhof (daily 6.30am–10pm).

rate of exchange and take a lower commission than a hotel or exchange booth (*Wechselstube*). The process takes a little bit longer, however, and, of course, restricts you to normal banking hours. The main Austrian high street banks are *Creditanstalt, Bank Austria* and *Die Erste Banke;* there's nothing to choose between them.

Banking hours vary but are generally Monday to Friday 8am to 12.30pm and 1.30 to 3pm, with late closing on Thursdays, at 5.30pm. Outside these hours, you will have to rely on the **Wechselstube**. The ones with the longest hours are in the Westbahnhof and Südbahnhof, and at the airport. There are also 24-hour automatic exchange machines dotted around the city centre if you have foreign cash.

Emergencies

When you buy your travellers' cheques, make a note of the emergency phone number given. On your trip keep a record of all cheques and note which ones you spend – and report any loss or theft immediately. All being well, you should get the missing cheques reissued within a couple of days. Things can be trickier if you lose your credit card: your bank should be able to give you details of the number to call if this happens, but you won't be provided with a replacement card until you get home.

Assuming you know someone who is prepared to send you the money, the quickest way to have funds sent out to you in an emergency is to do it through **Western Union**, who will wire the money to you in a couple of hours (some banks will also do this); get your sponsor to phone ☎0800/833833 in the UK or ☎1-800/325-6000 in North America. The Vienna office of *Western Union* is on the first floor of the offices of the *österreichische Verkehrskreditbank* in the Westbahnhof.

If you have a few days' leeway, you can simply get your bank to wire your money to an Austrian bank, a process that shouldn't take more than a couple of days. If you can last out for a week, then an **international money order**, exchangeable at any post office, is by far the cheapest way of sending money.

If you're in really dire straits, you can get touch with your **consulate** in Vienna, who will usually let you make one phone call home free of charge, and will – in worst cases only – repatriate you, but will never, under circumstances, lend money.

Telephones and mail

Dialling Codes

To Vienna
From Australasia ☎ 0011 43 1
From Britain & Ireland ☎ 00 43 1
From North America ☎ 011 43 1
Phoning from elsewhere in Austria, the Vienna city code is ☎ 0222

From Vienna
Australia ☎ 0061
Ireland ☎ 00353
New Zealand ☎ 0064
North America ☎ 001
UK ☎ 0044

Emergencies
Fire ☎ 122
Police ☎ 133
Ambulance ☎ 144

Local directory enquiries ☎ 1611

International operator ☎ 1616

Mail services

The **main post office** (*Postamt*) in Vienna is at Fleischmarkt 19, A-1001, just off Schwedenplatz. It's open 24 hours a day, seven days a week, as are the post offices in the Westbahnhof, Südbahnhof and Franz-Josefs-Bahnhof. All other branches have regular **opening hours** (Mon–Fri 8am–noon & 2–6pm, Sat 8–11am), with district post offices open until noon.

Air mail (*Flugpost*) between Austria and the UK usually takes three or four days, about a week to reach the US, and ten days to Australia and New Zealand. For stamps (*Briefmarken*) for postcards within the EU, you may be able to go to a tobacconist (*Tabak*), though for anything more complicated or further afield, you'll probably have to go to a post office, where they like to weigh everything.

Poste restante (*Postlagernd*) letters can be sent to any post office, if you know the address. At the main post office (see above) go to the counter marked *Postlagernde Sendungen*. Mail should be addressed using this term rather than "poste restante"; it will be held for thirty days (remember to take your passport when going to collect it).

Telephones

Austrian **phone booths** are easy enough to spot – usually dark green with a bright yellow roof and logo – and to use, some even having instuctions in four languages (including English). The dialling tone is a short followed by a long pulse; the ringing tone is long and regular; engaged is short and rapid. Although the minimum charge is öS1, you're likely to need much more than that in order to make even a **local call**, since Austria has one of the most expensive telephone systems in the world.

You can make an **international call** from any phone, though it's easier to do so with a **phone card** (*Telefonkarte*) rather than from a coin-operated phone. *Telefonkarten* are available from all post offices, tobacconists and some other shops, in öS50, öS100 and öS200 denominations. The other option is to go to one of the 24-hour post offices and use their **direct phone service** facility: a booth will be allocated to you from the counter marked *Fremdgespräche*, which is where you pay once you've finished. The post office is also the place to go if you want to make a collect call (*R-Gespräch*).

The Viennese phone system is currently being overhauled, so don't worry that the **telephone numbers** within the city vary in length. One further peculiarity is those numbers which end in -0. It's not necessary to dial the final 0, which simply signals that it's a line with extension numbers (if you know the extension you want, dial that after the number).

The media

The newspaper stands in the centre of the city stock a variety of **English-language newspapers**. You can usually get the European edition of the British broadsheet *The Guardian*, printed in Frankfurt, by mid-morning the same day. Similarly, the *International Herald Tribune* is widely available the same day. Other papers tend to be a day or so old. The only locally produced newspaper is the monthly *Vienna Reporter*, a thin broadsheet with good local news and selective lisings.

The **Austrian press** is pretty uninspiring, with nearly half the population reading either the *Neue Kronen Zeitung* or *Kurier* tabloids, both of which are fairly reactionary. Of the qualities, *Der Standard*, printed on pink paper, is more liberal compared with *Die Presse*. Best of the lot is *Falter*, the city's weekly **listings** tabloid, which is

lively, politicized and critical, and comes out on a Friday. Although it's entirely in German, it's easy enough to decipher the listings with the aid of a dictionary – or a few tips. If your German's good enough, the best place to leaf through a selection of newspapers and magazines is in a traditional coffeehouse – see p.279 for details.

Austrian **television** is is unlikely to win any international awards for cutting edge programming and presentation. The two state-run channels are ORF 1 and ORF 2; other channels regularly available include the ARD and ZDF German channels, which are pretty indistinguishable from the Austrian ones. Many hotels and pensions have satellite TV, bringing the joys of CNN and MTV into your room.

The state-run **radio** channels all feature a lot of chat, though Ö1 (87.8/92FM) offers a good dose of classical music, plus news in English and French at 8am. Blue Danube Radio (103.8FM) is the sort of channel you'll either love or hate, mixing AOR and transatlantic chat with the odd bit of news and weather in English, German and French. At 1pm, it has a "What's On in Vienna" slot. The BBC World Service broadcasts in English on 100.8FM.

Opening hours, public holidays and festivals

In general, Vienna's museums and galleries are open from Tuesday to Sunday from 10am to 6pm, though there are no hard and fast rules, so check in the margins beside each entry within the text of the *Guide* before setting out.

Churches in the centre of the city tend to stay open daily from 7am to 7pm or later, but many of those out in the suburbs only allow you to peep in from the foyer, except just before and after mass. Again, if a church has set opening times, we've said so in the margins beside the text of the Guide.

Shops in Vienna are obliged to comply with the state's very strict laws – similar to those in Germany – passed in a bid to counter national

Public Holidays

January 1 (*Neues Jahr*)

January 6 (Epiphany/*Dreikönigsfest*)

Easter Monday (*Ostermontag*)

May 1 (Labour Day/*Tag des Arbeit*)

Ascension Day (6th Thurs after Easter/*Christi Himmelfahrt*)

Whit Monday (6th Mon after Easter/*Pfingstmontag*)

Corpus Christi (*Fronleichnam*)

August 15 (Assumption Day/*Maria Himmelfahrt*)

October 26 (National Day/*Nationalfeiertag*)

November 1 (All Saints' Day/*Allerheiligen*)

December 8 (Immaculate Conception/*Maria Empfängnis*)

December 25 (*Weihnachtstag*)

December 26

workaholic tendencies. These laws were finally reformed in 1996 allowing shops to open regularly on Saturday afternoons. Even so, all shops must be closed by 6.30pm at the very latest from Monday to Saturday – in practice most close between 5 and 6pm – and all day on Sundays. The only exceptions to this rule, apart from pharmacists, are the shops in the main train stations and the airport, which are open late and at weekends.

Cafés, bars and restaurants tend to be open much longer hours. The traditional coffeehouses in particular often open as early as 7am and continue until 11pm or later. The trendier cafés stay open until 2am or later, and very few restaurants close before midnight.

Public holidays

On the national **public holidays** listed above, banks and shops will be closed all day. Museums and galleries will, somewhat confusingly, either be closed or open for free; for example, the vast majority are open for free on October 26, whereas most are closed on December 25. During the school summer holidays – July and August – you'll find Vienna quieter than usual, with many theatres and other businesses closed for all or some of the period.

Festivals

Vienna's calendar of events begins with the world-famous **New Year's Day Concert** (*Silvesterkonzert*) broadcast live from the Musikverein around the world.

The city's main cultural festival – featuring opera, music and theatre – is the **Wiener Festwochen**, which lasts from early May until mid-June. Once that's over, there's barely any breathing space before the city's big summer music festival, **Klangbogen Wien**, begins, lasting until early September. The festival includes a two-week Jazzfest in the first half of July.

October is the trendy month to visit, with the city's film festival, the **Viennale**, taking place towards the end of the month, and the **Wien Modern** festival of contemporary classical music continuing into November.

All Saints' Day (*Allerheiligen*) on November 1 is taken seriously in the whole of Austria, with huge numbers of Viennese heading out to the city's Zentralfriedhof to pay their respects to the dead. November 11 marks the official beginning of **Fasching**, the carnival (or more accurately ball) season which lasts until Ash Wednesday, though the balls don't really get going until after New Year. Towards the end of November, the city starts to get ready for Christmas. The biggest of the Christmas markets is the **Christkindlmarkt**, which takes place in front of the Rathaus. The other big pull for visitors is the **Mozart Festival**, which takes place in the run-up to Christmas.

In fact, such is the number of music festivals throughout the year, it's hard to turn up without coinciding with at least one.

Crime and personal safety

Vienna comes across as pretty safe compared to many capital cities. The Viennese themselves are a law-abiding lot, almost obsessively so. Old ladies can be seen walking their dogs in the city's parks late at night, and no one jaywalks. That said, crime does, of course, exist in Vienna as elsewhere and is on the rise, so it's as well to take the usual precautions.

Large sections of the **Gürtel ring road** double as a red-light district, and as such are best avoided. The **Karlsplatz** underpass and the **Stadtpark** both have dubious reputations, as do the major train stations, in particular the **Südbahnhof**, after dark. Even so, none of these places are strictly speaking no-go areas.

Almost all problems encountered by tourists in Vienna are to do with **petty crime**. Reporting thefts to the **police** is straightforward enough, though it'll take some time to wade through the bureaucracy. The Austrian police (*Polizei*) – distinguishable by their dark green uniforms and army-style officers' caps – are armed, and are not renowned for their friendliness, but they usually treat foreigners with courtesy. It's important to carry ID with you at all times (ideally your passport, or at the least a driving licence). Making photocopies of your passport and tickets is a very sensible precaution.

Emergency Phone Numbers	
Fire	☎ 122
Police	☎ 133
Ambulance	☎ 144

Travellers with disabilities

Like most western European countries, there are now regulations in force in Austria which mean that all public buildings must provide wheelchair access. As a result Vienna is becoming gradually more accessible for travellers with special needs.

That said, access to the **public transport** system is patchy, with only the new U3 and U6 lines fully equipped with lifts, escalators and a guidance system for the blind. Trams are not at all user-friendly, but some of the newer buses "kneel" to let people on and off. For a clearer picture, phone for the leaflet (in English) *Vienna for Guests with Handicaps* from the Austrian tourist board (see p.30) before you set off. This describes the level of access to U-Bahn stations, hotels and many tourist sights, and contains lots of other useful pieces of information.

Contacts for Travellers with Disablities

Australia
ACROD (Australian Council for Rehabilitation of the Disabled), PO Box 60, Curtin ACT 2605 (☎06/682 4333); 55 Charles St, Ryde (☎02/9809 4488).

Britain
Holiday Care Service, 2nd floor, Imperial Building, Victoria Rd, Horley, Surrey RH6 9HW (☎01293/774535).
Information on all aspects of travel.

RADAR, 12 City Forum, 250 City Rd, London EC1V 8AS (☎0171/250 3222; Minicom ☎0171/250 4119).
A good source of advice on holidays and travel abroad.

Ireland
Irish Wheelchair Association, Blackheath Drive, Clontarf, Dublin 3 (☎01/833 8241).
National voluntary organization working with people with disabilities with related services for holidaymakers.

New Zealand
Disabled Persons Assembly, PO Box 10, 138 The Terrace, Wellington (☎04/472 2626).

North America
Mobility International USA, PO Box 10767, Eugene, OR 97440 (Voice and TDD: ☎541/343-1284).
Information and referral services, access guides, tours and exchange programmes. Annual membership $25 (includes quarterly newsletter).

Society for the Advancement of Travel for the Handicapped (SATH), 347 5th Ave, Suite 610, New York, NY 10016 (☎212/447-7284; www.sittravel.com).
Non-profit travel-industry referral service that passes queries on to its members as appropriate; allow plenty of time for a response.

Twin Peaks Press, Box 129, Vancouver, WA 98666 (☎360/694-2462 or 1-800/637-2256).
Publisher of the Directory of Travel Agencies for the Disabled *and a number of other useful publications loaded with personal tips.*

The Guide

Chapter 1

Introducing the City

For all its grandiosity, **Vienna** is a surprisingly compact city: the centre is just a kilometre across at its broadest point, and you can travel from one side of the city to the other by public transport in less than thirty minutes. Although the **Danube** is crucial to Vienna's identity, most visitors see very little of the river, whose main arm flows through the outer suburbs to the northeast of the city centre.

Orientation

Vienna's central district is the old medieval town or **Innere Stadt** (Chapter Two), literally the "inner town". Retaining much of its labyrintine street layout, it remains the city's main commercial district packed with shops, cafés and restaurants. Chief sight here is **Stephansdom**, Vienna's showpiece cathedral and its finest Gothic edifice, standing at the district's pedestrianized centre. Tucked into the southwest corner of the Innere Stadt is the **Hofburg** (Chapter Three), the former imperial palace and seat of the Habsburgs, now home to a whole host of museums.

When the old fortifications surrounding the Innere Stadt were torn down in 1857, they were gradually replaced by a showpiece boulevard called the **Ringstrasse** (Chapter Four). It is this irregular pentagon-shaped thoroughfare that, along with the Danube Canal, encloses the Innere Stadt. Nowadays the Ringstrasse is used and abused by cars and buses as a ring road, though it's still punctuated with the most grandiose public buildings of late-imperial Vienna: the parliament, town hall, opera house and university, plus several museums. One of these – the **Kunsthistorisches Museum** – houses one of the world's finest art collections, detailed in Chapter Five.

Beyond the Ringstrasse lie Vienna's seven inner suburbs or **Vorstädte** (Chapter Six), whose outer boundary is comprised of the traffic-clogged Gürtel (literally "belt") or ring road. If you're travelling on any kind of budget, you're likely to find yourself staying somewhere out in the *Vorstädte*. Highlight here is the **Belvedere**, to

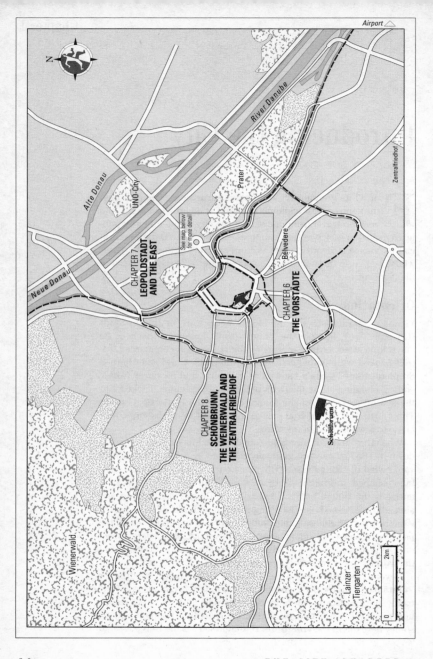

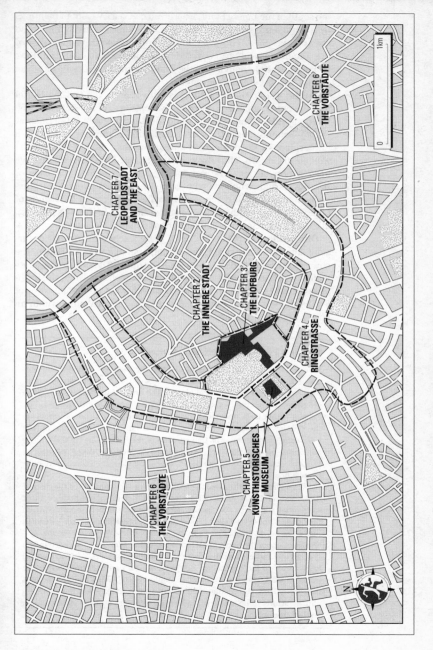

CHAPTER 6
THE VORSTÄDTE

CHAPTER 7
LEOPOLDSTADT
AND THE EAST

CHAPTER 2
THE INNERE STADT

CHAPTER 3
THE HOFBURG

CHAPTER 4
RINGSTRASSE

CHAPTER 5
KUNSTHISTORISCHES
MUSEUM

CHAPTER 6
THE VORSTÄDTE

1 km
0

N

the south of the Innere Stadt, where you can see a wealth of paintings by Austria's trio of modern artists, Egon Schiele, Gustav Klimt and Oskar Kokoschka. Those sections of the city worth visiting east of the Danube Canal are covered in **Leopoldstadt and the East** (Chapter Seven), though only the Prater, with its famous ferris wheel and funfair, is essential viewing.

On the whole, there's little reason to venture beyond the Gürtel into the outer suburbs or *Vororte*. Exceptions are **Schönbrunn**, the **Wienerwald** – Vienna Woods – and the **Zentralfriedhof** (all Chapter Eight). Schönbrunn is the Habsburgs' former summer residence, a masterpiece of Rococo excess and an absolute must if only for the wonderful gardens. The hilly woodland paths of the Wienerwald have been a popular rural retreat for the Viennese since the days of Beethoven and Schubert, who gained inspiration from their vine-backed slopes. Both composers now lie – along with thousands of other Viennese – at the opposite end of the city, in the far southeast, in the city's fascinating Zentralfriedhof (Central Cemetery).

Out of the city (Chapter Nine), there's scope for further excursions into the Wienerwald, the old imperial spa town of Baden, the court of the Esterházys at Eisenstadt, or up the Danube, to the spectacular monasteries of Klosterneuburg and Melk, to Tulln, the birthplace of Egon Schiele, or to the medieval, wine-producing town of Krems. All the above can be easily reached from Vienna within an hour by public transport.

Vienna's Postal Districts and Addresses

Vienna is divided into 23 **postal districts** or *Bezirke*, which spiral outwards from the first district (the Innere Stadt), in a clockwise direction, with only the odd geographical hiccup. The heart of the first district is the old town, though the Hofburg and Ringstrasse are also, strictly speaking, located within its boundaries. The city's second district (Leopoldstadt) is the old Jewish quarter, while the third to ninth districts make up the *Vorstädte* or inner suburbs that surround the old town. In 1890, Vienna's municipal boundaries were expanded to include the outer suburbs or *Vororte* – the tenth to twentieth districts – and since then three more have been added.

When writing **addresses**, the Viennese write the number of the district first, followed by the name of the street, and then the house number; most residential addresses also include an apartment number, separated from the house number by a slash. For example: 9, Löblichgasse 11/14, denotes Flat 14 at no. 11 Löblichgasse in the ninth district. We have used this system throughout the book. Sometimes you'll find addresses preceded by the postal code rather than the district, sometimes with an "A" (for Austria) hyphenated to the beginning. However, it's easy enough to decipher the postal district from the code, for example: A-1010 Wien denotes the first district, A-1020 the second, and so on. Lastly, there are a few common **abbreviations** to be aware of, including: –str. for –strasse, –g. for gasse, and –pl. for –platz.

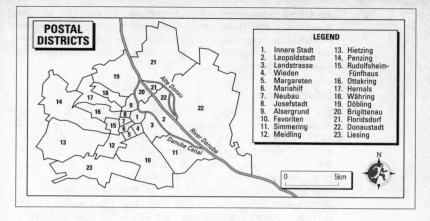

POSTAL DISTRICTS		LEGEND	

LEGEND

1. Innere Stadt
2. Leopoldstadt
3. Landstrasse
4. Wieden
5. Margareten
6. Mariahilf
7. Neubau
8. Josefstadt
9. Alsergrund
10. Favoriten
11. Simmering
12. Meidling
13. Hietzing
14. Penzing
15. Rudolfsheim-Fünfhaus
16. Ottakring
17. Hernals
18. Währing
19. Döbling
20. Brigittenau
21. Floridsdorf
22. Donaustadt
23. Liesing

0   5km

Arrival in Vienna

Flying into Vienna, you'll arrive at the city's **international airport**, Flughafen Wien-Schwechat, which lies around 20km southeast of the city. The airport is connected to the centre by the S-Bahn line S7; **trains** leave every thirty minutes between 5am and 10pm, taking twenty-five minutes to reach Wien-Mitte, where most people alight, and terminating at Wien-Nord. This is the cheapest way of getting into town, costing around öS17, plus the price of a travel pass (see below) which you can buy at the same time. **Buses** from the airport to the City Air Terminal bus station underneath the *Hilton Hotel* (adjacent to Wien-Mitte), are even more frequent, leaving every twenty minutes from 6.30am until 11.30pm, and every thirty minutes throughout the night; they take around twenty minutes to reach the city centre, and cost öS70 one way. There are also hourly buses to the Südbahnhof and Westbahnhof (see below). Taxis to the centre take twenty minutes or so and charge around öS380.

For a map of the U- and S-Bahn, see the colour insert at the back of this book.

Arriving in Vienna by train from the west, you'll end up at the **Westbahnhof**, five U-Bahn stops west of Stephansplatz in the city centre. Trains from eastern Europe, Italy and the Balkans terminate at the **Südbahnhof**, to the south of the city centre; you can either walk five minutes west to Südtiroler Platz U-Bahn station, or hop on tram #D into town. Of Vienna's other stations, **Franz-Josefs-Bahnhof**, in the northern suburb of Alsergrund, serves as an arrival point for services from Lower Austria and the odd train from Prague (take tram #D into town), while Wien-Nord (U-Bahn Praterstern), in Leopoldstadt, is used exclusively by local and regional trains, including the S-Bahn to the airport (see above).

International long-distance buses arrive at Vienna's **main bus terminal** beside Wien-Mitte, on the eastern edge of the city centre (U-Bahn Landstrasse). In the unlikely event of your arriving on one of the **DDSG boat** services from further up the Danube, or from Bratislava or Budapest, you'll find yourself disembarking at the Reichsbrücke, some way northeast of the city centre; the nearest station (U-Bahn Vorgartenstrasse) is five minutes' walk away, one block west of Mexicoplatz.

Information

The main **tourist office** of the Vienna Tourist Board (*Wiener Tourismusverband*) is at Kärntnerstrasse 38 (daily 9am–7pm; ☎513 88 92). It's a small office, with few leaflets on display, but if you have a specific enquiry, or just need directions, the staff will happily help out. It's worth asking for the latest *Museums* leaflet, listing all the current opening times, plus the *Young Vienna Scene* booklet, which contains some useful information, despite its cringe-making youth-speak; *Vienna Scene* is aimed at an older readership. Other leaflets include the tourist board's monthly *Programm* for opera, concert and theatre schedules, and upcoming exhibitions and events, and the monthly *Programm* of goings-on at the *Bundesmuseen* (State Museums). There are small information desks at the airport (24hr) and at the Westbahnhof (daily 7am–10pm) and Südbahnhof (6.30am–10pm).

The English-language monthly broadsheet *The Vienna Reporter* (öS25) carries selective **listings**, but for a more comprehensive run down you need the weekly tabloid *Falter* (öS28; published on Fridays). Even if your German isn't great, you should be able to decipher the pull-out *Wienprogramm & Lexicon* section, which contains the week's listings. A cheaper, trashier alternative is the weekly colour tabloid *City* (öS8), which also has a *Wienprogramm* in its centre pages.

City transport

There are maps of Vienna's public transport systems in the colour insert at the back of this book.

Vienna's city centre is best explored on foot, but for covering larger distances, you'll need to use the enviable **public transport system**, the *Wiener Linien*. Predictably enough, the trams and buses are punctual and the rapidly expanding metro – U-Bahn – is clean and very quick. A single journey **ticket** (*Fahrschein*), standard for all forms of public transport, costs öS17 from machines and ticket booths (*Vorverkauf*) at U-Bahn stations, and also from tobacconists (*Tabak-Trafik*). When you enter the U-Bahn, or board a tram or bus, you must punch (*entwerten*) your ticket in one of the blue machines. You can then make one journey, during which you can change buses, trams or U-Bahn lines as many times as you like. If you don't get it together to buy a ticket before boarding a tram or bus, you can buy a ticket for öS20 from the machines beside the driver – these need not be punched. Tickets for kids from six to fifteen cost öS9; under-6s travel free and under-15s travel free on Sundays, public holidays and during school holidays (you can pick up a calendar at a *Wiener*

Linien information office); women over sixty and men over sixty-five can buy a two-journey ticket for öS23.

If you're planning on making more than two journeys a day, you should invest in a **travel pass** or *Netzkarte*, which allows travel on all trams, buses, U- and S-Bahn trains within the city. You can buy a 24-hour ticket (öS50) or a 72-hour ticket (öS130) from machines and booths at all U-Bahn stations; when buying your ticket from a machine, select the central zone or *Kernzone* (*Zone 100*) which covers the whole of Vienna. You must punch your single *Netzkarte* at the beginning of your first journey – your 24 or 72 hours starts from that point. The much-touted *Vienna Card* (öS180) gives various discounts at local attractions as well as being a 72-hour *Netzkarte* (see p.33 for more details).

Another option is a **strip ticket** or *Streifenkarte*. The bargain is the green *Umwelt-Streifennetzkarte* (öS265), which is valid for eight (not necessarily consecutive) days' travel. It can be used by one or more people – one person for eight days, two people for four, and so on – simply punch one strip on the card for each person in the group. To do this you must fold the card over before inserting it in the blue machines, starting with strip 1. The other *Streifenkarten* available are the four-journey (öS68) and eight-journey (öS136) tickets.

If you're staying in Vienna longer than three days, it might be worth buying a **weekly card** or *Wochenkarte* (öS142), available only from the ticket offices at U-Bahn stations. The pass runs from 9am Monday to Monday so there's no need to punch the ticket. When you buy your first *Wochenkarte*, you need to ask for a *Zeitkarte*, which you must sign on the back, and on to which you must attach your (self-adhesive) *Wochenkarte*. The **monthly ticket** or *Monatskarte* (öS500), which runs for a calendar month, works in much the same way.

The Viennese being a law-abiding bunch, there are few **ticket inspectors**, but if you are caught without a valid ticket or pass, you'll be handed an on-the-spot fine of öS500 (plus the appropriate fare).

The U-Bahn

Vienna's **U-Bahn**, born in 1969, currently boasts five lines (U1–4 and U6), with further extensions planned. It's by far the fastest way of getting around the city, with trains running from between 5 and 6am to between midnight and 1am (the times of the first and last trains are posted up on each station). Not all U-Bahn lines are underground; the U4 and U6 lines run partly on the old overground Stadtbahn created in the 1890s, and both lines retain some of their original stations and bridges designed by Otto Wagner.

Trams and buses

Vienna has one of the largest **tram** – *Strassenbahn* or *Bim* (after the noise of the bell) as they're known colloquially – systems in the world, with more than thirty routes criss-crossing the capital. Electric trams were introduced in 1897 and they still sport the tradi-

There are Wiener Linien information offices at Stephansplatz, Karlsplatz and Westbahnhof (Mon–Fri 6.30am–6.30pm, Sat & Sun 8.30am–4pm).

There's a map of the U-Bahn system in the colour insert at the back of this book.

A couple of useful words to know on the U-Bahn are Ausgang (Exit) and Not (Emergency).

tional red-and-white livery. After the U-Bahn, trams are the fastest and most efficient way of getting around, running every five to ten minutes. They're pretty punctual, though some lines don't run on weekends or late at night so be sure to check the timetables posted at every stop (*Haltestelle*).

Buses (*Autobusse*) tend to ply the narrow backstreets and the outer suburbs, and despite having to battle with the traffic, are equally punctual. In the heart of the Innere Stadt, where there are no trams and only two U-Bahn stations, there are several very **useful bus services**: #1A, which winds its way from Schottentor to Stubentor; #2A from Schwedenplatz through the Hofburg to Burgring; and #3A from Schottenring to Schwarzenbergplatz. #13A wends its way through the fourth to the eighth districts of the *Vorstädte*.

S-Bahn and Regionalbahn

The **S-Bahn**, or *Schnellbahn* to give it its full name, is of most use to Viennese commuters. It's also the cheapest way of getting to and from the airport, and is useful for day trips to places like Klosterneuburg, Tulln and Krems. S-Bahn trains are less frequent than U-Bahn trains – running every fifteen to thirty minutes – and are strictly timetabled. You're even less likely to have to use the suburban railway system or **Regionalbahn**, unless you're heading out to Melk or Eisenstadt; trains leave from the mainline stations.

Taxis and night buses

Taxis are plentiful and fairly reliable in Vienna. Minimum charge is around öS25, followed by an extra öS10 or so per kilometre or couple of minutes. You can catch a cab at one of the taxi ranks around town, flag one down or phone for one: try ☎313 00, ☎401 00 or ☎601 60.

The only other way of getting home in the small hours is to catch one of the *Nightline* **night buses**, which run every thirty minutes from 12.30am to 4am; all 22 routes pass through Schwedenplatz at some point. A *Netzkarte* is not valid and tickets cost öS25; holders of monthly or yearly passes are eligible for the reduced öS10 fare.

Bicycles and Fiaker

Despite the fact that **cycling** isn't that popular in Vienna, there's a fairly good network of cycle paths – over 500km in total. If you haven't brought your own machine, you can rent bicycles (*Fahrräder*) cheaply enough from Westbahnhof, Südbahnhof and Wien-Nord for around öS100 a day, less if you've arrived by train. Bicycles can be taken on the U- and S-Bahn from Monday to Friday between 9am and 3pm and after 6.30pm, and on Saturdays and Sundays from 9am (you must buy a half-price ticket for your bike).

More expensive is a ride in a soft-top carriage or **Fiaker**, driven by bowler-hatted, multi-lingual coachmen; there are *Fiaker* ranks at Stephansplatz, Heldenplatz, Michaelerplatz and Albertinaplatz. It's

Guided Tours and Walks

Vienna Sightseeing Tours run a variety of **bus tours** around Vienna and the surrounding districts. Their standard city tour (daily 10.30am, 11.45am & 3pm; 1hr 15min; öS220) takes you round the Ringstrasse; pick up a leaflet at the tourist office or any hotel or pension. Alternatively, you can save yourself the commentary by hopping on tram #1 or #2, which circumnavigate the Ringstrasse clockwise and anti-clockwise respectively.

Every Saturday (11.30am & 1.30pm) and Sunday (9.30am, 11.30am & 1.30pm) from May to October, you can leap aboard a 1920s **tram** outside the Otto-Wagner-Pavillon on Karlsplatz and go on an hour-long guided tour, run by *Wiener Linien*; tickets cost öS200, and are available from Karlsplatz U-Bahn.

In summer (May–Oct) several companies run **boat trips** along the River Danube and the Danube Canal, leaving from the quayside of the latter by U-Bahn Schwedenplatz. *Donau Schiffahrt Pyringer-Zopper* is one of the least expensive, and offers a choice of tours lasting from just 75 minutes to more than three hours (öS120–170). Be warned, however, that Vienna's waterfront buildings are none too beautiful.

Most appealing of all are the **walking tours** organized by Vienna's official tourist guides. These cover a relatively small area in much greater detail, mixing historical facts with juicy anecdotes in the company of a local specialist. Subjects covered range from Jugendstil architecture to Jewish Vienna – the weekly *Third Man* tour takes you round the locations associated with the eponymous 1948 film (☎220 66 20) – you'll find most of them detailed in the monthly *Wiener Spaziergänge* leaflet from the tourist office. They tend to cost around öS110 and last about ninety minutes. Simply turn up at the meeting point specified.

best to settle on the price and duration of your ride beforehand; going rate is öS400 for twenty minutes or öS1000 for an hour.

Museums and monuments

The **opening hours and prices** listed on the following page (and in the text of the *Guide*) are the latest available, though bear in mind that some places are prone to raising their charges dramatically from year to year. A concessionary rate is generally available for students, under-18s, over-60s, soldiers and teachers; you'll need ID. Most museums are either closed or free on public holidays, and those marked * in the list below are free on Friday mornings until noon.

The only discount card of any interest to tourists is **The Vienna Card** (*Die Wien-Karte*), which costs öS180 and allows free travel on the public transport system for 72 hours. In addition, you also get discounts at sights such as the Hofburg and Schönbrunn, plus selected restaurants and shops. If you're in Vienna for a long weekend and intend to do quite a bit of sightseeing, then the ticket will probably pay for itself. However, the savings are less than they appear at first sight: a 72-hour *Netzkarte* costs just öS130 and the discounts rarely amount to more than öS20 per sight.

Akademie der bildenden Künste Tues, Thurs & Fri 10am–2pm, Wed 10am–1pm & 3–6pm, Sat & Sun 9am–1pm; öS30; ☎588 16-225; see p.118.

Albertina Mon–Thurs 10am–4pm, Fri 10am–1pm; öS45; ☎53 48 30; see p.96.

Belvedere Tues–Sun 10am–5pm; öS60; ☎795 57-0; see p.157.

* **Figarohaus** (Mozart Museum) Tues–Sun 9am–12.15pm & 1–4.30pm; öS25; ☎513 62 94; see p.47.

Freud-Museum July–Sept daily 9am–6pm; Oct–June 9am–4pm; öS60; ☎319 15 96; see p.178.

Heeresgeschichtliches Museum daily except Fri 10am–4pm; öS40, free on the first Sun of the month; ☎795 61-0; see p.168.

Hofburg

> *Burgkapelle* Jan–June & mid-Sept to Dec Tues & Thurs 1.30–3.30pm, Fri 1–3pm; öS15; Vienna Boys' Choir mass Sun 9.15am; free–öS250; ☎533 99 27; see p.88.
>
> *Kaiserappartements* daily 9am–5pm; öS70; ☎533 75 70; see p.80.
>
> *Prunksaal* (Nationalbibliothek) June–Oct Mon–Sat 10am–4pm, Sun 10am–1pm; Nov–May Mon–Sat 10am–noon; closed for the first three weeks of Sept; öS50; ☎53 410-0; see p.93.
>
> *Schatzkammer* daily except Tues 10am–6pm; öS60; ☎533 79 31; see p.85.
>
> *Winter Reitschule* (Spanish Riding School) training mid-Feb to June & late-Aug to early Oct Tues–Sat 10am–noon; öS100; performances March–June & Sept–Dec Sun 10.45am and less frequently Wed 7pm; öS240–800; see p.90.

* **Historisches Museum der Stadt Wien** Tues–Sun 9am–12.15pm & 1–4.30pm; öS50; ☎505 87 47; see p.126.

Jüdisches Museum daily except Sat 10am–6pm, Thurs 10am–9pm; öS70; ☎535 04 31; see p.54.

Kunsthistorisches Museum Tues–Sun 10am–6pm, Thurs 10am–9pm; öS100; ☎521 77-0; see p.137.

Museum für angewandte Kunst (MAK) Tues–Sun 10am–6pm, Thurs 10am–9pm; öS70; ☎711 36-0; see p.131.

Museum moderner Kunst Tues–Sun 10am–6pm; combined ticket öS60.

> *Palais Liechtenstein*; öS45; ☎317 69 00; see p.180.
>
> *20er Haus*; öS45; ☎799 69 00; see p.168.

Naturhistorisches Museum daily except Tues 9am–6pm; öS30; ☎521 77-0; see p.114.

* **Otto-Wagner-Pavillon** Tues–Sun 9am–12.15pm & 1–4.30pm; öS25; see p.124.

Riesenrad April 10am–11pm; May–Sept daily 9am–midnight; Oct daily 10am–10pm; Nov & Christmas Day–Epiphany daily 10am–6pm; rest of Dec Sat & Sun only; öS45; ☎512 83 14; see p.189.

Schönbrunn

> *Prunkräume* April–Oct daily 8.30am–5pm; Nov–March until 4.30pm; öS80–140; ☎811 13; see p.203.
>
> *Tiergarten* March daily 9am–5.30pm; April until 6pm; May–Sept until 6.30pm; Oct & Feb until 5pm; Nov–Jan until 4.30pm; see p.212.

Secession Tues–Fri 10am–6pm, Sat & Sun 10am–4pm; öS30; ☎587 53 07; see p.120.

Chapter 2

The Innere Stadt

T he **Innere Stadt** (Inner City), Vienna's first district, has been the very heart of the place since the Romans founded Vindobona here on the banks of the Danube in 15 BC. It was here, too, that the Babenburg dukes built their powerbase in the twelfth century, and from 1533, the Habsburgs established the Hofburg, their imperial residence (covered separately in Chapter Three). Consequently, unlike the older quarters in many European

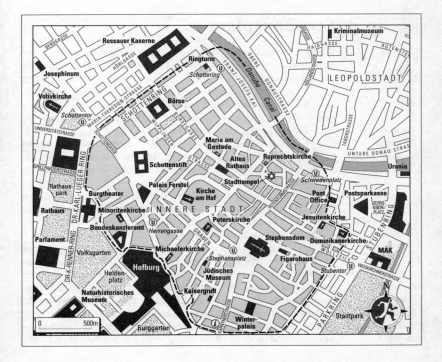

cities, the Innere Stadt remained the chief place of residence for the city's aristocracy throughout the Baroque period and beyond, its narrow, cobbled lanes the unlikely addresses of dukes and duchesses, princes and ambassadors. In fact, the city occupied pretty much the same space from the thirteenth century until the zig-zag fortifications, which had protected the city on two occasions against the Turks, were finally taken down in the mid-nineteenth century.

The focus of the Innere Stadt – and the one thing on all tourists' itineraries – is the city's magnificent Gothic cathedral, **Stephansdom**, whose soaring spire also acts as a useful geographical landmark. Close by are the chief shopping streets of **Kärntnerstrasse**, **Graben** and **Kohlmarkt**, which get progressively more exclusive the nearer you get to the Hofburg. There's a steady ebb and flow of folk along these streets at most times of the day, but the **Kaisergruft**, the last resting place of the Habsburgs, just off Kärntnerstrasse, is the only other sight which gets heavily clogged up with tour groups. Head off into the rest of the Innere Stadt, with its baffling medieval lanes, hidden courtyards and *Durchhäuser*, and you'll soon lose the crowds. For although most of the city's finest Baroque churches and palaces are to be found here, the dearth of premier league sights puts many off the scent.

Stephansplatz

The nearest U-Bahn is Stephansplatz.

The geographical heart of the Innere Stadt is **Stephansplatz**, a lively, pedestrianized square overlooked by the hoary Gothic bulk of the city cathedral. The square hasn't always been so central – the first church built here lay outside the medieval city walls, and the square itself was a graveyard until 1732. Nowadays, though, it's one of the best places for watching Viennese streetlife, from the benign young flame-haired punks who lounge around on the benches by the U-Bahn to the beleagured folk in eighteenth-century costumes wearily flogging tickets for classical concerts. The smell of horse dung wafts across the square from the fiacres lined up along the north wall of the cathedral.

Apart from the cathedral, the most dominant feature of the square is the **Haas Haus**, probably the singly most inappropriate building in the Innere Stadt and one which, not surprisingly, caused something of a furore when it was first unveiled in 1990. The real disappointment is that the architect, Hans Hollein, is clearly gifted (his equally uncompromising jewellery stores along Graben and Kohlmarkt are minor masterpieces). Here, though, the metal-coated glass and polished stone facade lacks subtlety, and the protruding turret is a veritable carbuncle; to cap it all, the interior is an unimaginative mini-shopping centre. The only conceivable reason to enter the building at all is to head up to the terrace of the *Haas Café*, which dishes out a great view over to the cathedral (and saves you from having to look at the Haas Haus itself).

For a review of the Do & Co *restaruant in the Haus Haus see p.286.*

Despite appearances, Haas Haus isn't in fact on Stephansplatz at all, it's on **Stock-im-Eisen-Platz**, a little known geographical entity which covers the no-man's-land between Graben, Stephansplatz and Kärntnerstrasse. The square takes its name – literally "stick-in-iron" – from the nail-studded, sixteenth-century slice of larch tree that stands in a glass-protected niche set into the grandiose **Equitable Palace** on the corner of Kärntnerstrasse. According to Viennese tradition, apprentice locksmiths/blacksmiths would hammer a nail into the trunk for good luck. The Equitable building itself is well worth exploring: built in the 1890s and recently restored, the ornate vestibule (originally designed to be a future metro entrance) is a superb example of the period, with lashings of marble and wrought iron, and a glass-roofed courtyard faced in majolica tiles.

In the paving between the Haas Haus and the cathedral, the groundplan of the **Chapel of St Mary Magdalene**, a charnel house which burnt to the ground in 1781, is marked out in red sandstone. Almost immediately below it is another church building, the Romanesque **Virgilkapelle**, which was discovered during the construction of the metro in the 1970s, and is now preserved in the metro station itself. The thirteenth-century chapel – at one time the family crypt of the Chrannests, one of whom was finance minister to the Habsburgs – is little visited, though the strangeness of its location and the simple beauty of its recesses, decorated with red wheel crosses, make it an intriguing sight. If the chapel is closed, you can satisfy your curiosity by looking down from the metro's viewing platform by the information office.

The Virgilkapelle is open Tues–Sun 9am–12.15pm & 1–4.30pm; öS25.

Stephansdom

The **Stephansdom** (St Stephen's Cathedral) still towers above the Innere Stadt and dominates the Viennese skyline as it has done for centuries. An obvious military target, it has endured two Turkish sieges, Napoleonic bombardment, and in the latter stages of World War II, the attentions of American bombers and Russian artillery. That it survived at all is a miracle, and has ensured it a special place in the hearts of the Viennese.

Visiting Stephansdom

Although the cathedral **opening hours** are daily 6am–10pm, tourists are discouraged from sightseeing during the religious services. In practice, this means that **visiting times** are restricted to Mon–Sat 9am–noon & 1–5pm, Sun 12.30–5pm. Entrance is free, though to have a proper look at anything beyond the transept, you really need to join a **guided tour** (*Domführung*). These run Mon–Fri 10am & 3pm, Sat 10am, 3 & 7pm, Sun 3pm; and cost öS40; you meet just inside the cathedral by the main door. Additional charges are made for the catacombs, the Pummerin and the Steffl itself (see below).

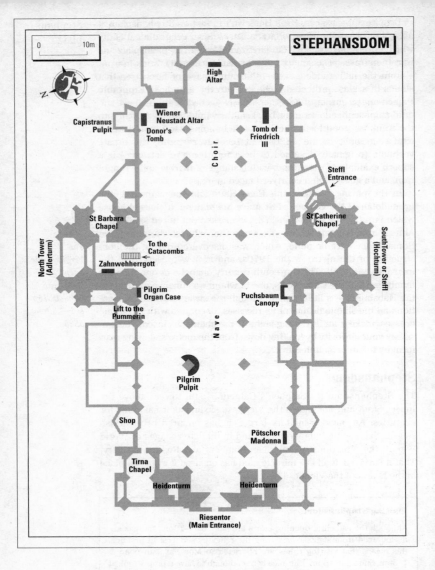

The first church on this site was a Romanesque basilica, begun in 1137, but replaced after a fire in 1193 by a transitional, early-Gothic variant, which was itself reduced to rubble in the fire of 1258. The foundation stone of the current building was laid in 1359 by Rudolf IV, who modelled his designs on the cathedral in Prague, which was being built by his rival, the Emperor Charles IV. Poor old Rudolf, however, could only secure collegiate status for his church, under the bishopric of Passau. In the end, it took more than a hundred years before an independent bishopric was established, yet another century before the final touches were added to the exterior; and it wasn't until the early twentieth century that the choir and several of the chapels were completed.

Stephans-platz

The cathedral's most magnificent feature is the sublime south tower (*Hochturm*) – ironically nicknamed "**Steffl**" (Little Stephen) by the locals – which soars to a height of around 137m. The planned north tower or Eagle Tower (*Adlerturm*) was to have been built along similar lines, but fell victim to cost-cutting during the build-up to the first Turkish siege of 1529, its half-built stump eventually receiving a copper cupola in 1556. You can climb (or take the lift) up the north tower to see the cathedral's great bell known as the **Pummerin** (Boomer), though the Steffl, a blind scramble up 533 steps, has better views. The current bell is a postwar rehash of the twenty-ton original, which was cast from a Turkish cannon captured during the 1683 siege.

The south tower is open March–Oct 9am–5.30pm; Nov–Feb 9am–4.30pm; öS20.

The cathedral's steeply pitched **roof** has been decorated with multi-coloured tiles since 1490, forming giant chevrons on the south side, and a double-headed imperial eagle on the north. The main entrance to the cathedral is via the **Riesentor**, a rare survivor from the present building's twelfth-century predecessor. Its name is usually translated as Giants' (*Riesen*) Gate, though another school of thought claims it is derived from the old German *Ristor*, meaning Draw Gate. Etymology aside, the sculpted figures are superb – though the iron railings and the ebb and flow of visitors make it hard to appreciate them. Flanking the Riesentor are two robust Romanesque towers, known as the **Heidentürme** (Pagans' Towers), which vaguely resemble Turkish minarets.

The north tower is open daily 9am–6pm; öS40 for the lift; öS20 if you walk.

The interior

The first thing that strikes you as you enter the gloomy, high vaulted interior of the cathedral is that, despite the tourists, Stephansdom is still very much a place of worship. At peak times, it can be difficult to get a seat in the area immediately to your right, facing the **Pötscher Madonna**, which sits below a delicate late-Gothic baldachin. Legend has it that the Madonna, an object of great veneration even today, wept tears from her unusually large eyes during the Battle of Zenta against the Turks in 1697, and in so doing miraculously secured victory against the infidels.

Another saviour of the city, Prince Eugène of Savoy, hero of the campaigns against the Turks in the early eighteenth century (see p.161), is buried in the **Tirna Chapel**, on the other side of the cathedral, off the north aisle – all of him, that is, except for his heart, which lies in Turin. Sadly, the chapel is usually shut behind heavy iron gates, which prevent even the slightest glimpse of the prince's tomb on the south wall. What you can see, though, is a fifteenth-century crucifix, whose statue of Christ sports a shaggy black beard of human hair, which, according to legend, is still growing. Close by, in the north aisle itself, another ornate Gothic baldachin shelters a Sacred Heart picture, in which Christ reveals his flaming, bleeding heart rather as one shows off a new T-shirt.

The highlight of the cathedral, though, is without doubt the early sixteenth-century carved stone **Pilgram pulpit**, with portraits of the four fathers of the Christian church (saints Augustine, Gregory, Jerome and Ambrose), naturalistically sculpted by the Moravian Anton Pilgram, who "signed" his work by showing himself peering from a window below the pulpit stairs. The filigree work above and below the staircase is masterly, as are the salamanders and toads (sadly now under protective perspex), symbolizing good and evil, pursuing one another up the bannister and culminating in a barking dog who keeps them all at bay. Pilgram can be spotted again on the wall of the north aisle, this time in polychrome, peeping out below another of his works, the now defunct organ case. The organ itself originally sat above the last of the cathedral's late-Gothic baldachins, whose lovely, lacy filigree work can be seen on the opposite side of the nave.

If you want to escape the crowds, head for the twin chapels at either end of the transepts. Though shut off behind wrought-iron railings, the **St Catherine Chapel**, to the south, boasts a beautiful baptismal font, made in 1481; the marble base features the four apostles, the niches of the basin are decorated with the twelve disciples, Christ and Saint Stephan, while the wooden lid is shaped like a church spire and smothered with sculpted scenes. Up above, there's a wonderful ceiling boss of Saint Catherine with her wheel and sword, on the end of a drooping pendant. To the north, the **St Barbara Chapel** also features hanging pendants, this time stamped with heraldic bosses. The chapel is dedicated to the those killed in concentration camps, and the small triangle in the crucifix below Christ's feet contains ashes from Auschwitz. On the wall opposite, as you leave the chapel, look out for a half-torso of Christ in suffering, known as the **Zahnwehherrgott** (Our Lord of the Toothache). According to Viennese legend, the three students who coined the nickname were immediately struck down with toothache, which no barber-surgeon could cure, until the young men had fallen prostrate before the statue and prayed for forgiveness.

The **choir**, beyond the transepts, is roped off, and only strictly visitable on a guided tour (see "Visiting Stephansdom" above). At the far end of the Women's Choir, however, you should just be able to make out the winged **Wiener Neustädter Altar**, a richly gilded masterpiece of late-Gothic art which dates from the mid-fifteenth century but was only brought to the cathedral in 1883. During the week, the altar's wings are closed and only twenty-four saints are depicted; on Sundays, the wings are opened to reveal twice that number; only on religious festivals, though, do you get to see the altar's showstopper – the Madonna and Child, the Birth of Christ, the Adoration of the Magi, the Coronation of Mary and the latter's death, all sculpted out of wood. Below the altar to the left lies the **Donor's Tomb**, adorned with sandstone effigies of Rudolf IV and his wife Catherine of Bohemia (they're actually buried in the catacombs; see below), which would originally have been richly gilded and peppered with precious stones.

In the Apostles' Choir to the south stands the glorious red marble **Tomb of Emperor Friedrich III**. In among the 240 statues, 32 coats of arms and numerous scaly creatures which decorate the tomb is the emperor's mysterious acronym composed of the vowels of the Roman alphabet, which has prompted numerous interpretations, ranging from the obvious A*ustria* E*rit* I*n* O*rbe* U*ltima* (Austria will be the last in the world), to the ingenious A*quila* E*lecta* I*ovis* O*mnia* V*incit* (The chosen eagle conquers all things). Friedrich himself revealed the German version to be A*lles* E*rdreich* I*st* Ö*sterreich* U*ntertan* (The whole world is subject to Austria), though some wags put forward the more appropriate A*ller* E*rst* I*st* Ö*sterreich* V*erloren* (In the first place, Austria is lost), since Friedrich had great difficulty keeping hold of Upper and Lower Austria and was in fact driven out of Vienna by the Hungarian king Matthias Corvinus in 1485.

In Latin, the letters "u" and "v" are both rendered as "V".

The catacombs

A stairway in the north transept leads down into the **catacombs** (*Katakomben*), which, initially at least, are a bit disappointing, having been over-restored in the 1960s. It's here that Rudolf IV and his wife are actually buried, along with other early Habsburg rulers, plus sundry priests, bishops and archbishops who served in the cathedral. Rudolf himself died aged twenty-six, though in his seven years' reign he managed to found both the cathedral and the university; he died in Milan in 1365 and was carried back to Vienna sewn into a cowhide to preserve his body. Last of all, there's a small chamber lined with cages filled with bronze caskets containing the entrails of the later Habsburgs.

The catacombs are open for guided tours only (every 30min) Mon–Sat 9–11.30am & 12.30–4.30pm, Sun 1–4.30pm; öS35.

From this point, you enter the damp, dimly lit labyrinth of eighteenth-century catacombs, which were closed in 1783 after the stench became too overpowering, and have been left more or less untouched by the city's otherwise over-zealous restorers. Around 16,000 locals are buried here, their bones piled high in over thirty rooms, and in the final chamber, there's a particularly macabre pile left over from a medieval plague pit. You exit from the catacombs via a secret staircase which deposits you outside the cathedral, by the place where Mozart's body was blessed before being buried in St Marxer Friedhof (see p.170). At the very northeastern corner of the cathedral, near the exit from the catacombs, is the **Capistranus**

The bodies of the later Habsburgs are buried in the Kaisergruft, see p.50; their hearts are buried in the Augustinerkirche, see p.95.

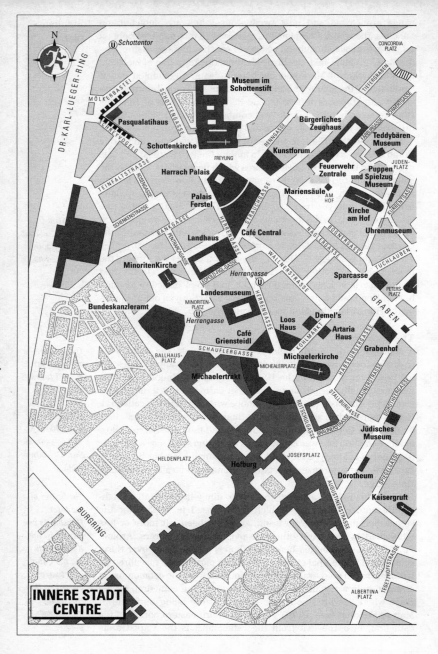

INNERE STADT
CENTRE

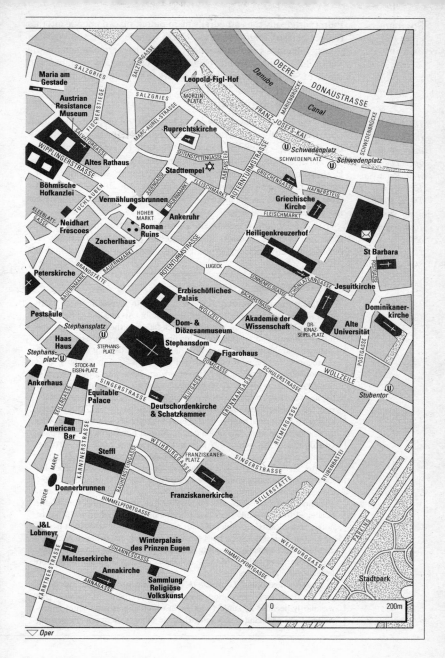

Pulpit, originally the cathedral's main pulpit, placed outside after its replacement by Pilgram's work. It was from here that the Venetian priest, Johannes von Capistrano, preached his sermons against the Turks during the fifteenth century; the extravagant sunburst and statue of St Francis trampling on a Turk are Baroque additions.

Around Stephansplatz

*The Dom- and
Diözesan-
museum is
open Tues,
Wed, Fri & Sat
10am–4pm,
Thurs 10am–
6pm, Sun
10am–1pm;
öS40.*

Badly bombed in the war, few of the buildings on Stephansplatz itself are worthy of mention. Even those that survived the bombs lack a little something – you'd hardly suspect that the two-storey building on the north side of Stephansplatz is in fact the seventeenth-century **Erzbischöfliches Palais** (Archbishops' Palace). Next door is the equally nondescript **Zwettlhof**, originally an abbey founded by Cistercians from Zwettl in Lower Austria, but bought by Rudolf IV for use as the cathedral priory.

The Zwettlhof now houses the **Dom- and Diözesanmuseum** on its first floor (access through the passageway at Stephansplatz 6). This is basically the dumping ground for a mishmash of the cathedral's

---

Mozart in Vienna

Wolfgang Amadeus Mozart (1756–91) moved to Vienna in March 1781 after a summons from his employer, the irascible Archbishop of Salzburg, Count Colloredo, who was visiting his sick father in the city. Within three months Mozart had resigned from his post as court organist to the arch-bishop or "arch-oaf" (*Erzlimmel*) as he called him, causing a rift with his overbearing father, who was assistant *Kapellmeister* in Salzburg. The relationship was further strained when Mozart, against his father's wishes, moved in with the all-female Weber family, and grew particularly attached to one of the daughters, Constanze. In August 1782 Mozart eventually married the nineteen-year old Constanze in the Stephansdom. Their union appears to have been happy, despite most biographers' misogynist attacks on Constanze as unworthy of his genius. Mozart himself hated to be parted from her, if his letters – "I kiss and squeeze you 1,095,060,437,082 times" – and the fact that he rarely left her side, are anything to go by.

After giving many concerts as conductor and pianist, Mozart turned his hand to opera, enjoying his greatest success in July 1782 with what is now his least-known operatic work, *Die Entführung aus dem Serail*. It was after hearing *Die Entführung* for the first time that the Emperor Josef II is alleged to have said: "Too beautiful for our ears, and an awful lot of notes, dear Mozart", to which Mozart replied "No more notes than necessary, Your Majesty!". Such tales have led to a popular belief that Mozart and Josef were constantly feuding over artistic debates: in his letters, however, Mozart's criticisms of the – notoriously stingy – emperor were on purely financial matters.

Mozart's next opera, *Le Nozze di Figaro*, was premièred in May 1786 to a decidedly mixed reception, running for just nine performances. This was partly because its subject matter, in which a lecherous count is prevented from seducing a servant girl by an alliance between the serving

---

most valuable treasures, church plate and artwork. There are, however, some arresting medieval sculptures in wood – Saint Dionysius (aka Denis) carrying his severed head to his place of burial (in 3D relief), Saint Aegydius (aka Giles) looking rather sadly at the arrow stuck through his hand – and some High Baroque, not to say high kitsch, pieces, like the shrine Madonna, whose cloak opens up to reveal God (forming her body), surrounded by a host of worshippers' faces. The highlight, though, is the dimly lit treasury of monstrances and macabre reliquaries, including St Leopold's hipbone, a piece of the Virgin Mary's belt and the cranium of Saint Stephen. Follow the signs to the "Kapelle", and you can experience the additional thrill of seeing one of Beethoven's quills.

Stephan-splatz

The Schatzkammer is open May–Oct Mon, Thurs & Sun 10am–noon, Wed 3–5pm, Fri & Sat 10am–noon & 3–5pm; Nov–April closed Fri morning & Sun; öS25.

The Church and Treasury of the Teutonic Knights
A much more intriguing ecclesiastical treasure trove can be seen at the **Schatzkammer des Deutschen Ordens** (Treasury of the Order of Teutonic Knights), spread over five rooms on the second floor of the Deutschordenshaus; enter from Singerstrasse 7, one block south

---

classes and his own long-suffering wife, was controversial – as a play it had already been banned in Paris and Vienna. Josef II obviously liked it, however, inviting the cast to give a special performance at his summer residence at Laxenburg. And *Figaro*'s subversive overtones went down a storm in Prague, where Mozart premièred two later operas, *Don Giovanni* and *La Clemenza di Tito*, both of which were written in Vienna.

Mozart's final work was his *Requiem*, which was commissioned anonymously by an "unknown messenger" in the last year of Mozart's life. Only after Mozart's death did the patron's identity became known: it was the recently widowed Count Franz Walsegg-Stuppach, who wished to pass the composition off as his own. In the end it became Mozart's own *Requiem*, since it was still unfinished when he died during the night of December 4–5, 1791, after two weeks' rheumatic fever. Few biographers have forgiven Constanze for not attending the funeral service at Stephansdom; others assert that she was too distraught to attend. She has also been criticized for having the *Requiem* completed by one of Mozart's pupils, Sussmayr, so as to get the final payment – though this seems fair enough for a widow left with two children to raise (and apparently Mozart had suggested this on his deathbed).

Yet more anecdotes surround the generally accepted rivalry with the *Kapellmeister* Antonio Salieri; though this, too, has been over-played. Salieri was exclusively an opera composer, while Mozart, at least until 1786, was known chiefly as an instrumental composer and virtuoso pianist. Some went as far as to suggest that Salieri himself poisoned Mozart, an allegation strenuously denied by Salieri on his deathbed years later, but to no avail: Alexander Pushkin dramatized it, Nicolai Rimsky-Korsakov made it into an opera, and most famously *Amadeus*, Peter Shaffer's play on the subject, was made into an Oscar-winning film by Miloš Forman. For the story of how Mozart was condemned to a pauper's grave, see p.170.

of Stephansplatz. The Teutonic Knights were one of the three main military-religious orders to emerge from the Crusades in the twelfth century and for many centuries had their base in Marienburg (in what is now Poland). When the Order split along religious lines in the sixteenth century, those still loyal to Catholicism moved their headquarters to Mergentheim in Bavaria, until 1809, when they were disbanded by order of Napoleon. Twenty-five years later the Order was reconstituted in Vienna, where it remains active as a charitable body.

The treasury's varied collection, assembled by seven centuries of Grand Masters (*Hochmeister*), ranges from the mundane – seals, coins and crosses – to the bizarre: an adder's tongue used for testing food for poison, a red coral salt cellar tree hung with the fossils of sharks' teeth, and two "chocolate sets", one with silver cups and saucers, complete with tiger-shell spoons sporting wonky silver handles, another in *Chinoiserie* style. There are other bizarre exhibits from the Kunstkammer collected by the Grand Master Archduke Maximilian III, like the set of three bezoars, petrifications of ibex stomachs, to which the Persians attributed great healing powers, and an onyx pendant depicting Jonah reclining on the tongue of a diminutive whale. The

---

On Mozart's Trail

It's almost as difficult to avoid images of Mozart in Vienna – on chocolate boxes, on tourist brochures, on flyers for concerts – as it is in his home town of Salzburg. For it was in Vienna that Mozart spent the last decade of his life, during which he composed almost all his most famous works. He moved thirteen times, for a variety of reasons, not least because he never managed to secure a permanent posting, which meant that he was always on the point of leaving. Today the streets of the Innere Stadt are littered with plaques marking his various addresses, though, in fact, only one – the Figarohaus – still stands.

Singerstrasse 7. On his arrival in March 1781, Mozart stayed here with the Archbishop of Salzburg in the House of the Teutonic Knights.

Petersplatz 11. In May, Mozart rented a room from the Weber family, but had to move out in early September, due to rumours about his liaison with one of the daughters, Constanze.

Graben 17. After leaving the Webers, he moved round the corner with the Arnsteins, the city's most privileged Jewish family.

Wipplingerstrasse 19. Following the success of his opera *Die Entführung aus dem Serail*, Mozart moved here in July 1782, to be joined after their marriage in August, by Constanze.

Wipplingerstrasse 14. In December 1782, the Mozarts moved down the street to a house belonging to a wealthy, converted Jew, Baron Wetzlar, where they lived in two rooms on the fourth floor.

Kohlmarkt 7. Three months later, in February 1783, Mozart moved again, as a favour to Wetzlar, who needed the rooms. Wetzlar waived the back rent, paid for the move, and paid for the Kohlmarkt lodgings.

Order's military past is represented by a collection of exotic arms and armour, including a wiggly sixteenth-century Malaysian sword and scabbard, and a poisoned dagger with a handle carved out of rhino horn into the Goddess of Death, with sapphire eyes and ruby eyebrows. And in the final room, there is the most amazing table clock, smothered in a garland of silver-gilded leaves studded with garnets and turquoise.

After the treasury, the Order's church, the **Deutschordenskirche**, on street level, can seem something of a let down. Incorporated into the Order's buildings in the fourteenth century, the church has retained its Gothic origins, despite remodelling in later centuries, and is decorated with the Order's numerous coats of arms. You're better off taking a stroll into the misshapen cobbled courtyard to the rear, an almost pastorally peaceful spot festooned with ivy and flower boxes. Brahms spent the best part of two years here in 1863–65, but inevitably it's Mozart who gets the plaque, for his brief sojourn here in the spring of 1781.

Stephans- platz

Devotees of the Deutschorden should view the order's monument off Schottenring (see p.108).

Figarohaus

The **Figarohaus**, home of Vienna's Mozart Museum, lies immediately east of the cathedral (to get there, pass through the *Durchhaus* at

---

Judenplatz 3. In April 1783, Mozart moved into "good accommodations", where his first child, Karl Thomas, was born (his wife's cries during labour are alluded to in his D minor String Quartet).

Graben 29. In January 1784, the Mozarts moved to the Trattnerhof, one of the most famous addresses in all Vienna at the time, owned by the wealthy publisher, Johann Thomas von Trattner, whose second wife, Maria Theresa, was one of Mozart's first pupils.

Schulerstrasse 8. In September 1784, the Mozarts moved into the Camesina House, behind Stephansdom (now the Figarohaus; see below).

Landstrasse Hauptstrasse 75–77. In April 1787, the Mozarts moved out of the Innere Stadt into a garden apartment in the third district of Landstrasse – here he composed *Eine kleine Nachtmusik*.

Tuchlauben 27. In December 1787, landlord problems forced them to move to the corner of Schultergasse and Tuchlauben.

Währingerstrasse 26. In June 1788, due to financial difficulties, the Mozarts moved again. Mozart's financial crisis was partly precipitated by the Turkish threat – 1788 was known as the *Türkenjahr* – and compounded by the French Revolution.

Judenplatz 4. They kept this address from January 1789 for almost two years. It was here that their fifth child died and Constanze's illness began – an ulcerated leg with fears of infection, which brought further financial worries, as she had to move to Baden to take the cure.

Rauhensteingasse 8. Mozart's last move – his thirteenth address – took place in September 1791, when it appears that he had largely overcome his money problems. During their time here the couple's sixth child, Franz Xaver, was born, Mozart wrote *Die Zauberflöte*, *La Clemenza di Tito*, and spent his last days working on his *Requiem*. The plot is now occupied by the *Steffl* department store, whose top floor contains a memorial to the composer.

---

*The
Figarohaus is
open
Tues–Sun
9am–12.15pm
& 1–4.30pm;
öS25.*

Stephansplatz 5a, and enter at Domgasse 5). Here, on the first floor, Mozart, Constanze and their son, Karl Thomas, lived for three years, during which the composer enjoyed his greatest success. It was Mozart's swankiest accommodation in Vienna, where he even had his own billiards room, and space for visitors. The composer, Johann Nepomuk Hummel, stayed here as Mozart's live-in pupil for two and a half years; Josef Haydn was a regular visitor, opining that Mozart was "the greatest composer that I know in person or by name".

Sadly, however, there's not a lot to see inside. Only one of the rooms retains the original decor of marble and stucco (the Camesina family, who owned the property, were stucco artists). There are none of Mozart's personal effects, no period furniture, no atmosphere, just a few facsimiles of original scores and reproductions of the composer and his circle of friends. Nevertheless, it's worth a visit, if only for the building's lovely courtyard, the views along Blutgasse, and the chance to hear some of Mozart's music on the headphones provided.

Kärntnerstrasse and around

As its name suggests, **Kärntnerstrasse** lies along the old road from Vienna to the southern Austrian province of Carinthia (Kärnten), and beyond to the Adriatic. Widened in the nineteenth century, badly bombed in World War II and pedestrianized in the 1970s, it retains only a few reminders of the days when it was home to the city's luxury retail trade. Today, it is more downmarket, with touristy cafés, delivery vans and buskers vying for space. Nevertheless, it's still a favourite street for promenading, especially in the afternoon/evening and at weekends, and for window shopping – the stratospheric prices mean you can do little else.

*The Lobmeyr
shop and
museum are
open Mon–Fri
9am–6pm, Sat
9am–1pm.*

One exception is **J. & L. Lobmeyr** at no. 26, which, as well as flogging expensive glass and crystal, also houses an informal glass museum. The assistants are quite happy for you to wander through to the back of the shop, where you'll find the stairs that lead to the second-floor balcony. The wonderful, mostly antique, exhibits here include an incredible range of chandeliers, culminating, in both senses of the word, in a copy of the 1960s chandelier which graces the New York Metropolitan Opera House. Downstairs in the shop itself, you'll see glassware sets still made to designs by Adolf Loos and Josef Hoffmann for the Wiener Werkstätte (see p.133).

The American
Bar, *on
Kärntner
Durchgang, is
a recently
restored archi-
tectural mas-
terpiece from
1908 by Adolf
Loos.*

The only other buildings of any architectural merit are no. 16, which sports quasi-medieval frescoes, and the **Malteserkirche** (Church of the Knights of Malta), directly opposite Lobmeyr. The latter is more difficult to miss, thanks to its imposing Neoclassical entrance, a misleading introduction to what is basically a simple, single-nave Gothic church. Inside is a splendid monument to Jean de la Valette, who in 1565 defended Malta from the Turks, two of whose moustachioed brethren hold up the Grand Master's monument.

Beyond, on the corner of Annagasse, is the street's oldest secular building, the modest three-storey Palais Esterházy, now a casino. Kärntnerstrasse continues south past the Staatsoper (see p.116), across the Ringstrasse to Karlsplatz (see p.120).

Neuer Markt

Kärntnerstrasse's most interesting sights lie off the street itself, most conspicuously in the **Neuer Markt** to the west, formerly the city's medieval flour market, now used as a car park. The centrepiece of the square is the **Donnerbrunnen**, a Baroque fountain designed by Georg Raphael Donner. The nudity of the figures perched on the edge of the fountain – they represent the four Austrian tributaries of the Danube: the Enns, March, Ybbs and Traun – was deemed too risqué by the Empress Maria Theresa, who had the lead statues removed in 1770 to be melted down into cannon. They were returned unharmed in 1801, and in 1873 replaced by bronze copies: the young male figure of Traun, in particular, depicted dipping his triton into the waters, clearly showed rather too much buttock for contemporary tastes, hence the judiciously placed fig leaf.

The original lead figures can be seen in the Unteres Belvedere, see p.160.

The buildings which surround the square are as undistinguished as those on Kärntnerstrasse itself – and that goes, too, for the **Kapuzinerkirche**. Yet this grim-looking church is one of the premier sights in Vienna, for since 1633, its crypt – the **Kaisergruft** – has been the unlikely resting place of the Habsburgs (with just a few notable exceptions). They chose the lowly, mendicant Order of the Capuchins as a gesture of modesty; to underscore the point, an elaborate ceremony was enacted at each Habsburg funeral. As the funeral cortege approached the church, the prior would ask "Who seeks entry here?". The grand master of the court would reply "I am His Majesty the Emperor of Austria, King of Hungary". The monk would then maintain "I know him not, who seeks entry?". "I am the Emperor, Apostolic King of Hungary, King of Bohemia, Dalmatia,

---

Meissl und Schadn

The Emperor Franz-Josef was famous for eating *Tafelspitz* (boiled rump of beef) for lunch every day. His courtiers, naturally, followed suit; one of the best places to sample the dish was at the legendary **Meissl und Schadn** restaurant on Neuer Markt, which regularly offered more than 25 varieties of *Tafelspitz*. The restaurant was also the scene of imperial Vienna's most famous political **assassination**. On October 21, 1916, the Prime Minister Count Karl von Stürgkh was shot dead, while enjoying his after-dinner cigar, by fellow diner, Friedrich Adler. The assassin, younger brother of the leader of the Social Democrats, Viktor Adler, was appalled by the slaughter of the war, and incensed by Stürgkh's refusal to reconvene parliament. He was sentenced to life imprisonment, but later released in an act of clemency by the Emperor Karl I, and went on to outlive *Meissl und Schadn* itself, which was destroyed in the air raids of World War II.

Croatia, Slavonia, Galicia, Lodomeria, Illyria, Jerusalem, Archduke of Austria, Grand-Prince of Transylvania, Grand Duke of Tuscany and Krakow, Duke of Lorraine, Salzburg, Styria, Carinthia and Carniola." The priest would insist "I know him not, who seeks entry here?. At this the grand master would kneel, saying "A humble sinner, who begs God's mercy" – only then would the coffin be allowed in.

The Kaisergruft

*The Kaiser-
gruft is open
daily
9.30am–4pm;
öS30.*

The **Kaisergruft** itself is entered from a doorway to the left of the church. While a monk relieves you of your money, notices demand a respectful *Silentium!* – but don't let them kid you, this place is a tourist attraction above all else. Inside, though the crypt is neither gloomy nor Gothic in any sense of the word, it is, nevertheless, an intriguing insight into the Habsburgs' fascination with Death.

To follow the tombs in chronological order, turn right immediately as you enter the crypt, and head for the small **Founders' Vault** on the right at the far end; here you'll find Matthias and his wife, Anna, who thought up the Kaisergruft, and whose bodies were transferred

*The Habsburgs'
entrails are
buried in the
catacombs of
Stephansdom,
see p.41; their
hearts are in
the Augustiner-
kirche, see
p.95.*

here in 1633 (a decade or so after their deaths). The tombs that line the **Leopoldine Vault** (along which you've just walked) are fairly modest seventeenth-century works, though when you consider that twelve of the incumbents are children, these are clearly pretty big coffins. The **Caroline Vault**, a continuation of the Leopoldine, marks the beginning of the monster Baroque sarcophagii. Those of Leopold I and Josef I were both designed by Johann Lucas von Hildebrandt, the latter sporting ghoulish skulls in full head armour and bat wings. Those of Karl VI and his wife are utterly his n' hers designs by Rococo artist, Balthasar Ferdinand Moll: his sits on lions, with toothy skulls sporting crowns at each corner; hers sits on eagles, with women in mourning veils at each corner.

The main focus and highlight of the crypt is the **Maria Theresa Vault**, almost entirely taken up with Moll's obscenely large double tomb for the empress and her husband, Franz Stephan, immediately to the left as you enter. Over three metres high and wide, six metres long, and smothered in Rococo decorations, the imperial couple are depicted sitting up in bed, as if indignantly accusing one another of snoring. Immediately below their feet lies the simple copper coffin of their son, Josef II, to whom such pomposity was an anathema. It was he who instigated the idea of a reusable coffin, and issued a decree enforcing its use in all funerals – not surprisingly, given the Viennese obsession with elaborate send-offs, the emperor was eventually forced to back down. Several more of Maria Theresa's sixteen children lie in the shadow of their mother, in ornate Rococo coffins, as does the only non-Habsburg among the crypt's 143 coffins, Karoline Fuchs-Mollard, the empress's governess.

It's all downhill architecturally, after the Maria Theresa Vault. The **Franz II Vault** contains only the fairly plain tombs of the emperor and his four wives. Ferdinand I and his wife share the **Ferdinand Vault** with thirty-seven others, though they're all buried in niches in the wall. At the far end of the crypt is the gloomy postwar bunker of the **New Vault**, which features jazzy, concrete, zig-zag vaulting. Star corpses here include Maximilian I, Emperor of Mexico, who was assassinated in 1867, and Marie Louise, Napoleon's second wife. Their son, the Duke of Reichstadt or "L'Aiglon", who died of consumption at the age of twenty-one, was also buried here until 1940, when Hitler had his remains transferred to Paris as a gesture of goodwill.

Kärntner-strasse and around

Finally, there's the **Franz-Josef Vault**, the emperor's sarcophagus, permanently strewn with fresh flowers. Even more revered, though, is his wife, Empress Elisabeth, who was assassinated in 1898, her tomb draped in Hungarian wreaths and colours. On the other side of the emperor is the coffin of their eldest son, Crown Prince Rudolf, who committed suicide in 1889 (see p.242).

For more on the Empress Elisabeth, see p.218.

The **Chapel** beyond contains the Kaisergruft's most recent arrival, the Empress Zita, who died in 1989 in exile and was buried here with imperial pomp and circumstance. In the corner is a bust of her dashing, bemedalled husband, the Emperor Karl I, who was deposed in 1918, and is buried on the island of Madeira, where he died of pneumonia in 1922.

East of Kärntnerstrasse

The Kaisergruft may be the main tourist attraction off Kärntnerstrasse, but there are a couple of other minor sights a short stroll east of the street. The most obvious is **Franziskanerplatz**, a pretty little square halfway along Weihburggasse, centred around a statue of Moses, and dominated by the Renaissance facade of the **Franziskanerkirche**, with its distinctive stepped gable. The interior, though, is High Baroque, with a high cherub count on just about every altar and ledge, and an incredible slab of sculpted drapery falling down in folds from the ceiling, on the left as you walk in. The St John of Nepomuk monument employs a similar theatrical effect – this time it's sculpted water flowing over the side – while the high altar features a huge Gothic Madonna set against a giant sunburst.

The Kleines Café, *on Franziskaner-platz, is one of Vienna's finest small Kaffee-häuser; see p.282.*

One block south, at Himmelpfortgasse 8, is the former **Winterpalais des Prinzen Eugen** (Winter Palace of Prince Eugène), a typically mighty Baroque palace strung out along a narrow street. Designed by Fischer von Erlach and extended by Hildebrandt, the palace now houses the Ministry of Finance; the only part visible to members of public is the staircase, executed in grandiose style despite the restricted space. Four writhing Atlantes flank the stairs, and a figure of Hercules stands in the niche above the landing; the ceiling painting of Apollo is by Louis Dorigny. To reach the staircase, pass through the main entrance and take the last door on the right before the Rococo courtyard. To view the equally splendid state

The Winterpalais is open Mon–Thurs 8am–4pm, Fri 8am–3.30pm.

*The Sammlung
is open Wed
9am–4pm &
Sun
9am–1pm;
öS25.*

rooms, where the prince received foreign dignataries, you must make a prior appointment; ☎514 33.

Another block south at Johannesgasse 8 is the **Sammlung Religiöse Volkskunst**, a department of the Folk Art Museum, housed in the city's former Ursuline convent (now the Academy of Music). Among the small collection of eighteenth-century folk paintings, travelling altars, and simple drawings illustrating the roads to heaven and hell, the highlight is, without doubt, the Baroque convent apothecary, built in 1747 and still *in situ*, with its pots and bottles arrayed in tall glass-fronted dressers.

One final block south is the pretty little pedestrianized street of Annagasse, lined with Baroque houses and named after its church, the **Annakirche**, an oasis of calm disturbed only by the odd snatch of muffled music coming from the nearby conservatoire. Built in the seventeenth century, the church was given a Baroque going over in the following century by the Jesuits, who employed David Gran to paint a series of superb ceiling frescoes, and the high altar painting of the Holy Family.

Graben and Kohlmarkt

The prime shopping streets of **Graben** and **Kohlmarkt** retain an air of exclusivity that Kärntnerstrasse has lost. Their shops, many of which are preserved in aspic, as if the Empire lives on, advertise branches in places such as Karlsbad, Leipzig and Prag. Others still sport the *K. K.* or *k.u.k* emblem – *kaiserlich und königlich* (Imperial and Royal) – the Austrian equivalent of "By Appointment to Her Majesty the Queen", flaunted by the shops of upper-crust London. In between these old-fashioned stores are several Art Nouveau edifices, and trendy new designer jewellers produced by the doyen of modern Austrian architecture, **Hans Hollein**.

Graben

Graben – its name translates as ditch – was once a moat that lay outside the Roman camp. It was filled in sometime in the thirteenth century, and, like Kärntnerstrasse, was widened at the beginning of the nineteenth century, from which era most of its buildings date. The most conspicuous monument on Graben is the **Pestsäule** (Plague Column), or Dreifaltigkeitssäule (Trinity Column) to give its full title, a towering, amorphous mass of swirling clouds, saints and cherubs, covered in a cobweb of netting to keep the pigeons off. On the south side of the column, Faith and a cherub can be seen plunging a flaming torch into the guts of an old hag (Plague). Ostensibly erected to commemorate the 1679 plague, similar monuments were raised throughout the Empire on the initiative of the Jesuits, often to celebrate deliverance from the Protestant or Turkish "plague". As such, they became symbols of the Counter-Reformation.

The Pestsäule, and the Hildebrandt-designed Bartolotti-Partenfeld palace at no. 11 on the corner of Dorotheergasse, are the only survivors of the Baroque era on Graben. The two most imposing buildings on the street were designed by Otto Wagner, best known for his Jugendstil architecture: the 1895 **Ankerhaus**, at no. 10, which forms the block between Spiegelgasse and Dorotheergasse, and the much earlier **Grabenhof**, whose red marble loggia forms the most eye-catching ensemble. If you look up at the roof of the Ankerhaus, you'll see a wrought-iron and glass superstructure, originally intended as Wagner's own purpose-built studio, now used by the architect Friedensreich Hundertwasser.

The **Sparkasse** at the far end on the right, is a classic post-Napoleonic, or Biedermeier, building, both in its function, as a savings bank for the burgeoning bourgeoisie (note the busy bee symbol on the facade), and in its severe, unadorned Neoclassicism. The latter became the officially sanctioned style of the Metternich era, its lack of ornament acting as a visual symbol of the latter's repressive, reactionary politics. The cluster of naked caryatids – the Graben nymphs – at the far end of the street are an unintentional reminder of the area's one-time associations as a red-light district, which stretch back to the Josephine era.

*For more on
Hundertwasser
see p.154.*

Designer Shops

The shops at street level on Graben and neighbouring Kohlmarkt are by no means all stuck in the Habsburg era; in fact, several are minor masterpieces of twentieth-century design. First off, there's the **Knize** tailors at no. 11, whose luxuriant black marble facade was designed by Adolf Loos in 1910. It's a typical example of Loos's work, which combines a love of rich materials with a strict aversion to unnecessary ornamentation. The sales room on the ground floor is tiny, but upstairs there's a much larger wooden-panelled fitting room, unchanged since Loos's day. Another characteristic Loos facade can be seen at Kohlmarkt 16, designed in 1912 for the bookshop **Manz**. Despite his name (and rumours to the contrary), Loos did not design the underground toilets on Graben, which are the work of Wilhelm Beetz.

After the war, Hans Hollein, of Haas Haus infamy (see p.36), continued where Loos had left off. The first real shot across the bows of the city's dour postwar architecture was his **Retti** candle shop at Kohlmarkt 8–10, designed in the 1960s, the doorway of its smooth aluminium facade shaped like a giant keyhole. Then, in the early 1970s, he gave the **Schullin** (now *Deutsch*) jewellers, Graben 26, a polished marble facade spliced by a seam of mercurial gold which trickles down into the door frame. The jewellers were clearly enamoured, and commissioned Hollein to design their branch at Kohlmarkt 7 in the 1980s; this time, he chose a more subtle interplay of shapes and materials rather than a single arresting image: slender wooden columns support a gilded industrial sheet metal pediment, while portholes serve as showcases, and brass snakes as doorhandles.

Peterskirche

Set back slightly from Graben, occupying a little square of its own, is the **Peterskirche**, completed by Hildebrandt in 1733, and without doubt the finest Baroque church in the Innere Stadt. From the outside, the great green oval dome overwhelms the church's twin towers; inside, the dome's fresco by Johann Michael Rottmayr is faded beyond recognition, leaving the High Baroque side altars, and *trompe l'oeil* painting in the choir, to create a sense of theatrics. The lavish gilded pulpit is truly magnificent, but the most dramatic work of art is the monument, designed by Lorenzo Matielli, opposite, depicting Saint John of Nepomuk being thrown off Prague's Charles Bridge by some nasty-looking Czech bully boys, with Václav IV in Roman garb directing the proceedings.

Dorotheergasse

Of all the streets that fan out from Graben, the most rewarding is **Dorotheergasse**, home of several famous Viennese institutions. The first two face each other at the bottom of the street: the bohemian, nicotine-stained, *Café Hawelka*, run by the same couple (now in their eighties) since World War II, and the ultimate stand-up sandwich bar, *Trzesniewski*, opposite. Further up on the left is the *Hotel Graben*, where, from 1914 until his death in 1919, the poet Peter Altenberg was a permanent guest; beyond stands the institution from which the street gets its name. The **Dorotheum** is the city's premier auction house, founded in 1707 by the Emperor Josef I as a pawnshop for the rich – the euphemism for those who had fallen on hard times was "going to visit Aunt Dorothy". Nowadays auctions take place daily, and you'll find almost anything up for sale from second-rate artworks, which go for a song, to Jugendstil furniture, for which you need to take out a second mortgage. *Schmuck* (jewels) and *Brillantschmuck* (diamonds) seem to feature most weeks. In the Glashaus, on the ground floor, there are even fixed-priced goods for sale over the counter, everything from Hoffmann chairs to utter tat; there's also a café on the second floor.

*Eating and
drinking in
the Innere
Stadt is
detailed on
p.273.*

*Viewing for
auctions takes
place Mon–Fri
10am–6pm,
Sat 9am–
12.30pm.*

Jüdisches Museum

A relatively new arrival on Dorotheergasse is the city's intriguing **Jüdisches Museum** (Jewish Museum), halfway up in the Palais Eskeles at no. 11. Vienna was home to the first Jewish Museum in the world, founded in 1896 but forcibly closed by the Nazis in 1938; it wasn't until 1989 that it was finally re-established. Lavishly refurbished with money from the city council, the museum now boasts state-of-the-art premises, including a swanky café and bookshop.

On the ground floor, the covered courtyard is dominated by a giant glass cabinet of Judaica etched with quotations from the Torah and other sources, whose prophetic nature is revealed on the walls, which are peppered with photographic images from the Holocaust.

On the whole, though, the curators have rejected the usual static display cabinets and newsreel photos of past atrocities. Instead, the emphasis of the museum's excellent temporary exhibitions on the first floor is on contemporary Jewish life.

On the second floor, visitors enter a seemingly empty room, with a quote from Marxist Jewish critic Walter Benjamin writ large on the white walls: "the past can only be seized as an image which flashes up at the instant when it can be recognised and is never seen again". It's a bold conceit, which the museum tackles admirably, by employing a series of free-standing glass panels imprinted with holograms – ranging from the knob of Theodor Herzl's walking stick to a short clip capturing an everyday instance of anti-semitism from 1911. These ghostly images, accompanied by judiciously selected soundbites (in German and English) on Zionism, assimilation and other key issues, pithily trace the history of Vienna's Jewry, juxtaposing the enormous achievements of the city's Jews – from Gustav Mahler to Billy Wilder – with its justified reputation as a hot-bed of anti-semitism. In an adjacent corridor, three CD-Rom terminals flesh out the history of Jews in Vienna (in German only).

Taking something of a different tack, the third floor contains the museum's *Schaudepot* or storage depot. The displays, in large moveable glass cabinets, of Hannukah candelabra and other ritual objects are deliberately haphazard – they constitute all that is left of the pre-1938 Jewish Museum and the community it served, and include many items pulled from the burnt embers of the city's synagogues, torched in *Kristallnacht*.

Kohlmarkt

The line of the old Roman moat continues down what is now Naglergasse, but most shoppers and strollers turn left at the end of Graben up **Kohlmarkt**, site of the old wood and charcoal market. The most striking aspect of the street is the perfectly framed vista of the Michaelertor, its green dome marking the main entrance to the Hofburg from the Innere Stadt. Before you head up Kohlmarkt, though, be sure to look up at the roof of the building on the corner, whose copper cupola is topped by a splendid Hussar, once used to advertise a shop.

Even more than Graben, Kohlmarkt is the last bastion of luxury retailing, perhaps best expressed by the various outlets of **Demel**, a very *k.u.k.* establishment, which still advertises itself as an imperial and royal confectioners. Established in 1786 as *Zuckerbäckerei* to the Habsburgs, its very famous and opulent *Kaffee-konditorei*, dating from 1888, is at no. 14, while opposite is *Demel*'s small seafood deli outlet. Another Viennese institution is the **Artaria Haus**, a Jugendstil building set back from the street at no. 9, and faced in marble by Max Fabiani in 1901, the bolted slabs on the first floor anticipating Wagner's Postsparkasse (see p.135). The bookshop of

Graben and Kohlmarkt

The Jüdisches Museum is open daily except Sat 10am–6pm, Thurs 10am–9pm; öS70.

For more on the city's Jews, see p.66.

For more on the shops of Kohlmarkt, see the box on p.53; for reviews of its eating and drinking options, see p.273.

the master mapmakers, *Freytag & Berndt*, occupies the ground floor, while *Artaria & Co* itself, publishers of musical tracts by the likes of Haydn, Mozart and Beethoven, live on the first floor.

Michaelerplatz, Herrengasse and Minoritenplatz

Michaelerplatz, the square at the top of Kohlmarkt, is the Hofburg's backdoor, and, like nearby **Herrengasse** ("Lords' Lane") and **Minoritenplatz**, has long been a high-prestige address due its proximity to the royal court. Once upon a time, every single house here was the town palace of some aristocratic family or another; these now serve as ministries and embassies, for the most part, making this something of a lifeless quarter. Nevertheless, both Michaelerplatz and Minoritenplatz are showpiece squares, and Herrengasse is worth exploring, if only for the Palais Ferstel, which houses Vienna's only nineteenth-century shopping arcade and the famous *Café Central*.

*The nearest
U-Bahn is
Herrengasse.*

Michaelerplatz

Michaelerplatz is dominated on one side by the exuberant arc of the neo-Baroque **Michaelertrakt**, begun in the 1720s by Fischer von Erlach's son, but only completed in the 1890s. Its curving balustrade is peppered with a lively parade of eagles, giant urns and trophies, while the gate's archways are framed by gargantuan statues of Hercules, and, at either end, fountains overburdened with yet more ungainly statuary: to the right, land power; to the left, naval power – though both were in short supply at the time the works were erected in 1897. The centre of the square is now occupied by a collection of archeological remains uncovered during work on the nearby U-Bahn station of Herrengasse. LED texts in several languages explain the significance of the rubble which lies exposed in a designer concrete trench (another of Hollein's works); most of what you see are heating ducts dating only from the last century – hardly heart-stopping stuff.

*The Hofburg
itself is covered in detail
in Chapter
Three.*

Much more significant is the **Loos Haus**, on the corner of Kohlmarkt and Herrengasse, which caused uproar when it was built in 1910–11 by Adolf Loos. Franz-Josef despised this "house without eye-brows" – in other words without the customary sculpted pediments which sit above the windows of most Viennese buildings. Work on the building was temporarily halted due to the protests, and only allowed to continue after Loos had acquiesced to adding bronze flower-boxes (to be filled with flora all year round). Today, it's difficult to see what all the fuss was about. The rich Greek columns that frame the main entrance look inoffensive enough, but the building's lack of ornamental dressing, particularly in the upper stories, was

Michaeler-
platz,
Herrengasse
and
Minoriten-
platz

shocking at the time. The original occupants, Loos's own tailors, *Goldman & Salatsch*, went bankrupt in 1925, but the current owners, *Raiffeisenbank*, have their name displayed in simple gilt letters across the upper facade, just as Loos originally instructed *Goldman & Salatsch*.

The next block along from the Loos Haus is taken up by the altogether more conventional late nineteenth-century Palais Herberstein, erected on the site of the **Café Griensteidl**, which was demolished in 1897. Reconstructed and reopened on the ground floor in 1990 to cash in on the current nostalgia for *fin-de-siècle* Vienna, the *Griensteidl* was, in its day, the preferred meeting place of the *Jung-Wien* (Young Vienna) literary circle, most notably Arthur Schnitzler, Hermann Bahr and Hugo von Hofmannsthal. The journalist, Karl Kraus, wrote his most famous diatribe, *The Demolished Literature*, against the "Young Vienna" circle, shortly after the destruction of the café, suggesting that the movement "would soon expire for lack of a foyer". Instead, the *Jung-Wien* posse simply moved down Herrengasse to the *Café Central* (see p.58), much to the annoyance of Kraus himself, who was a regular.

Michaelerkirche

The oldest building on Michaelerplatz, and the inspiration for its name, is the **Michaelerkirche**, first built in the thirteenth century, though the Neoclassical facade, added in 1792, somewhat obscures this fact. Inside, the church retains its plain Gothic origins, but it's the later additions which are of more interest, in particular the *Fall of Angels*, a Rococo cloudburst of cherubs and angels rendered in alabaster, tumbling from the ceiling above the high altar. From November to April you can get a closer look at this by simply walking in via the west door; from May to October you can only do so by entering from the *Durchgang* via the south door. After paying a small entrance fee (and picking up a confusing information sheet in English), you may then explore the church and the exhibition which spreads out into the adjoining monastery.

The church is open May–Oct Mon–Sat 10.30am–4.30pm, Sun 1–5pm; öS25.

By far the most interesting exhibits lie outside the main body of the church, though the gilded organ – the largest Baroque organ in Vienna – is very fine and there are regular recitals. The best place to start is the sacristy, to the right of the chancel, alive with stucco, frescoes and inlaid cabinets. Liturgical silverware lurks beyond in the summer sacristy, while the church's two stunning gold monstrances are displayed in the priests' secret choir behind the main altar. To the north of the choir lies the old sacristy, with an intriguing miniature chest of drawers containing tiny reliquary cases. From here, you cross a peaceful plant-filled courtyard to the wood-panelled refectory, whose cornice is richly decorated with acanthus leaves and cherubs holding writhing scrolls.

Michaeler-
platz,
Herrengasse
and
Minoriten-
platz

From a doorway in the north choir aisle, you can descend into the church's suitably gloomy, labyrinthine **crypt**, which stretches the length and breadth of the building. A brief guided tour (in German) takes you past piles of paupers' bones and numerous musty coffins taken from the now defunct graveyard which once occupied Michaelerplatz, many with their lids off revealing desiccated bodies, still clothed and locked in a deathly grimace. Before you leave, be sure to check out the bizarre collection of imperial funereal crowns from the church's days as parish church to the court, displayed just off the crypt's vestibule. Finally, there's a chance to glimpse one of the church's original Romanesque north doors from 1230, discovered only recently, having been hidden for several centuries at the back of a tool shed.

*Guided tours
of the crypt
take place
Mon–Fri 11am
& 3pm; öS20.*

Herrengasse

Herrengasse was the preferred address of the nobility from the time the Habsburgs moved into the Hofburg until the fall of the dynasty in 1918. Its name dates from the sixteenth century, when the Diet of Lower Austria built its **Landhaus**, which still stands at no. 13. As well as being a federal Land in its own right since 1922, Vienna was for centuries also the capital of Lower Austria (Niederösterreich) – the region which surrounds the city – until 1986. St Pölten is now the new capital but the Land continues to be run from the Landhaus in Vienna, and it was here that the Viennese revolution began on March 13, 1848. A large crowd of students, artisans and workers gathered outside the building demanding, among other things, freedom of the press and the resignation of the arch-conservative, Prince Metternich. At one o'clock, soldiers fired into the crowd killing several people, and sparking off a mass uprising in the city. Metternich resigned and fled the city the next day, disguised, so the story goes, as a washerwoman. The Emperor Ferdinand was a later casualty, abdicating in favour of Franz-Josef, but the revolt was eventually crushed on October 31.

*For more on
the 1848 revo-
lution, see
p.318.*

Next door to the Landhaus, at no. 9, is the little-visited, rather forlorn **Niederösterreiches Landesmuseum**, which clearly needs an injection of cash. If you've got children in tow, they might enjoy the stuffed birds, live lizards and snakes and the small aquarium of turtles, frogs and fish, but otherwise the whole collection is eminently missable. The building itself – the former Mollard-Clary Palace – is of more interest: the facade from 1698 was Hildebrandt's first commission, while the inner courtyards contain a beautiful wrought-iron fountain from the neighbouring Landhaus.

*The museum is
open Tues–Fri
9am–5pm, Sat
noon–5pm,
Sun 9.30am–
1pm; closed
Aug; öS25.*

Opposite the Landhaus is the grandiose Italianate **Palais Ferstel**, built in the Ringstrasse style (see p.106) by Heinrich Ferstel in 1860 for the National Bank of Austria (it also housed the Stock Exchange until 1877). More importantly, the palace has long been home to Vienna's most famous *Kaffeehaus*, **Café Central**, restored in 1986 primarily as a tourist attraction (though a very beautiful one at that). At the turn of the century, the café's distinctively decorated Gothic vaults were *the* meeting place of the city's intellectuals, harbouring not only the literary lights of the *Jung-Wien* movement, but also the first generation of

Michaeler-
platz,
Herrengasse
and
Minoriten-
platz

The Redl Affair

Without doubt the greatest scandal to hit the Habsburgs in their twilight years was the infamous affair of **Colonel Alfred Redl**, who committed suicide in the early hours of May 25, 1913. Not only had the head of counter-espionage in the imperial army had been uncovered as a Russian secret agent; worse still, he had been blackmailed into it because of his homosexuality, and had been in the pay of the Russians for the last seven years.

For some time, the Austrian military had been concerned about the leaking of classified information to the Russians. Then, early in April 1913, a letter was discovered to one "Nikon Nizetas", containing a considerable sum of money and the names and addresses of several Russian spies. It had been sent to the main post office in Vienna, but had remained unclaimed. Austrian counter-espionage decided to stake out the post office and wait for someone to pick up the incriminating letter. For six weeks, two agents sat in the building opposite waiting for a clerk in the post office to ring the bell, which had been specially installed to warn them of the arrival of "Nikon Nizetas".

When finally the bell rang at 5.55pm on May 24, one agent was having a pee, and the other was in the canteen. By the time they reached the street, they had missed their man, though they managed to take down the cab number. As the two men stood around considering their next move, the self-same cab miraculously reappeared outside the post office. Not only could they now continue the chase, but they also discovered that "Nizetas" had left the felt sheath for his dagger in the back of the cab. They eventually retraced "Nizetas" to the *Hotel Klomser*, in the Palais Battyány, Bankgasse 2. The agents were shocked to find that the man who answered to "Nizetas's" description was one of their own superiors, Colonel Redl, who had just returned to the hotel. The agents handed the sheath to the concierge and waited to see if Redl would reclaim it. Caught off-guard as he left the hotel, Redl accepted the sheath from the receptionist, and then realizing what he had done, took flight. After a brief chase through the Innere Stadt, Redl gave himself up. He was handed a loaded revolver and told to go to his hotel room and do the honourable thing.

The whole affair would have been successfully hushed up – suicide among the upper echelons was very common – if it hadn't been for the locksmith who was called in to break into Redl's Prague flat. The place was decked out like a camp boudoir with pink whips on the wall and women's dresses in the cupboard. Unfortunately for the authorities, the locksmith in question was supposed to be playing football with the investigative journalist, Egon Erwin Kisch. When he told Kisch why he had been unable to turn up, Kisch immediately sent the story to a Berlin newspaper, and on May 29, the War Ministry was forced to admit the real reasons behind Redl's suicide. Redl's lover, Lieutenant Stefan Hromodka, on whom he had spent a small fortune, was sentenced to three months' hard labour (he later married, had several children and lived for another fifty years). Kisch became a popular hero overnight, with the best table in the *Café Central* reserved for him on all his visits to Vienna.

Michaeler-
platz,
Herrengasse
and
Minoriten-
platz

Austrian Socialists: Karl Renner, Viktor Adler and Otto Bauer. The latter were occasional chess adversaries of Leon Trotsky, who whiled away several years here before World War I. At the entrance to the café is a life-size papier-maché model of the moustachioed poet Peter Altenberg, another of the café's *fin-de-siècle* regulars.

Further up Herrengasse, past the café, is the entrance to the **Freyung Passage** – built in the 1860s as part of the Palais Ferstel – an eminently civilized, lovingly restored shopping arcade, which links Herrengasse with Freyung (see below). The focus of this elegant marble passage is a glass-roofed, hexagonal atrium, with a fountain, crowned by a statue of the Donaunixen (Danube Mermaid), whose trickling water echoes down the arcade.

*For a review
of the* Café
Central, *see
p.281.*

Minoritenplatz

On the opposite side of Herrengasse, hidden away round the back of the Hofburg, is **Minoritenplatz**, a peaceful, cobbled square entirely surrounded by the Baroque former palaces of the nobility, now tranformed into ministries and embassies.

*The Minoriten-
kirche belongs
to the city's
Italian com-
munity.*

At its centre is the fourteenth-century **Minoritenkirche**, whose stunted octagonal tower is one of the landmarks of the Innere Stadt (the top was knocked off by the Turks during the 1529 siege). Inside, the Gothic church is impressively lofty, but it's the tacky copy of Leonardo da Vinci's *Last Supper*, on the north wall, which steals the show – only close inspection reveals it to be a mosaic, so minuscule are the polished mosaic pieces. The work was actually commissioned in 1806 by Napoleon, who planned to substitute it for the original in Milan, taking the latter back to Paris. By the time it was finished, however, Napoleon had fallen from power and the Emperor Franz I bought it instead, though it wasn't until 1847 that the Austrians managed to bring it back to Vienna.

On the south side of the square is a magnificent palace built for the Emperor Karl VI by Hildebrandt as the Court Chancery, and now the **Bundeskanzleramt** (Federal Chancery), home of the Austrian Chancellor and the Foreign Ministry, whose main entrance opens onto Ballhausplatz. It was in this palace that Prince Metternich presided over the numerous meetings of the Congress of Vienna in 1814–15 (see opposite), and here, in the Chancellor's office, that the Austro-fascist leader, Engelbert Dollfuss, was assassinated during the abortive Nazi putsch of July 25, 1934. On that day, 154 members of the outlawed SS entered the building, and in the melée, Dollfuss was shot; his demands for a doctor and a priest fell on deaf ears, and, after two and a half hours, he died of his wounds.

Freyung

The aforementioned Freyung Passage from Herrengasse brings you out onto **Freyung** itself, a misshapen square centred on the Austria-

Michaeler-
platz,
Herrengasse
and
Minoriten-
platz

The Congress of Vienna

The one time that Vienna truly occupied centre stage in European history was during the **Congress of Vienna**. Under the chairmanship of Prince Metternich, 215 European heads of state met in October 1814 to try and thrash out a balance of power following the collapse of the Napoleonic Empire. In addition to the Big Four of Austria, Prussia, Britain and Russia, there were innumerable smaller delegations, including 32 minor German royals, with their wives, mistresses and secretaries of state – there was even an unofficial deputation from the Jews of Frankfurt. Lord Castlereagh, Britain's chief emissary, thought the Congress would last four weeks at the most – in the end, it dragged on for nearly nine months. The Final Act of the Congress wasn't signed until June 1815, long after Napoleon's escape from Elba – "the Congress is dissolved" he announced on landing at Cannes – and just twelve days before the final showdown of Waterloo.

The Congress has gone down in history as the largest and longest party the city has ever seen, encapsulated in the famous quote by the Prince de Ligne*: *"le congrès danse, mais il ne marche pas"* (the Congress dances, but it doesn't work). For in order to distract the lesser participants from the futility of the Congress, a vast programme of entertainment was organized. Ironically, the Austrian Emperor Franz I, who ultimately footed the bill, was no great party animal himself. Nevertheless, every night dinner was served in the Hofburg at forty tables; 1400 horses were required to transport the royal guests to the palace. There were tombolas, fireworks, tournaments, ballooning, theatre performances, sleighing expeditions in the Wienerwald, concerts conducted by Beethoven himself, and lots of dancing. The Tsar, it was said, danced forty nights on the trot, his amorous adventures compounding his political rivalry with Metternich; the Russian princess Bagration, nicknamed "the naked angel" for her habit of displaying her *décolletage* publicly, was voted the most beautiful; and Lord Castlereagh was deemed the most ridiculous. He was later joined by the Duke of Wellington, who hated the whole charade: "the hot rooms here have almost killed me," he wrote home. At one ball in the palace's Redoutensaal, 6000 guests turned up instead of the 3000 invited, as the imperial bouncers resold the tickets. Appropriately enough, the congress's most lasting contribution to posterity was the popularization of the waltz.

---

* The prince, who was in his eighties, actually coined the epigram even before the congress had begun, repeating it on every possible occasion until his death in December, brought on a by a cold, contracted while waiting outside his house for his latest mistress.

Brunnen, unveiled in 1846 with bronze nymphs representing Austria and the key rivers in the Habsburg Empire at the time: the Danube, Po, Elbe and Vistula. In medieval times Freyung was a popular spot for public executions, and during the annual Christkindl Markt, held here in the eighteenth and nineteenth centuries, there were open-air theatre performances; the market has recently been re-established, and is held here on a much more modest scale in the run-up to Christmas. Freyung also boasts three major art galleries: the **Harrach Palais**, adjacent to the Freyung Passage, which hosts tem-

Michaeler-
platz,
Herrengasse
and
Minoriten-
platz

porary exhibitions put on by the Kunsthistorisches Museum; the
Kunstforum, a major venue for visiting exhibitions of fine art; and
the **Museum im Schottenstift**.

Schottenstift

Freyung – meaning "Sanctuary" – derives its name from the
Schottenstift (Monastery of the Scots), which dominates the north
side of the square, and where fugitives could claim asylum in
medieval times. The monastery was founded in 1155 by the
Babenburg Duke Heinrich Jasomirgott, though the Benedictine

*The
Schottenkirche
is used by the
city's French
community.*

monks invited over were, most probably, Irish and not Scottish. They
were eventually expelled, after having shocked Viennese society by
"trading in furs, initiating wild dances and starting games of ball".
The monastery's glory days may be over, but its highly prized grammar school, the Schottengymnasium, founded in 1807, remains one
of the most prestigious boys' schools in the country. The
Schottenkirche itself is worth skipping – instead, pass through the
archway to the left of the church's west door, and into a small courtyard, with a children's playground and tables and chairs belonging to
the nearby *Café Haag*.

*The museum is
open
Thurs–Sat
10am–5pm,
Sun
noon–5pm;
öS40.*

The first stairwell on the right leads up to the **Museum im
Schottenstift**, on the first floor, which houses the monastery's art collection, mostly seventeenth- and eighteenth-century Dutch and German
still lifes and landscapes. The prize exhibit, though, is the fifteenth-century winged altarpiece, which used to reside in the Schottenkirche.
Thirteen (out of the original sixteen) panels survive, set in a new, purpose-built mini-chapel: one side depicts scenes from the life of the
Virgin; the reverse side (shown only in the two or three weeks leading
up to Easter) features the Passion. The vivid use of colour, the plastic-
ity of the faces, and the daring stab at perspective, mark this out as a
masterpiece of late-Gothic art – a leaflet in English explains the significance of each panel. As a bonus, you also get to see the inside of the
vast Prälatensaal, decked out in pink and yellow Biedermeier style
around 1830 by Josef Kornhäusel, and now the setting for the
Schottenkirche's somewhat inferior Baroque high altar painting.

Mölker Bastei

*The nearest
U-Bahn is
Schottentor.*

The **Mölker Bastei**, one of the few remaining sections of the old zig-
zag fortifications that once surrounded the Innere Stadt, can be
found on Schreyvogelgasse, to the west of Freyung. The sloping cobbled lane should be familiar to fans of the movie *The Third Man*, for
it's in the doorway of no.8 that Harry Lime (played by Orson Welles)
appears for the first time.

*The museum is
open Tues–
Sun 9am–
12.15pm & 1–
4.30pm; öS25.*

High up on the Mölker Bastei itself at no. 8 is the **Pasqualatihaus**,
where Beethoven lived on and off from 1804 onwards (he stayed at
over thirty addresses during his thirty-five years in Vienna). The
composer's apartment is now a museum (one of three museums ded-

icated to Beethoven in Vienna), though, as usual, there's no indication of how the place might have looked at the time he lived there. Perhaps this is just as well – according to one visitor it was "the darkest, most disorderly place imaginable . . . under the piano (I do not exaggerate) an unemptied chamber pot . . . chairs . . . covered with plates bearing the remains of last night's supper". Instead, you're left to admire Ludwig's gilded salt and pepper pots and battered tin sugar container, or sit down and listen to some of his music through headphones.

Am Hof to Hoher Markt

The area of the Innere Stadt which lies between **Am Hof** and **Hoher Markt** is where Vienna began. It was here that the Roman camp of Vindobona lay, with Hoher Markt as its main forum; later, the Babenbergs established their royal court at Am Hof, with the city's medieval Jewish ghetto close by. Few reminders of those days remain – above ground at least – although Marc-Aurel-Strasse (which commemorates the bellicose Emperor Marcus Aurelius, who died here in AD 180), like neighbouring Wipplinger Strasse and Tuchlauben, is an old Roman road. There are few major sights in this part of the Innere Stadt, but several of the city's most beguiling alleyways are hidden deep within its matrix of streets, as is one of its finest Gothic churches, **Maria am Gestade**.

Am Hof

Am Hof is the largest square in the Innere Stadt, an attractive, tranquil spot, marred only by the surface protrusions of its underground car park. The name – *Hof* means both "royal court" and "courtyard" – dates from medieval times, when this was the headquarters of the Babenbergs, who lorded it over Vienna until the Habsburgs took the reins in 1273. Today the jousting tournaments, market stalls, religious plays and public executions have long gone, and the centrepiece is now the rather forbidding, matt black **Mariensäule** (Marian Column), erected by the Emperor Ferdinand III as a thank you to the Virgin for deliverance from the Protestant Swedish forces in the Thirty Years' War. At the base of the column, blackened cherubs in full armour wrestle with a dragon, lion, serpent and basilisk, representing the plague, war, hunger and heresy.

Dominating the square is the **Kirche am Hof**, from whose balcony the Austrian Emperor Franz I proclaimed the end of the Holy Roman Empire in 1806, on the orders of Napoleon. The church's vast Baroque facade, topped by a host of angels, belies the fact that this is, for the most part, a fourteenth-century Gothic structure. Inside, it's quite frankly a stylistic mess, with the old Gothic church struggling to get out from under some very crude later additions:

The Kirche am Hof belongs to the city's Croat community.

Corinthian capitals glued onto the main pillars, and the aisles turned into a series of side chapels, with stuck-on stucco porticos – only the coved and coffered ceiling of the choir works at all well. The adjoining former Jesuit seminary became the imperial war ministry, and as such was a prime target during the 1848 revolution. On October 6, the mob stormed the building, dragged out the War Minister Count Latour, and promptly strung him up from a nearby lamppost. Three railway workers were later hanged for the offence.

Opposite the church is another architectural illusion, for behind the palatial facade of no. 7–9 is the city's **Feuerwehr Zentrale** (Central Fire Station). The engines are hidden behind the series of double doors, while above them, on the first floor, is the little-visited **Feuerwehrmuseum** (Firefighting Museum). Prize attraction is the mock-up of the *Alte Türmestube* (look-out post) in the spire of Stephansdom; from 1534 until as recently as 1956 fires in the Innere Stadt were spotted from here, by a guy with a telescope and loud hailer. You should also be able to take a look at a couple of the older fire engines on the floor below. The firemen originally kept their equipment next door at no. 10 in the former **Bürgerliches Zeughaus** (Civic Armoury), suitably decorated with a panoply, several trophies, a double-headed eagle and crowned by a spectacular cluster of figures holding up a gilded globe.

The Feuerwehr-museum is open Sun & public holidays 9am–noon; free; Mon–Fri by appointment; ☎ 531 99.

Behind the Kirche am Hof

If you pass under the archway by the Kirche am Hof, and head down Schulhof, you can see the church's Gothic origins clearly in its tall lancet windows and buttresses. Watchmakers continue to ply their trade from tiny lock-ups in between the buttresses at the back of the church, while opposite stands the Baroque Obizzi Palace, home to the city's **Uhrenmuseum** (Clock Museum), ranged over three floors of Schulhof 2. Founded in 1917, this is the world's oldest museum of its kind, but sadly, it lacks the crucial information in either German or English to bring the collection alive. Nevertheless, you'll find evey kind of time-measuring device from sophisticated seventeenth-century grandfather clocks to primitive wax candles containing tiny lead balls which drop onto a metal dish as the candle melts. Other unusual exhibits include the smallest pendulum clock in the world, which fits inside a thimble, and a wide selection of eighteenth-century *zwiebeluhren*, literally "onion clocks", set within cases shaped like fruit, musical instruments and the like.

The Uhrenmuseum is open Tues–Sun 9am–4.30pm; öS50.

For most people, the **Puppen und Spielzeug Museum** (Doll and Toy Museum), next door on the first floor of Schulhof 4, holds more appeal, further enhanced by the building's well-preserved Baroque interior. It's an old-fashioned kind of a place, with ranks of glass cabinets and no buttons to press for younger kids. The majority of the exhibits are dolls – from Biedermeier porcelain figures to those portraying Chinese, Native American and African characteristics, which

The museum is open Tues–Sun 10am–6pm; öS60.

were all the rage between the wars – with just a small selection of teddies, toys and trains (for more teddies, see p.66). Also on show are a toy marionette stage, a Punch and Judy booth, a shadow screen and a dolls' toy shop, grocer's and house, complete with miniature Jugendstil coffee set.

Judenplatz

Taking either of the two alleyways which lead north from Schulhof brings you to **Judenplatz**, one of prettiest little squares in Vienna. As the name suggests, this was the site of the city's first Jewish ghetto, dating as far back as the twelfth century, when the square itself was known as Schulhof. It remained at the heart of the Jewish community on and off for centuries, and even today there's an orthodox Jewish prayer room at no. 8.

The oldest house on the square, **Zum grossen Jordan** (The Great Jordan), at no. 2, bears a sixteenth-century relief of the Baptism of Christ, commemorating the pogrom of 1421, when the Jews were driven out of Vienna: the lucky ones fled to Hungary, the rest were burned at the stake, or – to avoid that fate – killed by the chief rabbi, who then committed suicide himself. The Latin inscription reads: "By baptism in the River Jordan bodies are cleansed from disease and evil, so all secret sinfulness takes flight. Thus the flame rising furiously through the whole city in 1421 purged the terrible crimes of the Hebrew dogs. As the world was once purged by the flood, so this time it was purged by fire".

The square's Jewish associations are also recalled by the statue of the writer **Gotthold Ephraim Lessing** (1729–81), striding forward in a great trench coat. Lessing, himself an assimilated Jew, was a key figure in the eighteenth-century German Enlightenment, who pleaded for tolerance to be shown towards the Jews. Erected in 1935, the statue proved too much for the Nazis who had it destroyed; after the war, the sculptor Siegfried Charoux made a new model, but it wasn't returned to its original spot until 1982.

Perhaps to make amends, the city council decided in 1996 to erect a new memorial on Judenplatz to remember the Austrian Jews killed in the Holocaust. Designed by the controversial British artist, Rachel Whiteread, it consists of a giant concrete cast of a library. Initial objections from local residents and traders have been joined by protests from within the Jewish community, after excavations revealed the smoke-blackened remains of the synagogue burnt to the ground in 1421. The upshot of all this was that the monument was not unveiled on the 58th anniversary of *Kristallnacht* as had been planned, and the saga looks set to continue for some time yet.

The most elaborate edifice on the square is the former **Böhmische Hofkanzlei** (Bohemian Court Chancery), designed by Fischer von Erlach and so monumental its Baroque facade continues half way down Jordangasse. What you see on Judenplatz is, in fact, only the side of the building, whose elaborate main portal actually looks out

*The museum is
open daily
10am–6pm;
öS45.*

onto Wipplingerstrasse. It was from here that the Austrians ruled over the Czechs from 1627 onwards; the building now houses the country's supreme Constitutional and Administrative courts.

On the opposite side of the square, a short way down Drahtgasse, is the new **Teddybären Museum**, a private collection of antique teddy bears from all over the world. As well as the cuddly variety, there are china bears, bears on carousels and one of the very earliest battery-operated bears from before World War I, whose eyes light up in a way that would give most kids nightmares.

Altes Rathaus

On the other side of busy Wipplingerstrasse from the Böhmische Hofkanzlei is the **Altes Rathaus** (Old Town Hall), a dour-looking

---

Jews in Vienna

Nine tenths of what the world celebrated as Viennese culture of the nineteenth century was a culture promoted, nurtured or in some cases even created by Viennese Jewry.
The World of Yesterday Stefan Zweig, 1942

Most Jews have mixed feelings about Vienna: the city that nurtured the talents of Jewish geniuses such as Sigmund Freud, Gustav Mahler and Ludwig Wittgenstein also has a justifiable reputation as a hotbed of **anti-semitism**. The city where the father of Zionism, Theodor Herzl, spent much of his adult life (see p.224), is also seen by many as the cradle of the Holocaust, where Hitler spent five years honing his hatred; where in 1986, Kurt Waldheim was elected president, despite (or more likely thanks to) rumours that he had participated in Nazi atrocities in the Balkans; and where as recently as 1996, Jörg Haider's FPÖ achieved the largest vote of any extreme right-wing party in Europe.

Jews have lived in Vienna on and off for something like a thousand years, yet like most of the diaspora, they have been tolerated only when it suited the powers that be. They have been formally **expelled** twice, firstly in 1420, when the community was accused of supporting the Czech Hussite heretics (the real incentive for the expulsion was to boost the royal coffers by appropriating the Jews' property). The following year, those that remained – around 200 of them – were burned at the stake. Apart from a few individual exceptions, Jewish resettlement only took off again at the beginning of the seventeenth century, when Ferdinand II established a walled ghetto east of the Danube (now Leopoldstadt; see p.185). For around fifty years Jewish life flourished in the ghetto, but as the Counter-Reformation gathered pace, there was increasing pressure from Catholics to banish the Jews altogether. Finally, in 1670, Emperor Leopold I once more expelled the community.

The city suffered financially from the expulsion, and with the Turks at the gates of the city, a small number of Jewish financiers and merchants, hastily granted the status of *Hofjuden* or **"Court Jews"**, were permitted to resettle. The most famous of the Court Jews was Samuel Oppenheimer, who was appointed chief supplier to the imperial army by Leopold I in

---

Baroque palace that served as the city's town hall until 1885 (when the huge Ringstrasse Rathaus was finished, see p.109). The main courtyard is undistinguished but for Donner's wonderful **Andromeda Brunnen** from 1741, which depicts the Greek myth in lead relief. Andromeda, left at the mercy of a sea monster to appease the gods, looks unfeasibly calm as Perseus descends from afar on a winged horse to do away with the beast, which meanwhile spouts water noisily into the basin below.

The Altes Rathaus now houses, among other things, the highly informative **Austrian Resistance Museum**, which has a permanent exhibition on the Austrian anti-fascist resistance, with labelling in German and English throughout. The bulk of the displays cover resistance to the Nazi regime, but there's also a brief summary of the political

---

1677. Despite the elevated status of the Court Jews, their position was precarious, and it wasn't until Josef II's 1781 **Toleranzpatent** that they were allowed to take up posts in the civil service and other professions and to build their own synagogue. At the same time, the *Toleranzpatent* began the process of assimilation, compelling Jews to take German names and restricting the use of Yiddish and Hebrew.

After the **1848 revolution**, all official restrictions on Jews were finally abolished. At this point there were only around 2000 Jews living in Vienna. In the next sixty years, thousands arrived in the city from the Habsburg provinces of Bohemia, Moravia and Galicia, the majority of them settling, initially at least, in **Leopoldstadt**. By 1910, there were approximately 180,000 Jews in the city – almost ten percent of the total population and more than in any other German-speaking city. Though the majority of them were far from well-off, a visible minority formed a disproportionately large contingent in high-profile professions like banking, medicine, journalism and the arts. The Rothschilds were one of the richest families in the empire; virtually the entire staff on the liberal newspapers, *Neue Freie Presse* and the *Wiener Tagblatt*, were Jewish; the majority of the city's doctors were Jews, as were most of the leading figures in the Austrian Socialist Party. Other prominent Viennese Jews were the writers Arthur Schnitzler, Robert Musil, Stefan Zweig and Josef Roth; and the composers Arnold Schönberg, Alban Berg and the Strauss family.

Those Gentiles who found themselves sinking into poverty after the stock market crash of 1873 desperately needed a scapegoat. They eagerly latched onto anti-semitism, which began to be promoted by the Christian Social Party under Karl Lueger, the city's populist mayor from 1897 to 1910. Perversely, however, this virulent anti-semitism helped to save more Jews than in other more tolerant places, causing thousands to flee the country even before the 1938 Anschluss; by 1941, a total of 120,000 Viennese Jews had escaped. Nevertheless, some 65,000 died in the Holocaust. Right now, the community of around 7000 – many of them immigrants from the former eastern bloc – is enjoying something of a renaissance, much of it centred once again in Leopoldstadt, maintaining a dozen synagogues and several schools across the city.

---

*The Austrian
Resistance
Museum is
open Mon, Wed
& Thurs
9am–5pm;
free.*

upheavals of the inter-war republic, including a detailed section on the rise of Austro-fascism in the 1930s. Despite the high level of popular support for the Nazis, the Austrian resistance remained extremely active throughout the war, as a result of which 2700 of its members were executed and thousands more were murdered by the Gestapo.

No one knows where the city's original town hall stood, but by the fourteenth century, there was one located close to what is now the oldest part of the Altes Rathaus. The **Salvatorkapelle**, a Gothic chapel founded as the town hall chapel, is today hidden away at the opposite end of the courtyard from the fountain. It's a strange little building, much altered over the centuries, whose most handsome feature is its ornate Renaissance portal, flanked by richly carved columns, and visible only from Salvatorgasse.

Maria am Gestade

A more compelling ecclesiastical edifice by far is the Gothic church of **Maria am Gestade**, up Salvatorgasse, which is topped by an elaborate filigree spire depicting the Virgin's heavenly crown, a stunning sight after dark when lit from within. With its drooping, beast-infested pendants and gilded mosaics, the stone canopy of the tall, slender west facade is also worth admiring, best viewed from the steps which lead up from Tiefergraben. The unusual interior – the nave is darker and narrower than the choir and set slightly askew – is a product of the church's cramped site, lying as it does on the very edge of the old medieval town. Much of what you see, it has to be said, both inside and out, is the result of nineteenth-century over-restoration, as the church caught fire in 1809 when it was used by the Napoleonic forces as an arms depot.

In one of the side chapels, the remains of the city's little-known patron saint, Klemens Maria Hofbauer (1751–1820), can be seen in a gilded reliquary, set within a jazzy modern marble table beneath some rare medieval stained glass. As well as reviving the Marian cult, being a trained baker, and kick-starting Catholicism after the reforms of Josef II, Hofbauer was also made responsible for the welfare of the city's Czech community, which at its peak numbered over 100,000, and which the church has served since 1812. Incidentally, the church's name "am Gestade" means "by the riverbank"; the steep drop from the west door goes down to Tiefergraben, which used to be a minor tributary of the Danube.

Hoher Markt and around

*The Roman
Ruins are
open Sat &
Sun
11am–1pm;
öS25.*

It's difficult to believe that the **Hoher Markt**, now an unremarkable square surrounded by dour, postwar buildings and packed with parked cars, is Vienna's oldest square. Yet this was the heart of the Roman camp, Vindobona, a conduit of which you can see beneath the shopping arcade on the south side of the square (you enter through the arcade's sushi bar). In medieval times, Hoher Markt became a popular spot for public humiliations, the victims being displayed in a cage (later replaced by a pillory and gallows). That particular spot is now occupied by the square's centrepiece, Fischer von Erlach's **Vermählungsbrunnen** (Marriage Fountain), depicting the marriage of Mary and Joseph by the High Priest, for which there is no Biblical evidence and few iconographical precedents. Even more remarkable is the ornate bronze baldachin and gilded sunburst, held aloft by Corinthian columns with matching rams' head urns, under which the trio shelter.

The real reason folk crowd into Hoher Markt, however, is to see the glorious Jugendstil **Ankeruhr**, a heavily gilded clock designed by Franz Matsch in 1914, which spans two buildings owned by *Der Anker* insurance company on the north side of the square. Each hour, a gilded cut-out figure, representing a key player in Vienna's history, shuffles across the dial of the clock, and at noon tour groups gather to watch the entire set of twelve figures slowly stagger across to a ten-minute medley of slightly mournful organ music (the identities of the figures, which range from Marcus Aurelius to Josef Haydn, are revealed on the clock's street level plaque). Before you leave, check out the brackets on the underside of the clock bridge, which feature Adam, Eve, the Devil and an Angel.

There are a couple of other sights worth seeking out in the streets around Hoher Markt, in particular the secular medieval **Neidhart Frescoes** discovered in 1979, at Tuchlauben 19, during rebuilding works there. Executed around 1400, the wall paintings are patchy but jolly, some of them illustrating the stories of the *Minnesinger* (aristocratic minstrel) Neidhart von Reuenthal, others depicting a snowball fight, a ball game, dancing and general medieval merriment.

*The Niedhart
Frescoes are
open
Tues–Sun
9am–12.15pm
& 1–4.30pm;
öS25.*

Round the corner in Brandstätte is a rather more recent architectural highlight, the **Zacherlhaus**, a residential block with business premises on the ground floor, built by the Slovene Josip Plečnik in 1905. The exterior is all grim, grey granite, relieved only by the winged figure of the Archangel Michael above the ground floor, but it's the building's lens-shaped stairwell, hidden next door to a barber's at no. 2–4 Wildpretmarkt, that makes its way into the coffee-table books and postcards. Once you've made it down the black marble corridor, past the janitor, you can admire the weird and wonderful lamps whose twisted bronze stands topped by lighted globes punctuate each floor of the wood-panelled stairwell.

Bermuda Triangle

Since the 1980s, the area around the Ruprechtskirche has been known as the "Bermuda Dreieck" or **Bermuda Triangle**; the idea being that there are so many bars in these few narrow streets that you could get lost forever. And it's true, there are a staggering number of designer bars, late-night drinking holes, music venues and

*The nearest
U-Bahn is
Schwedenplatz.*

*For full list-
ings in the
Bermuda
Triangle, see
p.295.*

*The
Stadttempel is
open daily
except Sat;
free.*

restaurants literally piled on top of one another, particularly along Seitenstettengasse and Rabensteig. The clientele tends to be young(ish) and moneyed, well turned out but not that trendy. During the day, however, the scene is pretty muted, and you're more likely to rub shoulders with tourists who've come to appreciate the area's narrow cobbled streets and the two main sights: the Ruprechtskirche, the city's oldest church, and the Stadttempel, the only synagogue to survive *Kristallnacht*.

Stadttempel

Ironically, it was the building restrictions in force at the time the **Stadttempel** was built in 1826, that enabled it to be the only syna-gogue (out of twenty-four) to survive *Kristallnacht* in 1938. According to the laws enacted under Josef II, synagogues had to be concealed from the street – hence you get no hint of what lies behind 2–4 Seitenstettengasse until you've gone through the security proce-dures (take your passport) and passed through several anterooms to the glass doors of the temple itself. Despite its hidden location, it did suffer some damage in 1938, since the area was predominantly Jewish and the surrounding buildings were torched, though it has since been lavishly restored. Designed from top to bottom by Biedermeier architect, Josef Kornhäusel, it's a perfect example of the restrained architecture of the period, its top-lit, sky-blue oval dome dotted with golden stars and supported by yellow Ionic pillars which frame the surrounding two-tiered gallery. The slightly sinister presence of police with dogs and machine guns outside on Seitenstettengasse is a sad consequence of the terrorist attack on the Stadttempel which killed three people in 1983, and the continuing vandalism of Jewish property that takes place in Austria.

Ruprechtskirche and around

*The Ruprechts-
kirche is open
Mon–Fri
10.30am–
1.30pm; longer
hours during
exhibitions.*

Round the corner from the Stadttempel on Ruprechtsplatz stands the ivy-covered **Ruprechtskirche**, its plain, stout architecture attesting to its venerable age. Originally built as long ago as the eighth century, the current building dates partly from the twelfth century, though it has been much altered and expanded since. Inside, the vivid reds and blues of the modern stained glass are a bit overwhelming, detracting from the church's uniquely intimate ambience. Mass is still said here, and the space is also frequently used for art exhibitions.

Steps lead down from beside the Ruprechtskirche to **Morzinplatz** by the Danube Canal, a notorious address during the Nazi period. On the west side of the square stood the *Hotel Metropol*, erected to cope with the influx of visitors to the 1873 exhibition, but in 1938 taken over by the Gestapo, and used as their headquarters. Thousands were tortured here before the building was razed to the ground towards the end of the war. The plot is now occupied by the Leopold-

Figl-Hof, named after the country's postwar Foreign Minister, who passed through the *Metropol* en route to Dachau. A monument to the victims of fascism showing a prisoner surrounded by granite boulders from Mauthausen was erected in front of the apartments in 1985. There's also a permanent memorial round the back of the building, on Salztorgasse, where detainees were bundled in for interrogation.

For the duration of the war, O5, the Austrian resistance movement, had their headquarters right under the noses of the Gestapo at Ruprechtsplatz 5. Meanwhile, the tradition of anti-Nazi activities continues at Salztorgasse 6, at the Dokumentationszentrum headed by **Simon Wiesenthal**, which monitors ex- and neo-Nazis. Wiesenthal, in his eighties, is himself a survivor of the Holocaust, and is best known for pursuing fellow Austrian Adolf Eichmann, the SS chief who was hiding out in Argentina; Eichmann was eventually kidnapped, tried and executed by the Israelis in 1961.

Bermuda Triangle

The memorial is open Mon 2–5pm, Thurs & Fri 9am–noon & 2–5pm; free.

East of Rotenturmstrasse

East of Rotenturmstrasse, which stretches from Stephansplatz to Schwedenplatz, Vienna's intricate, medieval streetplan continues. It's this, more than any specific sight, that makes a wander in this quarter rewarding, though four churches, varying in styles from High Baroque to neo-Byzantine, punctuate the streets. Incidentally, the red tower that gave Rotenturmstrasse its name – it was actually a red and white chequered city gate – has long since disappeared.

Fleischmarkt and Postgasse

Fleischmarkt, the old meat market, straddles Rotenturmstrasse extending east as far as Postgasse. Greek merchants settled here in the eighteenth century, and following the 1781 *Toleranzpatent*, built their own Greek Orthodox church on Griechengasse. The only inkling you get that there's a church there is from the cupola and pediment, which face onto Hafnersteig. On Fleischmarkt itself, though, there's another more imposing stripey, red-brick **Griechische Kirche**, redesigned in mock-Byzantine style in 1861 by Ringstrasse architect, Theophil Hansen, its decorative castellations glistening with gilt. Opening hours are erratic, and you may not be able to get past the gloomy, arcaded vestibule – the best time to try is on a Sunday – to see the candle-lit interior, pungent with incense and decorated with icons and gilded frescoes. Next door to the church at no. 11, is the popular inn, *Griechenbeisl*, a Viennese institution for over five centuries; popular with the Greeks, with textile merchants from Reichenberg (Liberec) in Bohemia, and with the likes of Beethoven, Brahms, Schubert and Strauss – inevitably, it milks the connections.

East of
Rotenturm-
strasse

*The nearest
U-Bahn is
Stubentor.*

At the end of Fleischmarkt, turn right into Postgasse and you'll come to another neo-Byzantine edifice, the Greek-Catholic **Church of St Barbara**, a much lighter concoction, with a pistachio- and apricot-coloured facade. It's worth peeking inside at the pale pink and blue nave to see this Greek-Catholic church's Rococo iconostasis studded with medallion-style icons. Far more imposing, though, is the Italianate facade of the **Dominikanerkirche**, further south along Postgasse; the interior is a Baroque orgy of stucco and frescoes, rebuilt from scratch in the 1630s after being damaged in the first Turkish siege.

Dr-Ignaz-Seipel-Platz and Heiligenkreuzerhof

One block west of Postgasse along Bäckerstrasse lies **Dr-Ignaz-Seipel-Platz**, named after the leader of the Christian Socials, who became the country's chancellor in 1922. Son of a cab driver, a trained priest, and, ironically, one-time professor of moral theology, Seipel was one of the most vociferous anti-semites, who openly flirt-ed with the idea of re-ghettoizing the Jews. Given the eventual fate of Austria's Jews, this rather attractive little square might have been better left as Universitäts Platz, since its east side is still taken up by the **Alte Universität** (Old University), founded by Rudolf IV in 1365, and thus the second oldest (after Prague) in the German-speaking world. The current barracks-like building dates from the seventeenth century when many of the country's leading educational institutions were handed over to the Jesuits.

By the eighteenth century, the university had outgrown its original premises and a more fanciful Baroque extension – now the **Akademie der Wissenschaften** (Academy of Sciences) – was built on the opposite side of the square. The building's barrel-vaulted Freskenraum, decorated with frescoes by Franz Maulbertsch, is occasionally open to the public during the summer vacation for exhi-bitions (Mon–Fri 10.30am–5.30pm). Josef Haydn made his last pub-lic appearance here when he attended the première of his oratorio *Die Schöpfung* on his seventy-sixth birthday in 1808. It was at this concert that Haydn – commonly known, even during his lifetime, as "Papa Joe" – is alleged to have laid his hands on the kneeling Beethoven, saying "What I have started, you shall finish".

Next door to the university is the **Jesuitenkirche** (also known as the Universitätskirche), whose flat facade rises up in giant tiers that tower over the square. Begun in 1627 at the peak of the Jesuits' power, the church smacks of the Counter-Reformation and is by far the most awesome Baroque church in Vienna. Inside, the most strik-ing features are the red and green barley-sugar spiral columns, the exquisitely carved pews and the clever *trompe l'oeil* dome – the illu-sion only works from the back of the church; walk towards the altar and the painting is revealed as a sham.

Behind the Jesuitenkirche runs the picturesque, cobbled lane of **Schönlaterngasse** (Beautiful Lantern Lane); the ornate lamp, immortalized in the street's name, juts out of the wall of no. 6. At no. 5, there's a gateway into one of Vienna's hidden gems, the **Heiligenkreuzerhof**, the secret inner courtyard belonging to the Cistercian abbey of Heligenkreuz, which lies to the southwest of Vienna. Despite being used as an inner-city car park, this is a perfectly preserved slice of eighteenth-century Vienna. To visit the courtyard's winsome Bernhardskapelle – a favourite venue for posh weddings – you must ring the bell of the *Hauswart* (caretaker) and ask permission.

Chapter 3

The Hofburg

His gaze wandered up high walls and he saw an island – gray, self-contained, and armed – lying there while the city's speed rushed blindly past it.

Robert Musil, *A Man without Qualities*, 1930–43

Enmeshed in the southwest corner of the Innere Stadt, the Hofburg (Court Palace) is a real hotchpotch of a place, with no natural centre, no symmetry and no obvious main entrance. Its name is synonymous with the Habsburgs, the dynasty which, at its demise in 1918, ruled a vast multi-national empire, stretching the length and breadth of Europe. Nowadays, apart from the tiny proportion that has been retained as the seat of the Austrian president, the palace has been taken over by various state organizations, museums and, even more prosaically, a conference centre.

Seven centuries of architecture lie within the sprawling complex, much of it hidden behind anodyne, Baroque facades. Part of the reason for the palace's complicated groundplan was the unwritten rule among the Habsburgs that no ruler should use the rooms of his or her predecessor. Oddly enough, the most attention-grabbing wing of the palace, the vast Neue Burg, is a white elephant, only completed in 1913, and never, in fact, occupied by the Habsburgs.

Despite its plummet in status, two of Vienna's most famous attractions keep the Hofburg at the top of most visitors' agendas: the **Wiener Sängerknaben** (Vienna Boys' Choir) who perform regularly in the Burgkapelle, and the **Spanische Reitschule** (Spanish Riding School) who trot their stuff in the Winter Reitschule. The other chief sights are the dull **Kaiserappartements**, where the Emperor Franz-Josef I (1848–1916) and his wife Elisabeth lived and worked, the **Schatzkammer**, with its superb collection of crown jewels, and the **Prunksaal**, Fischer von Erlach's richly decorated Baroque library. The palace also boasts several excellent musuems and galleries: the **Albertina**, home to one of the world's great graphics collections, several departments of the Kunsthistorisches Museum, housed within the Neue Burg – the **Hofjagd- und Rüstkammer** (Court Hunting and Arms Collection), the **Sammlung alte Musikinstrumente** (Collection of Early Musical Instruments) and the **Ephesos Museum** (Ephesus Museum) – and the **Museum für Völkerkunde** (Museum of Ethnology).

The Hofburg in history

The first fortress to be built on the site of the Hofburg was erected around 1275 by the Czech King Otakar II, Duke of Austria. Three years later, the first of the Habsburgs, **Rudolf I** (1273–91), defeated and killed Otakar in battle, and set about expanding and strengthening the place. Rudolf's successor, Albrecht I (1291–1308), added a chapel to the palace, but it wasn't until **Ferdinand I** (1556–64) decided to make Vienna the Habsburgs' main base, that the Hofburg became established more or less permanently as the dynastic seat.

Although the palace was protected by the city walls until 1857, the Habsburgs left nothing to chance after **Friedrich III** (1440–93) and his family were besieged by the Hungarian King Mathias Corvinus, and forced to eat the pets – including the vultures who landed on the roof – in order to survive. Subsequent generations usually quit the palace (along with the imperial treasury) long before the enemy arrived. In 1683, with the Turks at the gates of Vienna, **Leopold I** (1657–1705) left in such haste, one eye-witness reported "the doors of the palace were left wide open". The same happened in 1805 and 1809, when Napoleon and his troops passed through, and in 1848, when the court fled, leaving the revolutionaries free to convene in the Winter Riding School.

Court life at the Hofburg reached its dramatic climax under Leopold I, who built a huge wooden theatre onto the palace fortifications, its three tiers of galleries seating up to 1500 under a *trompe l'oeil* ceiling of a Baroque church vault. Here, Leopold's own musical compositions were performed, along with numerous theatrical productions, in which the emperor himself often took the lead role. Inside the palace, courtiers had to wear the elaborate dress, and abide by the complex etiquette of the Spanish court, described by one former courtier as "a strange medley of Olympian revelry, of Spanish monastic severity, and the rigorous discipline of a barrack". To get away from such formalities, the emperor was as keen as the rest of the court to spend much of the year in the more informal atmosphere of the family's country retreats.

Though the Hofburg remained the Habsburgs' official winter residence, neglect of the complex became something of a recurring pattern with subsequent generations. Even under **Karl VI** (1711–40), who was responsible for building the incredible library and riding school, the palace remained lifeless for much of the year. **Maria Theresa** (1740–80) preferred the summer palace at Schönbrunn, even in winter, and after the death of her husband, Franz Stephen, in 1765, stayed there more often than not. The rooms they shared in

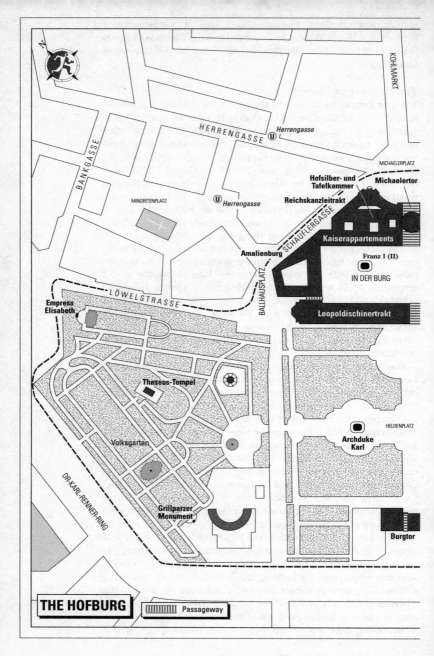

THE HOFBURG

|||||||| Passageway

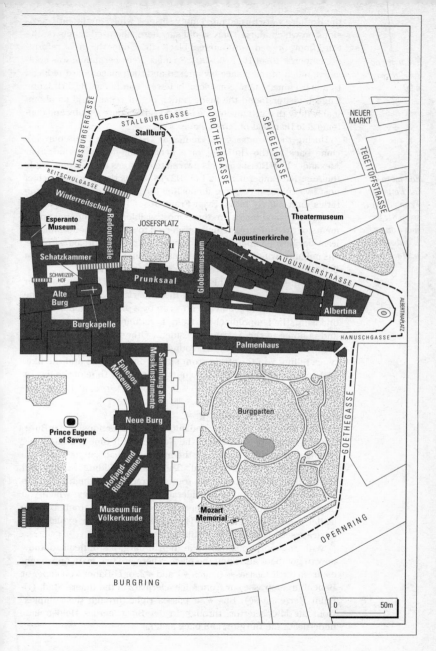

STALLBURGGASSE

HABSBURGERGASSE

DOROTHEERGASSE

SPIEGELGASSE

TEGETTOFFSTRASSE

NEUER MARKT

Stallburg

REITSCHULGASSE

Winterreitschule

Redoutensäle

Esperanto Museum

JOSEFSPLATZ

Globenmuseum

Theatermuseum

Augustinerkirche

Schatzkammer

SCHWEIZER-HOF

Prunksaal

AUGUSINERSTRASSE

Alte Burg

ALBERTINAPLATZ

Burgkapelle

Albertina

HANUSCHGASSE

Palmenhaus

Ephesos Museum

Sammlung alte Musikinstrumente

Burggarten

Neue Burg

Prince Eugene of Savoy

GOETHEGASSE

Hofjagd- und Rüstkammer

Museum für Völkerkunde

Mozart Memorial

OPERNRING

BURGRING

0   50m

the Hofburg were turned into empty shrines, while, on the rare occasions on which Maria Theresa did stay here, she used rooms on the third floor, draped with funereal black silk. Under the great reforming emperor **Josef II** (1780–90), Spanish court cermonial was abolished, much of the palace lay unused and the palace guard reduced to a mere ninety men, considerably fewer than today. By 1792, one English visitor found the place "much out of repair, and so abominably dirty that its appearance is (if possible) more shabby and contemptible than that of our St James's".

For more on Josef II, see p.90.

During the **Congress of Vienna** in 1815 (see p.61), court life came back to the Hofburg for a hectic nine-month period. Tsar Alexander II of Russia had his own suite of rooms in one wing, while the Austrian Emperor Franz I (1792–1835), as the congress's chief host, was obliged to serve dinner for forty tables of foreign dignitaries on a nightly basis. Even **Franz-Josef I** (1848–1916), whose austere personal tastes are those most visible in the imperial apartments of the Hofburg, actually preferred to stay at Schönbrunn, not least because he could drop in on his mistress for breakfast there. His unhappy wife, Elisabeth, spent as little time in the Hofburg (or at Schönbrunn) as possible, largely to get away from him.

For more on the Emperor Franz-Josef I, see p.81; for more on Elisabeth, see p.218.

After the downfall of the Habsburgs, the palace became more or less a state-run concern, though the imperial apartments and the court silver and porcelain are now run by a private company. Only one wing, the Leopoldischinertrakt, is retained for affairs of state, and is home to the Austrian president. Otherwise, the Hofburg is a relaxing place to wander round, mercifully free of officious types telling you to refrain from sitting on the steps and the like, and you can walk through the courtyards at any time of the day or night.

Approaching the Hofburg

The following account is divided into four main sections: In der Burg, the Alte Burg, Josefsplatz and the Neue Burg. If time is limited, the two most rewarding sights are the imperial Schatzkammer, and the Nationalbibliothek's Prunksaal. The Spanish Riding School and Vienna Boys' Choir are the top tourist attractions, though getting to see either of them takes considerable time and money, which you might well be better off spending elsewhere. The tourist office leaflet, *Spanische Reitschule/Wiener Sängerknaben*, explains the intricate schedules of both institutions.

With an amorphous mass like the Hofburg, it's difficult to know how to go about attacking the place. There are two main **approaches**: from the Ringstrasse (trams #1 and #2, or U-Bahns Volksoper or Babenburgerstrasse) or from Michaelerplatz in the Innere Stadt (U-Bahn Herrengasse). Bus #2a passes right through the complex, from the Michaelertor, through In der Burg, across Heldenplatz, underneath the Burgtor, and back again.

In der Burg

In der Burg is the largest of the Hofburg's enclosed courtyards, and the one which sees the most human traffic, mostly tourists and passengers alighting from bus #2a. It was once a much livelier place, the venue for the daily changing of the guard under the Habsburgs, and, in the Middle Ages, the scene of tournaments, military parades and executions. The courtyard's seemingly uniform Baroque facades are the result of a century of ad hoc imperial extensions, and not some grand plan. At the centre is an overblown monument to the **Emperor Franz**, dressed in a Roman toga, appropriately enough – as well as being (as Franz I, after 1804) the first Austrian Emperor, he was (as Franz II, until 1806) the last Holy Roman Emperor. Erected in the 1840s, the monument was a culmination of the patriotic cult of "Franz the Good", victor over Napoleon and host of the Congress of Vienna. Franz fever took off as soon as the emperor breathed his last in 1835, when aristocratic ladies fought over the feathers from the pillow on his deathbed.

In der Burg

The south side of the courtyard is occupied by the vast range of the **Leopoldischinertrakt** (Leopold Wing), with its lime green pilasters. Built by, and named after, Leopold I, and later occupied by the Empress Maria Theresa, it is now part of the president's official residence and is closed to the public. Opposite, the **Reichskanzleitrakt** (State Chancellery Wing), a giant, cream-coloured, Baroque confection, was built by a combination of Hildebrandt and the Fischer von Erlachs. Taking its name from the bureaucrats of the Holy Roman Empire, who resided here until 1806, it now houses the Kaiserappartements of Franz-Josef. The two wings are joined at the west end by the **Amalienburg**, built in the sixteenth century for the Emperor Rudolf II, though he preferred Prague to Vienna. It takes its current name from the widow of Josef I, who lived here until her death in 1742. Though essentially a Renaissance building, it sports a dinky little Baroque bell tower and weather vane, not to mention a sundial, a clock and a gilded globe which shows the current phase of the moon. Several subsequent emperors resided here, but the rooms now open to the public date from the time of the Empress Elisabeth, who died in 1898, and the Emperor Karl I (1916–18).

Kaiserappartements

*The Kaiser-
appartements
are open daily
9am–5pm;
öS70. A com-
bined ticket
with the
Hofsilber- und
Tafelkammer
costs öS90.*

Of all the sights within the Hofburg, it is the **Kaiserappartements** (Imperial Rooms) that are the most disappointing. Virtually every room is decorated in the same style: creamy-white walls and ceiling with gilded detailing, parquet flooring and red furnishings. There aren't even any guided tours in English to bring these mundane surroundings to life, nor is there any information or labelling in the rooms themselves. The ticket office and entrance are accessible through the main doorway of the Reichskanzleitrakt; after viewing the rooms, you exit onto Ballhausplatz.

The Kaiserappartements' current state is a legacy of their last full-time imperial occupant, the Emperor Franz-Josef, who, though a stickler for pomp and protocol at official functions, was notoriously frugal in his daily life. Despite being a field marshal, he almost invariably dressed in a simple lieutenant's uniform. His eating habits were equally spartan: a breakfast of coffee, *Semmel* and a slice of ham (except during Lent) was followed by a lunch of *Tafelspitz* or boiled rump. He distrusted telephones, cars and electricity, and his only concession to modern life was his use of the telegraph. For opulence, you need to see Maria Theresa's apartments at Schönbrunn (see p.203).

Franz-Josef's apartments

To get to Franz-Josef's apartments, you must first climb – just as courtiers and ambassadors did – the **Kaiserstiege** (Imperial Staircase), carved in heavy white marble and punctuated with huge

Emperor Franz-Josef I (1848–1916)

Emperor Franz-Josef I was Europe's longest serving monarch, and Austria's most popular. His sixty-eight year reign was the most sustained period of relative stability the country had ever known, and a stark contrast with what followed. Like his grandfather, Franz I – "Franz the Good"; see p.79 – he was a legend in his own lifetime, and, thanks to the Viennese love of nostalgia, the myth continues today. As historian William Johnston wrote, "Franz-Josef I symbolized more than he achieved". His aversion to innovation was legendary, epitomized by his addiction to the Spanish Court Ceremonial. At dinner, every guest had to cease eating at the moment the emperor finished each course. Since Franz-Josef was a very fast eater, his guests rarely got more than a few mouthfuls. Such dinners were also very silent, as no one was permitted to speak unless spoken to by the emperor – and he was more intent on eating. On his sickbed during a particularly severe illness, though he could barely speak, he is said to have reprimanded the doctor who was hastily summoned: "Go home and dress correctly." "Lord, this court is stuffy" remarked Edward VII, Prince of Wales.

Despite the pomp and protocol which surrounded him, Franz-Josef was a simple man. His dedication to his job was legendary: he woke at 4am (occasionally 3.30am), washed in cold water and would be at his desk by 5am. Twice a week he would give general audience to any of his citizens who wished to see him – as many as one hundred in a morning (the supplicants were, of course, vetted first). After finishing work around 5.30pm, he would tidy his desk and, towards the end of his life, be in bed by 8.30pm. He had no great love of the arts – "I go to the opera as a sacrifice to my country" he once wrote to his mistress. His only passions were hunting and mountain climbing, and his annual holiday was invariably taken in Bad Ischl, in the Salzkammergut.

Franz-Josef's personal life was something of a disaster. He was in awe of his powerful mother, the Archduchess Sophie, who arranged and then proceeded to sabotage his marriage to one of his cousins, Elisabeth (see p.218). Despite Elisabeth's indifference – she spent as little time as possible in his company – Franz-Josef remained dedicated to her all his life. Meanwhile, for over thirty years, he conducted a passionate relationship with the Burgtheater actress Katharina Schratt. However, although they went through the motions of an affair, propriety appears to have prevented the emperor from transforming it into physical fact. Matters outside the bedroom were no better. His brother Maximilian was executed in Mexico in 1867, his only son Rudolf committed suicide in 1887, and his wife was assassinated in 1898.

On the morning of November 20, 1916, at the age of 86, Franz-Josef rose at 3.30am for the very last time. His last words to his valet that night were: "tomorrow morning, half past three."

gilded urns. After a series of rooms hung with tapestries, you come to the **Guardroom**, where the emperor's personal *Trabanten-Liebgarde* kept watch day and night. Next is the **Audience Room**, whose formulaic Neoclassical frescoes glorifying the Emperor Franz I were executed by Johann Peter Krafft, a pupil of Jacques-Louis David, and commissioned by the emperor's fourth wife. Like Franz I, Franz-Josef, his grandson, would stand twice a week behind the high desk, next door in the **Audience Chamber**, to receive the hoi polloi – according to court etiquette, visitors had to bow three times at the beginning and end of the audience, backing out of the room so as not to display their *derrière* to the emperor. Of the imperial portraits in the room, the most familiar – reproduced on countless postcards across the city – is the easel painting of the octogenarian Franz-Josef, sporting his trademark bushy sideburns and slumped slightly in his chair the year before his death.

Passing swiftly through the pale turquoise Conference Room, where the emperor used to consult his ministers, you come to **Franz-Josef's Study**. On the wall hangs one of Franz Xavier Winterhalter's famous portraits of the Empress Elisabeth, *décolletée*, hair down and ready for bed. Here, the emperor used to sit at his rosewood desk poring over official paperwork, giving each document, however trivial, his close attention before signing it, and thus earning himself the nickname, "the first bureaucrat of the empire". A hidden door leads into a cramped room which was occupied by the emperor's personal valet. Franz-Josef went through valets "like candles", literally wearing them out with his early morning routine.

The **Emperor's Bedroom** features the simple iron bedstead in which he would sleep under a camelskin cover. The delights of a modern washbasin were alien to the ascetic emperor, hence the fold-away toilet set. It was only at the insistence of Elisabeth that Franz-Josef agreed to instal lavatories in the Hofburg; he himself preferred to use a bed-pan. The **Large Drawing Room** features Winterhalter's even more famous portrait of the empress, aged 28, again *décolletée*, and with jewelled stars in her hair. In the adjacent **Small Drawing Room** hang portraits of Franz-Josef's ill-fated brother, Maximilian, Emperor of Mexico, and his wife, Charlotte. Both rooms fell into disuse after Elisabeth's death in 1898.

Elisabeth's apartments

The empress's suite of rooms in the Amalienburg adjoins the Small Drawing Room, beginning with the **Empress's Living Room/Bedroom**. Any feminine touches there might have been have long since disappeared – as has the empress's simple iron bed, which was removed to another room during the day.

The **Empress's Boudoir** is the highlight of the tour, giving you a glimpse of Elisabeth's gymnastic equipment, on which she exercised daily, a practice considered highly unorthodox at the time. She even had wooden rings screwed into the gilded panelling above the doorway. Like the current Princess of Wales, the unhappy empress was a woman estranged from her husband and obsessed with her beauty, though unlike Di, she was in the habit of rising at 5am, and plunging into a copper bath full of cold water (she had the only bathroom in the Hofburg) – you can spy the bath through the bathroom door, reflected in the mirror. In order to maintain the inch-perfect waistline demanded of nineteenth-century women, Elisabeth undoubtedly suffered from eating disorders, which only exacerbated her melancholia. Significantly, apart from a bust of Elisabeth herself, the paintings in the room are not of the imperial family – whom she mostly despised – but of her horses and dogs.

In der Burg

For more on the Empress Elisabeth, see p.218.

In the **Large Drawing Room**, it's difficult to miss Antonio Canova's life-size marble statue of Napoleon's eldest sister, Elisa, which she presented to the Emperor Franz I in an effort to ingratiate herself. There's also a wonderfully idealized pen-and-ink portrayal of the imperial couple enjoying breakfast together; by the time depicted in the picture, they were barely speaking. In the **Memorial Room**, the cult of "Sisi" – as the Empress is still affectionately known by the Viennese – gathers pace with an entire glass cabinet of memorabilia, including a photograph of the dress she wore when she was assassinated in Geneva in 1898. Her apotheosis occurs in the shrine-like Small Entrance Room, at the far end of the **Grand Entrance Hall**, with a serene life-size white marble statue. The paintings of the numerous children of Franz-Josef's great-great-grandmother, Maria Theresa – she had sixteen in total – in the Great Entrance Hall itself, are by the court painter Martin van Meytens. Their jollity and frivolity comes as a complete contrast to the stiff portraits in the rest of the palace.

Alexander's apartments

The next four rooms are named after the Russian Tsar who stayed in the Hofburg for the best part of a year during the Congress of Vienna in 1815. The decor, as usual, is almost identical to the rooms in the rest of the palace, and there are no reminders of Alexander's time here. The **Memorial Room** features portraits of the last of the Habsburgs, Emperor Karl I (1916–18), who used a couple of the rooms during his brief spell on the throne, and his wife, the Empress Zita, who outlived Karl by more than 75 years.

Passing quickly through the Red Reception Room, hung with Gobelins tapestries, you come to the **Dining Room**, laid out as it would have been in the time of Franz-Josef, with silver and gold cutlery placed to the right of the plate, in accordance with the Spanish Court Ceremonial, and napkins folded according to a secret court formula. The strictures of eating with the emperor are described above; Elisabeth herself detested formal dinners, and on the few occasions when she did appear, refused to touch the food.

The final room in the Kaiserappartements, the **Small Drawing Room**, is a terse memorial to two of the three heirs to Franz-Josef's throne who suffered untimely deaths. On the larger of the two easels is an oil painting of Franz-Josef's only son, Crown Prince Rudolf, who committed suicide in 1889 (see p.242). Franz-Josef's younger brother, Karl Ludwig (1833–96), who was next in line for throne, is not represented, though he, too, cut short his life by insisting on drinking the holy (and contaminated) waters of the River Jordan.

The other easel picture is a photograph of Karl Ludwig's son, the Archduke Franz Ferdinand, who was assassinated in Sarajevo in 1914. The painting of Rudolf's wife, Stephanie, on the wall, is by Hans Makart. Conspicuous by her absence is Franz Ferdinand's morganatic wife, Sophie Chotek, who suffered the same fate as her husband, but who was snubbed by the court in death as in life. Despite the fact that a crown prince was expected to marry a princess of royal blood, Franz Ferdinand contracted a marriage of love to a mere countess, who ranked lower than over thirty archduchesses, who, however young, were entitled to walk ahead of her on ceremonial occasions. Even after her assassination, the Habsburgs refused to elevate her, and vetoed her burial in the Kaisergruft.

Hofsilber- und Tafelkammer

The Hofsilber-
und Tafel-
kammer is
open daily
9am–5pm;
öS65. A com-
bined ticket
with the
Kaiser-
appartements
costs öS90.

Beyond the ticket office, on the ground floor of the Reichskanzleitrakt, are six rooms devoted to the **Hofsilber- und Tafelkammer** (Court Silver and Porcelain Collection) – not to be confused with the Schatzkammer, in the Schweizerhof, which is where the crown jewels are displayed. The latter has universal appeal (and is described opposite), whereas the Court Silver and Porcelain Collection is something of an acquired taste. You really have to be seriously into dinner services to get the most out of it, though if you're visiting the Kaiserappartements anyway, it doesn't cost much more to get a combined ticket.

Among the star exhibits is the eighteenth-century green and gold Sèvres Service, originally made up of 290 separate pieces, given to Maria Theresa by Louis XV. Another monster is the early nineteenth-century Milanese centrepiece in gilded bronze, which stretches for 33m along a table strewn with classical figures and gilded bronze and crystal urns. Maximilian's vast Chinese-style Dinner Service was made in 1865, when he was already Emperor of Mexico; it seems unlikely he ever got to use it before his execution, some two years later. Less in-your-face are the Meissen Service from 1775, delicately and sparsely decorated with flowers, and the series of plates by the Vienna Porcelain Factory from 1803, featuring painted landscapes. Finally, don't miss the stone jugs and salvers, with which the Emperor and Empress used to wash the feet of twelve ordinary men and women every year on Maundy Thursday.

Alte Burg

The **Alte Burg** (Old Palace) lies at the very heart of the Hofburg, occupying roughly the same space as the first fortress built here in 1275, and gradually enlarged over the centuries by successive Habsburgs. A small section of the old moat, and the original drawbridge mechanism, can still be seen by the main entrance to the Alte

Burg, known as the **Schweizertor** (Swiss Gate), after the Swiss mercenaries who were employed to guard it under Maria Theresa. The gateway itself, with its maroon and grey banded columns and gilded relief, is the finest in the Hofburg. It was erected in 1552 under Ferdinand I, whose innumerable kingdoms are listed in the gilded inscription above the gateway, ending with the glorious "ZC", meaning "etc". Passing through the Schweizertor, you enter the inner courtyard of the Alte Burg, or **Schweizerhof** (Swiss Courtyard), given a unified, rather dull facade by Maria Theresa's court architect, Nicolo Picassi. The stairs on the right lead up to the Burgkapelle, where the Vienna Boys' Choir performs Mass every Sunday. Below is the entrance to the world-famous Schatzkammer, where the Habsburgs' most precious treasures reside.

Schatzkammer

Of all the museums in the Hofburg, the imperial **Schatzkammer** (Treasury) is far and away the most rewarding. Here you can see some of the finest medieval craftsmanship and jewellery in Europe, including the imperial regalia and relics of the Holy Roman Empire, not to mention the Habsburgs' own crown jewels, countless reliquaries and robes, goldwork and silverware. Much of it was collected by Ferdinand I for his *Kunstkammer*, and from his reign onwards, the collection became a sort of unofficial safety-deposit box for the Habsburgs. In the reign of Karl VI, the treasury was gathered together and stored on the ground floor of the Alte Burg; the iron door at the entrance is dated 1712. You can wander at will around the twenty or so rooms, but since the labelling is in German only, you might consider renting a headphone commentary (öS30) or signing up for an English guided tour (usually one a day; öS30).

The Schatzkammer is open daily except Tues 10am–6pm; öS60.

Insignia and mementoes of the Habsburgs

From the fifteenth century onwards, with only a brief caesura, the Habsburgs ruled as Holy Roman Emperors. Since the imperial insignia were traditionally kept in Nuremburg, they devised their own private insignia, which are displayed in the first two rooms. However, the most striking exhibit in room 1, a plain silver-gilt orb and sceptre made in Prague in the late fourteenth century, originally formed part of the Bohemian crown jewels. The centrepiece of room 2 is the stunning golden **Crown of Rudolf II**, studded with diamonds, rubies, pearls, and, at the very top, a huge sapphire – after 1804 it was used as the Austrian imperial crown. Along with an orb and a sceptre carved from a narwhal's tooth, these crown jewels were made in Prague at the beginning of the seventeenth century. There's a bronze bust of the moody, broody Rudolf by his court architect, Adriaen de Vries, displayed here too. In 1804, Franz II pre-empted the dissolution of the Holy Roman Empire by two years, declaring himself Emperor of Austria. For his son's coronation as King of Hungary in 1830, he commissioned for himself a glorious gold-embroidered purple cloak, with an ermine collar, and a long train, now displayed in room 3, alongside some lovely velvet hats for knights, sporting huge ostrich feathers. Room 4 contains the coronation regalia of the King of Lombardo-Venetia, territory awarded to the Habsburgs at the Congress of Vienna in 1815, and later lost by Franz-Josef in 1859 and 1866.

The sequence of rooms goes slightly awry at this point, so pass quickly through room 9, and turn left into room 5, where the mother of all cots resides, an overwrought, silver-gilt cradle with silk and velvet trimmings, made in 1811 by the City of Paris for Napoleon's son – known variously as the **Duke of Reichstadt** or "King of Rome" – by his second wife, Marie Louise, daughter of the Emperor Franz I. The poor boy must have had nightmares from the golden eagle which hovers over the cot, and it comes as no surprise that this sickly, sensitive child died of tuberculosis at the age of just 21 (see p.208). Also displayed here are mementoes of Franz-Josef's brother, the Emperor Maximilian of Mexico, including his Mexican gold sceptre, chain of state and crown.

Passing swiftly through the baptismal robes and vessels in room 6, some of which were embroidered by Maria Theresa herself for her grandchildren, you enter room 7, which contains the remnants of the **Habsburgs' private jewellery** (most of it was spirited out of the country on the orders of the Emperor Karl I in the last few weeks of World War I). There are some serious stones on display here, like the 2680-carat Columbian emerald the size of your fist, which was carved into a salt cellar in Prague in 1641, and the huge garnet, "La Bella", which forms the centre of a double eagle, along with an amethyst and an opal set in enamel. Another notable treasure is the solid gold Turkish crown of the rebel King of Hungary, István Bocskai, from 1605, inlaid with pearls and precious stones. More difficult to spot are the few pieces of the Empress Elisabeth's jewellery, looking a bit upstaged among such illustrious company. Finally, before you leave, don't miss the golden rose bush presented by the Pope to Franz I's wife, a traditional papal gift on the fourth Sunday in Lent to "the most worthy person".

Room 8 contains the so-called "**inalienable heirlooms**", two pieces collected by Ferdinand I, which the Habsburgs were very keen to hold onto: a fourth-century agate dish, stolen from Constantinople in 1204 and thought at the time to be the Holy Grail, and a 2.43m-long narwhal's horn, which was originally believed to have come from a unicorn and therefore to be a sacred symbol of Christ.

Geistliche Schatzkammer

At this point, you come to the five rooms (I–V) devoted to the **Geistliche Schatzkammer** (Sacred Treasury), which kicks off with a long corridor of ecclesiastical robes, plus a silver-gilt, gem-encrusted miniature of the Mariensäule on Am Hof (see p.63). Elsewhere there are a bewildering number of golden goblets, crystal crosses, jade candlesticks, huge monstrances, and best of all, reliquaries. In room IV, the star reliquary is the one purporting to contain the nail that pierced the right hand of Christ, though there's also a monstrance boasting a fragment of the cross, and Saint Veronica's sweatband. One of the most macabre items is the small seventeenth-century ebony-framed glass cabinet, filled with miniature skeletons partying round a glittering red and gold tomb.

Insignia of the Holy Roman Empire

Continuing a thematic tour through the Schatzkammer entails backtracking through the sacred treasury, followed by rooms 6 and 5, to return to room 9. Here, you'll find the **regalia of the Electoral Prince of Bohemia**, including matching gold lamé cloak, gloves and hat. Since the Holy Roman Emperor was automatically also King of Bohemia from the fourteenth century onwards, someone had to stand in for the latter during the imperial coronation. There are still more ancient royal insignia in room 10, which found their way into Habsburg hands via the Hohenstaufen dynasty. Among the most striking items have got to be the snazzy red silk stockings of William II of Normandy and the red silk mantle worn by Roger II, when he was crowned King of Sicily in the twelfth century.

The highlight of the whole collection are the **crown jewels of the Holy Roman Empire** in room 11, which were traditionally kept in Nuremburg, but were brought to Vienna in 1796 and retained by the Habsburgs after the abolition of the empire in 1806. The Nazis brought them back to Nuremburg in 1938, but the Americans made sure they were returned to the Austrians in 1945. The centrepiece is the octagonal imperial crown itself, a superb piece of Byzantine jewellery, smothered with pearls, large precious stones and enamel plaques. Legend has it that the crown was used in the coronation of Charlemagne in 800, but it now seems likely that it dates back only to that of Otto I, the first Holy Roman Emperor, in 962. Similarly encrusted with jewels are the eleventh-century imperial cross, the twelfth-century imperial orb, and the very venerable Purse of St Stephen, which belonged to Charlemagne himself and, so the story goes, contained earth soaked in the blood of the first Christian martyr. Also on display is the legendary **Holy Lance**, with which the Roman soldier pierced the side of Christ. The lance – which actually dates from the eighth century – was alleged to have magic powers, so that whoever possessed it held the destiny of the world in their hands. It was in front of this exhibit that the young Hitler is supposed to have had a mystical revelation, which changed the course of his life (and therefore of twentieth-century history), though the story is probably apocryphal.

Room 12 is given over to the **imperial relics**, many of them donated to the treasury by the Emperor Karl IV, who was a serious relic freak. What you see is a mere *soupçon* of the original collection – he is thought to have gathered together over two hundred relics (he apparently even stole one from the Pope). There's a tooth from John the Baptist, a bit of the tablecloth from the Last Supper, a bone from the arm of Saint Anne, a chip of wood from Christ's manger, and even a small piece of His bib.

The Burgundian Treasures

The last four rooms (13–16) of the Schatzkammer house the substantial dowry that came into Habsburg hands in 1477, when the Emperor Maximilian I married the only daughter and heiress of the Duke of Burgundy. By so doing Maximilian also became Grand Master of the **Order of the Golden Fleece**, the exclusive Burgundian order of chivalry founded in 1430, whose insignia are displayed here: heavy mantles embroidered with gold thread, a collar of golden links from which the "fleece" would hang, and the ram emblem, worn by the 24 knights of the order at all times. The Grand Master was responsible for replacing any collars that were lost in battle; to his financial embarrassment, Maximilian had to pay for four golden collars that vanished in hand-to-hand fighting during the Battle of Guinegate in 1479. After Maximilian, the Habsburgs became more or less hereditary sovereign Grand Masters of the Order, which still exists, albeit in a debased form, today.

Burgkapelle

The chapel is open Jan–June & mid-Sept to Dec for guided tours only: Tues & Thurs 1.30–3.30pm, Fri 1–3pm; öS15.

The **Burgkapelle** (Palace Chapel), up the stairs above the entrance to the Schatzkammer, was built in the late 1440s by the Emperor Friedrich III. Despite numerous alterations over the centuries, the interior retains its Gothic vaulting, its carved ceiling pendants, and much of its fifteenth-century wooden statuary protected by richly carved baldachins. It's a favourite venue for society weddings, but the public only get to see it on one of the rare guided tours. In any case, the real point of going there is to hear the Hofmusikkapelle, made up of members of the *Wiener Sängerknaben*, or **Vienna Boys' Choir**, supplemented by musicians from the Staatsoper.

For more on how to get to hear the Vienna Boys' Choir, see p.300.

Founded back in 1498 by the Emperor Maximilian I, the choir was closely linked to the imperial family, for whom they used to perform (famous *Sängerknaben* include Schubert and Haydn). In 1918, the choir went under with the dynasty, but was revived in 1924 and, dressed in ludicrous sailor's uniforms and caps, has since become a major Austrian export. There are, in fact, four choirs, who rotate jobs, one of which is to tour the world, and one of which is to sing Mass for the tourists on Sunday mornings (and on religious holidays) at 9.15am. The choir remain out of sight up in the organ loft for the whole of the Mass, and the only time you get a proper look at them is when they get their photos taken next to the congregation after the service.

Around Josefsplatz

Josefsplatz is without doubt one of the most imposing squares in Vienna, lined on three sides by the blank, brilliant-white Baroque facades of the Hofburg. The square started out as the churchyard of the **Augustinerkirche** (now masked by the south wing of the Augustinertrakt), and later served as the training ground for the **Spanische Reitschule** (now housed to the north). It's appropriate then, that the centre of the square features an equestrian statue of the Emperor Josef II – rather surprisingly the first ever public statue of a Habsburg when it was unveiled in 1807. It's Josef who lends his name to the square, which he opened to the public by tearing down the wall that enclosed it within the Hofburg.

The facades of the north and south wings, by Nicolo Pacassi, are typically severe and unadorned, but the middle wing – which houses the Prunksaal of the **Nationalbibliothek** – is a much earlier, more exuberant work by Johann Bernhard Fischer von Erlach, completed in 1735 by his son, Josef Emanuel. The attic storey bristles with marble statuary and urns, the central sculptural group above the main entrance featuring Minerva, goddess of wisdom, trampling Ignorance and Hunger with her four-horse chariot; on either side Atlantes struggle to contain a cluster of scientific instruments and two giant gilded globes from tumbling onto the cobbles below.

The north wing on Josefsplatz houses the **Redoutensäle**, originally the court theatre, but remodelled in the 1740s as a ballroom and banqueting hall. Mozart and Beethoven both conducted performances of their own works here, and the rooms became the traditional venue for the annual Hofball, held in February under the Habsburgs at the high point of the *Fasching*. Anthony Trollope's mother, Fanny, attended a masked ball here in 1836 at which over four thousand were said to be present, though "the press was almost intolerable, and the dust raised by it such as quite to destroy the beauty and effect of this very magnificent room". Sadly, the whole wing was badly destroyed by fire in November 1992, and is currently undergoing a massive restoration programme.

At the time of writing, the passageway allowing access to Josefplatz from the Schweizerhof was closed indefinitely for renovation.

Winterreitschule and Stallburg

Performances of the Spanische Reitschule (see p.92) take place regularly in the splendidly Baroque **Winterreitschule** (Winter Riding School), on the west side of Reitschulgasse. Purpose-built by Josef Emanuel Fischer von Erlach in 1735, the 55m-long Reitsaal is surrounded by a two-tiered spectators' gallery (with notoriously bad sightlines) held up by 46 Composite columns. Situated at one end of the Reitsaal, the former imperial box features an equestrian portrait of the Emperor Karl VI, to which all the

Emperor Josef II (1780–90)

If any Habsburg embodied the spirit of the Enlightenment it was the
Emperor Josef II. Born in 1741, the eldest son of the Empress Maria
Theresa, Josef was groomed for his role from an early age. After the death
of his father, Franz Stephan, in 1765, his mother appointed him co-regent
with her, and from 1780 he ruled in his own right. Though his reforming
zeal surpassed that of all his predecessors put together – it's estimated that
he published 6000 decrees and 11,000 new laws – he was in many ways
only continuing and furthering the work his mother had begun.

Josef's most famous reform was the 1781 **Toleranzpatent**, which
allowed freedom of worship for non-Catholics, and, significantly, lifted
many restrictions on Jews. In addition, he expelled the Jesuit order, and
dissolved and sold off four hundred contemplative or "idle" monasteries.
Though his policies incurred the wrath of the established church (including Pope Pius VI), Josef himself was a devout Catholic – his intention was
to reduce the power of the church in secular life, thereby giving him, and
his officials, a much freer hand. Other decrees had more altruistic motives:
aristocratic privilege before the law was abolished, with miscreant counts
made to sweep the streets as punishment in the same way as commoners
had for centuries. Among his most popular measures were the opening of
the royal gardens of the Prater and Augarten in Vienna to the public, and
of the court opera house to non-aristocratic patrons.

Josef's decrees didn't end with the general populace. During his reign,
the royal household was stripped of its former grandeur, and court ceremony virtually disappeared. One of his first acts as co-regent was to abolish the imperial birthdays and gala-days, forty of which were observed
annually. He wore simple, almost bourgeois clothing, drove through the
streets in a two-seater carriage and was often seen on foot with the people.
On becoming regent, he handed over his personal inheritance to the state

riders raise their hats on entering, in thanks for the wonderful
arena he bequeathed them. It was in these unlikely surroundings
that Austria's first democratically elected assembly met in July
1848 – the court having fled to Innsbruck – and voted to abolish
serfdom.

Visiting the Winterreitschule

Access to the Winterreitschule is either from the north side of
Josefsplatz, or from underneath the Michaelertor. The riding
school's complicated public schedule of training sessions and performances is written up outside both entrances. There are one or two
performances (*Vorführungen*) a week (usually Sun 10.45am, and
less frequently Wed 7pm) between March and June and September
and December, though for at least a month of the latter period, the
school is usually on tour. Seats **cost** öS240–800, and standing room
öS190. Even at those prices, the performances are booked solid
months in advance; to be sure of a place, you must **write in advance**
to: Spanische Reitschule, Hofburg, A-1010 Wien.

treasury and demanded that his brother Leopold do the same, much to the latter's disgust. He lived for most of the time in a small outbuilding in the Augarten (see p.194), boarding up much of the Hofburg and Schönbrunn to avoid the expense of having to guard them.

Despite his policies, Josef was a despot – "everything for the people, and nothing through the people" was his catchphrase – who listened to no advice, and whose invasions of his subjects' privacy did not endear him to them. He forbade the wearing of corsets, on health grounds; the superstitious practice of ringing of church bells to ward off lightning; the dressing of saintly images in real clothes; and the baking of honeycakes (which he considered to be bad for the digestion). Most famously, he banned the use of coffins, because of a shortage of wood, insisting corpses should be taken to the cemetery in reusable coffins, and buried in linen sacks to hasten decomposition, again on health grounds. In the end, he issued so many decrees that few of them could be effectively executed, and many were rescinded as soon as his reign was over.

"As a man he has the greatest merit and talent; as a prince he will have continual erections and never be satisfied. His reign will be a continual Priapism." Despite the Prince de Ligne's predictions, it was the emperor's wives who ended up dissatisfied. Though Josef clearly loved his first wife, Isabella of Parma, she had eyes only for his sister, Maria Christina. Isabella died of small pox in 1763, having given birth to two daughters, neither of whom survived to adulthood. Josef's second marriage, to Maria Josepha of Bavaria, was no love-match. "Her figure is short, thick-set, and without a vestige of charm. Her face is covered with spots and pimples. Her teeth are horrible," he confided to a friend on first setting eyes on her. He treated her abysmally, and it was a release for her when she too died of small pox in 1767. He never remarried, took no mistresses, and lived as a bachelor until his death of tuberculosis at the age of just 48 in 1790.

From mid-February to June and from late August until early October, the school also holds **training sessions** (*Morgenarbeit;* Tues–Sat 10am–noon), which are open to the public. Seats cost öS100 and are sold at the Michaelertor entrance box office; the queue for tickets is at its worst early on, but by 11am, it's usually easy enough to get in, as folk get bored. Another option, between April and June, and occasionally in the autumn, is to catch one of the training sessions with music (*Morgenarbeit mit Musik;* Sat 10am), for which tickets cost öS240. Cheapest of all is to watch a **video** on the riding school, which is shown daily from 10am to 6pm in the Palais Palffy, Josefsplatz 6; tickets cost öS50.

Stallburg

Sixty-five horses are kept in the **Stallburg** (Stables), an arcaded Renaissance palace, on the other side of Reitschulgasse, conceived in 1559 by Ferdinand I as a private residence for his son, Maximilian. Lack of finance delayed the project, and when Maximilian became emperor, he converted the building into the imperial stables. If

Spanische Reitschule

The Habsburgs' world-famous **Spanische Reitschule** (Spanish Riding School) has its origins with the Archduke Karl, brother of Maximilian II, who established several studs at Lipizza northeast of Trieste (now the Slovene town of Lipica) in the 1570s. By cross-breeding Spanish, Arab and Berber horses, the studs created the Lipizzaner strain, which subsequently supplied the Habsburgs with all their cavalry and show horses. However, it was only properly expanded by the Spanish-bred Emperor Karl VI, who gave the riding school a permanent home in the Hofburg. After World War I, the stud was moved to Piber near Graz, though the horses are now bred at both places.

Since an imperial decree in the early nineteenth century, only silver-white stallions have been used, though when they're born, Lipizzaner foals can be any shade of brown to grey, their coats turning white when they are at least four years old. They begin to learn the dressage steps from the age of seven, gradually progressing to the aerial excercises for which they are famous, and can live to the ripe old age of thirty-two. The highlight of the dressage is the cabriole, where the horse walks on its hind legs, with its hocks practically touching the ground and its front legs in the air. In deference to tradition (and with an eye to their tourist appeal) the riders wear period costume: black boots which reach above the knee, white buckskin jodhpurs, double-breasted, brown jackets, white gloves and a black bicorn hat.

The Spanish Riding School is such an intrinsic part of Vienna's Habsburg heritage industry, it's difficult not to feel a certain revulsion for the whole charade. That said, to witness the Lipizzaners' equestrian ballet is an unforgettable, if faintly ridiculous, experience; certainly those with any interest in horses will feel compelled to see at least a rehearsal. As Edward Crankshaw famously remarked more than half a century ago: "The cabrioling of the pure white Lippizzaners is, by all our standards, the absolute of uselessness. The horses, fine, beautiful, and strong, are utterly divorced from all natural movement, living their lives in an atmosphere of unreality with every step laid down for them and no chance whatsoever of a moment's deviation. And so it was with the nineteenth-century Habsburgs."

you're lucky you might catch a glimpse of the horses as they are taken over to the Winterreitschule for their morning exercise. The rest of the horses are kept in the stables of the Lainzer Tiergarten (see p.217).

Nationalbibliothek

Spread out across the Hofburg, the **Nationalbibliothek** (National Library) is first and foremost the country's largest working library, home to millions of books. Though the main reading room (in the Neue Burg) is open to the public, most visitors only ever see the library's Baroque Prunksaal, on Josefsplatz, which, though it holds some 200,000 venerable volumes, is primarily an architectural rather than a tourist attraction. You can also see the library's assortment of papyrus, musical manuscripts, globes and maps, and its off-shoots, the Esperanto Museum and Theatermuseum.

Around
Josefsplatz

Prunksaal

If the Karlskirche (see p.125) is Johann Bernhard Fischer von Erlach's sacred masterpiece, then the **Prunksaal** (Grand Hall) is his most stunning secular work. The library was begun in 1723, the year of his death, and, like so many of his projects, had to be finished off by his son, Josef Emanuel. It's by far the largest Baroque library in Europe, stretching the full length of the first floor of the central wing on Josefsplatz. Access to the Prunksaal is via the monumental staircase in the southwest corner of the square.

The first thing that strikes you on entering the library is its sheer size: nearly 80m in length and 30m in height at its peak. Not an architect to be accused of understatement, Fischer von Erlach achieves his desired effect by an overdose of elements: massive marble pillars and pilasters, topped by gilded capitals, punctuate the space, gilded wood-panelled bookcases, carved balconies accessed by spiral staircases, and from floor to ceiling, over 200,000 leather-bound books, including the 15,000-volume personal library of Prince Eugène of Savoy.

The space is divided into two quasi-transepts by a transverse oval dome, underneath which stands a statue of the Emperor Karl VI, just one of sixteen marble statues of Spanish and Austrian Habsburg rulers executed by the unlikely-named Strudel brothers, Peter and Paul. Directly above you (and Karl) is Daniel Gran's magnificent, colourful fresco, with the winged figure of Fame holding a rather misshapen pyramid. The emperor himself appears on a medallion just below Fame, flanked by Hercules and Apollo. Among the other celestial groups, there's a model of the library heading Karl's way – in case you miss it, one of the women depicted as Austrian magnanimity is pointing to it. At the lowest level, Gran has painted *trompe l'oeil* balconies, on which groups of figures hold scholarly discussions. If you're really keen to work out what's going on there's an inexpensive guide to the dome fresco available at the ticket desk.

The Prunksaal is open June–Oct Mon–Sat 10am–4pm, Sun 10am–1pm; Nov–May Mon–Sat 10am–noon; closed for the first three weeks of Sept; öS50.

Globenmuseum

There are several antique globes in the Prunksaal itself, but if that has only whetted your appetite, you can view lots more at close quarters in the two rooms of the **Globenmuseum**, situated next door on the third floor of the Augustinertrakt, the south wing on Josefsplatz. The majority of the globes date from the nineteenth century, though one of the oldest was made in 1541 by Mercator (of Projection fame) for the Emperor Karl V; another particularly fine example is Eimmart's celestial globe from 1705, which is decorated with pictorial symbols representing the constellations of the zodiac.

The museum also displays a selection of the library's **Kartensammlung** (Map Collection). Check out the upside-down map

The Globenmuseum is open Mon–Wed & Fri 11am–noon, Thurs 2–3pm; öS15.

of the world from 1154, and the sixteenth-century charts, one of which features a magnificent sea dragon happily swimming in the south Atlantic, while another depicts a bevy of parrots in the *terra incognito*, now known to us as South America.

Esperanto Museum

The museum is open July, Aug & the last week in Sept Mon, Wed & Fri 10am–6pm; Oct–May Mon & Fri 10am–4pm, Wed 10am–6pm; free.

One of the least-visited sights in the entire Hofburg complex is the **International Esperanto Museum** (Internacia Esperanto Muzeo) deep in the bowels of the palace. To get there, enter under the archway that leads from In der Burg towards Michaelerplatz, and take the elevator to the third floor; thereafter follow the signs. In addition to a library and a bookshop, there is a small historical exhibition on the language (captions are in German and Esperanto).

Esperanto is an artificial language, created by the Russian Jew, Dr Ludvik Zamenhof, in 1887, as an easy-to-learn, worldwide *lingua franca*. Though it has never caught on in the way its creator originally hoped – there are an estimated 30,000 Esperanto-speakers worldwide – the argument for such a language remains powerful. Translation budgets are a permanent drain on organizations such as the European Union, and opting for a language like English carries with it enormous political consequences. Yet although Esperanto carries less ideological baggage than English, it is still a deeply Eurocentric language for an international *lingua franca*. Its roots come almost exclusively from Latin-based, Romance languages, making it plain sailing for an Italian, but virtually impenetrable at first sight for, say, an Egyptian.

The curators of the museum are, understandably, die-hard Esperantists, and will gladly enthuse about (and in) the tongue. All kinds of Esperanto texts are on display, ranging from the first book published by Zamenhof, in 1887, to the latest Esperanto fiction, some of it written in the original. To continue the theme of artificial and obscure tongues is a version of *Asterix* in Romanisch and a Klingon/English dictionary (apparently *Hamlet* has recently been translated into Klingon, but that's another story).

Theatermuseum

The Theater-museum is open Tues–Sun 10am–5pm; öS40.

The **Theatermuseum** – not strictly speaking part of the Hofburg complex, but part of the Nationalbibliothek's collection – is a short distance from Josefsplatz. To get there, head up Augustinerstrasse and take the second street on your left. Here, on the corner, overlooking Lobkowitzplatz, stands the splendid, silver-white, Baroque Palais Lobkowitz. The museum's permanent collection focuses on the history of Austrian theatre and is likely to be somewhat mystifying to non-Austrians, particularly as the labelling is entirely in German. However, the building alone merits a visit.

From the main courtyard, which centres on a Hercules fountain, you ascend a grandiose stuccoed staircase to reach the marble-decked **Eroicasaal**, decorated with Jacob von Schuppen's colourful ceiling fresco. The Lobkowitz family were among Beethoven's many highly placed patrons, and the hall takes its name from the composer's Third Symphony, which was premièred here in 1804, to be followed by his Fourth Symphony three years later. Temporary exhibitions, on more contemporary theatrical themes, are held on the same floor as the Eroicasaal, and are likely to hold more interest than the permanent collection.

Around Josefsplatz

Another regular feature of the museum is the performances using the late Richard Teschner's rod puppets, which usually take place on Tuesdays at 7.30pm (check the current programme for details). In the basement, there's a **children's section**, reached by a huge metal slide from the ground floor, where kids' workshops are occasionally held. Here, too, you'll discover more puppets – glove, rod, string and shadow – plus a paper theatre and a wonderful *Geistertheater* (ghost theatre). Lastly, for the truly dedicated, there's an annexe to the museum round the corner at Hanuschgasse 3, with memorial rooms dedicated to the likes of Max Reinhardt, Hermann Bahr and Fritz Wotruba.

The Theatermuseum annexe is open Tues–Fri 10am–noon & 1–4pm, Sat & Sun 1–4pm.

Papyrussammlung and Musiksammlung

The library's **Papyrussammlung** (Papyrus Collection) is on the second floor of the Albertina (see below), in a small room off the Papyrus Library. What you see is but a minuscule selection of the 100,000 or more papyrii in the collection. The labelling and translations are all in German, so make sure you pick up the English leaflet available for a small sum. There are sample texts in numerous ancient tongues from Hebrew to Aramaic, many of them receipts of one sort or another or snippets of literature, with one or two quirkier items: a fourth-century BC Greek recipe for toothpaste, Arabic advice from the ninth century on how to mix up a laxative, and questions to ask the oracle from turn-of-the-milliennium Greece.

The Papyrussammlung is open Mon 9am–6.45pm, Tues–Fri 9am–1pm; öS15.

Two floors above, the **Musiksammlung** (Music Collection) contains original scores of Mozart's Requiem and the like. Again, there are display cabinets off the Music Library's reading room, but this is really more of a research facility than for general consumption. However, if you've a genuine interest, present yourself to the librarian on duty.

The Musiksammlung is open Mon, Wed & Fri 9am–1pm, Tues noon–3.45pm & Thurs noon–6.45pm; free.

Augustinerkirche

Masked by Picassi's bland facade, the **Augustinerkirche**, to the south of Josefsplatz, is one of the oldest parts of the Hofburg, dating back as far as the 1330s. The church was originally built for the monks of the adjacent Augustinian monastery, but was gradually swallowed up by the encroaching Hofburg, which adopted it as the court parish church in 1634. It was the scene of several notable Habsburg weddings, including those of Maria Theresa and Franz Stephan, Franz-Josef and Elisabeth, Crown Prince Rudolf and Stephanie, and the proxy marriage of the Archduchess Marie Louise

The Augustinerkirche is open Mon–Sat 10am–6pm, Sun 1–6pm.

to Napoleon in 1810 (his stand-in was the Archduke Karl who had defeated the French Emperor at Aspern the previous year).

Inside, the church has clearly taken a beating over the years, though it retains its lofty quadripartite Gothic vaulting. The chief attraction is Antonio Canova's Neoclassical **Christinendenkmal**, in the right-hand aisle, a lavish memorial to Maria Christina, favourite daughter of Maria Theresa, erected in 1805 by her husband, Albrecht, Duke of Saxony-Tetschen. A motley procession of marble mourners heads up the steps for the open door of the pyramidal tomb, while a winged spirit and a sad lion embrace on the other side, and another genius holds aloft the Duchess's medallion. They'd be disappointed if they ever got inside, for she's actually buried in the Kaisergruft. Canova himself was so taken with his creation that he repeated it for Titian's tomb, and his own mausoleum in Venice.

Several more monumental tombs can be found in the **Georgskapelle**, a self-contained, two-aisled chapel, built in the fourteenth century to the right of the chancel. In the centre of the chapel lies the empty marble tomb of the Emperor Leopold II, whose brief reign of less than two years ended in 1792. Balthasar Ferdinand Moll's gilded wall tomb to Count Leopold Daun, on the far wall, is significantly more extravagant, and includes a relief of the 1757 Battle of Kolín in which Daun trounced the Prussians. Also buried here is Maria Theresa's faithful physician, Gerhard van Swieten, who saw her successfully through fifteen pregnancies.

The Habsburgs' bodies are buried in the Kaisergruft, see p.50; their entrails are in the catacombs of Stephansdom, see p.41.

To get to the Georgskapelle, you must pass through the Lorettokapelle, at the far end of which lies the **Herzgrüftel** (Little Heart Crypt), where, arranged neatly on two semi-circular shelves, are 54 silver urns containing the hearts of the later Habsburgs. The two tiny grilles in the wrought-iron door are usually kept shut, so if you want to have a peek, you must make an appointment with one of the monks (call ☎533 70 99). Before you leave, take time to admire the richly gilded Rococo organ, on which Anton Bruckner composed and gave the première of his Mass no. 3 in F minor in 1872. The church still has a strong musical tradition, and a full orchestra accompanies Sunday morning Mass.

Albertina

At the far end of Augustinerstrasse, beyond the Augustinerkirche, the **Albertina** is a mish-mash of a building, incorporating parts of the former Augustinian monastery, the late eighteenth-century Taroucca Palace, and the southernmost bastion of the Hofburg. There are steps up to the latter, which overlooks the back of the Staatsoper, and is surmounted by a grand equestrian statue of the Archduke Albrecht, who vanquished the Italians at the Battle of Custozza, one of his few bright moments in the otherwise disastrous Austro-Prussian War of 1866. The Albertina is best known for its world-famous graphics collection, but it is also home to the

Nationalbibliothek's papyrus and music collection (see p.95), and the Filmmuseum. The latter is not, in fact, a museum, but a cinema, which shows a wide range of documentaries and full-length features drawn from its extensive archives.

Founded in 1768 by Albrecht, Duke of Saxony-Teschen (after whom the gallery is named), the Albertina boasts one of the largest collection of **graphic arts** in the world, with approximately 50,000 drawings, etchings and watercolours, and over a million and a half printed works. With such a vast archive, the gallery can only hope to show a tiny fraction at any one time, which it does by putting on a series of temporary exhibitions devoted either to one artist, period or theme. Within its catalogue, it has some 43 drawings by Raphael, 70 by Rembrandt van Rijn, 145 by Albrecht Dürer – more than any other gallery in the world – and 150 by Egon Schiele, plus many more by the likes of Leonardo da Vinci, Michelangelo, Peter Paul Rubens, Heironymus Bosch, Pieter Bruegel the Elder, Paul Cézanne, Pablo Picasso, Henri Matisse, Gustav Klimt and Oskar Kokoschka. A permanent exhibition of highlights in facsimile is usually on display, but the whole building is undergoing extensive renovation until at least 1998, so it's difficult to predict what exactly will be on offer.

*The Albertina
is currently
open Mon–
Thurs 10am–
4pm, Fri
10am–1pm;
öS50.*

Neue Burg

The last wing of the Hofburg to be built – completed in 1913 – was the **Neue Burg**, a piece of pure bombast crafted in heavy neo-Renaissance style by Gottfried Semper and Karl von Hasenauer. Semper originally planned to create a vast *Kaiserforum*, by enclosing Heldenplatz with another new palatial wing mirroring the Neue Burg, and by linking both wings to the nearby *Hofmuseen* via a pair of triumphal arches spanning the Ringstrasse. In the end, only the southern arc of the Neue Burg got built; the exterior was completed in 1913, but the interior was still being given the finishing touches long after the Habsburgs had departed, in 1926.

Heldenplatz (Heroes' Square) thus remains a wide, slightly meaningless, expanse, which nonetheless affords a great view across to the Rathaus and Parlament buildings on the Ringstrasse (see p.109). The square takes its name from Anton Fernkorn's two nineteenth-century equestrian statues, whose generals appear to be marshalling the surrounding parked cars into battle. The more technically remarkable of the two is the earlier one of the Archduke Karl, who defeated Napoleon at Aspern in 1809 (and then lost to him shortly afterwards) and whose horse is cleverly balanced on its hind legs. Fernkorn failed to pull off this unique trick with the statue of Prince Eugène of Savoy, and had to resort to using the horse's tail for extra stability; he died insane the following year.

The Neue Burg itself is now home to the Nationalbibliothek's main reading room, an offshoot of the Naturhistorisches Museum, and three departments of the Kunsthistorisches Museum. For the Viennese, though, it's forever etched in the memory as the scene of Hitler's victorious return to Vienna on March 15, 1938, when thousands gathered here to celebrate the Anschluss. "To say that the crowds which greeted him . . . were delirious with joy is an understatement," observed eye-witness George Clare before he fled the country. Hitler appeared on the central balcony of the Neue Burg and declared: "As Führer and Chancellor of the German nation and the German Reich I hereby announce to German history that my homeland has entered the German Reich."

To the west of Heldenplatz, the **Burgtor** cuts something of a pathetic figure as the official entrance to the Hofburg. Built into the walls in the 1820s – to commemorate the Battle of Leipzig in 1813, when the Austrians defeated Napoleon – it is the city's only surviving gateway. However, stripped of its accompanying walls, its classical lines and modest scale are at odds with everything around it. It was converted by the Austro-fascists in the 1930s to serve as Vienna's chief memorial to the fallen soldiers of World War I.

Neue Burg museums

The Neue Burg museums are open daily except Tues 10am–6pm; öS30.

Access to the museums within the Neue Burg is via the main entrance. A single ticket covers all three departments run by the Kunsthistorisches Museum: the Hofjagdt und Rüstkammer (Court Hunting and Arms Collection), the Sammlung alter Musikinstrumente (Collection of Early Musical Instruments), and the Ephesos (Ephesus) Museum. Free radiophone commentary (in German) is available for the first two collections. The Museum für Völkerkunde (Museum of Ethnology) has its own separate entrance, different opening hours and requires a separate ticket (see below).

Hofjagd- und Rüstkammer

The **Hofjagd- und Rüstkammer** or Waffensammlung (Weaponry Collection) boasts one of the world's finest assemblages of armour. Most items date from the fifteenth to the seventeenth century; for the arms and armour of the later imperial army, you must go to the Arsenal (see p.168). Chronologically, the collection begins in room 1, and continues in an anti-clockwise direction, finishing off with the great, curving, arcaded gallery of hunting weapons, at the top of the monumental marble staircase to the right of the main entrance.

Before you get to room 1, as you mount the stairs, admire the Albanian helmet from 1460, which sports a golden goat's head, and the fourteenth-century crested funereal helmet, which, weighing 7kg, was too heavy to be used for anything except tournaments. The two dog-snout-shaped visors – devised to replace the closed helmet, in which it was extraordinarily difficult to breathe – in room 1 probably come from the estate of Duke Ernst of of Austria (1377–1424), who was responsible for starting the weaponry collection. The two finely carved, ivory-encrusted saddles belonged to the Emperor Albrecht II (1365–95) and Ladislaus the Posthumous (1440–57).

Further on, in the first of the side galleries (A), there's a splendid array of **jousting equipment,** made for the knights of the Emperor Maximilian I. To try and minimize the death-rate among competitors, whose necks were particularly vulnerable, the helmets were attached to the armour. The High Renaissance **costume armour** in room 3 was meant only for show, its design deliberately imitating the fashionable clothes of the time: puffy sleeves, decorative bands inlaid with gilded silver, and slightly comical pleated skirts. It's difficult to imagine getting married in the wedding suit made for Albrecht of Brandenburg in 1526, with its huge pleated skirt, beetle-crusher shoes and grotesque helmet with wings and a beak.

There's some fabulous sixteenth-century **Milanese armour** crafted by Filippo Negroli in room 4, including an iron shield, embossed with a Medusa head, no doubt designed to turn the enemy into stone, and a suit of armour with a cap complete with naturalistic ears and curly hair. The museum's other great weaponry freak was the manic collector, Archduke Ferdinand of Tyrol (1525–95), who ordered the bank-breaking **Adlergarnitur** (Eagle Armour) in room 5, with its exquisite gilded garniture. The **gold rapier** in room 6, with its gilded cast-iron hilt, was a gift to Ferdinand from his brother, the Emperor Maximilian II, and is one of the finest works in the entire collection. Equally resplendent is the blue and gold suit of armour made for Maximilian, with vertical gold bands in imitation of contemporary Spanish court dress; the chain of the Order of the Golden Fleece can be seen around the neck. Also on display are several spoils from the sixteenth-century wars against the Turks.

Yet more richly decorated suits of armour fill room 7, including the "rose-petal" garniture ordered by Maximilian II for the tournament held in Vienna in 1571 to celebrate his brother Karl's wedding; equally fancy suits were created for his two sons, Rudolf and Ernst. There's more Milanese craftsmanship in room 8, including a rapier whose hilt features numerous moors' heads. A vast array of elaborate hunting rifles and pistols, dating from the early-seventeenth to the nineteenth century, concludes the exhibition.

Sammlung alter Musikinstrumente

If you've absolutely no interest in instruments of death, however beautifully crafted, you can skip the entire collection, and head straight for the early musical instruments. The Archduke Ferdinand of Tyrol is again responsible for many of the rare pieces, which were designed to be admired for their artistry rather than the sound they produced. With the later instruments, the opposite tends to be true, and those with a green spot on the label can be played.

The unique set of six sixteenth-century **dragon-shaped shawms,** in room 10, is from the *Kunstkammer* of Ferdinand of Tyrol.

However, the vertically strung **calvicytherium**, in room 11, richly inlaid with ivory, ebony, tortoise-shell and mother-of-pearl, was actually played by the Emperor Leopold I, who was a musician and composer in his own right. Room 12 is loosely based around Josef Haydn, featuring instruments from his day, plus a quadruple music stand for a string quartet; the extraordinarily lifelike beeswax bust of the composer sports a wig of real human hair.

The **tortoise-shell violin**, decorated with gold and ivory, in room 13, was bought by Maria Theresa for the Schatzkammer, and, like many such showpieces, is totally unsuitable for playing. Also in this room is an early nineteenth-century **glass harmonica** of the variety invented by the American statesman Benjamin Franklin. Next door the ornate **Marble Hall** (room 14) – still occasionally used as a concert venue – contains several instruments associated with famous composers: a cembalo owned by Haydn, a square piano used by Schubert, and a grand piano given to Beethoven by the famous piano makers Erard Frères.

Eye-catching exhibits in room 15 include a crystal flute, and a violin that doubled as a walking stick, both from the time of Schubert. An aluminium violin and a "dummy keyboard" – stringless, for silent practice – can be found in room 16, and in the final room there's an entire late nineteenth-century orchestra as well as a grand piano designed by Theophil Hansen and given to the Emperor Franz-Josef for his wife, Elisabeth, to play. A whole load of Bösendorfer grands, an early synthesizer, and a look at the inner workings of the piano through the ages, round off the collection.

Ephesos Museum

From 1866 until a ban on the export of antiquities from Turkey stopped the flow early this century, Austrian archeologists made off with a lot of first-class relics from the ancient city of Ephesus, on the coast of Asia Minor. It wasn't until 1978 that the loot was finally publicly displayed in the **Ephesos Museum**, occupying one half of the Neue Burg's monumental staircase.

The most significant find of the lot is the impressive forty-metre-long **Parthian Frieze**, sculpted in high relief around the second century AD, shortly after the Roman victory in the Parthian Wars. The relief formed the outer walls of a pantheon in honour of the commander of the Roman forces, Lucius Verus, who was joint emperor of the Roman Empire, along with his adoptive brother, Marcus Aurelius. The adoption of the two brothers by Antoninus Pius (himself adopted by the Emperor Hadrian), is depicted at the end of the corridor on the right, followed by battle scenes from the campaign, and finally Lucius Verus's apotheosis on the far left of the corridor (he was deified on his death in 169 AD).

Other notable finds include one side of the Octagon, a burial chamber with Corinthian columns, an Amazon from the Temple of Artemis – one of the Seven Wonders of the Ancient World – and a Roman bronze copy of a classical Greek sculpture depicting an athlete cleaning sand from his hands with a scraping iron. You can also see a vast wooden model of Ephesus (and lots of text in German on the excavations), and a model of the Temple of Artemis. Finally, there's a selection of minor finds from the Sanctuary of the Great Gods on the Aegean island of Samothrace, excavated in the 1870s by Austrian archeologists.

Museum für Völkerkunde

In the section of the Neue Burg nearest the Ring, the **Museum für Völkerkunde** (Museum of Ethnology) houses a bewildering array of secular and religious artefacts from around the world. Unfortunately, large sections of the museum are likely to be closed for renovation over the next few years as it drags itself into the twenty-first century. This is a good thing, as those galleries which have already been modernized are far more appealing than the old-style displays that linger on in some rooms.

The museum is open daily except Tues 10am–4pm; öS50.

The museum has a grandiose central atrium, with balconies held up by marble columns streaked like blue cheese. There's a coffee machine, and a few seats; temporary exhibitions are held in the rooms straight ahead. Much (but by no means all) of the labelling in the museum is in German and English; earphone commentary in German is also available for the upstairs galleries.

It's difficult to know where to start with such a wide-ranging collection. The ground-floor galleries, despite being badly in need of modernization, contain some interesting pieces from the **Far East**: check out the cheek-whipping device from China, dried frog from Korea and Japanese reed raincoat with matching rice straw boots. The ground floor also houses the Africa section, including one of the world's finest collection of bronze sculptures from **Benin**, bought at auction in London, where the former kingdom's finest art treasures were sold following the British invasion of 1897.

The new displays upstairs are a great deal more enticing to look at, beginning with the **Polynesia** section, much of it brought back from Captain Cook's expeditions, and then snapped up at auction in 1806 by the Emperor Franz I – who could resist the Hawaiian firelighter shaped like a giant penis? The highlight of the Americas section is undoubtedly the stunning sixteenth-century gilded **Aztec feather headdress** of the Emperor Montezuma II, who was stoned to death by his own people for his passivity in the face of Cortès, the Spanish imperialist. The section on **Native Americans** comes up to date with Apache-Power T-shirts, and information on life in the USA for the country's indigenous peoples. The new **Inuit** gallery is similarly contemporary, featuring a cramped wooden shack from Greenland, in which a family of seven lived until 1975.

Volksgarten

The **Volksgarten**, which forms a large triangular wedge to the north of Heldenplatz, was opened in 1820 on the site of the old Burgbastei,

*The
Volksgarten is
open daily
April–Oct
8am–10pm;
Nov–March
8am–8pm.*

*For more on
the Empress
Elisabeth's
tragic life and
death, see
p.218.*

blown up by Napoleon's troops in 1809. Appropriately enough, given its origins, it was laid out as a formal French garden, and quickly became a favourite resort of the nobility – especially the "Aristocratic Corner", for which an entry fee had to be paid. When the rest of the fortifications were torn down in 1857, the garden was extended, and it remained an upper-crust haunt long after that.

Focal point today is the Doric **Theseus-Tempel**, a replica of the Theseion in Athens erected in the 1820s. Originally commissioned by Napoleon to house *Theseus and the Minotaur* by Antonio Canova, it's been more or less permanently closed since the statue was transferred to the staircase of the newly opened Kunsthistorisches Museum in 1890. Plans in the 1930s by Carl Moll and Josef Hoffmann to turn the temple into a pantheon of Austria's musicians sadly came to nothing – and the building remains unused for the most part. In the far northern corner of the garden, a seated statue of the **Empress Elisabeth** (1837–98) presides over a melancholic, sunken garden of remembrance. The opposite corner of the Volksgarten shelters an equally imposing monument to **Franz Grillparzer** (1791–1872), the poet and playwright, seated before a marble backdrop with reliefs illustrating his plays.

Burggarten

The **Burggarten**, like the Volksgarten, came into being fortuitously after Napoleon blew up the bastions around the Hofburg. Unlike the Volksgarten, however, it was landscaped in the informal English style, and retained as a private garden for the Habsburgs until 1918. It now lies hidden, a bit seedy and a bit forgotten, behind the giant Neue Burg, though its entrance off the Ringstrasse is announced grandly enough by the marble **Mozart Denkmal** by Viktor Tilgner. Unveiled on Augustinerplatz in 1896 and moved to its present site in 1953, the plinth features frolicking cherubs, two reliefs from *Don Giovanni*, as well as representations of the composer's father and sister, with whom he used to tour Europe as a *Wunderkind*.

Elsewhere, in the shrubbery, there's an equestrian statue of Franz Stephan, Maria Theresa's husband, by Balthasar Ferdinand Moll, which has come down in the world since the bastion it used to adorn was blown up, and a rather downcast statue of Franz-Josef in his customary military garb. Incredibly, despite the omnipresence of the latter's image during his long reign – the emperor's portrait hung in millions of households across the empire – and the great trade in memorabilia since then, there was no public statue of Franz-Josef in Vienna until this one was erected by private individuals in 1957. On the far side of the garden is the elegant glass Palmenhaus (Palm House), designed by Friedrich Ohmann around 1900, and currently undergoing badly needed restoration.

Chapter 4

The Ringstrasse

From morning until late at night, I ran from one object of interest to another, but it was always the buildings that held my primary interest. For hours I could stand in front of the Opera, for hours I could gaze at the parliament; the whole Ring-Boulevard seemed to me like an enchantment out of The Thousand and One Nights.

Adolf Hitler *Mein Kampf*

On Christmas Eve 1857, the Emperor Franz-Josef I announced the demolition of the zig-zag fortifications around the old town and the building of a **Ringstrasse**, a horse-shoe of imperial boulevards to be laid out on the former glacis (the sloping ground between the walls and the suburbs). Vienna had been confined within its medieval walls since the last Turkish siege of 1683 – now, with the Ottoman threat receding, the Habsburgs could create a boulevard befitting an imperial capital. Twelve major public buildings were set down along its course between 1860 and 1890 – among them a court opera house and theatre, two court museums, a parliament building, a university and a town hall – all at no cost to the taxpayer. By the end of World War I, though, the Habsburgs were no more: as Edward Crankshaw wrote, "[the Ringstrasse] was designed as the crown of the Empire, but it turned out to be a tomb".

Today Vienna's Ringstrasse looks pretty much as it did in last days of the Habsburgs, studded with key landmarks. The monumental public institutions remain the chief sights: heading anti-clockwise, they include the **Börse**, **Votivkirche**, **Rathaus**, **Burgtheater**, and **Parlament** buildings, the two monster museums – the **Naturhistorisches** and **Kunsthistorisches** (covered in Chapter Five) – and the **Staatsoper**. Countless other cultural institutions occupy prime positions on the Ring, and neighbouring Karlsplatz, most notably, the **Musikverein**, the city's premier concert venue, the glorious Jugendstil **Secession** building, and three more excellent museums: the **Akademie der bildenden Künste**, the **Historisches Museum der Stadt Wien**, and the **MAK** (Museum of Applied Art). Last, but not least, Karlsplatz also boasts Vienna's most imposing Baroque church, the **Karlskirche**.

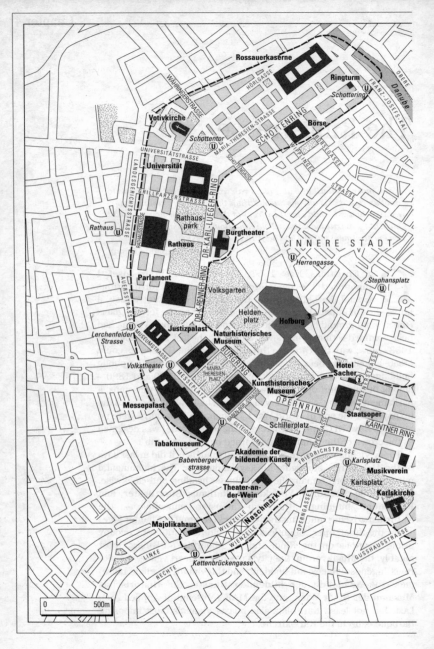

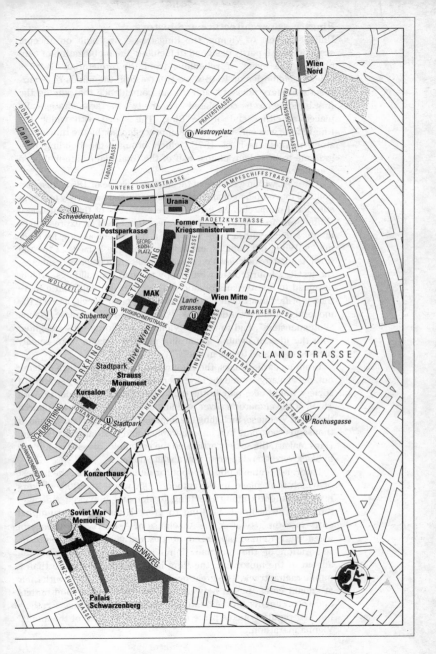

Ringstrasse architecture and history

Unlike the rest of Vienna, the Ringstrasse was built on an epic scale, its width partly designed to facilitate the mobilization of cannons in the event of rebellions from the proletarian districts beyond. Memories of 1848 were still fresh in the minds of Franz-Josef's military advisors, and it's no coincidence that among the first buildings to be completed were the two barracks strategically placed at either end of the Ring. The speed with which the Ringstrasse was constructed was unprecedented: by the time of the stock market crash of 1873, which brought the building programme to brief halt, almost half of the total real estate had been completed.

However, within a decade of the imperial decree of 1857, Austria's political make-up had changed from an undiluted autocracy to a constitutional monarchy. As a result, the emphasis of the Ringstrasse shifted, too, from an imperial showpiece to more of an expression of liberal values, with a town hall and a parliament among its landmarks. While the nobility, esconsed in Baroque palaces in the old town, tended to look down on the Ringstrasse as a place of residence, the wealthy **bourgeoisie** were happy to snap up buildings, which, designed to ape the aristocratic *palais*, were in reality little more than glorified apartment blocks. It was a popular deceit, as even the modernist architect Adolf Loos, who dubbed Ringstrasse Vienna "Potemkinstadt", had to admit: "Viennese landlords were delighted with the idea of owning a mansion and the tenants were equally pleased to be able to live in one".

From its earliest days, the Ring was a **fashionable** place to hang out, particularly around the new opera house, where every stratum of society would take part in the daily afternoon promenade. In April 1879, at the emperor's silver wedding celebrations, several hundred thousand Viennese, including the imperial family, watched as tens of thousands took part in a choreographed and costumed procession. Hans Makart, the society artist, led the ensemble, dressed as Rubens in black velvet, and mounted on a white horse.

Later, it became a popular spot for **demonstrations**, the largest of which took place in November 1905, when 250,000 workers marched silently along the Ring to demand universal suffrage. Similar crowds lined the Ring to greet Hitler on his triumphal entry into the city after the Anschluss of April 1938 – and again when Karl Renner appeared at the Rathaus to proclaim the restoration of the Austrian Republic. Unfortunately, with the advent of the motor car, the Ring has become little more than a public racing track. The great institutions remain, along with their attendant cafés, but in between, airline offices, fast-food outlets and travel agents predominate. Nowadays, the only mass gathering that regularly takes place here is for the last lap of the annual Vienna marathon.

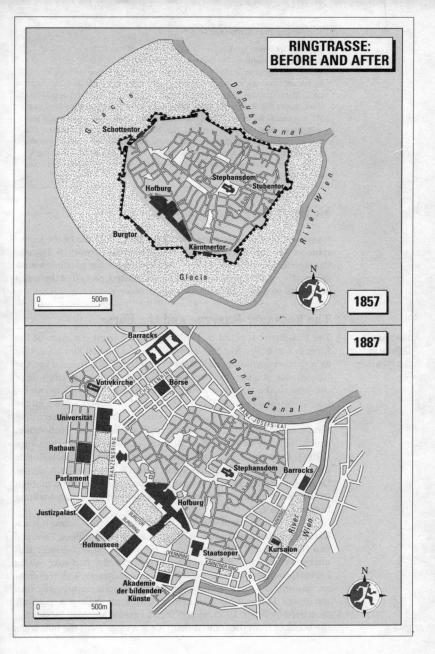

Schottenring

If you take the tram along any part of the Ring, it should be the northernmost section, **Schottenring**, which stretches from the Danube Canal to the Votivkirche. This is the least interesting portion to walk along, since none of the buildings can be visited, and all of them can be viewed well enough from the tram window.

The Rossauer-Kaserne and the Börse

The nearest U-Bahn is Schottenring.

The **Ringturm**, erected in 1955 at the very northern apex of the Ring, is one of the few high-rise buildings in central Vienna, acting as a marker (or so its architects like to think) for the start of the Ringstrasse. A more distinguished building, on the opposite side of the Ring, is the **Rossauer-Kaserne**, a fanciful, red-brick barracks, (currently used by the police). One of the first constructions on the Ring, occupying three blocks, it formed a strategic and architectural pendant to the former imperial barracks on Stubenring, which later became the War Ministry or Kriegsministerium (see p.135). Only the crenellated central block, with its mock-Gothic turrets and machicolations, is actually visible from the Ring, across Deustchmeisterplatz, which features a giant militaristic monument to the Order of the Teutonic Knights, topped by a flag-wielding bronze soldier.

The key public building on Schottenring is the **Börse** (Stock Exchange), designed in the 1870s by the Danish architect, Theophil von Hansen, one of the pioneers of the historicist architecure that characterizes the Ringstrasse. Here, exactly half-way along Schottenring, he chose to ape the Italian Renaissance – viz the arches, rooftop balustrade and corner towers – a style popularized with the opera house a decade earlier. The main hall was partially destroyed by fire in 1956, so you're not missing anything by viewing the building from the tram, though it's not clear from the building's solid exterior that much of its vast ground plan is in fact taken up with a large central, open courtyard.

Votivkirche

The first public building on the Ringstrasse – begun in 1854 even before the emperor had ordered the demolition of the city ramparts – was the **Votivkirche**, a monumental church built by the Vienna-born architect Heinrich Ferstel in the style of the great Gothic cathedrals of Cologne and Chartres. Built opposite the spot where a Hungarian tailor, János Libényi, had tried to stab the Emperor Franz-Josef the previous year – he was thwarted only by the emperor's collar and cap – the church was to be "a monument of patriotism and of devotion of the people to the Imperial House". Forever associated with the old order – the church and crown – the Votivkirche differed from the later Ringstrasse buildings, which derived much of their inspiration from the liberal ideology of the newly ascendant middle class.

The nearest U-Bahn is Schottentor.

For all its size, there is something spiritually lacking in the Votivkirche. Built partly to serve the large influx of soldiers to the capital following the 1848 revolution, the church has no natural parishioners, and the gloomy interior, badly damaged in World War II, remains underused and little visited. The one monument worth a look is the sixteenth-century marble tomb of Count Salm, who commanded Vienna during the Turkish siege of 1529.

Rathausplatz

Rathausplatz is the Ringstrasse's showpiece square, framed by no fewer than four monumental public buildings – the Rathaus, the Burgtheater, Parliament and the University – all completed in the 1880s. The architectural style of each building was carefully chosen to allude to its function: Flemish Gothic for the Rathaus, conjuring up municipal wealth and independence; hybrid Baroque for the Burgtheater, recalling the era in which theatre first flourished in Vienna; Neoclassicism for the Parliament building, in honour of the birthplace of democracy, Ancient Greece; and Italian Renaissance for the University, that bastion of secular scholarship.

Rathaus

The most imposing building of the four is the cathedralesque **Rathaus** (City Hall) – strictly speaking the Neues Rathaus – a powerful symbol of the city's late nineteenth-century political clout. Designed by the German architect Friedrich von Schmidt in imitation of Brussels' Gothic *Hôtel de Ville*, the Rathaus was open for business in 1884, though one can only feel sympathy for the city bureaucrats who had to work in its gloomy neo-Gothic chambers before the

Karl Lueger (1844–1910)

Karl Lueger, mayor from 1897 to 1910, is by far the most famous of Vienna's *Bürgermeister* – the section of the Ring that crosses Rathausplatz is named after him, and his statue occupies a prime site at the beginning of Stubenring. Brought up by his widowed mother, who ran a tobacco shop, Karl made it to the city's most prestigious private school, the Theresianum, as a day scholar, subsequently becoming a lawyer before entering politics as a left-wing Democrat in 1870.

His elegant appearance, impeccable manners and skillful oratory earned him the nickname "*der schöne Karl*" (handsome Karl), but his reputation will always be clouded by the **anti-semitic rhetoric** he adopted during the 1880s. In 1890, he made a speech in the *Reichsrat* suggesting that the city's Jews should be put on a ship, sent out to sea and sunk. By 1893, he had formed the **Christian Social Party**, whose blend of municipal socialism, Catholicism and anti-semitism proved irresistable to the Viennese petit bourgeoisie, in which Lueger had his roots. However, his election as mayor in 1895 was followed by two years of deadlock as the Emperor Franz-Josef refused to ratify his taking office, wary of his popularity and his crude anti-semitism. Once in power, Lueger toned down his anti-semitism, resorting to it when he needed to maintain his popular appeal, and dropping it when he needed co-operation of the city's wealthy Jewish financiers – hence his catchphrase, "*Wer a Jud is bestimm' i*" (I decide who is a Jew).

In his thirteen years as mayor, Lueger succeeded in laying the foundations for the municipal socialism that was greatly extended by the Social Democrats in the 1920s. He was responsible for much of the infrastructure the Viennese enjoy today: he piped in water from Styria, built gas works, established a green belt around the city, made provisions for cheap burials, built schools and old people's homes, enlarged the parks and electrified the tram and subway network. His funeral in 1910 was the largest the city had ever seen, with over 200,000 lining the streets, among them one of Lueger's biggest fans, the young, out-of-work artist, Adolf Hitler.

Free guided tours of the Rathaus take place Mon, Wed & Fri at 1pm if there is no city council session; call ☎ 525 50 to confirm, and meet at the information office in Schmidthalle.

advent of electricity. The central tower, which soars to a height of over 100m, is topped by a copper statue of a medieval knight in full armour, known affectionately as the *Rathausmann*; there's a replica of him at close quarters in the Rathauspark below.

You're free to walk through the town hall's seven courtyards, but to get a look at the ornate interior, home to the *Bürgermeister* (Mayor) and the *Gemeinderat* (City Council), you must join a 45-minute guided tour (in German). Concerts are occasionally held in the main Arkadenhof, and in July and August, free opera and classical concerts are beamed onto a giant screen on the town hall's main facade. Restaurants set up stalls selling food and beer, though these are as nothing compared to the number of stalls which fill the Rathauspark in the month leading up to Christmas, when the famous **Christkindlmarkt** takes place. As well as selling various folksy Christmas presents, the market runs workshops for making and baking presents, and there are sideshows for kids.

Burgtheater

Directly opposite the Rathaus, the **Burgtheater** seems modest by comparison – until you realize that the sole function of the theatre's two vast wings was to house monumental staircases leading to the grand boxes. In practical terms, though, the design by Gottfried Semper and Karl von Hasenauer was none too successful. Less than a decade after the opening night in 1888 the theatre had to close in order to revamp the acoustics, which were dreadful, and to modify the seating, some of which allowed no view of the stage at all. The auditorium was badly gutted by fire during the liberation of Vienna in April 1945, and has since been totally modernized. Thankfully, the staircase wings survived, and still boast their sumptuous decor, including ceiling paintings by Franz Matsch and Gustav Klimt.

When the Burgtheater opened, it was, of course, known as the *k.k. Hofburgtheater* (Imperial and Royal Palace Theatre), as the lettering on the facade still proclaims. The royals had their own entrance, directly from the Hofburg. Nowadays, it devotes itself solely to spoken drama, but the original Burgtheater, which stood on Michaelerplatz in the Innere Stadt, also functioned as the chief ballet and opera house. It was there that Mozart's *Die Entführung aus dem Serail*, *Figaro* and *Così fan tutte* were premiered, as well as Gluck's *Orfeo*, *Alceste* and *Paris and Helen*, and Beethoven's *Second Piano Concerto* and his *First Symphony*. It was also where the Emperor Franz-Josef first clapped eyes on the actress Katharina Schratt, who became his mistress for more than forty years.

Universität

The **Universität** (University) – strictly speaking the Neue Universität – is the most unassuming of the four public buildings on Rathausplatz. It's also the one which had to campaign longest to secure a prominent Ringstrasse site, due its radical past. Vienna's students had been among the most enthusiastic supporters of the 1848 revolution, forming their own Academic Legion, manning the barricades and dying in their hundreds. Finally in 1873, Heinrich Ferstel was commissioned to design new premises for the Law and Philosophy faculties in the ubiquitous neo-Renaissance style. More famously, in 1894, the painter Gustav Klimt was commissioned, along with Franz Matsch, to paint three murals for the university's Aula (Great Hall). Sadly, it's no longer possible to view these paintings, which caused possibly the biggest scandal in the university's history. Klimt and Matsch had already completed murals for the Burgtheater (1886–88) and the Kunsthistorisches Museum (1891), and the univeristy no doubt expected more of the same. However, by the time the first picture, *Philosophy*, was unveiled in March 1900, Klimt had broken with Vienna's mainstream artists' association and helped found the rebellious Secession (see p.120) – more important-

Rathaus-platz

The Burgtheater is closed July & Aug except for guided tours on Mon, Wed & Fri 1,2 & 3pm; öS50.

The Café Landtmann *by the Burgtheater has been a favourite with the city's politicians, actors and professors – Sigmund Freud was a regular – for over a century; see p.282.*

You may enter the university during working hours, and stroll around the arcaded main courtyard.

ly he had moved a long way from the university's original proposal for a painting to illustrate the triumph of light over darkness. It was this, as much as anything else, which caused 87 professors to sign a petition of protest. The painting's tangled mass of naked, confused humanity – "a victory of darkness over all" in the words of one critic – was certainly not what the Ministry of Culture and Education had had in mind.

The scandal drew 34,000 onlookers to see the painting in just two months. Unperturbed, Klimt exhibited the second of the murals, *Medicine*, the following year, its naked and diseased figures provoking further abuse. Questions were asked in parliament, where the artist was accused of "pornography" and "perverted excess". Eventually in 1905, having completed the last, but by no means least controversial, of the trio, *Jurisprudence*, Klimt returned his fee and claimed back the paintings. The industrialist August Lederer immediately bought *Philosophy*, while the artist Kolo Moser, co-founder of the Secession, purchased the other two in 1911. All three were placed in Schloss Immendorf for safe-keeping during World War II, but were destroyed in a fire started by retreating SS troops on May 5, 1945.

Parlament

*There are
guided tours of
Parlament
Mon–Fri 11am
& 3pm; mid-
July to Aug
also 9 & 10am
and 1 & 2pm.*

On the south side of Rathausplatz stands the Neoclassical **Parlament** (Parliament), one of five major Ringstrasse buildings by the Danish architect, Theophil von Hansen. From street level, it's difficult to see past the giant Corinthian portico and its accompanying wings and pavilions. Stand back, though, and it becomes clear that the main body of the building – home to the *Bundesrat* (Federal Council) and *Nationalrat* (National Council) of the Austrian parliament – is mostly hidden behind the projecting facade.

When it came to the building's **sculptural decoration**, there wasn't much of an indigenous democratic tradition to draw on. The main pediment frieze shows the Emperor Franz-Josef I granting the seventeen peoples of the empire a deeply undemocratic constitution, but for the most part, Hansen plumped for classical antiquity, with Roman horse-tamers and seated historians punctuating the two ramps. Between the ramps stands a gargantuan statue of Athene, goddess of wisdom, sporting a natty gilded plume in her helmet and presiding over a fountain served by four writhing mermen, representing the Danube, Inns, Elbe and Moldau. The attic of the main building, meanwhile, is peppered with 76 classical statues, 66 reliefs and four bronze chariot groups – these are best viewed from the sides of the building, where you'll find porticos held up by caryatids modelled on the Erechtheion on the Acropolis.

The Austrian parliament has had a chequered history since it moved into its new premises in 1883. Initially, it served as the *Reichsrat* (Imperial Council) for the Austrian half of the empire, a body deadlocked by nationalist factions of Croats, Czechs, Poles, Romanians, Slovenes and Germans. The nadir came in 1897 when the Polish Count Kasimir Badeni attempted to introduce his language ordinances, which would put Czech on an equal footing with German in the Czech Lands. Conservatives and German-Nationals organized an "Obstruction Concert", with whistles, sleigh bells, harmonicas, cowbells, gongs, toy trumpets, hunting horns and snare drums. During the din, one member delivered a twelve-hour filibuster which ended at 8.45am the following morning. Following the Badeni débacle, the Emperor bypassed parliament and ruled through the bureaucracy, until the introduction of universal male suffrage in 1907. Parliament was again prorogued shortly before World War I and didn't re-convene until after Franz-Josef's death.

On November 12, 1918, the *Reichsrat* held its last session, during which the Austrian republic – known officially as *Deutsch-Österreich* (German-Austria) – was declared from the ramps before parliament. The Babenburg colours of the new Austria, red-white-red, were hoisted on the tall masts either side of Athene; also present were the Pan-German nationalist students with their black-red-gold banners, and the Communist-dominated 41st battalion of the *Volkswehr* known as the *Rote Garde* (Red Guard). The latter tore up the Pan-German banners, and also removed the white from the Austrian banners, leaving red rags flying. Shots were fired, the *Rote Garde* tried to storm the parliament building; two people were killed and 45 injured. Five months later, there were more revolutionary rumblings as a posse of Communists, spurred on by the Soviet republics in Bavaria and Hungary, broke in and set fire to the parliament building. In the street fighting that followed, five policemen and a woman were killed.

On the Ides of March, 1934, democracy was put on hold indefinitely as the Austro-fascists ordered police to block the entrance to the building to prevent parliamentary members from assembling. On siezing power, one of the Austro-fascists' first acts was to remove the **Monument of the Republic**, erected to the south of the parliament building after World War I, and featuring the busts of the Socialist politicians: Jakob Reumann, Viktor Adler and Ferdinand Hanusch. Strangely, the monument wasn't destroyed, but simply put into storage (rather like Austrian democracy itself), and returned to its rightful place after World War II.

Justizpalast

Set back slightly from the Ring, behind the Monument of the Republic, lies the **Justizpalast**, a dour neo-Renaissance monolith that holds a special place in Austrian history. On July 15, 1927, the day after three right-wing activists were acquitted of murdering a socialist man and boy, a spontaneous demonstration of several thousand workers descended on and set fire to the Justizpalast. Chaos

*The nearest
U-Bahn is
Volkstheater.*

ensued, with mounted, armed police charging the crowd, and police reinforcements shooting, leaving eighty odd people dead, and up to 1000 wounded. The Socialists promptly called a general strike, which was deftly crushed by the heavily armed *Heimwehr*, the right-wing militia, who acted as strike breakers, and civil war was put off for a few more years.

Burgring

On the other side of **Burgring** from the Hofburg stand the two so-called *Hofmuseen* (Court Museums), which were opened to the pub-lic in the late nineteenth century. The **Kunsthistorisches Museum** (History of Art Museum), which houses one of the world's top art col-lections, is covered in detail in Chapter Five; the **Naturhistorisches Museum** (Natural History Museum) is described below. Designed in pompous neo-Renaissance style, with giant copper-domed cupolas and colossal wings, they are both the work of Karl von Hasenauer, and as such, virtual mirror images of each other. The overall plan was thought up by the great Dresden architect, Gottfried Semper, who envisaged a monumental *Kaiserforum*, linking the museums to the Neue Burg via a pair of triumphal arches spanning the Ringstrasse. The project was interrupted by World War I, and then binned altogether after the fall of the Habsburgs. Today, the muse-ums remain cut off from the Hofburg by the traffic roaring round the Ring. They stare blankly at one another across a formal garden, pep-pered with topiary and centred on a gargantuan monument to the Empress Maria Theresa with eight of her aides.

*The
Kunsthistor-
isches Museum
is covered in
Chapter Five.*

Naturhistorisches Museum

*The museum is
open daily
except Tues
9am–6pm;
öS30; the first
floor closes at
3pm in the
winter. The
nearest
U-Bahn is
Babenbergerst-
rasse.*

In many ways very little has changed at the **Naturhistorisches Museum** since it opened in 1889. Whereas most European cities have tried to pep up their natural history collections with automated dinosaurs, ecological concerns and the like, the hard sell has passed Vienna by. The display cabinets are over a century old, as is the exclusively German labelling – places as distant as Illyria (present-day Slovenia) and Galicia (part of present-day Ukraine) are still described as if part of Austria – the dim panes of glass are almost pre-industrial, and the stuffed animals have all succumbed to a uniform, musty, grey hue. It's really only as a museum of museums that the Naturhistorisches continues to be of any interest.

The ground floor (or Parterre as it's called) kicks off with five rooms of minerals (I–V) in the east wing, among them some impres-sive slabs of green malachite, a sculpture carved from Siberian graphite and a huge chunk of transparent quartz. Polished marble tiles are accompanied by illustrations of buildings within the old Empire which feature the materials. The final room contains several meteorites which fell on the Empire in the late nineteenth century, and various objects made from precious and semi-precious stones – perhaps the most interesting section for the non-specialist.

The paleontology section is currently under wraps, with the exception of room X – a huge hall decorated with caryatids struggling with weird, evolutionary beasts – where you can find the skeleton of a Diplodocus and various fossils. The prehistoric section begins in room XI with the **Venus of Willendorf**, by far the most famous exhibit in the entire museum. This tiny fertility symbol – a stout, limestone figure with drooping breasts – stands just a few centimetres high, but is something like 25,000 years old, and as such is an object of some fascination. Sadly, what you actually see is a replica (the real thing is far too precious to be put on display), accompanied by another much larger reproduction.

The west wing includes finds from the prehistoric Beaker folk and various implements, jewellery and arms from Iron Age burial tombs at Halstatt in the Salzkammergut. There's some impressive Thracian silver jewellery, a reconstructed funereal chariot from the Iron Age, and a staggering collection of human skulls. The Kindersaal, beyond, is the museum's one concession to modernization, though this tired playroom, built in the 1970s, isn't going to impress kids brought up on interactive, hands-on displays.

Zoology occupies the top floor, progressing from starfish, corals and sea shells in the east wing to a bevy of bears, cats and monkeys in the west. Some may find the pickled fish and lizards, the jars of snakes and reptiles, and the dissected frog, more than they can stomach. However, if you want to get the best out of this section, come on a bright, sunny morning when the light is at its best.

Messepalast (Museumsquartier)

If you stand between the two *Hofmuseen* with your back to the Hofburg, you are confronted with the **Messepalast** (Trade Fair Palace), built in the eighteenth century as the imperial barracks by Johann Bernhard Fischer von Erlach, but greatly enlarged following the 1848 revolution. This vast complex of buildings was earmarked way back in the 1980s to become a new *Museumsquartier*, which its backers hoped would rival the likes of the Pompidou Centre in Paris, housing, among other things, the city's collection of modern art, currently on show at the Liechtenstein Palace (see p.180).

You'll find one of Vienna's nicest garden restaurants, Glacisbeisl, hidden round the back of the Messepalast (see p.288).

The architectural partnership, Ortner & Ortner, won the competition to develop the barracks. However, they provoked a barrage of criticism in the press, both over their plan to do away with most of Fischer von Erlach's existing barracks, and over their proposed Leseturm, a 56-metre-high library tower. Several of the city's politicians jumped on the bandwagon, hoping to boost their popularity with the Viennese voters, who were seen as being against the design. It now looks increasingly unlikely that Ortner & Ortner's vision will ever got off the ground.

In the meantime, there's just a handful of attractions within the scruffy courtyards: the **Kindermuseum** (Mon–Fri 8.30am–6pm, Sat & Sun 10am–6pm; closed July & Aug), which puts on temporary exhibitions aimed primarily at Austrian kids; the **ArchitekturZentrum Wien** (daily 11am–7pm), whose temporary exhibitions on the city's architecture are often worth a look; and the contemporary art installations at the **Kunstraum Wien** (Tues–Fri 2–7pm, Sat 11am–7pm). To locate these places, pick up a free plan of the complex from the main entrance.

Tabakmuseum

The museum is open Tues–Fri 10am–5pm, Sat & Sun 10am–2pm; öS50. The nearest metro is Babenbergerstrasse.

The one permanent museum in the Museumsquartier to date is the **Österreichisches Tabakmuseum** (Austrian Tobacco Museum), an exhaustive collection of *objets d'art* and smoking paraphernalia housed in the Klosterhof (accessible from Mariahilferstrasse). Funded by the state tobacco monopoly, *Austria Tabak*, the overall tone is celebratory – you can even smoke while inside the museum. You'll find no health warnings, nor tales of the darker side of the tobacco industry, and only the odd historical anecdote: to be allowed to smoke in public was one of the demands of Prussian revolutionaries in 1848. Ask for the English notes, in order to identify the various snuff boxes made out of gold, agate, ivory, tortoiseshell, mother-of-pearl and horn, and the huge pile of pipes, ranging from simple clay versions to the Giant Pipe of the Waldviertel, an ornamental monstrosity made for the Emperor Franz-Josef in 1910. It took four years to carve and depicts the 1278 Battle of Marchfeld in which Rudolf of Habsburg defeated the Bohemian King Otakar II.

Around Oper

The human congestion around **Oper** – the opera house – makes this the busiest section of the Ringstrasse. It's here that the shoppers of Kärntnerstrasse cross the Ring, and descend into the Opernpassage, which stretches south as far as Karlsplatz (see p.120). In the late nineteenth century, this crossroads became known as the "Sirk Ecke", after the then fashionable *Sirk Café* on the corner of Kärntnerstrasse and Kärntner Ring. The latter, which runs down to Schwarzenberg Platz, quickly became the Viennese Corso, where, according to one French visitor, "every branch of society from the great world, to the *demi-monde*, to the 'quarter world', as well as the world of diplomacy and the court" promenaded in the afternoon. Nowadays most people prefer to stroll along Kärntnerstrasse rather than battle with the roaring Ringstrasse traffic.

The nearest U-Bahn is Karlsplatz.

Staatsoper

That the **Staatsoper** (State Opera House) was the first public building to be completed on the Ringstrasse – opening in May 1869 with a performance of Mozart's *Don Giovanni* – is an indication of its importance in Viennese society. Designed in heavy Italian Renaissance style – even the Austrians deferred to Italy as the home of opera – it's a suitably grandiose exterior, with a fine loggia beneath which the audience could draw up in their carriages. However, compared with the other monumental edifices on the Ringstrasse the opera house sits low. This was the most common criticism of the building when it was completed, and when the Emperor Franz-Josef was heard to concur with his aides on this issue, one of the architects, Eduard van der Nüll, hanged himself. Van der Nüll's grief-stricken friend and collaborator on the project, August Siccard von Siccardsburg, died two months later of a heart attack; neither architect lived to witness the first night. Thereafter Franz-Josef always chose the safe riposte "*Es war sehr schön, es hat mir sehr gefreut*" (It was very beautiful, I enjoyed it very much) whenever he was asked his official opinion.

The Staatsoper has always had a special place in the hearts of the Viennese, besotted with their musical heritage, so it was a particularly cruel blow when the building caught fire during the air raid of March 12, 1945. The main auditorium was rebuilt in a much plainer style, and is now pretty undistinguished. Shortly after the withdrawal of the Allied Powers and the declaration of independence in November 1955, the building re-opened with a performance of Beethoven's *Fidelio*. Prestigious past directors include Gustav Mahler, Richard Strauss, Herbert von Karajan and Claudio Abbado, though each one had notoriously difficult relationships with the opera house. It still receives massive state subsidy, and hundreds of – relatively cheap – tickets are sold each day on a first-come-first-served basis (standing room only).

Behind Oper

Vienna's top three hotels – the *Sacher*, the *Bristol* and the *Imperial* – are all within a stone's throw of the opera house. The most famous of the trio, directly behind the Staatsoper, is the **Hotel Sacher**, built in the 1870s on the site of the old Kärntnertor Theater, where Beethoven's *Ninth Symphony* premièred in 1824. Founded by Eduard Sacher, it became the aristocrats' favourite knocking shop, particularly after 1892 when it was run by Eduard's widow, the legendary, cigar-smoking Anna Sacher, until her death in 1930. Without doubt, the most famous incident that took place here was when the Archduke Franz Ferdinand's younger brother, the flamboyant Archduke Otto, appeared in the hotel lobby naked except for his sword and the Order of the Golden Fleece around his neck – later he was forced to wear a leather nose to hide the ravages of the syphilis that killed him in 1906. The *Sacher*'s continuing popularity, though, rests on its famous *Sachertorte* invented by Eduard's father, Franz, who was Prince Metternich's chef. *Sachertorte* is, of course, avail-

Around Oper

Schedules for guided tours are listed beneath the arcade on the east side of the building; öS 50.

For more on how to obtain tickets for the opera, see p.299.

*For more on
Vienna's cakes
and cafés, see
p.280.*

able all over Vienna, but only at the *Sacher* does it come with a layer of apricot jam beneath the icing.

The Philipphof, a typically ornate Ringstrasse-style building which was home to the exclusive Jockey Club, originally stood to the north of the *Sacher*. However, during the air raid of March 12, 1945, the building received two direct hits, killing several hundred people sheltering in the basement. The lot remained vacant until the 1980s, when the city council commissioned Alfred Hrdlicka to erect a Holocaust memorial – a controversial move given the site's history and its extreme prominence. Planned to be unveiled in time for the fiftieth anniversary of the Anschluss and *Kristallnacht*, an almighty row meant that the **Monument against War and Fascism** was three years behind schedule. Hrdlicka's final design, a small bronze sculpture, made no direct mention of the Holocaust, but showed instead a crouching Jew scrubbing the pavement, recalling the days following the Anschluss, when some of the city's Jews were forced to clean up anti-Nazi slogans with scrubbing brushes dipped in acid. Many Jews found the image degrading, among them Simon Wiesenthal, who successfully campaigned for a proper Holocaust memorial to be erected in Vienna, though this, too, has also run into controversy (see p.65).

Akademie der bildenden Künste

*The perma-
nent collection
is open Tues,
Thurs & Fri
10am–2pm,
Wed 10am–
1pm & 3–6pm,
Sat & Sun
9am–1pm;
öS30.*

Set back from the Ring, the **Akademie der bildenden Künste** (Academy of Fine Arts) occupies an imposing neo-Renaissance building by Theophil von Hansen on Schillerplatz, to the southwest of the Staatsoper. The Academy itself was founded in 1692, and its main purpose continues to be teaching, but the school also houses a small, much overlooked study collection. To see the paintings, follow the signs to the **Gemäldegalerie**: turn right after the porter's lodge, up the stairs to the second floor, then right again to the end of the corridor. The **Aula** – straight ahead as you pass through the main entrance – is also worth a glimpse, both for its decor and for the regular wacky student installations.

Badly lit and indifferently hung, the Academy's collection is tiny compared with the Kunsthistorisches Museum. Nevertheless, it does have one star attraction: *The Last Judgement* triptych by **Hieronymus Bosch** (c.1450–1516). The action in the left panel, Paradise, is a taster for the central panel, the Last Judgement itself, most of which is taken up with strange half-animal devil figures busy torturing sinners in imaginatively horrible ways; the right panel, Hell, looks even less fun. Overall, the possibility of salvation seems painfully slim, with only a lucky few having made it to the small corner of the painting given over to heaven.

Flemish and Dutch paintings make up the core of the Academy's collection, with an early Rembrandt portrait, a self-portrait by Van Dyck aged just fourteen, preparatory studies for the Jesuit Church frescoes in Antwerp by Rubens, plus works by Jordaens, Ruisdael

Hitler in Vienna

Although he was born and grew up in Upper Austria, **Adolf Hitler** (1890–1945) spent five-and-a-half formative years in Vienna. He arrived in the city aged just seventeen, hoping to enrol at the Academy of Fine Arts. However, though he passed the entrance exam, his portfolio, mostly architectural sketches of Linz, was rejected as "inadequate". Saying nothing about his failure to his family, he stayed in Vienna for a whole year, living fairly comfortably off his father's inheritance and, following the death of his mother, his orphan's pension. In September 1908, Hitler tried once more to get into the Academy: this time he failed the entrance exam. These two rejections hit hard, and still rankled with Hitler two years on, as he wrote to a friend, "Do you know – without any arrogance – I still believe that the world lost a great deal by my not being able to go to the academy and learn the craft of painting. Or did fate reserve me to some other purpose?"

Very little is known about the rest of Hitler's time in Vienna, though he spent a good three years in a men's hostel in the eastern district of Brigittenau, abutting Leopoldstadt, where he sold his mediocre paintings mostly to Jewish frame dealers. (As the saying goes, some of his best friends were Jewish, though Hitler never allowed anyone to get too close.) The evidence is scanty, but Hitler appears to have worked for brief periods as a snow shoveller at the Westbahnhof, and as a painter and decorator at the Kunsthistorisches Museum – he even auditioned for a part in the chorus at the Theater-an-der-Wien, but was rejected when he couldn't produce the right clothes for the part.

Though there is no proof to back up the rumour that Hitler contracted syphilis from a Jewish whore while in the city, it is possible that he may have contracted some minor sexually transmitted ailment, hence his obsession with syphilis and prostitution – both of which he rails against at length in *Mein Kampf*. Other accounts portray Hitler as some kind of proto-hippy, with beard and long hair, practising yoga and tripping on mescaline. Again, there's no concrete evidence, though Hitler certainly experienced a period of homelessness in the winter of 1909, after which he became increasingly unkempt, wearing his beard and hair long.

For much of his stay in Vienna, Hitler was a draft evader – something he neglects to mention in *Mein Kampf* – since he should have signed up in 1909. By the end of 1912 he was liable to a year in prison and a large fine; it was this which eventually led him to flee to Germany in 1913. After a 25-year gap, Hitler returned to Vienna under rather different circumstances in March 1938, following the Anschluss. He stayed at the *Hotel Imperial* on the Ring, gave a speech to the multitude from the Neue Burg on Heldenplatz, and within twenty-four hours, was on a plane back to Germany.

and David Teniers the Younger. After Bosch, the other outstanding masterpiece is the *Family Group in a Courtyard* by **Pieter de Hooch** (1629–84), with its sublime tranquility and clever play on perspective. The Italian works are disappointing in comparison, with the exception of Titian's *Tarquin and Lucretia*, a late work replete with loose brushwork and brooding, autumnal colours.

Other works to look out for are Murillo's sentimental *Two Boys Playing Dice*, a *Crucifixion* by Memlinc, Lucas Cranach the Elder's moralistic-erotic *Ill-Matched Couple*, and paintings by Guardí and Lorrain. In the final corridor, there's a brief selection of twentieth-century Austrian art, including works by Friedensrich Hundertwasser, Fritz Wotruba and Herbert Boeckl.

Karlsplatz

The nearest U-Bahn is Karlsplatz.

Overlooked by the city's most awesome Baroque church, several key Ringstrasse institutions, the gilded Secession building and Otto Wagner's wonderful Art Nouveau pavilions, **Karlsplatz** should be one of Vienna's showpiece squares. Instead, the western half is little more than a vast traffic interchange, with pedestrians relegated to a set of seedy subways that stretch north as far as Oper. There has never been any grand, overall plan at Karlsplatz – the Naschmarkt was held here until the 1890s, and when it moved to the nearby Wienzeile, the heart was ripped out of the square. The city council provided a site for the Secession, but the avenue that should have connected it with the Karlskirche never materialized. As a result, it's actually impossible to stand back and admire the Secession building without seriously endangering your life. The latest abomination is Adolf Krischanitz's Kunsthalle, a mustard yellow and blue pre-fab steel box used for large scale art exhibitions. It was originally erected in 1992 in the Messepalast (see p.115), and moved only temporarily to Karlsplatz until such time as the Museumsquartier was finished. Now that that project has folded (see p.115), the Kunsthalle looks as though it's here to stay.

Secession

The Secession building is open Tues–Fri 10am–6pm, Sat & Sun 10am–4pm; öS30 for the Beethoven Frieze; öS60 for the temporary exhibitions.

In 1898, Joseph Maria Olbrich completed one of the most original Jugendstil works of art in Vienna, the headquarters for the **Secession** movement. The dome of gilded bronze laurel leaves is obviously the most startling feature – the Viennese dubbed it the "golden cabbage" – though all the building's decorative details are unusual. On the side, three wise owls suddenly emerge from the rendering, while the main entrance is adorned with a trio of Medusas, a pair of salamanders and copious gilded foliage; above is the group's credo "For every age its art; for art its freedom", replaced after being removed by the Nazis. Don't miss the tortoises at the feet of the ornamental bowls, Georg Klimt's bronze doors with snake handles, and Arthur Strasser's bronze statue of an overweight Mark Anthony on a chariot drawn by panthers (originally displayed at the group's fourth exhibition in 1899).

The main hall upstairs stages provocative contemporary art installations, while downstairs in the basement Gustav Klimt's **Beethoven**

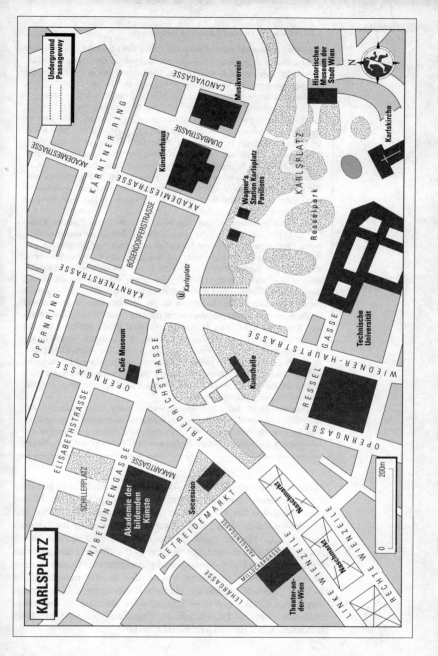

KARLSPLATZ

Undergrowund
Passageway

N

CANOVAGASSE

Musikverein

Historisches Museum der Stadt Wien

KÄRNTNER RING

Künstlerhaus

DUMBASTRASSE

Karlskirche

AKADEMIESTRASSE

AKADEMIESTRASSE

Wagner's Station Karlsplatz Pavilions

KARLSPLATZ

BÖSENDORFERSTRASSE

Resselpark

KÄRNTNERSTRASSE

Ⓤ Karlsplatz

OPERNRING

Café Museum

WIEDNER-HAUPTSTRASSE

OPERNGASSE

Kunsthalle

RESSEL-GASSE

Technische Universität

FRIEDRICHSTRASSE

ELISABETHSTRASSE

OPERNGASSE

SCHILLERPLATZ

MAKARTGASSE

200m

Secession

GETREIDEMARKT

NIBELUNGENGASSE

Akademie der bildenden Künste

Naschmarkt

PAPAGENOGASSE

Naschmarkt

LEHARGASSE

MILLÖCKERGASSE

LINKE WIENZEILE

RECHTE WIENZEILE

Theater-an-der-Wien

0

A Brief Guide to the Viennese Secession

In 1897, a number of artists broke away from the Künstlerhaus, Austria's leading mainstream artists' association, and set up their own organization, which they named the **Secession**. The second half of the nineteenth century had seen the ossification of the arts in Vienna, exemplified in architecture by the heavy-handed historicism of the Ringstrasse, and epitomized in painting by the flattery of Hans Makart (1840–84). Broadly speaking, the aims of the new group were to regenerate the arts in Vienna, and to promote "art for art's sake", in particular the latest style, Art Nouveau, known in German as *Jugendstil* (literally "Youth-style"). "We want to declare war on sterile routine, on rigid Byzantinism, on all forms of bad taste," declared the critic Hermann Bahr, one of the literary champions of the movement. The other major thrust, which sat less happily with the Secession's other commitments, was to strip off the mask of historicism and, as Otto Wagner put it, "to show modern man his true face".

The first president of the Secession was the artist **Gustav Klimt** (1862–1918), who became the group's driving force over the next eight years. Klimt himself had begun his career as a promising young master of the old ideology. In the movement's striking, purpose-built headquarters, in full view of the Künstlerhaus, he now helped put on a series of exhibitions of new work. Initially, the reception among the Viennese critics and public was good; the emperor himself visited the exhibition, and several of the Secessionists went on to receive faculty appointments at the Arts and Crafts School. However, the movement ran into trouble when Klimt exhibited *Medicine* here, part of his controversial mural intended for the University. The ensuing public scandal (see p.111), and the mixed reception given to group's fourteenth exhibition in 1902, for which Klimt painted the *Beethoven Frieze* (see p.120), eventually prompted Klimt, along with a number of his followers, to leave the Secession and retreat from public life for several years, before returning to the public arena with the *Kunstschau* exhibitions (see below).

Between 1898 and 1903, the Secession group also published *Ver Sacrum*, a successful arts journal employing lavish Jugendstil typography and lay-out. Instrumental in its production and design were two of the Secession's co-founders, **Josef Hoffmann** (1870–1955) and **Kolo Moser**

Frieze is on permanent display. The frieze was intended to last only for the duration of the fourteenth exhibition held in 1902 – in the end it was preserved but not shown to the public again until 1986. The centrepiece was a heroic nude statue of Beethoven by the German sculptor Max Klinger (now in the entrance of Leipzig's Neues Gewandhaus, with an incomplete copy in the Historisches Museum der Stadt Wien). For the opening of the exhibition, Gustav Mahler conducted a new orchestration of the fourth movement of Beethoven's *Ninth Symphony*. Auguste Rodin deemed Klimt's frieze "tragic and divine", but most visitors were appalled by the whole exhibition, with its bare concrete chambers designed by Josef Hoffmann, and it proved a financial disaster.

(1868–1918). Hoffmann and Moser went on to pursue their interest in applied art, forming the craft-based Wiener Werkstätte in 1902 (see p.133), and eventually leaving the Secession in 1905 along with Klimt. All three later worked together to organize the *Kunstschau* exhibitions of 1908 and 1909 (see p.130), which in many ways represented the swan-song of the Secessionists. Hoffmann himself was strongly influenced by the more elongated, geometric style of Scotland's Charles Rennie Mackintosh, and later became one of Vienna's most intriguing early modernists, both in his architectural work and in his applied art (his villas on the Hohe Warte and in Hietzing are described on p.228 and p.216).

Though only a peripheral character in the Secessionist organization, the architect **Otto Wagner** (1841–1918) was a seminal figure in the Viennese art world throughout the period – as Hermann Bahr wrote, "without Wagner, there would be no Secession, no Klimt group, no applied art". Wagner not only completed more buildings than any other Secession architect, he also designed the entire Stadtbahn system from 1894 to 1901, including all the stations and bridges, many of which are extant on the U4 and U6 metro lines. As such, he remains the most high-profile exponent of the Secession style, though his works in fact range from nineteenth-century historicism to twentieth-century modernism. He began his career as a Ringstrasse architect, and had become something of an establishment figure by the time he joined the Secession in 1899. In the decade that followed he executed some of his finest work, initially opting for ornate curvilinear motifs derived from nature, but later moving towards more rectilinear, abstract forms. Wagner's shift towards minimalism and his enthusiastic adoption of new materials such as concrete and aluminium – best seen in his Postsparkasse (see p.135) – make him a key figure in the emergence of modernism.

Last, but not least, it's worth mentioning **Adolf Loos** (1870–1933), who published two articles in *Ver Sacrum*, one of which was a stinging attack on Ringstrasse architecture. Loos's relationship with the Secession was brief, however, and in 1908 he published a thinly veiled criticism of the movement in an article entitled *Ornament is Crime*. As an architect, Loos went on to design some of Europe's first, truly modernist buildings, most notably the Loos Haus (see p.56) and his series of villas in Hietzing (see p.216).

With much of the mural consisting of huge blank spaces framed by floating maidens, Klimt's frieze looks strangely half-finished. In between the blank spaces are three painted sections: *Longing for Happiness*, where the weak, represented by three naked emaciated figures, appeal to a knight in golden armour; *Hostile Forces* features a slightly comical giant ape, with a serpent's tail and wings, and his three daughters, the Gorgons, backed up by the figures of Disease, Madness and Death, and surrounded by decorative sperm and ovaries; and finally *Ode to Joy*, which culminates in an embracing couple, offering, in Schiller's words, "this kiss to all the world". There's an excellent English commentary available, which explains in greater detail the symbolism behind the frieze; also on display are Klimt's preparatory sketches.

Klimt and his followers used to meet at the nearby Café Museum, *see p.282.*

Resselpark

The central, traffic-free section of Karlsplatz is the leafy **Resselpark**, named for Josef Ressel, the Czech inventor of the screw propellor. Despite thinking up the device some ten years before John Ericsson, Ressel was prevented from experimenting with it by the Habsburg bureaucracy, and was thus confined to relative historical obscurity. Ressel's statue stands close to that of another hapless innovator, the tailor Josef Madersperger, who invented a sewing machine in 1815, but died penniless because no Austrian would market it. Johannes Brahms, who died in 1897 at Karlgasse 4, now a part of the nearby Technische Universität, is also represented.

The exhibition pavilion is open May–Oct Tues–Sun 9am–12.15pm & 1–4.30pm; öS25.

Resselpark is chiefly remarkable, however, for Otto Wagner's duo of Jugendstil entrance pavilions for the now defunct **Station Karlsplatz**, erected in 1899. Wagner broke with his usual design here, partly in deference to the presence of the nearby Karlskirche, adding gold trimmings and a sunflower motif. The green, wrought-iron framework, which was a feature of all his Stadtbahn stations, forms an essential part of the overall design, framing a series of thin marble slabs and creating a lovely, curving, central canopy. Today, one of the pavilions has been converted into a café (daily 10am–7pm), while the other holds exhibition space for the Historisches Museum der Stadt Wien; both have retained some of their original interior decor.

From the terrace between the pavilions, you can also admire two key institutions on the north side of Karlsplatz, both executed in Ringstrasse style. The neo-Baroque **Künstlerhaus** was built in 1881 as the exhibition hall of Austria's leading artists' association (from which the Secession group split in 1897); its diminutive extension was converted into a mid-scale theatre in the 1970s. Next door stands the **Musikverein**, Vienna's number one concert hall, designed by the ubiquitous Theophil von Hansen in the 1860s. The classical terracotta exterior apes the opera house with its front loggia, but you really need to attend a concert in the Grosser Saal to appreciate the unbeatable acoustics and the sumptuous decor with its parade of gilded caryatids. Home to the world-famous Vienna Philharmonic, the Musikverein's most prestigious event is the annual New Year's Day concert, which is transmitted live around the world to an estimated 1.3 billion viewers.

The concert hall also has a place in musical history as the place where the composer Arnold Schönberg and his followers unleashed atonal music – Schönberg preferred to call it "the emancipation of dissonance" – on an unsuspecting and unready Viennese public. The worst disturbance took place on March 31, 1913, at a concert conducted by Schönberg, during which two of Alban Berg's *Altenberg Lieder* were premièred. Programmes were used as missiles, blows were exchanged and the concert had to be abandoned after an ambulance was sent for. Schönberg of all people later complained that Berg's *Altenberg Lieder* were "so brief as to exclude the possibility of extended thematic development". Berg was mortified and the *Lieder* remained unheard and unpublished until seventeen years after his death in 1935.

Karlskirche

Rising majestically above everything around it, the **Karlskirche** is, without doubt, the city's finest Baroque church. A huge Italianate dome with a Neoclassical portico, flanked by two giant pillars modelled on Trajan's Column, and, just for good measure, a couple of hefty Baroque side towers, it's an eclectic and rather self-conscious mixture of styles, built to impress. Even surrounded by the mess that is now Karlsplatz, the church is an awesome sight – and must have been even more so when there was nothing between it and the Hofburg except the open space of the glacis.

The Karlskirche is open Mon–Sat 9–11.30am & 1–5pm, Sun 1–5pm.

The story goes that the Emperor Karl VI vowed to build a church during the plague of 1713. Architect Johann Bernhard Fischer von Erlach won the competition to design the building; his son, Johann Michael, completed the job in 1737. The church is actually dedicated to the sixteenth-century saint, Carlo Borromeo, who was canonized for his ministrations during the famine and plague in Milan. However, the fact that the emperor and saint shared the same name no doubt played a part in Karl VI's choice, conveniently glorifying both of them at the same time. The Karlskirche's dual nature – votive and imperial – is nowhere more evident than with the columns, imperial symbols, whose reliefs, rather than portraying the Emperor Trajan's campaigns, illustrate the life of Borromeo. As if to emphasize the point, the columns are topped by giant gilded Habsburg eagles, and, above the lanterns, the imperial crown.

Thanks to the windows and lantern in the oval dome, the interior is surprisingly sparse and light, allowing a much better appreciation of Johann Michael Rottmayr's vast fresco than you get of the artist's work in the Peterskirche (see p.54). The subject is the apotheosis of

Carlo Borromeo, along with a bit of Counter-Reformation Luther-bashing – note the angel setting fire to the German's bible. Everything else in the church finds it rather hard to compete with the sublime beauty of the dome, though Fischer von Erlach's sunburst above the main altar is definitely worth a closer look. Interwoven with the golden rays are stucco clouds and cherubs accompanying Saint Carlo as he ascends into heaven.

Historisches Museum der Stadt Wien

The museum is open Tues–Sun 9am–4.30pm; öS50.

Housed in an unprepossessing modernist block to the side of the Karlskirche, the **Historisches Museum der Stadt Wien** (Historical Museum of the City of Vienna) is foolishly overlooked by many visitors. The permanent collection may be uneven, but it does contain, among other things, an excellent *fin-de-siècle* section, which alone more than justifies a visit: there are paintings by Gustav Klimt, Egon Schiele, Carl Moll and Richard Gerstl, an interior by Adolf Loos, and several cabinets of Wiener Werkstätte pieces. There are also excellent temporary exhibitions on the ground floor.

The ground and first floors

The historical rundown on the city kicks off on the ground floor with the **Roman and Gothic** section – like much of the museum rather a ragbag assortment. There's a fifteenth-century gilded leather helmet topped with a female figure whose arms are in the process of being swallowed by a giant fish, and the Albertinischer Plan, the oldest map of the city from 1421. The most interesting pieces here, though, are the stained-glass windows and sandstone statues salvaged from the Stephansdom after the bomb damage of World War II, and the wonderfully beastly gargoyles from the Minoritenkirche.

The museum owns a welter of paintings, including works by the key artists of the **Baroque** period, displayed on the first floor. There are several representative works – though no masterpieces – by the three artists whose frescoes adorn so many churches in the former empire: Paul Troger, Johann Michael Rottmayr and Franz Anton Maulbertsch. Also on display are a smattering of spoils from the city's two Turkish sieges in 1529 and 1683: a vast red silk banner, Turkish horse plumes sporting crescent moons, and the odd turban.

See p.107 for a map of Vienna in 1857.

Before you head upstairs be sure to take a look at the model of Vienna, which shows the city shortly before the old zig-zag fortifications were torn down in 1857.

The second floor

To continue viewing the exhibits chronologically, turn left at the top of the stairs into the section devoted to the **Biedermeier** era (1815–48), which marked a return to simple, bourgeois values, after the excesses of the Baroque period. Just past Angelica Kauffmann's portrait of a dashing young noble, there's an entire room decorated in "Pompeii style" from a now demolished old town palace where, in the early nineteenth century, the wealthy Geymüller family entertained a coterie of artists. Among the guests was the Austrian poet and playwright Franz Grillparzer, whose musty living quarters are lovingly preserved further on. Surrounding Grillparzer's room are more than enough mawkish Biedermeier paintings for most people, epitomized by Ferdinand Georg Waldmüller's sentimental depictions of rural folk and flattering portraits of the bourgeoisie. Slightly more appealing are the exquisitely kitsch *objets d'art*, such as the mother-of-pearl candle lampshade and clock, which contains a whole miniature Tivoli scene with moving carriages.

Moving on through the modest collection of 1848 revolutionary memorabilia, you come to a sultry portrait of a society lady from thirty years later by Hans Makart. In his day Makart was lionized by the Viennese, but his art has since been more or less eclipsed by his most famous pupil, **Gustav Klimt**. Klimt's own *Pallas Athene* from 1898 hangs nearby, and marks his first use of gold, which was to become a hallmark of his work. The centrepiece of this section, though, is another model of Vienna, this time from after the construction of the great Ringstrasse buildings of the late nineteenth century, accompanied by before and after photos. To the side is an entire living/dining room designed in 1903 by the modernist architect **Adolf Loos** for his first marital home on nearby Bösendorferstrasse. Despite his diatribes against ornament of any kind, Loos loved rich materials – marble, mahogany and brass – and created for himself a typically plush interior.

Dotted around the next two rooms are various works of art from Vienna's golden age at the turn of the century. The copy of Max Klinger's nude statue of Beethoven, which formed the centrepiece of the Secession exhibition of 1902 (see p.122), is displayed here, albeit without its coloured marble drapery and seat. Carl Moll contributes two gloomily Expressionist views of the interior of his Haus Moll, designed by fellow Secessionist Josef Hoffmann. There are several glass cabinets – including one designed by Kolo Moser – stuffed with Wiener Werkstätte produce. Max Kurzweil's portrait of a *Woman in Yellow*, lounging luxuriantly on a sofa, is a classic *fin-de-siècle* painting, but it's the five works by **Egon Schiele** which really stand out. A typically distraught study of sunflowers from 1909 and the harrowing *Blind Mother II* hang beside a fondly painted view of the artist's bedroom in Neulengbach, a clear homage to Van Gogh, executed shortly before his brief imprisonment on a charge of "displaying an erotic drawing in a room open to children". The characteristically angular portraits of the art critic and collector Arthur Roessler and his wife Ida – loyal friends and patrons throughout Schiele's life – are among the artist's earliest commissioned portrait oils.

For more on the Wiener Werkstätte, see p.133.

Naschmarkt

The River Wien, which used to wend its way across Karlsplatz, was, by all accounts, an unsavoury stretch: "this black and vilely-smelling ditch is a foul blot upon the beauty and neatness of this lovely city, and must certainly produce a miasma extremely prejudicial to health," noted Anthony Trollope's mother, Fanny, in the early nineteenth century. So it was no doubt with some relief that it was eventually paved over in the 1890s, allowing the **Naschmarkt** to move from the square to its present site over the old course of the river, the Wienzeile. The market is now the city's premier source of fruit and vegetables, and is one of the few places where you get a real sense of the city's multi-cultural make-up: Turks, Arabs, Slavs and Chinese stallholders vie for customers all the way to the Kettenbrückengasse metro station. On Saturdays, the market extends even further west as the weekly flea market joins in.

The market is open Mon–Sat 9am–6pm.

The Linke and Rechte Wienzeile, which run parallel to each other on either side of the market, now function as a six-lane motorway. There are, however, a couple of sights along the Linke Wienzeile which make a stroll through the market doubly rewarding. First off, at no.6, there's the **Theater-an-der-Wien**, which opened in 1801 under the directorship of Emanuel Schikaneder, who is depicted as the bird-catcher Papageno from Mozart's *Die Zauberflöte* (Magic Flute) above the main portico. Schikaneder wrote the libretto for the opera and was instrumental in supporting Beethoven, putting the theatre at his disposal, and even allowing him to live there. Beethoven's opera *Fidelio* premièred here on November 20, 1805, exactly a week after the French had marched into Vienna. Under such extreme conditions – French soldiers made up much of the audience – it's hardly surprising that the opera flopped, running for just three performances. The theatre is also intimately connected with many other Austrian classics: Franz Grillparzer's *Ahnfrau*, almost all of Johann Nestroy's farces, Johann Strauss's *Die Fledermaus* and Franz Lehár's *Die lustige Witwe*, were all first performed here. After World War II, while the Staatsoper was being repaired, the theatre once more staged operas, though it now concentrates on musicals.

A good 500m further west on the same side are two of Otto Wagner's most appealing Secession buildings from 1899, the apartment blocks of **Linke Wienzeile 38** and **40**, next to each other overlooking the market. Wagner's ultimate aim was to transform the Wienzeile – which leads eventually to Schönbrunn – into a new Ringstrasse, though stylistically both buildings signal a break with the Ringstrasse style. Eschewing any pretensions to resemble a palace, the separation between the commercial ground floor and the residential apartments above is deliberately emphasized. The right-hand building (no. 38) is richly embossed with gold palm leaves and medallions – the latter designed by Kolo Moser – and even features an elaborate top-floor loggia with Art Nouveau swags, urns and a couple of figures. The left-hand building (no. 40) is more unusual, its pollution-resistant cladding of majolica tiles giving rise to the nickname, **Majolikahaus**. To contemporary eyes, the facade looks highly decorative, but what mattered to the Viennese was that – as with the Looshaus – there was virtually no sculptural decoration, and no mouldings or pediments above the windows. Instead, Wagner weaves an elaborate floral motif – a giant, spreading rose tree or a vine of sunflowers – on the tiles themselves.

From Schwarzenberg Platz to Stubenring

The last stretch of the Ringstrasse – Schubertring, Parkring and Stubenring respectively – runs more or less in a straight line from Schwarzenberg Platz to the Donaukanal. With fewer landmark buildings than the rest of the Ringstrasse, it does, however, boast the city's most congenial central green space, **Stadtpark**, Vienna's superb applied arts museum, the **MAK**, and Otto Wagner's seminal exercise in modernism, the **Postsparkasse**.

Schwarzenberg Platz

Faced with the din of cars and trams whizzing across its cobbles, it's difficult to believe that the large, rectangular, traffic intersection of **Schwarzenberg Platz** was once a fashionable address. The aristocracy, though they owned up to a third of the property on the Ring, usually turned their noses up at actually living there – with Schwarzenberg Platz they made an exception. The square became the nobility's own personal enclave, centred on an equestrian statue of one of their own, Prince Karl von Schwarzenberg, a member of one of the most powerful Austrian families, commander-in-chief at the Battle of Leipzig in 1813.

The Café Schwarzenberg *is one of the smartest Ringstrasse cafés; see p.283.*

At the southern end of the square, dramatically floodlit at night and spurting water high into the air, stands the **Hochstrahlbrunnen** (High Jet Fountain), erected in 1873 as a celebration of the city's nascent modern water supply system. Once the focal point of the square, it is now thoroughly upstaged by the bombastic **Russen Heldendenkmal** (Russian Heroes' Monument), which rises up behind the jet of water. A giant curving colonnade acts as the backdrop to the central column, crowned by the Unknown (Soviet) Soldier in heroic stance, flag aloft, gilded shield in hand; on the red granite plinth are the names of the fallen and a quote from Stalin (after whom the square was briefly renamed in 1945). For the Viennese, though, it's more a grim reminder of the brutality of the liberators and the privations suffered by those in the city's postwar Russian zones. No doubt aware of their unpopu-

From Schwarzenberg Platz to Stubenring

For a review of the Hotel im Palais Schwarzenberg, *see p.268.*

larity, the Soviets made sure that a clause ensuring the proper upkeep of the monument was written into the 1955 Austrian State Treaty.

Before the erection of the Soviet war memorial, the backdrop to the fountain was the **Palais Schwarzenberg**, Lucas von Hildebrandt's grandiose Baroque palace, built for Count Mansfeld-Fondi in 1704 and now hidden behind foliage. It was bought by the Schwarzenbergs who employed Hildebrandt's arch rival, Fischer von Erlach, to further embellish it in 1716. A bomb lopped off the central dome in World War II, and destroyed most of the frescoes by Daniel Gran, but the palace is otherwise well preserved. The Schwarzenbergs still live here, though they've turned the best rooms into a hotel and restaurant, and rented out one of the outbuildings to the Swiss Embassy. Sadly, the palace and its extensive gardens are closed except to hotel and restaurant guests, or embassy staff.

Konzerthaus

The nearest U-Bahn is Stadtpark.

The most illustrious concert venue in Vienna after the Musikverein (see p.124) is the **Konzerthaus**, on Lothringerstrasse, home to the Vienna Symphony Orchestra, three concert halls, the Akademietheater and a studio theatre. Built in late Secession style in 1913 by the great Austrian theatre-building firm, Helmer and Fellner, it boasts a lovely, illuminated wrought-iron and glass canopy, surmounted by octagons and a half-moon gable. Shortly before the Konzerthaus was built, Klimt and his followers, who had left the Secession in 1905 (see p.122), staged their own exhibition, *Kunstschau Wien 1908*, on this very site. Josef Hoffmann designed the pavilion and formal garden as a sort of stripped-down summer house, Oskar Kokoschka designed the poster, the Wiener Werkstätte took part and the centrepiece was a retrospective of Klimt's work hung in a room designed by Kolo Moser. The show was an outstanding success, and even before the exhibition closed, the Austrian state had purchased Klimt's *The Kiss* (now in the Belvedere, see p.157).

The next year, with Klimt's blessing, Egon Schiele exhibited his work for the first time at the *Kunstschau Wien 1909*, but the scandal which Kilmt dreaded never materialized. Instead, it came from the *Kunstschau*'s garden theatre, where Kokoschka's brutal, sexually aggressive play, *Murderer, Hope of Women*, was premièred. Some imperial army soldiers from Bosnia in the audience took exception to the play and started a riot. The Archduke Franz Ferdinand, reading the newspaper reports the next day, memorably opined, "every bone in that young man's body should be broken". Though Kokoschka avoided that particular fate, his art school stipend was withdrawn at the instigation of the Ministry of Culture.

Stadtpark

From
Schwarzen-
berg Platz to
Stubenring

Straddling the canalized River Wien much as the glacis once did, the **Stadtpark** is the largest of the Ringstrasse parks. Opened in 1862 as the city council's first public park, it's best known for Edmund Hellmer's eye-catching **Strauss Monument** from 1925, with its statue of the "Waltz King", Johann Strauss Junior, violin in hand. Gilded from head to toe and dramatically floodlit at night, the composer stands framed by an stone arch of naked, swirling naiads. Tour groups turn up at regular intervals to admire the monument, while the benches close by are a favourite spot for Vienna's elderly population. Vienna's younger generation also like to hang out here, too, smoking, drinking on the grass, and selling dope; the authorities occasionally move the scene on a few hundred metres or so, but without any great enthusiasm.

*For more on
the Strauss
family, see
p.193.*

Several other artistic types are honoured with statues in this park, but none deserve much attention. You're better off heading for the much diminished River Wien itself, where the Wienflussportal – a series of rather wonderful Jugendstil pavilions and quaysides – was constructed in 1905, nicely complementing Otto Wagner's adjacent Stadtbahn station, which survives as Stadtpark U-Bahn. The other architectural landmark is the **Kursalon**, built in neo-Renaissance style at the same time as the park, daubed in soft *Kasiergelb* (imperial yellow) and still a prime venue for waltzing.

MAK

North of the Stadtpark, the **Österreichisches Museum für angewandte Kunst** (Austrian Museum of Applied Art) – better known simply as the **MAK** – is one of the most enjoyable museums in Vienna. The highlights of its superlative, highly eclectic selection of *objets d'art*, stretching from the Romanesque period to the twentieth century, are Klimt's *Stoclet Frieze* and the unrivalled collection of Wiener Werkstätte products. But what really sets it apart is the museum's provocative redesign, completed in 1993. Giving free rein to some of Austria's leading designers, the MAK has created a unique series of rooms, each one individually designed.

*The MAK is
open Tues,
Wed, Fri–Sun
10am–6pm,
Thurs
10am–9pm;
öS90; öS30 if
there's no special exhibition.
The nearest
U-Bahn is
Stubentor.*

The MAK was founded as a Museum of Art and Industry in the 1860s by Rudolf von Eitelberger, who was inspired by a visit to what is now London's Victoria and Albert Museum. Built by Heinrich Ferstel in a richly decorative neo-Renaissance style in 1872, the building was later extended to house the Arts and Crafts School (now the Academy of Applied Arts), where Kokoschka and Klimt both trained. At the turn of the century the school became a stronghold of the Secession movement, handing out faculty positions to Josef Hoffmann and Kolo Moser, and promoting the work of the Wiener Werkstätte. At the ticket office in the beautiful, glass-roofed courtyard, with its double-decker loggia, you'll be given a plan of the museum in German and English. On the wall of each room there's a slightly pretentious, bilingual introduction by the designer, and a leaflet in English cataloguing and explaining each exhibit. Temporary exhibitions are held, for the most part, in the museum annexe, whose main entrance is on Weiskirchnerstrasse.

The MAK café is open Tues–Sun 10am–midnight, see p.283.

Romanesque to Rococo

To follow the collection chronologically, you should begin with the **Romanik, Gotik, Renaissance** room, on the ground floor where the minimalist display cabinets are beautifully offset by deep cobalt-blue walls. The designers have deliberately restricted the number of items on show, allowing you to pay detailed attention to each exhibit, though inevitably you also end up with a slightly staccato history of the applied arts. Aside from a few pieces of furniture and some very early thirteenth-century canonical garments, most of the exhibits are items of Italian sixteenth-century majolica, decorated with mythological scenes and grotesque faces.

The main focus of the next-door room – **Barock, Rokoko, Klassizismus** – is a room within a room. Acquired by the museum in 1912, the mid-eighteenth-century Porcelain Room was removed piece by piece from the Palais Dubsky in Brno and been reassembled here. It derives its name from the ceramics that have been used to decorate everything right down to the wall panelling, candelabra, chandeliers and table-tops. Outside the Porcelain Room exhibits include two huge maple and walnut marquetry panels, a large section of Chinese wallpaper portraying an idealized landscape, and a pair of pink, gilded double doors salvaged from the Palais Paar in the Innere Stadt in 1938.

Renaissance to Art Deco and the Orient

There's a slight chronological hiccup as you cross the main courtyard to the **Renaissance, Mittelalter** room. From this point, the rooms' designers begin to impose themselves more emphatically. This particular room consists of two long, central glass cabinets hung from the ceiling displaying Bohemian, Silesian and Venetian glass, with examples of Italian, French and Flemish lacework set against a black background all along the walls. The Empire-style **Biedermeier** room is much quirkier. A parade of early nineteenth-century Viennese chairs, arranged as if for a game of musical chairs, occupies the central space, while, up above, the cornice is broken by fast-moving, multi-lingual LED text. To take it all in, sit down on the aluminium mock-Biedermeier sofa.

The museum's *pièce-de-résistance*, though, in terms of design, comes in the **Historismus, Jugendstil, Art Deco** room – a wordy title for what is a very simple conceit. Two parallel shadow screens, running the length of the room, create a corridor down which you can stroll, while admiring the changing geometry of chair design over the last hundred years in silhouette. If you want a 3D look at the chairs, you can simply go round the back of the screens. The exhibits

Wiener Werkstätte

After the Secession, probably the most important Austrian art movement was the **Wiener Werkstätte** (Vienna Workshop), founded in 1903 by the architect Josef Hoffmann, the designer Kolo Moser and the rich Jewish textile merchant, Fritz Waerndorfer. Hoffmann and Moser, both founder members of the Secession, were initially inspired by William Morris and the English Arts and Crafts Movement. As with *Morris & Co*, the idea was to grant designers and craftsmen equal status – all Wiener Werkstätte produce bears the WW monogram, and the name of both the artist and craftsman. The other parallel with *Morris & Co* was the sheer range and breadth of the WW, whose work encompassed furniture, glassware, metalwork, porcelain, fashion, children's toys, postcards and even wrapping paper.

Artistically, the WW drew on a wide range of talents, including the likes of Oskar Kokoschka, Egon Schiele and Gustav Klimt. However, the strongest influences on Hoffmann and Moser were the Glaswegians, Charles Rennie Mackintosh and his wife, Margaret Macdonald, who exhibited at the Secession in 1900 – their rectilinear, geometrical style became the hallmark of the WW in their first decade. In 1907, the WW made a big splash in Vienna with the opening of the legendary *Cabaret Fledermaus* on Kärntnerstrasse, which they had designed from the toilets to the cutlery. However, despite winning numerous international prizes, and opening shops as far afield as New York and Zürich, the WW proved less successful financially. Unlike *Morris & Co* or Bauhaus, their works were not meant for mass production, and they remained attached to the old-fashioned idea of the single, unrepeatable object, designed for rich patrons, the majority of whom recoiled from such avant-garde designs. Though from 1915 onwards, Dagobert Peche's softer, more decoratively playful style, dubbed *spitzbarok* (spiky Baroque), significantly widened the appeal of the WW, the company eventually folded in 1932.

Although the most complete WW work – the 1905 Palais Stoclet designed by Hoffmann (in collaboration with Klimt) – is in Brussels, the room devoted to the WW in the MAK is the next best thing. There are also exhibits in the Historisches Museum der Stadt Wien (see p.126) and in the *Lobmeyr* glass shop (see p.48).

range from heavy neo-Baroque to modernist designs by the likes of Josef Hoffmann, Otto Wagner and Adolf Loos. By the turn of the century, the bentwood Thonet chair had become a cheap, classic design which sold by the million all around the world.

The final ground-floor room is devoted to tiles and carpets from the **Orient**, laid on the walls and floors, creating a mosque-like atmosphere. The carpets, mostly from the sixteenth and seventeenth centuries, were avidly collected by the Habsburgs. Star turn is the world's only surviving sixteenth-century silk Egyptian Mamluke carpet, spread out on the floor to the left as you enter.

The twentieth century

Three rooms on the first floor are given over to the permanent collection. One room is devoted to the **Wiener Werkstätte** (see above), whose archives were donated to the the museum in 1955. The range and scope of the WW is staggering, and just about every field in which they were active is represented here from jewellery and metalwork, primarily by Peche and Hoffmann, to an upper gallery containing the WW's prolific fashion off-shoot. One of the finest works is Kolo Moser's wood-inlaid writing-desk, which includes a retractable armchair that can be slotted into place to make the whole thing appear like a chest of drawers.

The **Jugendstil, Art Deco** room is dominated by Gustav Klimt's working designs for his *Stoclet Frieze*, a series of mosaics commissioned in 1904 for the dining room of the Palais Stoclet in Brussels. Predominantly gold, with Byzantine and Egyptian overtones, the frieze marks the climax of Klimt's highly ornamental phase (the finished product was inlaid with semi-precious stones). The tree of life is the central motif, the birds of prey in its branches symbolizing death, and the figures beneath it representing paradise. Aside from the Klimt, there's furniture by the likes of Otto Wagner and Kolo Moser, along with contemporaries Charles Rennie Mackintosh and Margaret Macdonald, and an amazing selection of Bohemian glass – from the Lötz factory's iridescent, plantlike Art Nouveau vases to monochrome, geometric bowls from Haida (NoZ Bor) – displayed in a glass cabinet suspended from the ceiling. A staircase leads up to an entire room of contemporary applied art.

More recent work is displayed in the adjacent **20. Jahrhundert, Architektur, Design** room. Among the more bizarre exhibits are a monochrome room installation by Jasper Morrison, architectural models by the Austrian deconstructionists Coop Himmelblau, and a wonderful cardboard armchair by Frank O. Gehry.

Studiensammlung

If you've got the time and energy, head off down to the museum's **Studiensammlung** (Study Collection), hidden away in the basement. The rooms here are as crowded as those in the permanent collection are sparse. The first room, **Ostasien**, displays a whole variety of stuff from the Far East, from wood, stone and bronze Buddhas to Chinese ceramic beasts, nephrite vases, porcelain bowls, rhino-horn beakers, and wooden boxes inlaid with mother-of-pearl. Top marks, though, go to the three rooms devoted to **Möbel** (Furniture), for the staggering pile of furniture stacked right to the ceiling. In a truly democratic display, painted chests from the fifteenth century share space with bean bags, De Stijl chairs, classic Wiener Werkstätte works and a Dutch cardboard sleeping box for the homeless.

The two **Keramik, Glas** rooms boast a collection ranging from Meissen porcelain figures to Jugendstil and Wiener Werkstätte produce; the glass, which kicks off with medieval stained-glass windows, ends with another incredible display of Jugendstil and Art

Nouveau glassware similar to that in the permanent collection, with works from Gallé, Tiffany and Lobmeyr as well as from several Bohemian factories. In the **Metall** room, a watering can from Wolverhampton sits happily among gold goblets, silver chalices, Art Nouveau candelabra and a collection of teapots. Finally, the **Textil** rooms hold ecclesiastical robes, dating from medieval times to the twentieth century, the majority displayed in giant pull-out cases.

From Schwarzen-berg Platz to Stubenring

Postsparkasse and around

The final segment of the Ringstrasse, from Stubentor to Urania, was the last to be laid out, erected mostly in the decade before World War I. The two biggest public buildings built here were the new Kriegsministerium (War Ministry) and the central office of the **Postsparkasse** (Postal Savings Bank). The latter was a state-funded attempt to counteract the perceived threat of Jewish capital, in particular that of the Rothschilds. With this duo in place, the Ringstrasse had, in many ways, come full circle: it had begun with a barracks and a church – the Votivkirche – in the 1850s; it was to end with another reassertion of the army and Catholicism.

The Postsparkasse is open Mon–Wed & Fri 8am–3pm, Thurs 8am–5.30pm.

Despite the reactionary politics behind the Postsparkasse, the design with which Otto Wagner won the competition for its construction was strikingly modern. The building is by no means entirely devoid of ornament – this is, after all, a prime Ringstrasse site – for a start, there's a pergola hung with laurel wreaths on the roof, flanked by two winged Victories. The rest of the building, though, looks something like a giant safety deposit box, its otherwise smooth facade studded with aluminium rivets, used to hold the thin grey marble slabs in place. Aluminium – a new and expensive material – is also used for the delicate glazed canopy over the entrance, and, most famously, for the heating cowls, which rise up into the main banking hall like giant curling tongs. Sadly, some of the interior furnishings have been carelessly modified, but the curving glass ceiling and the thick glass tiles in the floor survive intact. There's also a model of the building and regular exhibitions on modern architecture on display in the main banking hall.

You can still see the Emperor Franz-Josef's ceramic bust *in situ* above the main staircase, though moves by the Christian Socials to have the bust of the Postsparkasse's founder, government bureaucrat **Georg Coch** (1842–90), placed in the new building were foiled, allegedly by high-placed Jewish opposition. The anti-semitic mayor Karl Lueger (see p.110) stepped into the breach and got the square named after Coch, and – with Wagner's consent – placed Coch's bust on a plinth in the centre.

The Archduke Franz Ferdinand remained unimpressed by Wagner's architecture, and made sure the competition for the **Kriegsministerium**, situated opposite the Postsparkasse, was won

From
Schwarzenberg Platz to
Stubenring

by Ludwig Baumann's conservative neo-Baroque entry. Completed in 1912, it's a throughly intimidating building, smacking of reactionary, bombastic militarism, personified by the equestrian figure of Marshal Josef Radetszky, scourge of the 1848 revolution in northern Italy, which stands in front of the main entrance. Grim busts of the empire's soldiers keep watch from the keystones above the ground-floor windows, while armed cherubs and a vast military panoply guarded by a giant double-headed eagle with wings outstretched look down from the pediment. The building now houses various governmental departments.

Kunsthistorisches Museum

I n a city somewhat overloaded with museums, the **Kunsthistorisches Museum** (Art History Museum) stands head and shoulders above the rest. Thanks to the wealth and artistic pretensions of successive Habsburg rulers, it contains not only the fourth largest collection of paintings in the world, but also Egyptian, Greek and Roman antiquities, plus sundry *objets d'art* from this millennium. So numerous are the exhibits that several of the museum's departments are now housed in the Neue Burg wing of the Hofburg (see p.97).

The vast majority of the art collection is comprised of sixteenth- and seventeenth-century masters. Most people come to see the collection of **Bruegels** – the largest in the world – which forms part of a superlative early Netherlandish and Flemish section. Thanks to the Habsburgs' territorial acquisitions, the museum is also loaded with **Venetian** works, and a goodly selection of **Velázquez** portraits. In addition, there are numerous works by **Rembrandt, Cranach, Tintoretto, Veronese** and **Dürer**, and whole rooms devoted to **van Dyck, Rubens** and **Titian**. Lastly, don't miss the unrivalled collection of Mannerist works from the court of Rudolf II, especially the surrealist court painter, **Giuseppe Arcimboldo**.

One of the glories of the Kunsthistorisches Museum is, of course, the **building** itself, especially the main foyer and staircase, which is sumptuously decorated, from the monochrome marble floor to the richly stuccoed dome. Note the lunettes, spandrel and intercolumnar murals on the first-floor balcony, which illustrate the history of art from ancient Egypt to Florence. Hans Makart was commissioned to undertake the work, but only managed to complete the lunettes before his death from syphilis in 1884. The spandrel and intercolumnar murals were completed, very much in Makart's classical style, by the youthful trio of Franz Matsch, Ernst Klimt and his more famous brother Gustav; diagrams point out which mural was painted by which artist.

The museum is open Tues–Sun 10am–6pm; öS100. The picture gallery is also open Thurs until 9pm, while some of the ground-floor galleries close at dusk in winter.

Visiting the museum

Admission to the Kunsthistorisches Museum is currently öS100 – a lot of money for what is supposed to be a public institution – a fee that includes entry into the museum's temporary exhibition, whether you like it or not. If you arrive between exhibitions, you'll pay less, and it's free on public holidays. There's no **readmission** into the museum, and even if you spend the whole day here, you'll be pushed to see everything, so it's best to concentrate on just one or two areas. You'll also be extremely hungry, since the only place to eat is the overpriced, very ordinary **café** in the upper foyer.

The painting titles are all in German; in our account they're given the English names by which they're usually known. There are information sheets in each room of the Gemäldegalerie, though these occasionally go walkabout. **Guided tours** of the museum in English set off daily at 3pm and cost öS30.

The Gemäldegalerie

The **Gemäldegalerie** (Picture Gallery), on the first floor, has around 800 paintings on display at any one time, a mere tenth of the museum's total catalogue. It's easy to become overwhelmed by the sheer

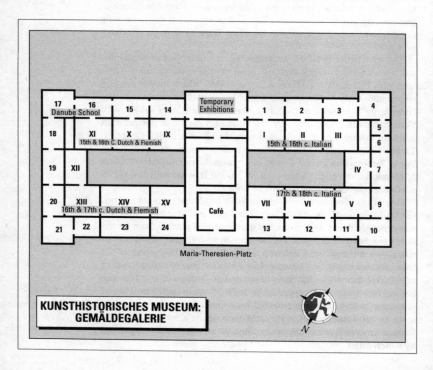

volume of art, most of which dates from the sixteenth and seventeenth centuries. Unlike most big galleries the Kunshistorisches makes no attempt to cover a broad span of art history – the collection has changed very little since the Habsburgs bequeathed it. Consequently, British and French artists, and the early Italian Renaissance, are all under-represented, and the collection stops at the late eighteenth century.

The paintings are arranged in parallel rooms around two courtyards: the Italians, plus a few French and Spanish, lie to one side; the Germans, Dutch and Flemish to the other. The larger rooms which face onto the courtyards sport Roman numerals (I–XV), while the smaller outer rooms use the standard form (1–24), though the latter are often unmarked. It would be difficult to concoct a more confusing numerical system, but at least both wings are laid out (vaguely) chronologically. The account below starts, for want of a better place, with the Bruegels and continues in an anti-clockwise direction to Vermeer; then it switches back to Titian and ends with Canaletto. However you plan your itinerary, be sure to avail yourself of one of the great virtues of the Gemäldegalerie, the comfy leather sofas in the larger rooms.

Bruegel and his contemporaries

Before you get to the Bruegel room you must pass through room IX, which contains works by the likes of **Pieter Aertsen** (c.1508–75), a contemporary of Bruegel's who also worked in the peasant genre. *Still Life with Christ at the House of Mary and Martha* is typical of his style, with the detailed still-life of the feast upstaging the religious episode played out in the background. **Frans Floris**, a painter more famous in his day than Bruegel ever was, contributes a gruesome *Last Judgement*, while **Lucas van Valckenborch**'s months of the year (only five of them survive) are modelled on Bruegel's, which you'll see in the next room.

The great thing about the museum's works by **Pieter Bruegel the Elder** (c.1525–69), in room X, is the breadth and range of the collection from innovative interpretations of religious stories to allegorical peasant scenes. Though well connected in court circles in Antwerp and, later, Brussels, Bruegel excelled in these country scenes, earning himself the soubriquet "Peasant Bruegel" – the story goes that he used to disguise himself in order to move freely among the peasantry. A classic example of the genre is his *Children's Games*, an incredibly detailed picture with more than 230 children playing 90 different games. Perhaps the most beguiling of all Bruegel's works within the peasant genre are the cycle of seasons, commissioned by a rich Flemish banker. Three (out of six) hang in this room: *The Gloomy Day*, *The Return of the Herd* and, the most famous of the lot, *Hunters in the Snow*, in which Bruegel perfectly captures a monochrome wintry landscape.

Several of Bruegel's peasant works clearly have a somewhat high-handed moral message, too, as in the *Peasant Dance*, where the locals revel irreverently, oblivious to the image of the Madonna concealed in the top right-hand corner. Similarly, the *Peasant Wedding* comes over less as a religious occasion than as another excuse for gluttony. Others, such as *The Peasant and the Bird-Thief* are more difficult to interpret, though it's thought to illustrate the inscrutable Flemish proverb: "He who knows where the nest is, has the knowledge; he who robs it, has the nest."

In *The Procession to Calvary*, we are confronted with a typically vigorous Bruegelian crowd, who seem utterly unmoved by the tragedy quietly and inconspicuously unfolding in their midst. Gruesome characters, revealing the influence of Bosch, inhabit *The Fight between Carnival and Lent*, a complex painting in which the orgy of Shrove Tuesday is contrasted with the piety of Ash Wednesday. *The Tower of Babel* (inspired, it's thought, by the Colosseum in Rome) is more straightforward, illustrating the vanity of King Nimrod – the detail on both the tower and the city below it is staggering, but get too near and you'll set off one of the alarms.

Bruegel lived through a particularly turbulent period in the history of the Netherlands, which were under Spanish Habsburg rule at the time, and many have tried to read veiled allusions to contemporary political events into his paintings (the troops accompanying Christ in *The Procession to Calvary* are Austrian). However, the most oft-quoted example, *The Massacre of the Innocents*, was, in fact, painted prior to the appointment of the Duke of Alba, and therefore cannot refer to the duke's Council of Blood, during which 12,000 were executed, despite what some art historians might say.

Early Netherlandish painting

Works by the generation of Flemish painters who preceded Bruegel are displayed in the adjoining rooms 14 and 15. **Jan van Eyck** (c.1390–1441), by far the most famous, is represented by two extremely precise portrait heads. There's a similar realism in **Hugo van der Goes'** (1440–82) diptych, *The Fall of Man and the Lamentation of Christ*; the story here given a misogynist twist by the portrayal of the serpent with a woman's head. Also in this room is the museum's one and only work by **Heironymus Bosch** (c.1450–1516), *Christ Carrying the Cross*, a canvas packed with a crowd of typically grotesque onlookers.

The three panels of *Altarpiece with the Crucifixion and Two Donors* by **Rogier van der Weyden** (c.1400–64) are cleverly unified by the undulating landscape that continues across all three frames. Uniquely, the two donors, positioned to the right of the cross in the main scene, and the holy figures, are given almost equal importance. The triptych by van der Weyden's pupil **Hans Memlinc** (1440–94) is altogether more Italian in form, with its carefully balanced symmetry and rich architectural framing.

Dürer, Cranach and Holbein

If you continue with the smaller rooms, you come to the excellent German collection, in particular the so-called "Danube School", a loose title used to group together various sixteenth-century German-speaking painters inspired by the landscape of the Danube. The collection begins in room 16 with a colourful *Adoration of the Trinity* by **Albrecht Dürer** (1471–1528). Amid his gilded throng are the donor, Matthäus Landauer (lower row, to the left), his son-in-law (lower row, to the right) and, with his feet firmly on the ground, Dürer himself (bottom right). The frame (a modern copy of the original) bears closer inspection, too, with those not heading for heaven being chained up and devoured by the devil. Dürer also appears, somewhat incongruously dressed in black, in the centre of his *Martyrdom of the Ten Thousand*; amid scenes of mass murder, he strolls, deep in conversation, with his recently deceased friend, the humanist Conrad Celtes.

Room 17 contains more Dürer, including his portrait of Maximilian I, from the year of the latter's death; the emperor holds a pomegranate, symbol of wealth and power. A prime example of the Danube School of painting is *The Crucifixion* by **Lucas Cranach the Elder** (1472–1553), one of his earliest works, with its gory depiction of Christ, spattered with, and vomiting up, blood, set against a rugged Danubian landscape. Cranach went on to become court painter to the Elector of Saxony, after which his style became more circumspect. His depiction of the *Stag Hunt of Elector Frederick the Wise*, in which numerous stags are driven into the water so the royals can pick them off with crossbows, is almost playful, with little sense of the subsequent bloody slaughter; his son, Lucas Cranach the Younger (1515–86), contributes an equally jolly scene of slaughter in *Stag Hunt of the Elector John Frederick*, which hangs close by. Also in room 17 are several melo-dramatic religious paintings by **Albrecht Altdorfer** (c.1480–1538), another artist of the Danube School, who reveals his penchant for the pornographic in the incestuous *Lot and his Daughters*.

The portraits in room 18 by **Hans Holbein the Younger** (1497–1543), who was almost a generation younger than Cranach and Dürer, date from his period as court painter to the English King Henry VIII. One of his first royal commissions was a portrait of *Jane Seymour*, lady-in-waiting to Henry VIII's second wife, Anne Boleyn, who, after the latter's execution, became his third wife (she died giving birth to Henry's one and only son, the future Edward VI). *Emperor Karl V with his Ulm Mastiff*, by Austrian artist **Jakob Seisenegger** (1505–67), helped popularize the full-length portrait among the European nobility, and was undoubtedly the model for Titian's more famous portrait of the emperor, which hangs in the Prado in Madrid.

Arcimboldo, Spranger and Van Dyck

In room 19, you enter the court of Rudolf II (1576–1612), the deeply melancholic emperor who shut himself up in Prague Castle surrounded by astrologers, alchemists and artists. It is Rudolf, whose portrait by **Hans von Aachen** (c.1551–1615) hangs in the room, we have to thank for the Bruegels and Dürers in the museum. One of Rudolf's favourite court artists was **Giuseppe Arcimboldo** (1527–93), whose "composite heads" – surrealist, often disturbing, profile portraits created out of inanimate objects – so tickled the emperor that he had portraits made of every member of his entourage, right down to the cook. Among the four in the Kunsthistorisches, all of which are allegorical, are *Water*, in which the whole head is made of sea creatures and *Fire*, where it's a hotchpotch of burning faggots, an oil lamp and various firearms. Rudolf also enjoyed the works of Mannerist artists like **Bartholomäus Spranger** (1546–1611), who pandered to the emperor's penchant for depictions of erotic, mythological dream-worlds as in his *Vulcan and Maia* and *Venus and Adonis*.

Room 19 also contains several works by the son of "Peasant Bruegel", **Jan Brueghel the Elder** (1568–1625), whose detailed still lifes of flowers were highly prized, his luminous paintwork earning him the nickname "Velvet Brueghel". One of his most famous, nonflowery paintings is his reverential *Adoration of the Kings*, a beautifully detailed work that's a firm favourite on Christmas cards. **Anthony van Dyck** (1599–1641) predominates in the adjacent room (XII): some pieces, like *The Apostle Philip*, date from the time when van Dyck was working closely with Rubens, hence the chracteristic, "ruffled" brushstrokes; others – mostly portraits – from after van Dyck's appointment as court painter to the English King Charles I.

Rubens

Thanks to the Habsburgs' long-term control of the southern Netherlands, the Kunsthistorisches boasts one of the largest collections of paintings by **Peter Paul Rubens** (1577–1640) in existence, spread over three rooms (rooms 20, XIII & XIV). As is clear from his self-confident self-portrait at the age of sixty-two, in room XIII, Rubens was a highly successful artist, who received so many commissions that he was able to set up a studio and employ a group of collaborators (among them van Dyck and Jordaens). Rubens would supply the preliminary sketches – witness the sketches for giant high-altar paintings commissioned by the Jesuits in room XIV, and the end result, in the same room.

Perhaps the best known of all the Rubens works is *The Fur*, in room XIII, a frank, erotic testament to the artist's second wife, Hélène Fourment, who was thirty-seven years his junior. Rubens was clearly taken with his sixteen-year-old wife, who appears as an angel, saint or deity, in two other of his late works: the *Ildefonso*

Altar and the *Meeting near Nördlingen*. The loose brushwork and painterly style in these two bears comparison with Titian's late work in room I, and Rubens pays tribute to the Italian in his *The Worship of Venus*, a veritable chubby cherub-fest set in a classical landscape.

Rembrandt, Vermeer and the Brits

Rubens' Baroque excess is a million miles from the sparse, simple portraits of **Rembrandt van Rijn** (1606–69), five of which hang in room XV. There's a sympathetic early portrait of his mother, the year before she died, depicted in all the fragility and dignity of old age, and a dream-like later study of his son, Titus, reading. The other three are self-portraits from the 1650s, when, as the art critics love to point out, Rembrandt was beginning to experience financial difficulties. Whether you choose to read worry into Rembrandt's face or not, these are three superb studies of the human face.

Next door, in room 24, is the museum's one and only painting by **Jan Vermeer**, *Allegory of the Art of Painting*, considered by many to be one of his finest. The bright light from the onlooker's left, the yellow, blue and grey, the simple poses, are all classic Vermeer trademarks, though the symbolic meaning, and even the title, of the work have provoked fierce debate. Close by are the museum's only **British paintings**: a gentle, honey-hued *Suffolk Landscape* by Thomas Gainsborough, a portrait of painstaking realism by Joseph Wright, an unfinished portrait of a young woman by Joshua Reynolds, and a portrait by Henry Raeburn.

Titian and the Venetians

Over in the west wing, the museum boasts an impressive selection of Venetian paintings, especially works by **Titian** (c.1488–1576), which span all sixty years of his artistic life. Very early works like *The Gypsy Madonna* in room I reveal Titian's debt to Giovanni Bellini, in whose studio he spent his apprenticeship. The colours are richer, the contours softer, but the essentially static composition is reminiscent of Bellini's own *Young Woman with a Mirror* (see below). The largest canvas in room I is Titian's *Ecce Homo*, from his middle, Baroque period, in which, amid all the action and colour, Christ is relegated to the top left-hand corner.

In *Girl in a Fur* and the portrait of Benedetto Varchi, Titian shows himself equally capable of sparing use of colour, allowing the sitter's individual features maximum effect. By contrast, Titian's very last portrait, of the art dealer Jacopo Strada, whom the painter disliked, is full of incidental detail, colour and movement. Towards the end of his life, Titian achieved a freedom of technique in his own personal works (as opposed to those produced for commission by his studio), in which "he used his fingers more than his brush" according to fellow painter Palma il Giovane. His masterpiece of this period is the *Nymph and Shepherd*, painted without a commission, using an autumnal palette and very loose brushwork.

Giovanni Bellini's *Young Woman with a Mirror* hangs in the adjacent room 1, along with a sculptural *St Sebastian* by Bellini's brother-in-law, **Andrea Mantegna** (c.1430–1506), and three fragments of an altarpiece by Antonello da Messina, who is credited with introducing oil painting to northern Italy. Next door, in room 2, the subject matter of the *Three Philosphers* is almost as mysterious as its painter, **Giorgone**. All we know about him is that he was tall, handsome and died young (possibly of the plague); as for the painting, no one's sure if it depicts the Magi, the three stages of man's life or some other subject. Giorgone's sensuous portrait, *Laura* – fur and naked breasts are a recurring theme in the gallery – is one of his few works to be certified and dated on the back.

Colourful, carefully constructed, monumental canvases by **Paolo Veronese** (1528–88) fill the walls of room II – the *Anointing of David* is a classic example, with the subject matter subordinated to the overall effect. In room III, there are several impressive portraits by **Tintoretto** (1518–94), and a voluptuous *Susanna and the Elders*, full of contrasts of light and shade, old age and youthfulness, clothed and naked. However, it's the horizontal panels, depicting scenes from the Old Testament and intended for use on furniture, which draw your attention, not least for their refreshing immediacy and improvised brushstrokes.

Raphael, Bronzino and Caravaggio

In room 3, the scene shifts across northern Italy to the Mannerist school of Emilia. **Antonio Correggio** (c.1489–1534) puts his bid in for the gallery's most erotic painting with *Jupiter and Io*, in which the latter is brought to the verge of ecstasy by Jupiter in the form of a cloud. *Self-portrait in a Convex Mirror* by **Parmigianino** (1503–40) was just the sort of tricksy art that appealed to Rudolf II, in whose collection it appeared in 1608. Florentine art proper starts in room 4 with the masterly *Madonna in the Meadow*, a study in Renaissance harmony and proportion, painted by **Raphael** (1483–1520) at the tender age of 22. Further on, in room 7, there's a typically icy *Holy Family* by **Agnolo Bronzino** (1503–72).

Caravaggio (1571–1610) was nothing if not controversial. His chief artistic sin, in the eyes of the establishment, was his refusal to idealize his Biblical characters, frequently using street urchins as his models, as in his *David with the Head of Goliath*; he also painted his own self-portrait as the severed head of Goliath. He may have managed to outrage more than a few of his religious patrons, but his works had a profound effect on seventeenth-century artists like Rubens and Bruegel, both of whom at one time or another owned the *Madonna of the Rosary*, now in room V.

Velázquez, Bellotto and Canaletto

If the Italians start to get you down – and there is a lot of less-than-fantastic seventeenth-century art out there – head for the Spanish in rooms 9 and 10. Here you can see Alonso Sánchez Coëllo's portrait of Don Carlos, Philip II's mentally and physically handicapped son, who was incarcerated by his father some four years later, and died shortly afterwards. The museum's smattering of works by **Diego Velázquez** (1599–1660), most of them gifts from the Spanish Habsburgs to the Austrian side of the family, include a portrait of Queen Maria-Anna of Spain, whose hair-do is twice the size of her face, and two of Charles II of Spain, though neither is as grotesque as the early portrait by Juan Carreño de Miranda – it's scary to think that he probably looked even worse in real life. The most famous works are those of the Infanta Margarita Teresa, who was betrothed to her uncle, the future Emperor Leopold I, from the age of three, and another of the sickly Philip son of Philip II, who died shortly after the painting was finished.

Lastly, you might want to take a look at the eighteenth-century views of Vienna in room VII, commissioned by the court from **Bernardo Bellotto**, to see how little the view from the Upper Belvedere has changed over the centuries. The Viennese insisted on calling Bellotto "Canaletto", though he was in fact the latter's nephew and pupil. For real Canalettos, you must go next door, to room 13, where his picture-postcard views of Venice hang alongside his compatriot, Francesco Guardi.

The ground-floor galleries

The ground floor is laid out entirely chronologically using only Roman numerals: it kicks off with the Egyptian and Near Eastern Collection (I–VIII), passes through Greek and Roman Antiquities (IX–XVIII) and heads off into Sculpture and Decorative Arts (XIX–XXVII). However, for what seems like an eternity now, rooms XXVIII onwards, and the Coin Cabinet, have been closed for renovations, with just eight rooms from this collection remaining open.

Egyptian and Near Eastern Collection

Immediately to the right as you enter the museum are the purpose-built galleries of the **Egyptian and Near Eastern Collection**, which sport appropriately hieroglyphic decorations. Pink granite papyrus-stalk columns from around 1410 BC are even incorporated into the construction of room I, which is devoted to the **Egyptian death cult**. The entrance to the room is guarded by two statues of the fearsome, lion-headed goddess, Sekhmet; the museum owns just four out of the six hundred which once formed a colossal monument to the deity erected at Thebes by Amenophis III.

In the room itself, there's only one actual mummy, wrapped in papyrus leaves, but there are numerous wooden inner coffins in the

The Egyptian and Near Eastern galleries close at dusk in the winter.

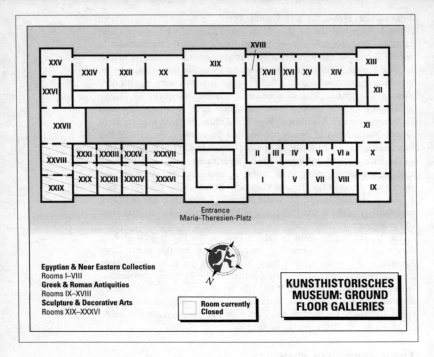

shape of mummies, smothered with polychrome symbols and hieroglyphs. Below the mummy cases are the tiny canopic jars, used for
storing the entrails removed during mummification, with lids carved
in the shape of animal deities. Elsewhere, there are cabinets full of
shabti figurines, in wood, stone and pottery, which were placed in
the tomb in order to perform any task the gods might require (there
had to be at least 365 in each tomb, plus 36 overseers). Another display cabinet to make for, in room III, contains the mummies of various animals, including cats, falcons, snakes, crocodiles and a bull's
head, alongside figurines evincing the strength of Egyptian animal
cults.

The Kunsthistorisches owns some superb examples of **Egyptian
sculpture**, beginning in room V with an unusual depiction of a lion
tucking into a bull, and Isis, sporting cow's horns, a solar disc and a
vulture headdress, breast-feeding Horus as a child. Horus appears in
his adult, falcon-headed form in rather wonderful duo in room VII,
seated alongside King Horemheb, who was the power behind the
throne of Tutankhamun. Also in this room is a winsome blue pottery
hippo, whose body is tatooed with papyrus leaves, lotus flowers and
a bird, pictoral elements from its natural swamp habitat. Room VIII
contains one of the collection's most prized possessions, the so-

called **Reserve Head** from around 2450 BC, a smooth, stylized head carved in limestone, which exudes an extraordinary serenity. Excavated by an Austrian archeological team early this century at Giza, it is thought to be a surrogate head for the immortal *ka* or cosmic double which the Egyptians believed was born with every person.

In the smaller side room IV, notice the cabinet of heart scarabs, that were placed upon the chests of mummies, bearing a spell that implored the deceased's heart not to bear witness against him or her during the Judgement of Osiris. The statuette of the woman servant making bread, in room VI, would also have been placed inside the tomb to provide the *ka* with food in the after-life. The miniature wooden pleasure boat – known as a "solar boat" by archeologists – was thought to provide the *ka* with a method of transport through eternity. Don't miss the prehistoric fertility symbols in this room – small men with inordinately large erections and rotund women showing off their labia – not to mention the penis fragments. Last, but not least, room VIA contains the complete *mastaba* or **Tomb Chamber of Kaninisut** from Giza. Hieroglyphs and relief cartoons decorate the cramped chamber where the *ka*-priest, in charge of tending to the deceased in the after-life, would offer food, burn incense and sprinkle water.

Greek and Roman Antiquities

The **Greek and Roman Antiquities** begin in room X, though one of the most prominent statues here – the **Youth of Magdalensberg** – is in fact a sixteenth-century bronze copy of the Roman original, something that was only discovered in 1983 when research was being conducted into the methods used in the casting. The vigorous high relief on the **Amazonian Sarcophagus**, also in room X, from the fourth century BC, depicts the struggle between the Greek heroes and the mythical women warriors.

There are more Greek antiquities from Ephesus in the Neue Hofburg, see p.100.

At the centre of the large, arcaded room XI, is the magnificent fourth-century AD **Theseus Mosaic**, discovered in a Roman villa near Salzburg. Theseus and the Minotaur are depicted in the middle of a complex geometric labyrinth, out of which the hero escapes with the help of the red thread given to him by Ariadne, who is pictured abandoned to the right. The extraordinarily busy **Lion-Hunt Sarcophagus**, from the late third century AD, has two of its main characters' heads uncarved – proof that funerary art was often produced before actually being commissioned.

Those in search of **Greek vases** need look no further than room XIV, which contains an excellent selection, from early Geometric vases from the eight century BC to the sophisticated black- and red-figure vases of the Classical period. Among the many onyx cameos in the adjoining room XV is one of the finest in the world, the **Gemma Augusta**, a mere 19cm in height. The upper scene depicts the Emperor Augustus in the guise of Jupiter, seated on a bench alongside Roma, with the emperor's star sign, Capricorn, floating between them; the lower scene shows the Romans' victory over the Dalmatians under Tiberius.

The last three small rooms (XVI–XVIII) contain **gold work**, much of which, strictly speaking, post-dates the collapse of the Roman Empire. The chain of honour with 52 pendants is an excellent example of early Germanic gold, its centrepiece a bead of smoky topaz, mounted with two tiny pouncing panthers. The most impressive haul is the treasure from Nagyszentmiklós (Sînicolaul Mare) in Romania, twenty-three pure gold vessels, weighing a total of 20kg, with runic inscriptions that continue to fox the experts.

Sculpture and Decorative Arts

The majority of the **Sculpture and Decorative Arts** galleries have been under wraps for some time now, but the seven rooms which remain open give a fair indication of the wealth of the collection. Most of the exhibits were collected or specially commissioned for the various *Kunstkammern* (Chambers of Marvels), which became *de rigueur* among German-speaking rulers during the Renaissance – the most avid collectors were the Archduke Ferdinand II of Tirol (died 1595) and the Emperor Rudolf II (1576–1612). The latter took the whole thing very seriously indeed, even going so far as to incarcerate the Augsburg clockmaker, Georg Roll, when the celestial globe he made for him broke down, while the one supplied to his brother, the Archduke Ernst, continued to work.

Room XIX contains objects made from precious and semi-precious stone, and sets the tone – slightly vulgar, exquisitely executed kitsch – of much of the collection. A prime example is the gold vase holding tulips made from agate, jasper, chalcedony and rock crystal, or the gold chain, inset with rubies and made up of forty-nine portraits of the Habsburgs carved in shell. Most of the exhibits have no function, but the rock-crystal dragon-lions were something of a party piece: liquid poured into their tails would gush into a shell through nozzles in the beast's breasts.

In the seventeenth century, highly complex **ivory sculptures** became all the rage with royalty; examples in room XX include Leopold I trampling a Turk and one of the Hesperides feeding the dragon with golden apples. Also on display is the heavy gold breakfast service of Maria Theresa, and the matching toilet set of her husband, Franz Stephan – over seventy pieces in total – which were donated to the collection after the death of the empress.

In room XXV you can see an elaborate piggy bank belonging to the Archduke Ferdinand II of Tirol, but the most famous exhibit in the entire collection is Benvenuto Cellini's **Saliera**, in room XXVII, a slightly ludicrous sixteenth-century salt cellar, in which the gold figures of Neptune, holding a phallic trident, and Earth, squeezing her own nipple, appear to be engaged in some sort of erotic see-saw.

Chapter 6

The Vorstädte

Once the Turks were beaten back from the city gates in 1683, Vienna could, at last, spread itself safely beyond the confines of the medieval town walls. A horseshoe of districts, known as the **Vorstädte**, quickly grew up and engulfed the villages around the old town, beyond the *glacis* (the sloping ground outside the city walls). In 1704, the great military leader, Prince Eugène of Savoy, ordered the construction of a second, outer line of fortifications or *Linienwall*, to protect the new suburbs. Later, the *Linienwall* became the municipal boundary, where, in a Habsburg custom going back to the Middle Ages, every person entering the city had to undergo a thorough search, and pay a consumer's tax on goods purchased outside the city.

As the city spread still further out into the *Vororte* or rural parishes, the *Linienwall* was finally demolished in 1890, and became what's known today as the **Gürtel** – literally "belt" – a thunderous ring road, which has the added indignity of doubling as the city's red-light district. The seven districts of the Vorstädte – the third to the ninth – are neatly confined between the Ringstrasse and the Gürtel. They have remained residential, for the most part, though each one is cut through with a busy commercial thoroughfare, the largest of which is the city's main shopping drag, **Mariahilferstrasse**, which divides the sixth and seventh districts. Sights in the Vorstädte are widely dispersed, so it pays to be selective – a *Netzkarte* and a grasp of the transport system are essential (see p.30). Our account goes round in a clockwise direction, beginning with the third district and finishing with the ninth.

For more on the postal districts of Vienna, see p.28.

The one sight in the Vorstädte that no visitor should miss is the **Belvedere**, in the third district, with its formal gardens and twin-set of Baroque palaces, which house some wonderful works of art, including the city's finest collection of paintings by Gustav Klimt and Egon Schiele. Two other sights that positively heave with visitors in summer are the **Hundertwasserhaus**, also in the third district, and the **Freud Museum** in the ninth. The former is a wacky piece of council housing by an old hippy and, as such, is some kind of must, since opinion is so divided on the building. As for Freud's apartment, there's really not much to see, yet it remains the pilgrim's choice.

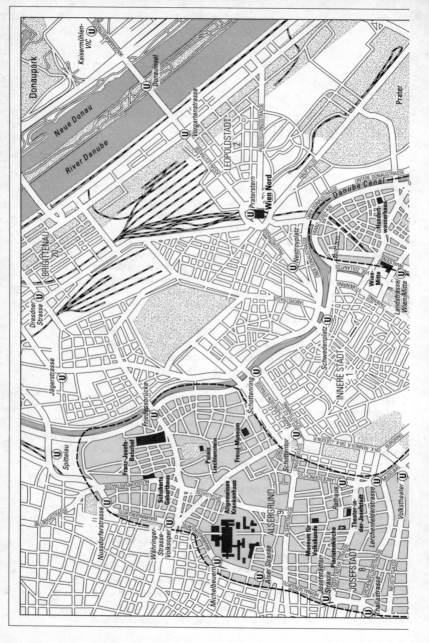

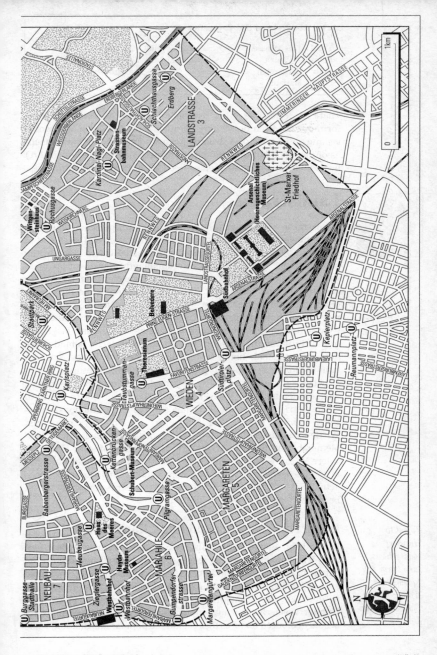

There are, of course, other reasons to explore the Vorstädte. Even for those not keen on military paraphernalia, the **Arsenal** is worth visiting for its quasi-Moorish architecture alone, and the two branches of the city's **Museum moderner Kunst** (Museum of Modern Art) boast under-visited permanent collections of twentieth-century art.

Landstrasse

Landstrasse – Vienna's third district – lies to the east and southeast of the Innere Stadt, framed to the east by the Danube Canal, and to the west by Prinz-Eugen-Strasse and Arsenalstrasse. By far the largest of the Vorstädte, it's a predominantly working-class area, with a high immigrant population, mostly refugees from the former eastern bloc and Yugoslavia. The one exception is the diplomatic quarter around the **Belvedere**, where Prince Eugène of Savoy's summer palaces house a feast of fine art from medieval times to the early twentieth century. Contemporary art has its own gallery, just south of the Gürtel, in the **Museum des 20. Jahrhunderts**; behind it lies the city's **Arsenal**, home to the **Heeresgeschichtliches Museum** built to glorify the Imperial Army in the nineteenth century.

Other sights are more widely dispersed. The **Hundertwasserhaus**, an idiosyncratic housing development in the nub of land to the north of the district, is now one of Vienna's top tourist attractions, something which cannot be said for the nearby modernist **Wittgensteinhaus**, designed by the famous philosopher. An incredible number of diehard fans make it out to the **St Marxer Friedhof**, where Mozart is buried – infinitely more than accompanied his coffin in 1791 – despite the fact that no one is quite sure where his bones actually lie. Finally, for tram-lovers, the **Strassenbahnmuseum** beckons in the far east of the district.

Hundertwasserhaus and KunstHausWien

To get to Hundert-wasserhaus, take tram #N to Hetzgasse from Schwedenplatz U-Bahn.

In 1983 the ageing hippy artist Friedensreich Hundertwasser (see box) was commissioned to redesign some council housing on the corner of Löwengasse and Kegelgasse, in an unassuming residential area of Landstrasse. Following his philosophy that "the straight line is godless", he transformed the dour apartment block into **Hundertwasserhaus**, a higgledy-piggledy, kitsch, childlike jumble of brightly coloured textures that caught the popular imagination, while

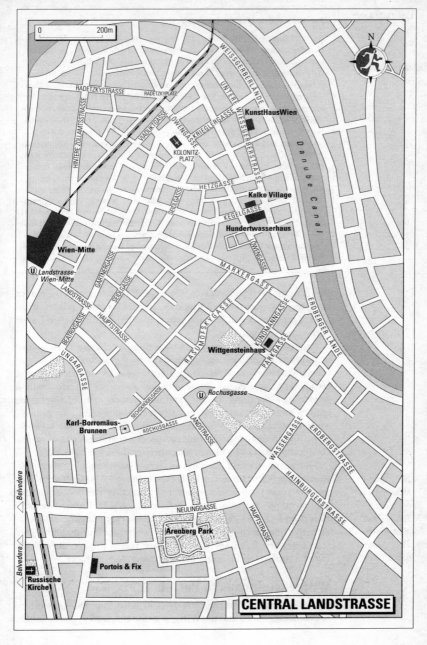

CENTRAL LANDSTRASSE

Friedensreich Hundertwasser

Born Friedrich Stowasser in Vienna in 1928, **Friedensreich Hundertwasser** adopted his *nom de plume* in 1949, having spent just three months training as an artist at the Akademie der bildenden Künste. He first made it as an artist in the 1950s, using distinctive coiling forms to produce "kaleidoscopic landscapes", reminiscent of Gustav Klimt, with a dash of Paul Klee. In the late 1960s, at the height of the hippy era, he achieved even greater notoriety for his speeches given in the nude, one of which was his architecture boycott manifesto *Los von Loos* (Down with Loos), in which he attacked the establishment in the form of modernism.

In many ways, Hundertwasser anticipated the current, widely accepted critique of modernism – that its emphasis on machine-like, undecorated flat surfaces was de-humanizing and alienating – stressing green issues and arguing for architectural variety. However, as an unrepentant hippy, experienced self-publicist and shrewd businessman, he has made no small number of enemies along the way, not least among contemporary Viennese architects, who feel his forays into their art form – his "painted boxes" – have been crass, irreverent and populist. As one critic put it, his wavy lines and individually designed windows are akin to "a nineteenth-century quack flogging his bottles of coloured horsepiss as a miracle cure for all diseases".

enraging the architectural establishment. It certainly runs the gamut of styles; a frenzy of oriel windows, loggias, ceramic pillars, glass embellishments, a gilded onion dome, roof gardens, and even a slice of the pre-1983 building.

Understandably, the residents were none too happy when hordes of pilgrims began ringing on their doorbells, asking to be shown round, so Hundertwasser obliged with an even tackier shopping arcade opposite, called **Kalke Village**, providing a café (with a stream running along the bar) and information centre to draw the crowds away from the apartments (which are closed to the public), while simultaneously increasing the sales outlets for his artwork. Here, you can get the full Hundertwasser experience, the most disconcerting aspect of which is his penchant for uneven floors.

There's another of Hundertwasser's Gaudi-esque conversions, **KunstHausWien**, three blocks north up Untere Weissgerberstrasse, though it has been less successful at attracting visitors; it features another shop and café, and a gallery devoted to Hundertwasser's own paintings. The gallery also hosts temporary exhibitions (another öS80; combined ticket öS120) by other headline-grabbing contemporary artists. Hundertwasser's most recent project, the rebuilding of a rubbish incineration plant, is described on p.227.

The Kunst-HausWien is open daily 10am–7pm; Mon öS40; Tues–Sun öS80.

Wittgensteinhaus to Portois & Fix

One sure way to lose the crowds is to head four blocks south to Kundmanngasse 19 and the **Wittgensteinhaus**, a grey, concrete-rendered house built in the modernist spirit of Adolf Loos, the very architect Hundertwasser spoke out against in 1968. It's a one-off design, executed in the late 1920s by the philosopher Ludwig Wittgenstein – as rigorous in his architecture as in his philosophical thinking, advocating an austere functionalism – with the help of the architect Paul Engelmann. The house was commissioned by Wittgenstein's sister, Gretl, herself a leading light among the Viennese intelligentsia and a personal friend of Freud's. Gretl no doubt saw the funny side of making Klimt's highly decorous portrait of her the focal point of the house's implacably minimalist interior. The building now belongs to the Bulgarian embassy – hence the bronze statues of the Slav saints, Cyril and Methodius, in the garden – and is open only during the exhibitions regularly held there.

The Wittgenstein-haus is open during exhibitions Mon–Fri 9am–12.30pm & 2–6pm; the nearest U-Bahn is Rochusgasse.

To the west, on the other side of Landstrasser Hauptstrasse, two blocks up Rochusgasse, is the little-known and rather unusual **Karl-Borromäus-Brunnen**, erected in 1909 by the sculptor Josef Engelhart, one of the founders of the Secession (see p.120), and the Slovene architect, Josip Plečnik. Set within its own little sunken square, whose entrances are flanked by flower pots sporting rams' and eagles' heads, the fountain is one of the hidden gems of Landstrasse. Centring on a plain triangular obelisk, it is shaped like a three-leaved clover, and covered with salamanders, bog-eyed frogs and reptiles of various kinds. Rings of cherubs holding hands dance beneath the leaves, while above three groups of diminutive, free-standing figures tell the story of the saint, to whom the Karlskirche is also dedicated (see p.125).

Another arresting sight in the vicinity is the **Portois & Fix** building, one block west of the fountain, and then south on Ungargasse to no. 59–61. Designed by Max Fabiani in 1900, this Jugendstil building copies Otto Wagner's innovative use of tiling for the facade of his Majolikahaus (see p.129). Instead of Wagner's more conventional floral pattern, however, Fabiani creates a strikingly modern, abstract, dappled effect with his tiles in various shades of lime green and brown, topped by a decorative, wrought-iron balustrade.

Along Rennweg

"East of Rennweg, the Orient begins", is one of Prince Metternich's much-quoted aphorisms, though he clearly meant a bit further along the road than his own house at no. 27 (now the Italian embassy), where he lived until forced to flee the city in 1848. **Rennweg** begins at Schwarzenbergplatz and runs for several kilometres through Landstrasse towards Hungary, but the section close to the Belvedere has always had a certain cachet. Nowadays, the streets immediately to the north are more desirable, dotted with embassies, among them the German, British and Russian legations. The last two are provided with their own churches, a red-brick Anglican one and an onion-domed Orthodox one, both on Jaurèsgasse.

Ludwig Wittgenstein

*Whatever can be said can be said clearly, and that of which one
cannot speak, one must remain silent about.*

Tractatus Logico-Philosophicus

With such pithy aphorisms, **Ludwig Wittgenstein** (1889–1951) – who
published only one complete text in his entire lifetime – made his name as
one of the world's greatest philosophers. The youngest of a large, wealthy,
cultured family in Vienna, Ludwig was raised a Catholic like his mother,
though his father, a leading industrialist, was a Protestant convert of
Jewish descent. Sceptical from an early age, Ludwig rejected his comfortable upbringing, reportedly never wearing a tie after the age of 23, and dis-
persing the fortune he inherited from his father to struggling writers such
as Rainer Maria Rilke and Georg Trakl.

Like all the Wittgenstein children (three of whom comitted suicide),
Ludwig was educated at home, entering the Gymnasium in Linz at the
age of fourteen (Adolf Hitler, almost the same age as Wittgenstein, was
a fellow pupil). From 1906 to 1908, he studied mechanical engineering
in Berlin, completing his research in Manchester. From there, his interests shifted to mathematics and eventually to philosophy, which he
studied at Cambridge under Bertrand Russell, who took a shine to the
eccentric young Austrian, considering him a genius, "passionate, profound, intense and domineering". From 1913, Wittgenstein lived in a
hut in Norway for two years, meditating and writing a series of notes on
logic, which he put forward as his degree, only to be turned down when
he refused to add a preface and references. During World War I, in
between winning several medals for bravery, and being taken prisoner
on the Italian front, he completed his *Tractatus Logico-philosophicus*,
seventy pages of musings on a wide range of subjects, including logic,
ethics, religion, science, mathematics, mysticism, and, of course,
linguistics.

Rennweg itself is now too busy with traffic to be truly fashionable,
but when **Otto Wagner** built himself a "town house" here in 1891, at
no. 3, it was clearly still des res. Now known as the Palais Hoyos and
occupied by the Yugoslav embassy, this early Wagner work is very
much in the Ringstrasse style (see p.106), with its elaborate
wrought-iron balconies, but you can discern hints of his later work in
touches such as the projecting cornice and the very fine reliefwork in
the upper floor. Wagner also designed the much less ornate houses
on either side, including no. 5, where Gustav Mahler lived from 1898
to 1909.

Just up from Wagner's trio, towards Schwarzenbergplatz, is the
Gardekirche, originally completed by Maria Theresa's court architect, Nicolo Picassi, in 1763, but refaced in a rather dour,
Neoclassical style just six years later. The Rococo interior, however,
was left alone, and still retains its richly gilded stucco work, ribbed
dome, bull's eye windows and lantern. Built as the chapel of the
imperial hospital, it was handed over to the Polish Guards in 1782.

After the war, Wittgenstein inherited still more of his father's fortune, this time handing it over to his brothers and sisters. He trained as a teacher, writing a spelling dictionary for schools, and working in several villages south of Vienna. Prone to pulling a pupil's hair if he or she failed to understand algebra, he wasn't greatly liked by the locals, and eventually returned to Vienna to design a house for his sister, Gretl (see p.154). During this time, he fell in love with a Swiss friend of his sister's called Marguerite, who refused his marriage proposal. In 1927, Wittgenstein became part of the **Vienna Circle**, a group of philosophers, scientists and mathematicians, including Karl Popper, Kurt Gödel, Rudolf Carnap and Moritz Schlick, who rejected traditional philosophy and espoused instead logical positivism. The Circle had chosen *Tractatus* as their working text, but their interpretation of it as an anti-metaphysical tract infuriated Wittgenstein, who preferred to dwell on its ethical and mystical aspects.

He was persuaded to return to Cambridge in 1929, putting forward *Tractatus* as his PhD, and consoling his examiners – among them Russell – with the remark, "Don't worry, I know you'll never understand it". He became a legend in his own lifetime: scruffily dressed, discussing philosophy with his chambermaid, devouring American pulp fiction, delivering lectures without notes, gesticulating violently and cursing himself at his own stupidity or maintaining long silences. Such was his ambivalence towards the smug, unnatural world of academia, and his conviction that philosophy precludes improvement, that he frequently tried to dissuade his students from continuing with the subject. He succeeded in persuading his lover, a promising young mathematician called Francis Skinner, to give up his studies and become a factory mechanic. After Skinner died of polio in 1941, Wittgenstein gave up his post, considering it intolerable to be teaching philosophy in time of war. He took a job as a porter at London's Guy's Hospital, and later worked researching wound shock. In 1946, he fell in love with another undergraduate, a medic forty years his junior called Ben Richards, with whom he stayed until his death from prostate cancer in 1951.

The Gardekirche stands directly opposite the entrance to the Belvedere, but the great green dome which features so prominently in the view from the top of the Belvedere, is, in fact, the **Salesianerkirche**, further up on the south side of Rennweg. Along with its neighbouring convent, it was founded by Amalia, widow of Josef I, in 1716, as her own private residence and as a college for daughters of the nobility (it's now the Botanisches Institut). Josef Emanuel Fischer von Erlach assisted in designing the exterior, which has more spatial interplay than the Gardekirche; the interior is less interesting, however.

Gardekirche serves the city's Polish community.

The Belvedere

Forget the Hofburg or even Schönbrunn – the **Belvedere**, to the south of Rennweg, is the finest palace complex in the whole of Vienna, at least from the outside. Two magnificent Baroque mansions, designed in the early eighteenth century by Lukas von

Hildebrandt, face each other across a sloping formal garden, commanding a superb view over central Vienna. The man for whom all this was built was **Prince Eugène of Savoy**, Austria's greatest military leader, whose campaigns against the Turks enabled the city, at last, to expand beyond the walls of the old town. Today, the loftier of the two palaces, the Oberes Belvedere, houses one of the most popular art galleries in Vienna, with an unrivalled collection of paintings by Gustav Klimt, Egon Schiele and Oskar Kokoschka.

Prince Eugène himself was a great patron of the arts, but he left no direct heirs, and after his death in 1736, a distant cousin, Anna Victoria, inherited the estate, and sold off the prince's possessions. The statues from Herculaneum were bought by the court of Dresden; nearly two hundred paintings were purchased by the King of Sardinia, head of the house of Savoy; the menagerie fell into disrepair; but the Emperor Karl VI succeeded in buying the prince's personal library, which now resides in the Prunksaal of the Nationalbibliothek (see p.93). Finally in 1752, the Belvedere itself was snapped up by the Empress Maria Theresa, who decided to house the Habsburgs' own court art collection here, and who opened the palace gardens to the public in 1779.

The imperial art collection eventually moved into the purpose-built Kunsthistorisches Museum in the 1890s. In 1903, the Unteres Belvedere became home to the new Moderne Galerie (later to become the Österreichisches Galerie), while the Oberes Belvedere was taken over by the **Archduke Franz Ferdinand** until his assassination in Sarajevo in 1914. He stayed here only occasionally, preferring to reside at his Bohemian castle of Konopiště, near Prague, since his wife was snubbed by the Habsburgs (see p.84). Thanks to the patronage of the Emperor Franz-Josef's daughter, the Archduchess Valerie, the ailing composer, **Anton Bruckner**, was granted the ground-floor flat in the gatehouse of the Oberes Belvedere in July 1895 until his death sixteen months later.

After World War I, both palaces were used as state art galleries (as they are today), though under the Austro-fascists (1934–38), Chancellor Kurt Schuschnigg also chose to reside here, before he was interned by the Nazis following the Anschluss. In 1955, the

---

Belvedere Opening Times

A single **ticket** (öS60), lets you into the Oberes Belvedere and the Unteres Belvedere, both of which are **open** from Tuesday to Sunday 10am to 5pm, and are run by the Österreichisches Galerie. The same ticket also gets you into the latter's Gustinus Ambrosi-Museum in the Augarten (see p.194), so keep it just in case. There are **guided tours** in English during the summer: Saturday at 2.30pm for the Oberes Belvedere, and Sunday at 2.30pm for the Unteres Belvedere. Entry to the gardens is free. If you're in need of refuelling, there's a very pleasant café on the ground floor in the east wing of Oberes Belvedere.

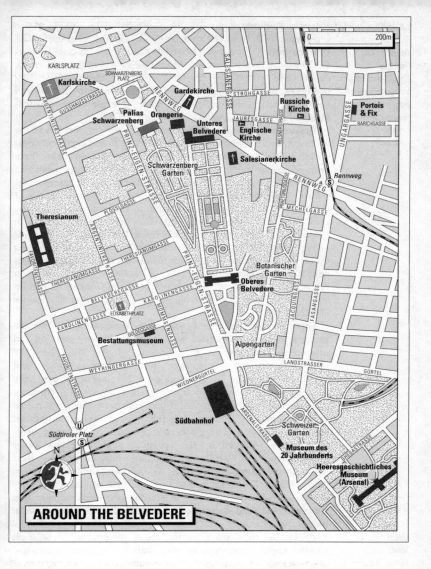

AROUND THE BELVEDERE

Austrian State Treaty, or *Staatsvertrag*, was formally signed by the Allied Powers, in the Marmorsaal of the Oberes Belvedere. Fifteen years later, the superpower Stategic Arms Limitation Talks (SALT) were officially opened in the same room by the then Foreign Minister, Kurt Waldheim.

Unteres Belvedere

Completed in 1716 at the very bottom of the formal gardens, the **Unteres Belvedere** (Lower Belvedere) is a relatively simple, one-storey garden palace, built for Prince Eugène's personal use, rather than for affairs of state or entertainment. Inside, however, it actually preserves more of its lavish original decor than the Oberes Belvedere, and for that reason alone it's worth exploring the **Barock-Museum** now installed in its rooms.

To get to the Unteres Belvedere, take tram #71 one stop from Schwarzen-bergplatz – or just walk.

The museum possesses a representative sample of works by all the leading Austrian painters of the late seventeenth and eighteenth centuries, including Johann Michael Rottmayr, Daniel Gran, Paul Troger, Johann Martin Schmidt and Franz Anton Maulbertsch. The highlight of the palace, though, is the richly decorated **Marmorsaal** (Marble Hall), which extends over two floors at the central axis of the building. The whole hall is a hymn to Prince Eugène's military prowess, white stucco trophies and reliefs contrasting with the rich red marbling. Extra depth is given to the walls through *trompe l'oeil* niches and balconies, and to the ceiling by illusory moulding, leading up to Martino Altomonte's fresco featuring Prince Eugène himself enjoying his apotheosis in the guise of Apollo. At ground level, you can admire the original lead statues from the Donnerbrunnen on Neuermarkt (see p.49), sculpted by Georg Raphael Donner (1693–1741).

There are more works by Donner in the adjoining room, once the prince's bedroom, decorated with yet more illusory painting and Altomonte frescoes. At the far end of the wing lies the **Groteskensaal**, with a "grotesque" decor of birds and beasts, and fanciful floral murals. The inspiration for this style of painting, very fashionable in its day, came from ancient Roman wall decoration, discovered during excavations of underground rooms. The rooms became known as "grottos" and the style of decor was dubbed "grotesque". Displayed here is a series of bizarre, hyper-realist "character heads", carved by the eccentric sculptor Franz Xaver Messerschmidt (1732–83), each depicting a different grimace. Next comes the **Marmorgalerie**, a richly stuccoed white and red reception room built by Prince Eugène to house his trio of classical statues from Herculaneum. These, now in Dresden, provided the inspiration for the Neoclassical sculptures by Domenico Parodi, which stand in niches along the walls.

A secret door in the Goldkabinett leads to a toilet; if the place isn't too crowded, the attendant might let you use it.

By far the most mind-blowing room, though, is the adjacent **Goldkabinett**, a cabinet of mirrors, dotted with oriental vases and adorned with yet more "grotesques" painted onto a vast expanse of gaudy, 23-carat gold panelling. Dominating this small room is *Apotheosis of Prince Eugène*, an explosion of marble by Balthasar Permoser, in which a tangle of figures struggles to stay on the plinth. The prince is depicted in full armour, trampling on the enemy, while attempting modestly to muffle the horn of Fame.

The Goldkabinett marks the end of the Barock-Museum, but there are further artistic treasures in the former orangery, down the steps from the palace. Converted into stables by Maria Theresa, the orangery now houses the **Museum mittelalterlicher Kunst** (Museum of Medieval Art). The sculptures and paintings here range from the twelfth to the sixteenth centuries, though the greater part

---

Prince Eugène of Savoy (1663–1736)

The Austrians have never enjoyed the greatest of military reputations, so it comes as little surprise that their most revered military figure is, in fact, a Frenchman, **Prince Eugène of Savoy**. His first taste of military warfare came at the age of twenty, when he offered his services to the Emperor Leopold I, partly to avenge his brother, Louis Julius, who had recently died fighting the Turks. Eugène immediately fought in the front line against the 1683 Turkish siege of Vienna, earning himself a pair of golden spurs for his bravery. Subsequently, he was given command of a regiment by Leopold; by thirty, he was a field marshal. His victory over the Turks at Zenta in 1697 helped win back Hungary for the Habsburgs, and he was made president of the Imperial War Council. His capture of Belgrade in 1718 was the single most important act in making western Europe safe from the Ottomans. In between times, he even fought against his fellow countryman, Louis XIV, in the Spanish Wars of Succession (1701–14), assisting the Duke of Marlborough in the victories at Blenheim, Oudenarde and Malplaquet. Meanwhile, back in Vienna, he became one of the greatest patrons of the arts the city has ever known, building fabulous Baroque palaces, and amassing a huge library, art collection and menagerie.

If the prince's military achievements and artistic endeavours are well documented, very little is known about his childhood or his later personal life. There are no memoirs, and nothing written about him by anyone who was close to him. Born in Paris into a leading aristocratic family, Eugène was brought up in the most extraordinary circumstances. His mother, the Countess of Soissons, was not only one of Louis XIV's mistresses, but also a wild party animal, with a penchant for intrigue and black magic. She was eventually exiled from France in 1680, on suspicion of having poisoned her husband, and of plotting to kill the king himself. Whether the infant Eugène participated in the transvestite orgies conducted in his childhood home, will never be known for sure. He remained unmarried all his life, and there is no mention of him ever having taken a mistress. Again, whether this was due to his own sexual preference, his troubled relationship with his mother, or his notoriously unprepossessing appearance, remains a mystery. Certainly, the Duchess of Orléans' description of him as a boy is far from flattering: "It is true that his eyes are not ugly, but his nose ruins his face; he has two large teeth which are visible all the time. He is always dirty and has lanky hair which he never curls . . . and an upper lip so narrow that he cannot close his mouth." As a result of the child's physical deficiencies, Louis XIV decided he should be brought up for the church rather than follow a military career. Given his mother's reputation, it's hardly surprising that Eugène was denied admission into the French army by the king in 1683, though Louis lived to rue his decision when the prince went on to humiliate him on the battlefield on several occasions.

THE VORSTÄDTE

dates from the fifteenth. One of the most remarkable altarpieces is the high-relief crucifixion scene from Znaim (Znojmo) in South Moravia from 1450. The five pictures by Tyrolean artist Michael Pacher are also worth noting, representing, as they do, the transition between the more static, one-dimensional art of the Gothic period and the love of perspective that heralds the Renaissance.

The gardens

The formal **gardens** of the Belvedere are laid out on a wide slope, punctuated with box hedges, fountains, waterfalls and statuary, and centred on a grand vista culminating in the magnificent Oberes Belvedere itself. Prince Eugène began buying up land for the gardens way back in 1693, employing Dominique Girard to use the skills he learnt at Versailles to create the perfect Baroque landscape. In the prince's day, the gardens would have been much more lavishly laid out, and the schematic arrangement of the sculptures far more complex: the lower section was put aside as the domain of the elements, while the upper section belonged to the gods. Today, this elaborate allegorical scheme only partially survives.

The central axis, flanked by statues of the Eight Muses, leads up to the **Lower Cascade**, a giant shell held up by tritons and sea-nymphs. On either side of the central axis are sunken bosquets, or hedge gardens, two circular and two square, with statues of Pluto and Proserpina from the Underworld. The balustrades, which line the steps either side of the cascade, are peppered with putti representing the seasons, and, beyond, the first of the sphinxes for which the Belvedere is famous. Fearsome beasts spurt water over the crest of the **Upper Cascade**, from where the water flows over a set of steps. The upper section of the garden was meant to represent Olympus, but the statues of the Greek gods were replaced in the nineteenth century by yet more sphinxes.

The main entrance lies to the south of the Oberes Belvedere, on Landstrasser Gürtel, its wonderful wrought-iron gateway flanked by standing lions clasping the Savoy coat of arms. The prince himself was a keen gardener, bringing rare and exotic plants and trees from all over the world to his garden. He also established a **menagerie**, situated to the east of the Oberes Belvedere (the ground plan of radial paths is all that survives), and an **aviary** (originally facing the orangery but now converted into apartments), where he kept numerous species of rare birds, and his favourite pet eagle that he himself fed by hand every day.

The Alpengarten is open April–July daily 10am–6pm; öS35.

To the east of the main entrance on Landstrasser Gürtel is the small **Alpengarten** (Alpine Garden), founded in 1793. It's a small, walled garden, packed with heathers, shrubs and hardy alpine flowers that stick close to the rockery to escape the chilling winds. To the north of the Alpengarten lies the university's **Botanischer Garten** (Botanical Garden), founded in 1754, and as large again as the formal gardens in the Belvedere. The overall layout is more like an English park, with a woodier section popular with red squirrels, sloping down to another pseudo-alpine shrubbery near the Mechelgasse entrance.

Oberes Belvedere

Completed in 1724, the **Oberes Belvedere** (Upper Belvedere) is at least twice as big and twice as grand as the Unteres Belvedere. Its unusual roofline, like a succession of green tents, seems deliberately to echo the camps erected by the Turks during the siege of Vienna; others have even interpreted the domed octagonal pavilions as quasi-mosques. The whole building was purpose-built for the lavish masked balls, receptions and firework displays organized by the prince. Guests would pull up in their coaches underneath the central *sala terrena*, thickly adorned with white stucco, its four columns decorated with military trophies and held up by writhing Atlantes.

Originally an open arcade, the *sala terrena* was glassed in during the nineteenth century and now serves as the ticket office and entrance area of the museum. To the right is the *trompe l'oeil* frescoed **Gartensaal**, the first in a series of ground-floor rooms used for temporary exhibitions; to the left lies the bookshop and the changing displays of **Art after 1918**, beyond which lies the café. There isn't enough space to display all the gallery's post-1918 works; instead, temporary exhibitions are mounted around a particular theme, with a representative sample of paintings on show. Some of these are taken from the permanent galleries upstairs, so you may not find things on the first floor exactly as described below. In addition, it is hoped that the galleries on the second floor will eventually display works from the early nineteenth century.

Most visitors, though, head straight upstairs to the **Marmorsaal**, a lighter and loftier concoction than the one in the Unteres Belvedere; it was here that the Austrian State Treaty of 1955 was signed, guaranteeing the withdrawal of foreign troops in return for Austria's neutrality. There's a painting of the event in the hall, in which you can pick out the chief representatives of the four Allied Powers: Molotov, for the Soviets, Pinay for the French, Macmillan for the British and Dulles for the Americans. There's also a photograph of Chancellor Leopold Figl, brandishing the *Staatsvertrag* to cheering crowds from the balcony.

The permanent collection of **Art around 1900** begins in the room to the right of the Marmorsaal with the *Plain at Auvers* painted by **Vincent van Gogh** a month before his suicide in 1890. Alongside it hangs *Rack Railway on the Kahlenberg*, painted by fellow depressive Richard Gerstl, in a similar, though slightly less intense, style; **Egon Schiele**'s *Interior 1907* also pays homage to the Dutch genius. Auguste Rodin's bust of Mahler, and a small terracotta study

Landstrasse

The Botanischer Garten is open Easter–Oct daily 9am–one hour before dusk; free.

To get to the Oberes Belvedere, take tram #D from the Ringstrasse.

for the Victor Hugo Monument, in which the author is overwhelmed by allegorical figures from his own imagination, can also be found in this room.

Gustav Klimt

The first of the gallery's works by **Gustav Klimt** (1862–1918) is in the second room, along with works by his contemporaries, Kolo Moser, Carl Moll and Max Kurzweil. Klimt's ethereal, slightly aloof *Portrait of Sonja Knips*, from 1898, marked his breakthrough as an independent artist, and was the first of several portrait commissions of the wives of the city's wealthy Jewish businessmen. Two later examples hang in the adjacent room: the *Portrait of Fritza Riedler*, from 1906, in which Klimt's love of ornamentation comes to the fore, and the *Portrait of Adele Bloch-Bauer I*, painted at the height of his "golden phase" in 1908, with the subject almost engulfed in gilded Mycenaean spirals and Egyptian eyes, or as one critic put it, "mehr Blech als Bloch" (more rubbish than Bloch).

The culmination of Klimt's golden age is his monumental work, *The Kiss*, displayed behind a protective glass shield, and depicting Klimt himself embracing his long-term mistress, Emilie Flöge. Klimt's use of gilding – derived partly from his father, who was an engraver – proved extremely popular, and the painting was bought for the Austrian state during the *Kunstschau* of 1908 (see p.130), a rare seal of official approval for an artist whose work was mostly frowned upon by the establishment. Another of Klimt's famous works is *Judith I*, an early gold work from 1901, with the Jewish murderess (modelled by Adele Bloch-Bauer) depicted in sexual ecstasy having beheaded Holofernes. Note that the original is far smaller than many reproductions, and therefore easy to miss here.

Also displayed in the room with *The Kiss* are eight landscapes on square canvases arranged in two neat rows on one wall. Every summer Klimt spent his vacations at the Flöge family house on the Attersee in the Salzkammergut. As a way of relaxing, he liked to paint landscapes *al fresco* straight onto canvas, without preliminary sketches. Like Monet, he often used to row out into the middle of the lake and set up his easel on board, finishing the works off after the holidays in his Vienna studio. The results are rich, almost flat, one-dimensional tapestries of colour – some almost *pointilliste* – which are easy on the eye and which sold extremely well in the salons.

The final room of Klimt's work is from his later period, when, having dispensed with gold, he was influenced by Japanese art and the primary colours of Fauvists such as Matisse. The results can be seen in the doll-like *Portrait of Adele Bloch-Bauer II*, painted in 1912, just four years after the gilded version in the previous room. Klimt regularly worked on several canvases at once, often painting his models in the nude before clothing them, as is clearly demonstrated in *The Bride*, discovered unfinished in his studio at his death, along with the Fauvist *Portrait of Johanna Staude*.

From the last room of Klimt's work, you can look down into the richly gilded, octagonal, palace **chapel**, designed by Hildebrandt to extend over two floors, looking pretty much today as it would have in Eugène's day.

Egon Schiele

Klimt actively supported younger artists like **Egon Schiele** (1890–1918) – to whom the next two rooms are devoted – introducing them to his patrons, allowing them to exhibit in shows he organized, and even, in the case of Schiele, passing on his young models after he'd finished with them. Such was the case with the seventeen-year-old Wally Neuzil, with whom Schiele enjoyed a four-year affair. *Death and the Maiden* is a disturbingly dispassionate farewell portrait to Wally, painted in 1915, the year they split up. In it, Wally clings to Schiele, depicted in deathly, detached decay. Also in this room is one of Schiele's most famous, erotic oil paintings, *The Embrace*, a double nude portrait of the artist and his model.

Schiele went on to marry Edith Harms, who came from a respectable middle-class family, the same year. *The Artist's Wife*, in the next room, was bought by this very gallery, though only after the director had got Schiele to repaint Edith's tartan skirt, which he felt was too "proletarian". Edith's pregnancy in spring 1918 was the inspiration for *The Family*, Schiele's last great painting, which remained unfinished at the time of his death from the influenza epidemic that had claimed Edith's life just three days earlier (and Klimt's eight months before that). Schiele is the father figure, the child is Schiele's nephew, Toni, but Edith had reservations about posing nude, and is clearly not the model for the mother. (Though melancholic, the painting is positively upbeat compared with the harrowing *Mother with Two Children* from 1915, in the next room, with its skeletal mother, and two mannequin-like children.)

The other works in the second room are portraits commissioned by the sitters, Herbert Rainer, Hugo Koller and Eduard Kosmak. The latter was an amateur hypnotist, which may explain his somewhat intense stare. Displayed alongside Schiele's works is Richard Gerstl's manic *Laughing Self-Portrait* from 1908, a deeply disturbing image given that its subject was, in fact, in a deep depression at the time – his lover, Mathilde, had gone back to her husband, the composer Arnold Schönberg. Gerstl committed suicide the very same year at the age of just 28.

Oskar Kokoschka and others

The work by **Oskar Kokoschka** (1886–1980), on permanent show in the last two rooms, mostly dates from his first ten creative years when he lived in Vienna. After 1915, Kokoschka only occasionally returned, usually staying with his mother, an affectionate portrait of whom hangs in the first room. Kokoschka's portraits, several of which hang in this room, contrast sharply with those of Schiele. "A person is not a *still* life" Kokoschka insisted, and he encouraged his sitters to move about and talk, so as to make his portrayals more animated. Among the portraits in this room is one of fellow artist, Carl Moll, who was stepfather to Alma Mahler (widow of the composer) with whom Kokoschka had a brief, passionate affair. Moll committed suicide in 1945 when the Russians liberated Vienna, along with his daughter, Marie, and her husband.

The last room features more work by Kokoschka, including his *Still-Life with Dead Mutton* from 1909, painted in the kitchen of the art collector Dr Oskar Reichel, who had commissioned him to paint a portrait of his son. There's a smattering of other artists' works in this room, too, among them a characteristically dark, intense work by Emil Nolde, a Cubist offering from Fernand Léger and Max Oppenheimer's evocative *Klingier Quartet*.

Historicism, Realism, Impressionism

The seven rooms in the west wing, on the other side of the Marmorsaal, are given over to more turn-of-the century paintings. In the first room, it's difficult not to be somewhat taken aback by the gargantuan *Judgement of Paris* by Max Klinger, in which a bored Paris is confronted by a boldly naked goddess, while the two others get ready to strip in the wings. Giovanni Segantini's *Evil Mothers* is a misogynist piece of anti-abortion propaganda, donated by the Secession to the gallery shortly after its foundation in 1903. Auguste Rodin's *Eve* and Auguste Renoir's *Victorious Venus*, also displayed in this room, continue the feminine theme. The next two rooms are crowded with further works by French Impressionists, among them Edouard Manet, Claude Monet and Camille Corot.

Less well known, and less well thought of now, is the Austrian artist **Hans Makart** (1840–84), whose influence went far beyond painting. He was a high society figure, and, appropriately enough, the room devoted to his works has been decked out with sumptuous furnishings much as Makart's own, much frequented studio was. On one side hangs the gigantic, triumphant flesh-fest of *Bacchus and Ariadne*; on the opposite wall in long vertical panels are four of the *Five Senses*, featuring typically sensuous Makart nudes.

In the adjacent room, you can admire more work by Makart, whose fame eclipsed several of his more innovative contemporaries, among them **Anton Romako** (1832–89), so much so that the latter's death was rumoured to be suicide. Compared with Makart's studied flattery, it's easy to see why Romako's uncomfortably perceptive psychological portraits were less popular – consider how far removed from official portraiture Romako's portrait of the Empress Elisabeth is, with its gloomy palette and its emphasis on Sisi's defensive body language. Romako's most famous work, *Tegetthoff at the Naval Battle of Lissa*, hangs in the final room, and again reveals his unconventional approach; there's no hint of heroics, but simply fear and foreboding in the expressions of the crew.

Südbahnhof and around

Vienna lost all its wonderful nineteenth-century railway stations in World War II, and the Südbahnhof, on the other side of the Landstrasser Gürtel from the Belvedere, is a typically grim postwar building. Trains from the former eastern bloc tend to arrive here, a fact which has given the area something of a seedy reputation.

From the Südbahnhof, Prinz-Eugen-Strasse runs north along the side of the Belvedere to Schwarzenbergplatz. En route it passes the innocuous-looking *Kammer für Arbeiter und Angestellte* (Chamber of Workers and Employees), at no. 20–22. Before World War II, this was the site of the Palais Rothschild, where **Adolf Eichmann** set up the Nazis' euphemistically named "Central Office for Jewish Emigration", which oversaw the "final solution". At his trial, Eichmann remembered his days there as "the happiest and most successful of my life". Round the corner, on Thersianumgasse 16–18, another former Rothschild palace served as the headquarters of the Nazi SD, the security service of the SS. Both palaces were destroyed in World War II.

West of Prinz-Eugen-Strasse lies **Wieden** – Vienna's fourth district – which is worth a mention for the **Theresianum**, on Favoritenstrasse. Originally built in the early seventeenth century by the Habsburgs, and known as the Favorita, it was the chief imperial summer residence before Schönbrunn was completed; Leopold I, Josef I and, most famously, Karl VI all died here. The latter expired unexpectedly, having eaten a "pot of mushrooms which changed the course of history" as Voltaire put it, and left no male heir. The Empress Maria Theresa, who succeeded Karl, turned the palace over to the Jesuits, and it eventually became the most prestigious school in the country. Nowadays the school shares its premises with a college for diplomats and civil servants and the state radio and television company *Österreichischer Rundfunk* (ORF).

The Theresianum is not open to the public.

Bestattungsmuseum

The only sight as such in Wieden is the **Bestattungsmuseum** (Undertakers' Museum), run by the state funeral company, at Goldeggasse 19. Since the guided tours are in German only, this is really only for those who share the strong, morbid fascination with death for which the Viennese remain famous. The custom of magnificent funerals – known as having a "beautiful corpse" or *schöne Leich* – is one to which many Viennese still aspire (only 18 percent opt for cremation).

The museum is open Mon–Fri noon–3pm for guided tours by appointment only; ring ☎ 501 95.

Inside the museum, you can admire the elaborate costumes of undertakers over the years, their banners, équipage and so on, and learn about some of the more bizarre rituals associated with Viennese funerals. Dead Habsburgs, for instance, used to have their faces smashed in, to make them appear more humble in the eyes of God, and it was common practice to install a bell inside the coffin, which the deceased could ring in case they came back to life. There are some wonderful examples of funereal merchandising: matches, photo albums, toy cars, and, best of all, undertakers' cigarettes, with the motto *Rauchen sichert Arbeitsplätze* (Smoking guarantees work). The *pièce de résistance*, though, is the reuseable coffin instigated by Josef II (see p.90).

Museum des 20. Jahrhunderts

The museum is open Tues–Sun 10am–6pm; öS25, more if there's a temporary exhibition. It is near the terminus for tram #D and bus #13A; tram #O and #18 also stop nearby.

A short distance south of the Südbahnhof, down Arsenalstrasse, lies the **Museum des 20. Jahrhunderts** (Museum of the Twentieth Century), one of Vienna's two permanent modern art galleries. It's housed in an unprepossessing prefab building that went down well in the 1958 Brussels Expo for which it was originally constructed, but like many such one-offs would have been better left as such. The gallery hosts large contemporary art exhibitions on the ground floor, while maintaining a permanent collection of international modern art, dating from the 1960s to the present day, upstairs.

For more twentieth-century modern art, see the Palais Liechtenstein on p.180.

The first floor collection, mostly derived from previous exhibitions held in the gallery, is arranged in "–isms", with pretentious (and unintentionally hilarious) commentaries in German and English. The works displayed here are the kind that give modern art a bad name: two prime examples are Bertrand Lavier's *Crashed Peugeot 103* or the three entirely grey paintings by Roman Opalka. However, armed with a sense of humour, you can enjoy such treats as Pino Pascali's giant furry blue spider, and Erwin Wurm's *22 degrees Celsius Room Temperature*, which consists of a large square glass box kept at said temperature by means of a small electric heater.

Arsenal and the Heeresgeschichtliches Museum

Further south still, down Arsenalstrasse, lies the city's former **Arsenal**, a huge complex of barracks and munitions factories, built on strategic heights above the city in the wake of the 1848 revolution. At the same time the Emperor Franz-Josef I ordered the construction of the city's first purpose-built museum, the **Herresgeschichtliches Museum** (Museum of Military History), designed to glorify the Imperial Army. The winning design is a wonderful red-brick edifice, adorned with diapers and crenellations, and completed in neo-Byzantine style by the Ringstrasse architect Theophil Hansen in 1856.

The ticket office and cloakroom of this vast museum are in the vaulted foyer or **Feldherrnhalle** (Hall of the Generals), which is crowded with life-size marble statues of pre-1848 Austrian military leaders. To follow the collection chronologically, you should begin in the **Ruhmshalle** (Hall of Fame), on the first floor, a huge domed hall of polished marble, decorated with worthy frescoes depicting Austrian military victories over the centuries. It's a heady mixture of architectural styles, gilded and arcaded rather like a Byzantine church or Moorish palace.

From the Thirty Years' War to the Austro-Prussian War

The first room of the west wing, to the left as you reach the top of the stairs, concentrates on the seventeenth century, and features twelve huge battle paintings by Peeter Snayers portraying the decisive encounters of the Thirty Years' War (1618–48). The rich pickings to be had during the **Turkish Wars** proved a useful incentive to the imperial troops fighting the Ottomans, and a fine selection of trophies is displayed here.

Among the most impressive are the horse tails that formed the insignia of the Ottoman army, and the Great Seal of Mustafa Pasha. The latter, which the Grand Vizier wore round his neck as a symbol of his absolute authority, and which had never before fallen into enemy hands, was **Prince Eugène of Savoy**'s prize trophy from the battle of Zenta in 1697. Other bits and bobs relating to Prince Eugène include his breastplate, his marshal's baton and the pall and cortège decorations from his magnificent state funeral.

The end room of the west wing contains yet more Turkish spoils, including the vast tent of the Grand Vizier, Damad Ali-Pasha, killed at the battle of Peterwardein in 1716, in which Prince Eugène triumphed over an Ottoman army more than twice the size of his. Also displayed here is the "Mortar of Belgrade" that caused the explosion of the powder magazine during the Turkish occupation of 1717.

To continue chronologically, you need to retrace your steps and walk to the far end room of the east wing, where you'll find a French hot air balloon captured by the Habsburgs in 1796. Most of the items displayed here relate to the **Napoleonic Wars**: Field-Marshal Radetzky's hat, map bag and sword, Prince Karl von Schwarzenberg's hat, sword and medals, and Napoleon's Russian greycoat, thought to have been worn during his exile on Elba. The room closer to the Ruhmshalle is filled with splendid early nineteenth-century military uniforms, and concludes with paintings of the disastrous **Austro-Prussian War**, which the Habsburgs lost at Könniggrätz in 1866.

The road to World War I and the Navy Hall

A large section of the ground-floor west wing is taken up with the glorious **uniforms of the Imperial Army**, and their opponents. At the beginning of the twentieth century, the Habsburgs could at least boast that they had the best dressed army in Europe – while the other superpowers were donning various dull khakis as camouflage, their pristine white and cream won the prize for the most elegant uniform at the 1900 Paris Exhibition. The uniforms were at their most resplendent during the ball season, and certainly had the right effect on many female guests, as Anthony Trollope's mother, visiting in 1836, swooned: "I really know nothing at once so gorgeous and picturesque as the uniform of the Hungarian noble body-guard, with their splendid silver accoutrements, their spotted furs, uncut, hanging at their backs, and their yellow morocco boots. The rich and beautiful skins which they all carry, apparently in the very shape in which they came off the animal, give the most striking air of primitive and almost barbarous magnificence." The Imperial Army also clung to other outdated practices, such as the code of honour, which meant that an officer's challenge to a duel had to be obliged (a practice only discontinued in 1911). Officers were automatically accepted at court, and like the aristocracy, used the familiar *du* with one another.

By far the most famous exhibits in this wing, though, relate to the **Archduke Franz Ferdinand**, in particular the splendid Gräf & Stift convertible in which the archduke and his wife, Sophie, were shot dead on June 28, 1914, by the Bosnian Serb terrorist, Gavrilo Princip. Even more macabre is the archduke's reverentially preserved bloodstained light-blue tunic and his unblemished, slightly comical hat with green feathers. The final rooms of the wing are devoted to **World War I** memorabilia. There are some great posters and paintings, including Albin Egger Lienz's chilling *To the Unknown Soldier*, whose repetitive image of advancing infantry perfectly captures the mechanical slaughter of modern warfare.

For more on Josef II's burial ordinance, see p.90.

The east wing of the ground floor begins with the **Navy Hall**, an interminable collection of model ships, figureheads and nauticalia. Though the Habsburgs were never much of a naval power, and enjoyed few significant naval victories, the museum makes the most of their chief moment of glory on the seas, their defeat over the Italians at Lissa in 1866, under the command of Rear Admiral Tegetthoff. An additional thrill is the model of the U-27 submarine, commanded by Georg Ritter von Trapp of *Sound of Music* fame.

St Marxer Friedhof

In the 1780s, the Emperor Josef II closed all the inner-city cemeteries, and decreed that all burials, for health reasons, should take place outside the city walls. The first of these out-of-town graveyards was the **St Marxer Friedhof** (St Mark's Cemetery), founded in 1784 near the Landstrasser Gürtel, closed down in 1874, and also known as the Biedermeier cemetery since its corpses date mostly from that era. The main reason tourists trek out here is because it was here, on a rainy night in December 1791, that Mozart was given a pauper's burial in an unmarked mass grave with no one present but the gravediggers.

Though to contemporary minds the bare facts of Mozart's final journey seem a particularly cruel end for someone considered by many to have been the greatest composer ever, the reality is less tragic. In the immediate period after Josef II's reforms mass burials were the rule; only the very wealthy could afford to have a family vault, and the tending of individual graves was virtually unknown. Funeral services took place in churches (Mozart's in the Stephansdom), and it was not customary for mourners to accompany the funeral cortège to cemeteries. In fact, bodies were only allowed to be taken to the cemetery after nightfall, where they were left in the mortuary overnight for burial the next day.

By the mid-nineteenth century, the Viennese had adopted the lavish tastes for funerals and monuments for which they remain famous to this day, and it was in this context that it became a scandal that no one knew where Mozart was buried. In 1844, his wife Constanze returned to try to locate the grave, but to little avail as graves were usually emptied every eight years and the bones removed to make way for more corpses. The most that Constanze discovered was that he had most likely been buried three or four rows down from the cemetery's central monumental cross. In 1859, the **Mozartgrab** was raised around this area, featuring a mourning angel and a pillar, broken in half to symbolize his untimely death.

Nowadays, the St Marxer Friedhof gives little indication of the bleak and forbidding place it must have been in Mozart's day, having been tidied up earlier this century and planted with a rather lovely selection of trees. To get to the Mozartgrab, head up the main avenue and bear left; you'll also find the graves of several other eighteenth-century artists here (a plan at the entrance to the cemetery locates the most famous graves).

Strassenbahnmuseum

Occupying three brick-built sheds in the eastern corner of Landstrasse, the **Strassenbahnmuseum** (Tram Museum) houses examples of just about every type of rolling stock that has trundled over the tramlines of Vienna, with a few buses thrown in for good measure. The vast majority of the trams sport the familiar municipal red livery, with the exception of the war-time exhibits, the horse-drawn trams from the 1870s, and the wonderful steam tram (still working). Children will be disappointed not to be able to climb on any of the exhibits, although the model tram railway in the ticket office might just mollify them. You can also take a ride on a 1920s tram: there are **sightseeing tours** every weekend between May and September (11.30am & 1.30pm, Sun also 9.30am; 1hr; öS200); trams leave from beside the Otto Wagner pavilions on Karlsplatz.

The cemetery is open daily 7am–dusk; April & Oct until 5pm; May & Sept until 6pm; June–Aug until 7pm; four stops on tram #18 from Südbahnhof, or five stops from Schwarzenberg Platz on tram #71.

The museum is open May–Sept Sat & Sun 9am–4pm; öS20; the nearest U-Bahn is Schlachthausgasse.

Mariahilf, Neubau and Josefstadt

Mariahilf and Neubau – Vienna's sixth and seventh districts – lie on either side of Mariahilferstrasse, the city's busy, mainstream shopping street, which stretches for more than 2km from the Kunsthistorisches Museum in the west to the Westbahnhof in the east. A few minor tourist sights are scattered across both districts, but the only area which actually merits a stroll is the narrow network of eighteenth and early nineteenth-century streets in Neubau known as **Spittelberg**, the liveliest spot in the entire Vorstädte. You might also find yourself wandering up Burggasse or Neustiftgasse, further north, in search of some of the area's numerous restaurants, cafés and pubs. The eighth district, **Josefstadt**, to the north, is a slightly more homogenous residential area, created in the eighteenth century. It, too, has its sprinkling of sights; it's also popular with students, due to its proximity to the university.

For details of the cafés, pubs and restaurants of the three districts, see p.273.

On and off Mariahiliferstrasse

Unlike most Western capitals, Vienna has relatively few big department stores, but those it does have are almost exclusively to be found on **Mariahilferstrasse**. Apart from the multinational *Virgin Megastore* and *C&A*, most are Austrian affairs like *H&M*, *Herzmansky*, *Gerngross* and *Leiner*. Perhaps the best insight into Mariahilferstrasse's contemporary character, though, is the **Generali-Center**, at no. 77, one of Vienna's few indoor shopping malls. It marks the start of the so-called *Strasse der Sieger* or "Avenue of Champions", a series of footprints, handprints and signatures in the pavement, belonging to the country's fifty most famous sports stars, and "as significant for sports fans as Hollywood's 'Walk of Fame' is for film enthusiasts", as the promotional bumf rather hopefully describes it. The first half – among them Arnold Schwarzenegger and Franz Klammer – are inside the shopping precinct; the next twenty-five – starring Thomas Muster, Niki Lauda, and Gerhard Berger – punctuate the street as far as Webgasse.

Take the U-Bahn to Neubaugasse to get to the Strasse der Sieger.

The district of Mariahilf takes its name from the **Mariahilferkirche**, a big Baroque church set back from the street between no. 55 and 57. Just behind the church is one of Vienna's five unsightly **Flacktürme** (anti-aircraft towers). Built during World War II, and capable of housing up to 30,000 troops, these tall, concrete monstrosities are some of the few visible legacies of the Nazi period. Many Viennese view them with acute embarassment; others argue that they serve as a useful and indelible reminder of that period. The real reason for their survival, though, is that, with walls of reinforced concrete up to 5m thick, they would be very costly to demolish. The only Flacktürme to have been put to use is the one in Esterházy-Park, which is daubed around the rim with the gnomic "smashed into pieces (in the still of the night)" in German and English. The interior now houses the eminently missable **Haus des Meeres** (Marine House), a claustrophobic collection of reptiles, amphibians and fish. The tanks are just too small for these big creatures, and the only conceivable reason to come here is if you have very bored children in tow.

Bundesmobiliensammlung and the Haydn-Museum

Back on Mariahilferstrasse itself, at no. 88, is the **Bundesmobilien-sammlung** (Federal Collection of Period Furniture), successor to the Court Furniture Depot established by Maria Theresa in 1750. In that efficient Austrian way, all furniture from the imperial palaces that was no longer required was stored here, and from 1924 to 1993, part of the collection was put on public display. The museum is currently under renovation and unlikely to open again until at least 1998.

For dedicated museum fans, there may be some compensation in the form of the **Haydn-Museum**, at Haydngasse 19, two blocks south of Mariahilferstrasse. Josef Haydn (1732–1809) spent much of his life in the service of the Esterházy family at their seats in Eisenstadt (see p.247) and Esterháza (now in Hungary), but with the death of his chief patron, Prince Nikolaus Esterházy in 1790, the composer was free at last to settle permanently in Vienna. He bought this single-storey house in 1793, adding an extra floor in which he lived until his death in 1809. Here he wrote, among other works, his great oratorio, *Die Schöpfung* (The Creation) and spent the last few months of his life sitting at home, silently handing visitors a specially printed calling card, which began with a quote from one of his own texts, "Gone is all my strength...". At the time of his death, Vienna was occupied by Napoleonic troops, but such was his renown, that – so the story goes – Napoleon himself ordered straw to be laid down on the road outside Haydn's house, so the noise of his cavalry riding past would not disturb the dying composer. Sadly, none of the original fittings survive from Hadyn's day, and you'll learn little about the composer's life from this formulaic museum. The house also contains an equally unenlightening memorial room dedicated to Johannes Brahms (1833–97), who lived near Karlsplatz.

The Spittelberg Quarter

Few areas in the Vorstädte have retained their original eighteenth- or early nineteenth-century appearance – the exception is the half dozen parallel narrow cobbled streets between Siebensterngasse and Burggasse known as the **Spittelberg Quarter**. Traditionally a working-class and artisan quarter, it also doubled as the red-light district, conveniently backing onto two sets of barracks, full of sex-starved soldiers. Bypassed by the late nineteenth-century, the area was saved from demolition in the 1970s, its Baroque and Biedermeier houses carefully restored – and inevitably gentrified – and many of the streets pedestrianized.

Mariahilf, Neubau and Josefstadt

The Haus des Meeres is open daily 9am–6pm; öS65.

The nearest U-Bahn is Zieglergasse.

The Haydn-Museum is open Tues–Sun 9am–12.15pm & 1–4.30pm; öS25.

For details of the area's cafés, pubs and restaurants, see p.273.

Mariahilf, Neubau and Josefstadt

The nearest U-Bahn is Volksoper.

A small **craft market** takes place on Saturdays along and around Spittelberggasse in the summer; daily during Easter and the month leading up to Christmas. Spittelberg also boasts one of the densest concentrations of bars, cafés and restaurants in the Vorstädte, not so much throbbing as gently swaying until the early hours. There's a sort of spill-over on to nearby **Sankt-Ulrichs-Platz**, a small, sloping square to the northwest, pedestrianized and dominated by the Baroque Ulrichskirche, where Christoph Willibald Gluck was married, Schubert's requiem was celebrated and Strauss the Younger was christened.

The Otto Wagner-Archiv is open Mon–Fri 9am–noon; July–Sept also at other times by appointment, ☎ 523 22 33; free.

Those with an interest in the work of Otto Wagner should stroll a couple of blocks northwest of Ulrichsplatz to the **Otto Wagner-Archiv**, on the first floor of Döblergasse 4. This was Wagner's town apartment and studio until his death in 1918, and there are plans to turn the place into a commemorative museum. Both Döblergasse 4, and the corner apartment block of Neustiftgasse 40 were designed by Wagner himself in 1912, and the only decoration on their austere facades are the bands of indigo blue glass tiles and the sparing use of aluminium – it's the closest Wagner, better known for his Jugendstil works, ever came to the kind of austere functionalism later championed by the modernists. Inside, a few of the original fittings have survived, and there are some interesting architectural drawings of Wagner's numerous, unrealized projects.

Josefstadt

The nearest U-Bahn is Rathaus.

Josefstadt – Vienna's eighth district – was laid out in the early eighteenth century and named after the Emperor Josef I (1705–11). Almost immediately, the Piarists were given a large slice of the land for their monastery, the Maria-Treu Kloster, which now forms a pleasant square with its own Marian column, three quarters of the way along Piaristengasse. Overlooking the square is the splendid convex Baroque facade and twin towers of the monastery church, better known as the **Piaristenkirche**, originally designed by Hildebrandt, but only completed in 1753. The light interior is a glorious slice of High Baroque, full of playful oval shapes and faded frescoes by the youthful Franz Anton Maultbertsch. It was on the church's still extant nineteenth-century organ that the young Anton Bruckner was examined, after which one of the judges exclaimed: "He should have been testing us!"

Tram #J runs along Josefstädter Strasse.

Close by the monastery, on the other side of Piaristengasse, facing Josefstädter Strasse, is the **Theater in der Josefstadt**, founded in 1788 as a variety theatre, but remodelled in Neoclasscial style by Josef Kornhäusel, and reopened in 1822 with a première of Beethoven's *Consecration of the House* overture, conducted by the composer himself. Between the wars, the theatre was under the direction of Max Reinhardt, the great theatrical innovator who helped found the Salzburg Festival, staged incredible large-scale productions, and eventually fled to Hollywood in the 1930s. Today, the theatre has returned to its light-entertainment roots, staging comedies, melodramas and farce.

Three blocks north of the theatre, in the Palais Schönborn on Laudongasse, is the **Österreichisches Museum für Volkskunde** (Austrian Museum of Folk Art), a collection that seems out of place in such an urban setting. The museum, founded in 1894, has been recently modernized, though the exclusively German labelling is unfortunate (as complaints in the visitors' book testify). Still, there's enough variety to keep you entertained for an hour or so, with exhibits ranging from grass raincoats and magnificent Tirolean wardrobes to an incredible limewood shrine to the Emperor Karl I.

Mariahilf, Neubau and Josefstadt

The museum is open Tues–Fri 9am–5pm, Sat 9am–noon & Sun 9am-1pm; öS45; tram #5 from Josefstädter Strasse U-Bahn.

Alsergrund

Alsergrund – Vienna's large, roughly triangular ninth district – is dominated by its medical institutions and associations. A vast swathe of land is taken up with the **Allgemeines Krankenhaus** (General Hospital), established by Josef II in 1784, and now more than double its original size. The following year, Josef founded the **Josephinum**, an academy for training military surgeons, next door. Since then, various university science faculties have relocated here, and the area remains popular with doctors and medical students, as it has been since **Freud**'s day – his museum is now Alsergrund's chief tourist attraction. Alsergrund also boasts one of the few aristocratic summer palaces to survive into the modern era, the **Palais Liechtenstein**, now Vienna's premier modern art museum.

Allgemeines Krankenhaus

The **Allgemeines Krankenhaus** (General Hospital) was one of the most modern medical institutions in the world when it was founded in 1784 to replace the Grossarmenhaus (Great Poor House). The original buildings, designed around spacious courtyards, lie to the north of Alserstrasse and to the east of Spitalgasse; the scandal-ridden modern hospital lies to the northwest, on the other side of Spitalgasse. There's little reason to head this way – unless you're ill, that is, or wish to visit the **Museum of Pathological Anatomy** in the former lunatic asylum of the Narrenturm.

Vienna was the "medical Mecca" of the empire, and from its foundation, the overriding philosophy of the Allgemeines Krankenhaus was therapeutic nihilism. At its best, this meant letting nature take its course, rather than relying on the quack remedies popular at the time. At its worst, it meant neglecting patients while they were alive, and then concentrating on autopsy as a means of prognosis instead. By 1850, it was claimed that the only medicine used at the hospital was cherrry brandy. Even at the turn of the century, conditions were

To get to the Allgemeines Krankenhaus, take tram #43 or #44 two stops up Alserstrasse.

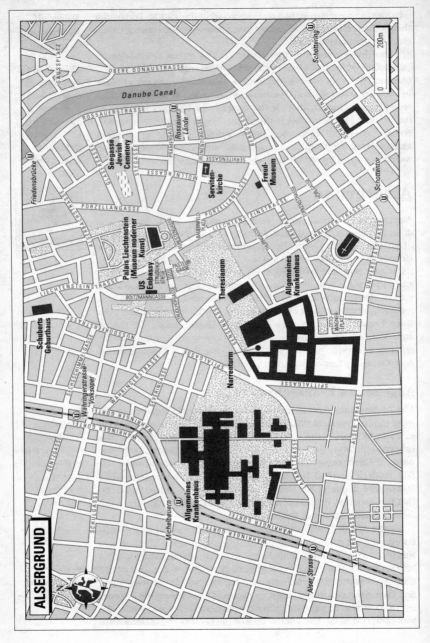

ALSERGRUND

THE CITY: CHAPTER 6

dire, with nurses forced to work 24-hour shifts, and paid so badly they had to sell coffee and demand tips to make up their wages.

Narrenturm

The circular **Narrenturm** (Fools' Tower) is an unprepossessing building, that looks something like a converted gasometer, situated in a scruffy, neglected courtyard of the old Allgemeines Krankenhaus. It was built in 1784 as a lunatic asylum with five floors, each housing 28 cells which feed off a circular corridor; its nickname was the "Guglhupf", after the popular, circular cake. Despite its forbidding, prison-like design and slit windows, conditions were exceptionally humane for the period. It fell into disuse in 1866, and now houses the **Pathologisch-anatomische Bundesmuseum** (Federal Museum of Pathological Anatomy). Locating the Narrenturm can be tricky as there are several entrances to the Allgemeines Krankenhaus – on Garnisongasse, Spitalgasse and, most conveniently, Alserstrasse – and whichever you choose, you'll need to consult the map inside each of the gateways in order to find your way to courtyard no. 6.

The museum is popular with medical students, and it certainly helps to have a strong stomach. The ground floor cells contain a mock-up of Dr Robert Koch's 1882 discovery of the bacillus that causes tuberculosis, an apothecary from 1820, a section on artificial limbs, a mortuary slab, wax models of TB sufferers and the odd piece of anatomy preserved in formaldehyde. If you're already feeling queasy, don't, whatever you do, venture upstairs where the cells and corridors are filled with yet more examples of abnormalities and deformities preserved in formaldehyde from autopsies conducted around a hundred years ago.

The Narrenturm is open Wed 3–6pm, Thurs 8–11am & first Sat of the month 10am–1pm; free.

Josephinum

Founded in 1785 to the northeast of the Allgemeines Krankenhaus, the **Josephinum** is housed in an austere silver-grey palace, set back from Währinger Strasse behind a set of imposing wrought-iron railings. Having observed the primitive techniques used by army surgeons at first hand during his military campaigns, the Emperor Josef II decided to set up an Institute for Military Surgery. The institute was closed in 1872, and the building now houses the Pharmacological Institute for Medicine and History of Medicine Institute instead – plus a museum run by the latter.

Aside from the leech cups, amputation saws, dental instruments and the odd pickled stomach, the chief attraction of the institute's museum is its remarkable collection of anatomical wax models, or Wachspräparate Sammlung, commissioned by Josef II from a group of Florentine sculptors in 1780. The models are serene life-size human figures, for the most part, presented as if partially dissected, revealing the body's nerves, muscles and veins in full gory technicolour. Equally beautiful are the original display cases, fashioned from rosewood and

The Josephinum is open Mon–Fri 9am–3pm; öS10.

Sigmund Freud (1856–1939)

Few people are so intimately associated with one place as **Sigmund Freud** is with Vienna. He may have been born to a Jewish wool merchant in Freiberg in Moravia in 1856, and died in 1939 in exile in London, but in the intervening eighty-three years, he spent most of his life in Vienna. The family moved to the capital when Freud was just four years old, and in 1873 he entered the university's medical faculty determined to be a scientist. He took three years longer than usual to complete his degree, and then decided to switch tack and train as a medic at the Allgemeines Krankenhaus. In 1887 Freud began practising as a neuropathologist, experimenting with cocaine, electro-therapy and hypnosis, before eventually hitting upon the "pressure technique", using a couch for the first time and asking questions, while pressing his hand on the patient's forehead. He later switched to the method of "free association", during which the patient says whatever comes into their mind. "The aim is modest," Freud said when describing his new science: "to turn neurotic misery into common unhappiness."

In 1896, Freud coined the term "psychoanalysis", and four years later published the book which established his originality, *The Interpretation of Dreams*. In it, Freud argued that "all dreams represent the fulfillment of wishes", and that these wishes are often (but not always) sexual. Freud's impact on twentieth-century thought has been profound, and several of his discoveries – the death wish, the Oedipus complex, transference, the Freudian slip, penis envy, the oral, anal and phallic stages of childhood, and so on – have become common parlance. (Much of this popularization has come at the expense of Freud's original meaning – "Freudian symbols", for example, used exclusively by Freud for dream interpretation, are now widely used simply as a day-to-day form of sexual innuendo.)

In 1902, Freud founded the Psychoanalytical Society, which met every Wednesday evening in his apartment, his wife serving *Gugelhupf* and coffee, while academic papers were read and discussed. Freud ruled his disciples with an iron hand, ejecting anyone who disagreed with him, most famously Carl Jung, the Swiss psychoanalyst, in 1913.

Though Jung accused Freud of having slept with his wife's attractive younger sister, Minna, who lived with the family in Berggasse, Freud was

---

fitted with huge, bobbly, hand-blown panes of Venetian glass. There's also a model of the Allgemeines Krankenhaus and the Narrenturm as they would have appeared in 1784, just for good measure.

Freud Museum

*The Freud
Museum is
open
July–Sept
daily
9am–6pm;
Oct–June until
4pm; öS60.*

Sigmund Freud moved to the second floor of Berggasse 19 in 1891 and stayed here until June 3, 1938, when, unwillingly, he and his family fled to London. His apartment, now the **Freud Museum**, is a place of pilgrimage, though he himself took almost all his possessions – bar his library, which he sold – with him into exile (where they can still be seen in London's Freud Museum). As a result, an exhibition of photographs, rather like a giant family album, with captions in English in fact a disappointingly conventional Viennese *paterfamilias*. "What a terrible man! I am sure he has never been unfaithful to his wife. It is quite abnormal and scandalous," reported one of his fans, the French poet Countess Anna de Nouailles, after meeting him. He was happily married all his life to Martha Bernays, a good Jewish *Hausfrau*, who gave birth to and brought up six healthy children. He saw patients without appointment daily from three to four in the afternoon, using the proceeds to buy the (occasionally erotic) antiquities that filled his study; afterwards he would write until as late as three in the morning. Every afternoon, he would walk the entire circuit of the Ringstrasse at a brisk pace; every Saturday evening he played the card game Tarock, every Sunday in summer, the family would dress up in traditional Austrian peasant gear, right down to their leather underpants, and go mushroom picking in the Wienerwald.

In 1923, he was diagnosed as having cancer of the jaw (he was an inveterate cigar-smoker) and given just five years to live. A year later, aged 68, he was granted the freedom of Vienna, two years earlier than was the custom. As he joked to a friend, they clearly thought he was going to die. In the end, he lived another sixteen years in some considerable pain, taking only aspirin, undergoing thirty-three operations, and having his mouth scraped daily to accommodate an ill-fitting prosthesis.

Shortly after the Anschluss in March 1938, the SS raided Freud's flat. Martha, ever the accommodating host, asked them to put their rifles in the umbrella stand and to be seated. The Freuds' passports were subsequently confiscated and their money (öS6000) taken from the family safe. Freud dryly commented that *he'd* never been paid so much for a single visit. Later he was forced to sign a document before being allowed to leave the country to the effect that he had been treated with respect and allowed "to live and work in full freedom" after the Anschluss. This he did, but he asked to be allowed to add the following sentence "I can heartily recommend the Gestapo to anyone".

Only through the efforts of his friends was Freud able to escape to Britain on June 3, 1938. Four of his sisters were not allowed to join him and died in the Holocaust. Finally, just over a year after having arrived in London, Freud's doctor fulfilled their eleven-year-old pact, and, when the pain became too much, gave him a lethal dose of morphine.

and German, is pretty much all there is to see. His hat, coat and walking stick are still here, and there's home movie footage from the 1930s, but the only room with any original decor – and consequently any atmosphere – is the waiting room, which contains the odd oriental rug, a cabinet of antiquities, and some burgundy-upholstered furniture, sent back from London by his daughter Anna.

Servitenkirche and the Seegasse Jewish cemetery

If you're heading from Freud's apartment to the modern art museum (see below), it's worth taking a slight detour to visit the **Servitenkirche**, an early Baroque gem of a church up Servitengasse, designed in the mid-seventeenth century by Carlo Carnevale, and the only church in the Vorstädte to survive the 1683 Turkish siege. Its oval-shaped nave, the first to be built in Vienna, was a powerful influence on the layout of the Peterskirche and Karlskirche. You can only peek through the exquisite wrought-iron railings, but that's enough to get a feel for the cherub-infested, stucco-encrusted interior, which features an exuberant gilded pulpit by Balthasar Moll. To the side of the entrance are two side chapels worth noting, especially the one to the north, with its stucco relief of Saint John of Nepomuk taking confession from the Bohemian queen, and its very own grotto of the Virgin Mary.

A couple of blocks to the north, at Seegasse 9–11, is Vienna's oldest surviving **Jewish cemetery**, with gravestones dating back to 1540. In disuse now for two centuries, today it remains hidden from the street behind a supremely ugly modern old people's home, which occupies the site of the former Jewish Hospital and Old People's Home, demolished in 1972. It's possible to visit the cemetery at any reasonable time by simply walking through the foyer to the back of the building, where the graves that survived the Nazi desecration shelter under tall, mature trees. One of the most famous people to have been buried here was Samuel Oppenheimer (1630–1703), the first of the Court Jews to be allowed to settle in Vienna after the 1670 expulsion (see p.66). He supplied the Habsburg army for its war with France, and organized the logistics of the defence of Vienna in 1683. When he died, however, the Habsburgs refused to honour their debts to his heirs, causing the family to go bankrupt, which in turn caused a major European financial crisis. His protégé, Samson Wertheimer (1658–1724), who became chief administrator of financial affairs to three successive Habsburg emperors, is also buried here.

Palais Liechtenstein (Museum moderner Kunst)

At the turn of the seventeenth century, when the enormously wealthy Liechtenstein family commissioned Domenico Martinelli to build a summer palace, Alsergrund was still a rural idyll. Now hemmed in by nineteenth-century apartment blocks, the Baroque **Palais Liechtenstein** comes as something of a surprise, hidden away down the backstreet of Fürstengasse. It's built on a giant scale, with an imposing entrance hall, two grandiose marble staircases and frescoes by the likes of Johann Micheal Rottmayr and Andrea Pozzo.

*The Museum
moderner
Kunst is open
Tues–Sun
10am–6pm;
öS45; take
tram #D three
stops from
Schottentor
U-Bahn.*

Though the family used to house their own vast art collection here (since removed to Vaduz, Liechtenstein), it's still a somewhat incongruous setting for Vienna's **Museum moderner Kunst** (Museum of Modern Art). The uneasy arrangement, which began in 1979, is meant to be temporary, with the collection eventually being rehoused in the Museumsquartier (see p.115). For now, the permanent collection is housed on the first and second floors of the palace, with badly translated pretentious commentaries on the more important work in German and English. There's a café in the entrance hall, which spills out into the palace gardens in the summer.

The permanent collection

The gargantuan works of contemporary Austrian art on the twin staircases set the tone of the museum: Franz Gertsch's photo-realist *Johanna I*, on the one hand, and Jörg Immendorff's cartoon-like *Museum of Modert Art*, which depicts a whole load of artistic luminaries, including Josef Beuys and Marcel Duchamp, hobnobbing in an art gallery.

The huge rooms on the first floor are given over to large-scale installations, such as Jean-Luc Vimouth's didactic *Café Whale Songs*, its walls hung with graphic photos of slaughtered whales. There's also a good showing of **1960s Pop Art**, with Robert Rauschenberg's "neo-dada" cardboard collages and John Chamberlain's anti-consumerist scrap-metal sculptures filling the ornate *trompe l'oeil* Marmorsaal. The pope of Pop Art, **Andy Warhol**, is given a whole room to himself; *Mick Jagger* and the morbid *Orange Car Crash* are among the silkscreen prints displayed. The greater part of the gallery's collection, though, is housed in the more cramped rooms on the second floor.

Oskar Kokoschka's portrait of his friend, the feisty journalist Karl Kraus, kicks off the proceedings in room A, along with Max Oppenheimer's much more flattering portrait of the journalist's wife, Rosa Kraus, painted fifteen years earlier. Kokoschka was closely associated with the Dresden Brücke group, led by **Ernst Ludwig Kirchner**, whose sickly green *Grünes Haus* reveals his debt to the French Fauvists as clearly as does the self-portrait by Alexei Jawlensky, a painter from Munich's Blaue Reiter group. The influence of African art is discernible in room B in André Derain's *Crouching Figure* and **Pablo Picasso**'s bronze head of his first mistress Fernande Olivier, both sculpted in 1907. One artist who had a profound influence on both Kokoschka and Schiele was the Belgian sculptor **George Minne**, whose emaciated *Kneeling Boy*, sculpted in marble in the 1890s, is a perfect example of the "fleshless Gothic bodies" described and admired by Kokoschka.

Room C features a couple of minor Cubist paintings by Fernand Léger, and three works by the Czech **František Kupka**, an early pioneer of abstract art. Room D is devoted mostly to sculptures by the likes of the Romanian **Constantin Brancusi**, Bauhaus artist Oskar Schlemmer and the Lithuanian, Jacques Lipchitz. You have to backtrack through the last two rooms to get to the Surrealists in room E, where **Réne Magritte**'s *Voice of Blood* (a painting of a tree, in case you hadn't guessed) shares space with works by Giorgio de Chirico and Max Ernst, a collage and an iron with nails in it by Man Ray, and a tender portrait from 1960 by Picasso of Jacqueline Roque, who became his second wife the following year.

Abstract paintings by Paul Klee and Vassily Kandinsky, and a colourful mobile by kinetic artist, Alexander Calder, are the high-

An annexe of the museum, displaying modern art from the 1960s onwards, is described on p.168.

lights of room F. Next door, in room G, a very small and squiggly Jackson Pollock and an attenuated Alberto Giacometti statue rub shoulders with two "over-paintings" – in which works by great artists are painted over in thick, usually black, paint – by **Arnulf Rainer**, one of Austria's leading contemporary artists. There's more Rainer in room H, along with works by the leading figures of **Wiener Aktionismus**, Vienna's very own extremely violent version of 1960s performance art. Their last happening, *Art and Revolution* by Günter Brus, in which the latter displayed himself naked, urinated and dipped his penis into a foaming beermug, resulted in a six-month prison sentence for "degrading Austrian symbols" (presumably the beermug) and a "gross and public violation of public morality and decency". The relics of such events, such as *Altar*, a blood on canvas work by Hermann Nitsch, are inevitably a little anticlimactic.

There's more Pop Art in room I, including the inevitable crushed car by César. The slightly grubby, wrapped *Package* of unidentified objects is an early work by **Christo**, before he managed to convince anyone to fund the much larger projects for which he's now famous. Things reach something of a climax – if that's the right word – in room J, where **Yoko Ono**'s *White Chess Set* sits beside Nam June Paik's piano, which has been rendered unplayable thanks to the various objects which have been glued to it. The latter is accompanied by the curator's illuminating comment that "if it were not already in a museum, Paik could change it again any time". How true. It would be churlish not to mention the final two rooms, K and L, which boast a canvas across which the artist Otto Mühl has walked with bare, paint-daubed feet, Gloria Friedmann's shamanistic concoctions made from iron, glass and raven feathers, and Guillaume Bijl's *Death Chamber of Johannes Vogl*, which consists of an entire room of the deceased man's furniture.

Further north; the Strudlhofstiege and Schubert

If you've just emerged from the Palais Liechtenstein, you might as well take a stroll up the **Strudlhofstiege**, an imaginative set of Jugenstil steps designed by Johann Theodor Jäger, that link Pasteurgasse with Strudlhofgasse above it. They may not have the fame nor the setting of Rome's Spanish Steps, but they are a beguiling vignette of *fin-de-siècle* Vienna, and provided the inspiration for a long novel of the same name written in 1951 by Heimito von Doderer, which is dear to the hearts of many Viennese.

Schuberts Geburthaus

Further north still, at Nussdorfer Strasse 54, is **Schuberts Geburthaus**, the unassuming, two-storey house where the composer was born in 1797. Inside, the charming courtyard has been lovingly restored, with wooden balconies festooned with geranium flower boxes. As so often with Vienna's musical memorials, however, there has been no attempt to reconstruct Schubert's family home, which would have consisted of just one room and a kitchen (the latter survives). In any case, Schubert would have had very little recollection of the place as the family moved down the road, to Säulengasse 3, when he was four years old. So, beyond admiring the composer's broken spectacles and his half-brother's piano, there's little to do here but listen to the excerpts from his music on the headphones provided. However, fans of **Adalbert Stifter**, the writer and artist from the Böhmerwald who slit his throat in 1868 rather than suffer cancer of the liver, fare a little better than those on Schubert's trail. Although Stifter had nothing whatsoever to do with Schubert, several rooms in the museum have been given over to his idyllic Biedermeier landscapes, and for an extra öS10, you can view them at your leisure.

Schubert's brother's house – 4, Kettenbrückengasse 6, near the Naschmarkt – in which the composer died, has been made into a similarly unenthralling museum for the truly dedicated; times and prices as for Schuberts Geburthaus.

Schuberts Geburthaus is open Tues–Sun 9am–12.15pm & 1–4.30pm; öS25; take tram #38 or #39 five stops from U-Bahn Schottentor.

Franz Schubert

Of all the composers associated with Vienna, **Franz Schubert** (1797–1828) fulfils more Romantic criteria than most. He died of syphilis at the age of just 31 (younger even than Mozart), he really was penniless (unlike Mozart, who was just a spendthrift), and never lived to hear any of his symphonies performed (the first one wasn't published until fifty years after his death). The picture would be complete had he died while writing his *Eighth (Unfinished) Symphony* – in fact, he abandoned it before he died, and went on, instead, to complete a *Ninth Symphony*.

Schubert was born the eleventh child of an impoverished teacher. At the age of nine or ten, he was sent to study with the organist at the local church on Marktgasse, where he had been baptized. He went on to become the church organist, and composed his first mass for the church at the age of 17. In between times, he served as a chorister at the Burgkapelle, where he studied under Antonio Salieri, Mozart's famous court rival, before working as an assistant teacher at his father's school for three years. At the end of this period, he became a freelance musician, thanks to financial help from his friends, and spent two summers as music tutor for the Esterházys (see p.243). His intensely lyrical chamber music, fragile songs and melodic piano works were popular among the Viennese bourgeoisie, and he performed at numerous informal social gatherings, which became known as "Schubertiaden". In his personal life, he was fairly dissolute; a heavy drinker, who frequented "revolutionary" circles, he remained unmarried all his life, his sexual appetite confined to prostitutes. Towards the end of his short life, he fulfilled a lifetime's ambition and met up with his hero Beethoven, though there are no reliable details of the encounter. He was one of the torchbearers at the great composer's funeral, and was buried, according to his wishes, three graves away from him in Währinger Friedhof the following year (he now lies with Beethoven in the Zentralfriedhof, see p.234).

Chapter 7

Leopoldstadt and the east

L eopoldstadt – the city's second district – is separated from
the centre of Vienna by the Danube Canal, and, along with the
district of Brigittenau, forms a misshapen island bordered to
the east by the main arm of the Danube. For the most part, it's a drab
and uninteresting residential suburb, only redeemed by the **Prater**,
the vast city park, with its funfair, ferris wheel, woods and numerous
recreational facilities. Leopoldstadt also boasts a long history as the
city's foremost Jewish quarter, though few traces of the old community remain. More recently, the area has been settled by a wave of
immigrants from Turkey and the Balkans. It's also still something of
a red-light district, with a sprinkling of strip joints and sex shops in
the backstreets between Taborstrasse and Praterstrasse.

Jewish Leopoldstadt

*In Leopoldstadt, where the humbler Jews mostly congregate, there
was suddenly an endless concourse of new, strange figures – men in
long gabardines, tiny circular caps of silk or velvet on their heads,
and corkscrew curls meandering down the sides of the face; women
with wigs and ancient finery, blooming young Esthers and
Susannahs ambling along with downcast eyes. Along the quays of the
Danube Canal there was an endless procession of these – a new edition of Hebrew fugitives mourning by the waters. Rabbis in every
costume and of every degree of holiness were scattered amongst
them all.*

Wolf von Schierbrand,
an American journalist stationed in Vienna in the late nineteenth century.

It was probably Leopoldstadt's physical separateness that persuaded
the Emperor Ferdinand II to choose the area in 1624 as a site to
establish a walled Jewish ghetto. For around fifty years the Jewish
quarter flourished, the financial acumen and clout of its wealthiest
burghers happily used by the Habsburgs to fund the Thirty Years'
War. At the end of the 1660s the population peaked at around 3000
or 4000, but as the Counter-Reformation gathered pace, there were

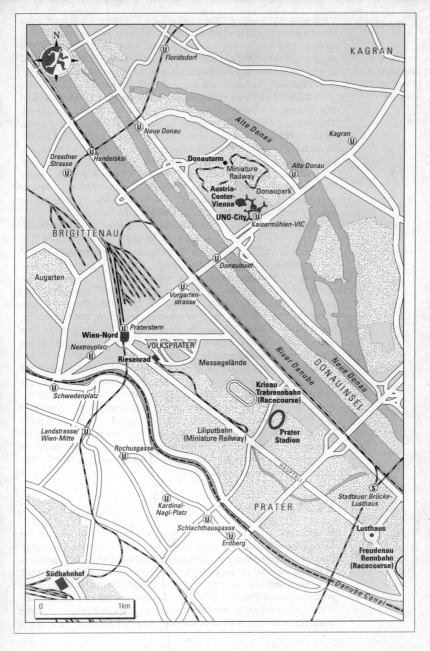

For more on the plight of Vienna's Jews, see p.66.

increasingly vociferous calls from devout Catholics – not least from the city council and the Emperor's Spanish wife – to banish the community entirely. In 1670, the Emperor Leopold I bowed to the zealots' pressure and expelled Jews from the city on the charges of spying for the Turks and blasphemy against the Virgin Mary.

Fortuitously, Leopoldstadt enjoyed a second period of Jewish settlement in the decades following the 1848 revolution, when official restrictions on Jews within the empire were finally abolished. Thousands took the opportunity to leave the *shtetls* of Bohemia, Moravia, Hungary and Galicia and migrated to the capital, the majority arriving by train at Wien-Nord or the now defunct Nordwestbahn, and settling, initially at least, in the surrounding district of Leopoldstadt, where housing conditions were poor and rents cheap. The Strauss family, Sigmund Freud, Gustav Mahler, Arthur Schnitzler and Theodor Herzl all lived here at some point, before moving up in the world to the city's richer suburbs.

This time around, Leopoldstadt was only ever an unofficial Jewish quarter – even at their numerical peak, in 1910, the district's 60,000 Jews only constituted a third of the population – though the area had the appearance of an old walled ghetto, partly due to the high proportion of orthodox Hasidic Jews, with their distinctive dress. With the richer Jewish families moving out at the earliest opportunity, and poorer families constantly arriving to fill their place, the area remained trapped in a cycle of poverty, attracting the underprivileged ranks of Viennese society. By the turn of the century the area was notorious as a hotbed of prostitution, much to the delight of the city's numerous anti-semites.

During World War II, the Nazis turned Leopoldstadt back into the official ghetto, and forced the city's remaining Jews into its confines. The deportations to the camps began in earnest in 1941 and by the end of the following year the ghetto's Jewish population was reduced to a few thousand, most of whom were married to gentiles. A mere 500 Jews returned to Vienna after the war, but with more recent Jewish immigration from the former eastern bloc, these numbers have increased to around 7000, many of whom have chosen to settle once more in Leopoldstadt.

Prater

Of all the places in Leopoldstadt, it is the **Prater** – derived from the Spanish *prado* (plain) – which draws the biggest crowds. This large, flat tract of land, taking up almost half the island, includes vast acres of mixed woodland, sports stadiums, racecourses, a miniature railway, allotments, a trade fair centre, a planetarium, an amusement park, and, most famously of all, the Vienna's giant ferris wheel. Aside from the Wienerwald, the Prater is by far the most popular weekend destination for any Viennese searching for a breath of fresh air, a stroll in the woods, a jog in the park, or, according to the city's current fad, a spot of rollerblading.

Traditionally a royal hunting preserve, the Prater was opened to the public in 1766 by Josef II, and soon became a popular spot for Viennese society, as the eighteenth-century Irish opera singer, Michael Kelly, noted: "there are innumerable cabarets, frequented by people of all ranks in the evening, who immediately after dinner proceed thither to regale themselves with their favourite dish, fried chicken, cold ham, and sausages; white beer, and Hoffner wines, by way of dessert; and stay there until a late hour: dancing, music, and every description of merriment prevail; and every evening, when not professionally engaged, I was sure to be in the midst of it." In 1791, Mozart broke off work to go and watch Francois Blanchard go up in a hot-air balloon, with the Archduke Franz himself cutting the rope. Throughout the nineteenth century, the Prater continued to be *the* place to be seen, particularly along the long, central Hauptallee. On Sundays, the latter was the scene of the *Praterfahrt*, when, as one observer put it, "the newest shape in carriages, the last 'sweet thing in bonnets', the most correct cut of coat *à la Anglais*, is to be seen, walking, riding, or driving up and down".

In 1873, the Prater was the venue for the empire's *Weltausstellung* or **World Trade Fair**, bringing unprecedented numbers of tourists to Vienna. Some 50,000 exhibitors from 40 countries set up displays in the exhibition's rotunda, topped by a huge cupola 108m in diameter (the rotunda burned down in 1938). Unfortunately, just eight days after the emperor opened the fair on May 1, the Vienna stock exchange collapsed and what had been touted as a celebration of the empire's thriving liberal economy became a charade. In July, to further dampen the mood, a cholera epidemic broke out in the city, claiming 3000 victims. By November, seven million admissions were recorded – thirteen million less than expected – and the fair was forced to close.

Traditionally, the **First of May** was a holiday to celebrate the arrival of spring, during which something like half the population of the city would turn up for the *Praterfahrt*. In 1890, this tradition was appropriated by the Socialist leader Viktor Adler, who helped organize the first May Day parade of workers down the Hauptallee, though he himself was in prison on the day itself. There was panic among the ruling classes; "soldiers are standing by, the doors of the houses are being closed, in people's aparments food supplies are prepared as though for an impending siege, the shops are deserted, women and children dare not go out into the street," reported the *Neue Freie Presse*. Even so, thousands took part, marching four abreast, carrying red flags and singing, and the demonstration passed off peacefully. The May Day parade quickly became a permanent fixture in the city's calendar of celebrations, though in these post-communist times, it's a pale shadow of its former self.

Visiting the Prater

The Prater is vast, and its backbone is the chestnut-lined Hauptallee which runs dead straight for 5km, from the ferris wheel and tacky Volksprater in the northwest, to the woodier section around the Lusthaus to the southeast. The easiest way of **approaching the Prater** is from the northwest, from Wien-Nord station (U-Bahn Praterstern), the terminus for tram #5 and #O, and a stop on tram #21. Alternatively, tram #N from U-Bahn Schwedenplatz has its terminus right by the Hauptallee, a third of the way down from the ferris wheel. Halfway down, bus #80B and #83A cross the Hauptallee en route to and from U-Bahn Schlachthausgasse. Finally, bus #77A from the same U-Bahn will take you all the way to or from the Lusthaus, even travelling some of the way down the Hauptallee itself.

    Getting around the Prater, you can walk, jog, rollerblade, cycle, take a fiacre, or rent one of the pedal carriages, which seat two adults (plus two kids if you wish). Another possibility is to buy a one-way ticket on the miniature railway or Liliputbahn, which will get you almost halfway down the Hauptallee.

Volksprater

The easiest point of access from the city centre – and by far the busiest section of the Prater – is the northwest end, where you'll find the park's permanent funfair, known as the **Volksprater**. (It's also known as the *Wurstelprater*, not for the sausages sold in abundance here, but for the Punch-like character of Hanswurst, whose puppet booths were once a common sight.) Tourists flock to the Volksprater for the Riesenrad, but the Viennese come here for the other **rides,** a strange mixture ranging from high-tech helter-skelters and white-knuckle affairs to more traditional fairground rides like ghost trains, dodgems and strength contests judging participants from *Weichling* (weakling), through *Fräulein* (girly) to *Weltmeister* (world champion). The fair has an impressive range of bad-taste attractions, too, including a tawdry "Sex-Museum" and a "Jack the Ripper" dark ride, with mock graves of the victims on the outside. For the kids, there are bouncy castles, horse rides and even a rather sad sleigh carousel pulled by real ponies.

    The atmosphere is generally fairly relaxed during the day, though it can get a little bit more charged at night. If you get lost, you should be able to orientate yourself by one of the two open areas, Rondeau and Calafattiplatz, named after the man who set up the first carousel in the Prater in 1840. The easiest point of reference of all is, of course, the Riesenrad. Sadly, there are no longer over fifty restaurants and pubs to choose from as there were a hundred years ago, but if you're peckish, there's no shortage of *Wurst* stands, plus a few more appetizing options, such as the famous *Schweizer Haus* (see p.291), whose roast pig is legendary.

The Volksprater is open Easter–Oct daily 8am–midnight; the nearest U-Bahn is Praterstern.

Riesenrad

Taking a ride on the **Riesenrad** (Giant Wheel) is one of those things you simply have to do if you go to Vienna; it's also a must for fans of the film *The Third Man*, as the place in front of which Orson Welles does his famous "cuckoo clock" speech. Built in 1898 for the Emperor Franz-Josef I's golden jubilee celebrations, the Riesenrad was designed by the British military engineer Walter Basset, who had constructed similar ferris wheels in Blackpool and Paris (both long since demolished). The cute little red gondolas were destroyed during World War II, and only half were replaced after 1945 in deference to the Riesenrad's old age. Acrophobes can reassure themselves with the fact that the gondolas, which hold up to twelve people standing, are entirely enclosed, though they do tend to wobble around a bit, and reach a height of over 65m. You should also be prepared for the fact that the wheel doesn't so much spin as stagger slowly round, as each gondola fills up with passengers; once you've done a complete circuit, you've had your twenty-minute ride.

The Riesenrad is open April daily 10am–11pm; May–Sept daily 9am–midnight; Oct daily 10am–10pm; Nov, Christmas–Jan 6 until 6pm; rest of Dec Sat & Sun only; öS45.

Prater Museum and Planetarium

If you've no interest in the amusements at the Volksprater, you're probably best off heading instead for the nearby **Prater Museum**, which records the golden age of the funfair. Old photographs of the likes of Semona, the fiery Amazonian snake charmer, and Liliputstadt, an entire miniature city inhabited by dwarves, give you something of the nineteenth-century flavour. Also displayed here are some of the characters from Hanswurst, various antique slot machines (some of which you can play on) and a model of the 1873 *Weltausstellung*. The museum is housed in one room of the **Planetarium** (closed Aug to mid-Sept), founded by the German optician Carl Zeiss in 1927, which puts on a varied programme, with commentary nearly always in German. Pick up one of the leaflets to find out the latest listings.

The Prater Museum is open Tues–Fri 9am–12.15pm & 1–4.30pm, Sat & Sun 2–6.30pm; closed Aug; öS25.

Beyond the Volksprater

The quickest method of escape from the Volksprater is by the miniature railway, known as the Liliputbahn, which runs from near the Riesenrad over to the main Stadion, a return trip of around 4km. The engines are mostly diesel, but some steam trains run in the summer. There are three stations: Praterstern by the ferris wheel, Rotunde, named after the now defunct exhibition hall of the 1873 *Weltausstellung*, and Stadion. En route, you pass the Hockey-stadion and Bowling-halle to the south, the ugly, expansive Messegelände (trade fair grounds) and the Krieau Trabrennbahn (trotting-racecourse), to the north.

The Liliputbahn runs April to mid-Oct daily 10am–11pm; öS20 one-way; öS35 return.

Prater Stadion

Beyond the Trabrennbahn, the **Prater Stadion** (aka the Wiener or Ernst-Happel-Stadion) opened in July 1931 with the International Workers' Olympics. The playing field was transformed into a giant stage, on which 4000 musicians, actors and gymnasts re-enacted the struggle of Labour over Capital from the Middle Ages to the present day. As a grand finale, the giant gilt idol, representing capitalism, was toppled, thousands of youths dressed in white marched forward carrying red flags and the crowd sang the *Internationale*. The show was repeated four times that year before a total audience of 260,000, and proved the cultural highpoint of inter-war "Red Vienna" (see p.227).

The museum is open Mon & Fri 10am–1pm, Tues & Thurs 2–6pm; closed Jan, Feb & school holidays; öS30.

The stadium itself – the largest in Austria, holding just over 60,000 spectators – was given a face-lift in the 1980s, including the addition of a technically remarkable roof; invisible from the outside, it's a self-supporting light steel structure that hangs gracefully over the terraces. Despite this, the stadium remains underused, hosting no regular soccer matches, only the odd European or international match, plus sporadic large-scale pop concerts. On the north side of the stadium, along Meiereistrasse, is the **Fussball-Museum**, which traces the history of Austrian soccer, whose golden days were back in the early 1930s before the Austro-fascists took over.

Beyond the Stadion

Notwithstanding the Autobahn and the railway line that cut across the southeastern half of the Prater, the woods beyond the Stadion are among the most peaceful sections of the entire park, perfect for a picnic. If you've no provisions, walk to the far end of the Hauptallee where

For details of the Lusthaus *and* Altes Jägerhaus, *see p.291.*

you'll find the **Lusthaus** restaurant, a pretty octagonal building, remodelled from a hunting lodge into a pleasure palace by Isidor Canevale in 1783. During the Congress of Vienna, it served as the centrepiece for a mass picnic laid on for 18,000 soldiers on the first anniversary of the 1813 Battle of Leipzig. It now forms the island of a roundabout, but preserves its original frescoed interior, and is still a popular spot for lunch, as is the more rustic *Altes Jägerhaus*, opposite.

To the southeast of the Lusthaus lies the **Freudenau Rennbahn**, a lovingly restored racecourse from the late nineteenth century. The racing season traditionally opens on Easter Sunday and reaches its apogee during the annual Derby, organized by the Austrian Jockey Club since 1868, the year it was founded. Held on a Sunday in June, the Derby used to be attended almost unfailingly by the emperor himself, with various aristocrats often among the riders, and the wealthy young Viennese crowd dressed to the nines.

Central Leopoldstadt

Though Leopoldstadt's days as a flourishing Jewish quarter are a distant memory, the pockets of kosher shops on Hollandstrasse and Tempelgasse, and the new Jewish school on Castellezgasse, are evidence of the area's modest Jewish renaissance. The surviving wing of the district's largest synagogue, the neo-Byzantine **Leopoldstädter Tempel**, on Tempelgasse, gives a vague idea of the building's former

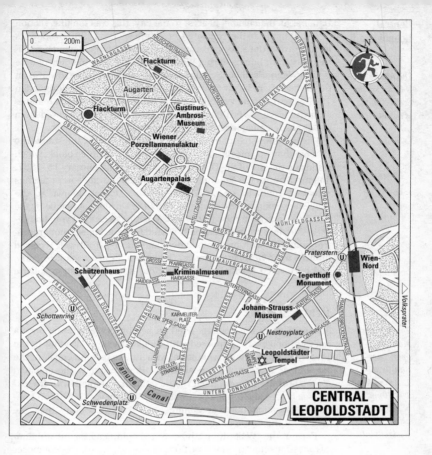

Map showing CENTRAL LEOPOLDSTADT, with a scale of 0–200m. Labelled features include: Flackturm, Augarten, Gustinus-Ambrosi-Museum, Wiener Porzellanmanufaktur, Augartenpalais, Schützenhaus, Kriminalmuseum, Schottenring, Johann-Strauss-Museum, Nestroyplatz, Leopoldstädter Tempel, Praterstern, Wien-Nord, Tegetthoff Monument, Volksprater, Schwedenplatz, and Danube Canal. Streets labelled include Wasnergasse, Rauscherstrasse, Nordbahnstrasse, Taborstrasse, Am Tabor, Obere Augartenstrasse, Unter Augartenstrasse, Castellezgasse, Heinestrasse, Grosse Stadtgutgasse, Mühlfeldgasse, Malzgasse, Novaragasse, Blumauergasse, Grosse Sperlgasse, Pfarrgasse, Haidgasse, Rotensterngasse, Obere Donaustrasse, Franz-Josefs-Kai, Holland-strasse, Kleine Sperlgasse, Karmeliter-platz, Lilienbrunngasse, Krakauerstrasse, Tabor-strasse, Grosse Pfargasse, Praterstrasse, Czerningasse, Zirkusgasse, Tempelgasse, Ferdinandstrasse, Gredlerstrasse, Untere Donaustrasse, Franzensbrückenstrasse.

glory; there's a mosaic from the missing central section on the facade of the Desider Friedmann building on the corner of Ferdinandgasse and Tempelgasse. Elsewhere, at Kleine Sperlgasse 2a and Malzgasse 7, plaques record two of the locations used by the Nazis to round up the city's Jews for deportation to the camps. Otherwise, there's really very little to see in contemporary Leopoldstadt, beyond the **Johann Strauss-Museum**, and, perhaps, the collection of sculptures in the **Gustinus Ambrosi-Museum**. And if Meissen porcelain is your thing, the Augarten **Porzellanmanufaktur** will not disappoint.

The Danube Canal

The **Danube Canal** (Donaukanal), which separates Leopoldstadt from the old town, is the narrowest of the four arms of the River

*The nearest
U-Bahn for the
Schützenhaus
is Schottenring.*

Danube. As the channel nearest to the city, this was the first section of the Danube to be regulated, as far back as 1598. Despite its human proportions, its banks are by no means pretty, having been an easy target for bombs during World War II. The only building of note is Otto Wagner's dinky **Schützenhaus** (literally "defence tower"), on the embankment below Obere Donaustrasse, a late work designed in 1907 as part of a now defunct weir. Clad in white marble, it features a playful wave pattern of cobalt blue tiles, and is best viewed from the opposite embankment below Franz-Josefs-Kai.

Further downstream from the Schützenhaus, at no. 95, stands the IBM building, a typically unimaginative corporate office block, which stands on the site of the Diana Rooms, where, on February 15, 1867, **Johann Strauss the Younger** first performed the city's most famous signature tune *An der schönen, blauen Donau*, known to the English-speaking world simply as *The Blue Danube*. A plaque by the building's entrance records the fact. What it doesn't tell you, however, is that the waltz was originally scored for male chorus, not orchestra, complete with ludicrous lyrics, and wasn't at all well received after its inept first performance. Only when Strauss took it to Paris, and performed it with an orchestra, did it become a stratospheric success.

Praterstrasse

*The Strauss-
Museum is
open Tues–
Sun 9am–
12.15pm &
1–4.30pm;
öS25; the near-
est U-Bahn is
Nestroyplatz.*

Johann Strauss the Younger lived on nearby **Praterstrasse**, once a majestic boulevard, peppered with Yiddish theatres, leading to the Prater, now just a busy, wide street with little to recommend it. At the far end of Praterstrasse, nearest the Prater, stands the splendid **Tegetthoff Monument**, a tall rostral column, complete with frolicking sea horses and topped by a statue of Wilhelm von Tegetthoff himself, celebrating the rear admiral's 1866 naval victory over the Italians at the Battle of Lissa.

Fans of the "Waltz King", however, should head for the **Johann-Strauss-Museum** on the first floor of no. 54, where the composer lived from 1863 until the death of his first wife, the singer Jetty Treffz, in 1878. In contrast to most of the city's musical museums, some attempt has been made here to re-create a period interior; one room, decorated with ceiling panels of cherubs, contains his grand piano, house organ and standing desk at which he used to compose. There's also a fascinating collection of ephemera from the balls of the day, with various gimmicky dance cards – one laid out in the form of a staircase – and quirky ball pendants, which were kept as a sort of memento of the evening.

Kriminalmuseum

Leopoldstadt's most popular museum is the **Kriminalmuseum** (Museum of Crime), a prurient overview of Vienna's most gruesome

The Strauss Family

Of all the many tunes associated with Vienna, perhaps the best known are the waltzes composed by the Strausses. Born in Vienna to a Jewish innkeeper in Leopoldstadt, **Johann Strauss the Elder** (1804–49) kept quiet about his origins, though it was the Nazis themselves who felt the need to falsify the parish register of Vienna's Stephansdom, in order to make the Strauss family appear as true Aryans (a similar leniency was shown towards Hitler's much-loved composer Franz Léhar, whose wife was Jewish). Strauss began his career serenading diners in Viennese restaurants, along with the likes of Josef Lanner, who was to become his chief musical rival. However, it was in the dance hall of *Zum Sperl* in Leopoldstadt that Strauss the Elder made his name as a band leader, conducting a mixture of dances, orchestral phantasies and more serious music. His gypsy-like features, and wild, vigorous conducting style soon became very popular in Vienna. Later, he and his orchestra achieved a modicum of fame touring Europe, and he was eventually appointed *k.k. Hofballmusikdirektor* (Imperial-Royal Director of Music for Balls). Strauss's touring took its toll on domestic life, and he created a public scandal in 1842, when he left the family home and moved in with a young seamstress, who bore him several illegitimate children.

His eldest son, **Johann Strauss the Younger** (1825–99), followed in his footsteps, writing his first waltz at the age of six, though much against the latter's wishes (he wanted him to be a banker). It was, in fact, Johann's long-suffering mother, Anna, who directed her sons into musical careers. Father and son soon became rivals, both musically and politically. In 1848, while the Elder was busy conducting his famous *Radetsky March*, the signature tune of the *ancien régime*, the Younger was composing stirring tunes such as the *Revolution March* and the *Song of the Barricades*. Fourteen years after his father's death, Strauss the Younger was appointed *k.k. Hofballmusikdirektor* in 1863, rapidly surpassing even his father's enormous fame. He was one of the world's first international celebrities, feted on both sides of the Atlantic. On one memorable occasion in Boston in the US, he conducted *The Blue Danube* with 20,000 singers, an orchestra of over 1000, and 20 assistant conductors, to an audience of more than 100,000. Johann's operetta, *Die Fledermaus*, written to take Viennese minds off the economic crash of 1873, was another huge success – by the end of the decade, it was playing in some 170 theatres.

Despite his success, Johann, a difficult character like his father, was something of an outsider. He was also constantly irked by his lack of acclaim among serious musical critics, and his several attempts at straight opera flopped. Again like his father, he too caused a scandal, divorcing his second wife, Lili, in order to marry his mistress Adele. As the Vatican would not annul his marriage, he was forced to convert to Lutheranism and become a citizen of Saxony, though he continued to live in Vienna until his death in 1899.

As for the remaining Strauss sons, Johann's two younger brothers, **Josef** – "the romantic-looking, chaotically pale" Strauss as he was dubbed by one Viennese critic – and **Eduard**, were also musicians (again against their absent father's wishes). Josef was a successful composer in his own right, but died at the age of forty-three, while Eduard became *k.k. Hofballmusikdirektor* after Johann in 1872 and was left in charge of the Strauss orchestra.

*The Kriminal-
museum is
open Tues–
Sun 10am–
5pm; öS60.*

*To get to the
Augarten, take
tram #31 two
stops from
U-Bahn
Schottenring.*

*The museum is
open Tues–
Sun 10am–
5pm; öS60;
take tram #5
from U-Bahn
Praterstern.*

*The Porzellan-
manufaktur is
open Mon–Fri
9am–6pm, Sat
9am–noon;
free.*

*The Augarten-
palais is closed
to the public.*

crimes, at Grosse Sperlgasse 24. In between the voyeuristic photos of autopsies, there are some interesting sections on the city's social and political history, though with labelling in German only, these are lost on most foreign visitors. To cap it all, there's a fairly gratuitous section on flagellation, while the biggest criminals of the lot – the Nazis – get only the very briefest of mentions. All in all, it's worth giving this museum a wide berth.

Augarten

The **Augarten**, in the north of Leopoldstadt, is one of Vienna's oldest parks, laid out in formal French style in 1650, and opened to the public in 1775 by Josef II. Sadly, it's come down in the world since its fashionable halcyon days when Mozart gave morning concerts here, and, a century later, Strauss the Younger championed Wagner's overtures. Old-age pensioners are the park's main visitors now, and the melancholic air is further compounded by the forbidding presence of not one, but two World War II Flacktürme (see p.172). These sinister concrete hulks put the dampeners on the formal section of the park; the only way to escape them is to head off into the woody network of chesnut-lined paths to the north.

Hidden in this dense section of the park, by the eastern boundary, is the intriguing **Gustinus-Ambrosi-Museum**, a little-visited offshoot of the Österreichische Galerie, which runs the Belvedere (the same ticket is valid for both). It's devoted to the prolific Austrian sculptor, Gustinus Ambrosi (1893–1975), whose larger works are clearly influenced by Auguste Rodin. However, Ambrosi is at his best with his bronze portrait heads, of which there are plenty here, his subjects drawn mainly from the artistic and political circles of the inter-war period. Note the emaciated Otto Wagner the year before his death, a suitably overblown Nietsche, and a youthful Mussolini (with hair).

On the ruins of the Alte Favorita, Leopold I's summer palace, which was burnt to the ground by the Turks in 1683, Josef II erected a long, low-lying garden pavilion. From 1782, the pavilion's restaurant was the venue of the fashionable musical matinées conducted by the likes of Mozart and Beethoven; the building now serves as the headquarters of the **Wiener Porzellanmanufaktur**, founded in 1718, eight years after Meissen. The factory's famous "flower and figure" porcelain is exhibited in the Hofsilber- und Tafelkammer in the Hofburg (see p.84), though temporary exhibitions are also staged in the showroom foyer. The factory's current offerings – from gaudy Rococo to more subtle designs by the likes of Josef Hoffmann – are sold in the adjacent shop.

The **Augartenpalais**, to the east of the Porzellanmanufaktur, was designed by Johann Bernhard Fischer von Erlach at the end of the seventeenth century, and bought by the Emperor Josef II in 1780. Unfortunately, you can't get a good look at the building, as it's now the boarding school of the *Wiener Sängerknaben* (Vienna Boys'

Choir), for more on which see p.88. Those boys whose voices have broken are housed in the **Kaiser-Josef-Stöckl**, a pavilion hidden behind the palace, designed by Isidor Canevale in 1781 for Josef II, who preferred the Augarten above all his other residences.

Central
Leopoldstadt

Donauinsel and Kaisermühlen

In the second half of the nineteenth century, the main course of the River Danube was straightened to allow larger vessels to dock. A parallel channel, the slow-flowing Neue Donau, was cut in the 1970s, thus creating a long, thin, artificial island, officially known as the **Donauinsel**, though dubbed variously Spaghetti Island or Copa Cagrana (after the end station on the nearby U-Bahn line). The original course of the Danube, to the east of the Neue Donau, was simultaneously dammed to create the semi-circular nub of land known as **Kaisermühlen**, home to Vienna's UNO-City and the accompanying Donaupark. Neither deserves to top your itinerary, but each provides an interesting insight into modern Viennese life.

Donauinsel

To be perfectly honest, the **Donauinsel** – measuring 20km by just 200m – is pretty bleak, a situation not helped by the views over to the unsightly east bank. Nevertheless, the Viennese flock to the beaches here in the summer, when the island's numerous bars, discos and food stalls, centred around the Donauinsel U-Bahn station, open for custom. Joggers, skateboarders and cyclists also use the island, and every June it becomes the focus for the *Donauinselfest*, an open-air rock festival with fireworks. To the north, there's a huge water sports complex, *Aquadrom*, with a 200m-long water slide, boat rental, windsurfing and the like. To the south, there are fixed barbecue spots, and a nudist beach (FKK).

There are two U-Bahn stations on the Donauinsel: Donauinsel in the centre, and Neue Donau, to the north.

Vienna International Centre and the Donaupark

Since 1979, the **Vienna International Centre** – known as VIC to its inmates, and UNO-City to the mapmakers – has been the United Nations' number-three base, after New York and Geneva. The idea for this was first mooted by the then UN Secretary General, Austrian Kurt Waldheim, and its construction nearly bankrupted the country. The UN functionaries, until then housed in the Hofburg, were none too happy either. Today, the VIC is home to, among other bureaucracies, the International Atomic Energy Authority, the Commission for Infectious Diseases, and the ever-busy High Commission for Refugees (UNHCR).

The nearest U-Bahn is Kaisermühlen-Vienna International Centre.

Of the 4000 folk employed here, only a third are Austrians, but the place is clearly an important source of income for the city, and has ensured Vienna a bit part on the international stage. The adjacent

Donauinsel and Kaisermühlen

There are guided tours of the VIC Mon–Fri 11am & 2pm; öS40.

The Donauturm is open daily April–Sept 9.30am–midnight; Oct–March 10am–10pm; öS60.

conference centre – the imaginatively named Austria Center Vienna – completed in 1987 at a cost of millions, has proved less of a money-spinner. However, whatever the financial benefits, UNO-City is not a beautiful place to visit. Within earshot of a roaring Autobahn, cordoned off with wire fencing, and bristling with armed police and CCTV cameras, the whole place is intimidating and, essentially, ugly. The six Y-shaped, glass-fronted high-rise offices rise to a height of 110m, and radiate from a central block like a three-legged man on the run. The interior is generously sprinkled with works of art by contemporary Austrian artists, and you can sign up for a guided tour should you so wish; tours start from Checkpoint One.

It's with a certain amount of relief that you descend from the VIC to the adjacent **Donaupark**, laid out on an old rubbish dump in 1964 as part of the Vienna International Garden Show. The most pleasant section is around the artificial lake, Irissee, and in the rose garden and walled Chinese garden beyond. An added incentive for kids is the miniature railway, the **Kleinbahn**, which wends its way around the park (round-trip öS35). Last, but not least, there's the futuristic **Donauturm** (Danube Tower), which reaches a height of 252m. For a not insignificant sum (öS60), you can take the lift to the viewing platform, and for even more money, you can eat in one of the tower's two revolving restaurants.

Chapter 8

Schönbrunn, the Wienerwald and the Zentralfriedhof

V ienna's outer suburbs or *Vororte* have little to recommend them for the most part. Until 1890, they lay beyond the city limits of the Gürtel, and since then have been ruthlessly built over in order to properly accommodate the city's population.

There are, of course, exceptions, the prime one being **Schönbrunn**, the Habsburgs' former summer residence to the west of the city centre, which is one of Vienna's most popular tourist sights after the Hofburg. The palace boasts some of the best Rococo interiors in central Europe, while the surrounding **Schlosspark** is home to the **Tiergarten**, Vienna's zoo, the **Schmetterlinghaus** (Butterfly House) and the **Palmenhaus** (Palm House). To the west of the neighbouring villa district of **Hietzing** is the much wilder parkland of the **Lainzer Tiergarten**, a former royal hunting ground that's now a haven for wildlife.

The rest of the suburbs have a scattering of interesting museums and sights that call for a targeted approach, relying on the tram system to get you around. Vienna is very lucky to have the **Wienerwald** (Vienna Woods) on its doorstep, and a trip up to one of its forested hills is rewarded with glorious views over the entire city. Finally, there's the **Zentralfriedhof**, Vienna's truly awesome Central Cemetery, with a population almost twice that of the city itself, and featuring the graves of the likes of Beethoven, Schubert, Brahms, Schönberg and the Strauss family.

Schönbrunn

Compared with the hotchpotch that is the Hofburg, the Habsburgs' summer residence of **Schönbrunn** is everything an imperial palace should be: grandiose, symmetrical and thoroughly intimidating. Built

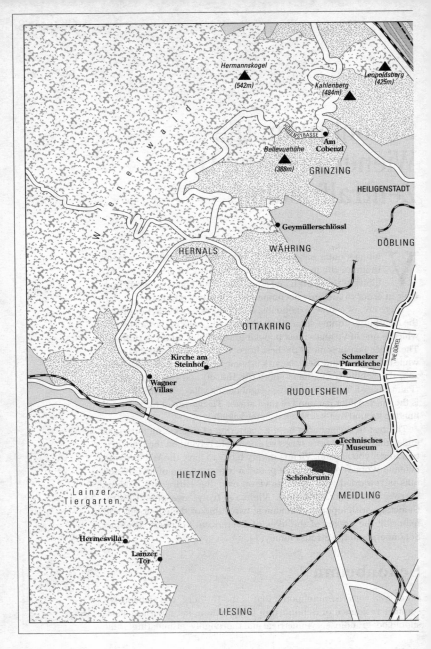

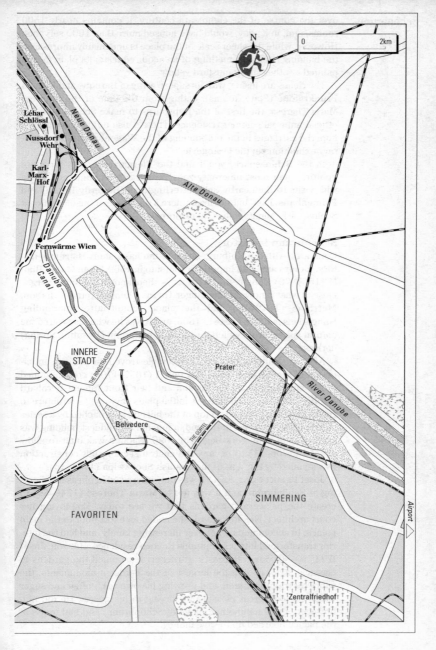

over the course of the eighteenth century, it contains nearly 1500 rooms, and, in its day, would have housed more than 1000 servants. However, while the sheer scale of the place is undeniably impressive, the building itself is something of an acquired taste, its plain facade painted a rather sickly mustard yellow.

The riches are inside, with its superb array of Baroque and Rococo **Prunkräume** (State Rooms), dating from the time of the Empress Maria Theresa, the first of the Habsburgs to make Schönbrunn the official imperial summer residence. There's also a fine collection of imperial carriages in the outbuilding of the **Wagenburg**, plus temporary exhibitions in the **Orangerie**.

In the **Schlosspark**, you'll find the **Tiergarten** (Zoo), far more uplifting than most inner-city zoos, which can be combined easily with visits to the nearby **Schmetterlinghaus** (Butterfly House) and **Palmenhaus**. Last, but not least, there's the whole of the magnificent Schlosspark, and its follies, to explore.

Schönbrunn in history

Compared with the Hofburg, Schönbrunn has a short Habsburg history. It only came into imperial ownership in 1569, when **Maximilian II** (1564–76) bought the property – then known as Katterburg – close to what is now the Meidlinger Tor, as a hunting retreat. His son, **Matthias** (1612–19) had the place rebuilt after marauding Hungarians laid it to waste in 1605, and it was he who discovered the natural spring, from which the name Schönbrunn (Beautiful Spring) derives.

After the Habsburgs themselves had destroyed the place in anticipation of the Turks in 1683, **Leopold I** (1657–1705) commissioned a new summer palace for his son and heir from Johann Bernhard Fischer von Erlach. The latter's initial plans envisaged a structure to rival Versailles, perched on top of the hill and approached by a series of grandiose terraces. In the end, a much more modest building was agreed upon, and work began in 1696. Enough was built to allow **Josef I** (1705–11) to occupy the central section, but construction was stymied by the War of the Spanish Succession (1701–14).

Josef I's successor, Karl VI, was only interested in pheasant-shooting at Schönbrunn, and it was left to **Maria Theresa** (1740–80) to create the palace and gardens that we see today. Employing her court architect, Nicolo Pacassi, she added an extra floor to the main palace, to accommodate her ever increasing family, and had the interior transformed into a sumptuous Rococo residence. Her son, **Josef II** (1780–90), an enthusiastic gardener, rearranged the gardens in classical style, adding the largest of the garden's monuments, the Gloriette triumphal arch, and growing his own tea, coffee and sugar which he took great pleasure in serving to his guests. He did not, however, share his mother's love of Schönbrunn, and had much of the palace boarded up to save money.

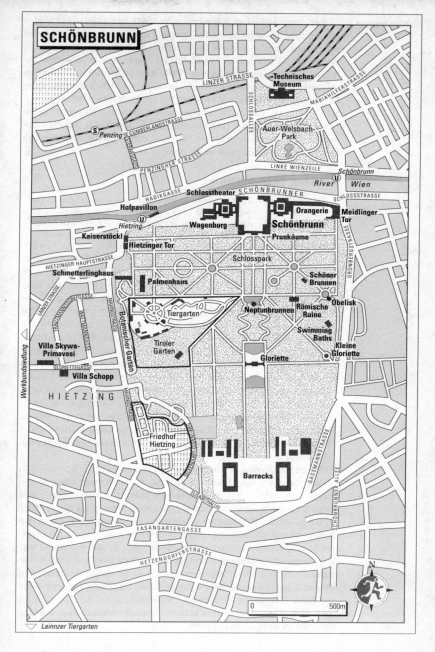

SCHÖNBRUNN

- LINZER STRASSE
- Technisches Museum
- SCHLOSSALLEE
- MARIAHILFERSTRASSE
- Auer-Welsbach Park
- Penzing
- CUMBERLANDSTRASSE
- OSTMARKGASSE
- PENZINGHER STRASSE
- LINKE WIENZEILE
- Schönbrunn River
- Wien
- SCHLOSSSTRASSE
- HADIKGASSE
- SCHÖNBRUNNER
- Schlosstheater
- Hofpavillon
- Hietzing
- Wagenburg
- Orangerie
- Schönbrunn
- Meidlinger Tor
- Kaiserstöckl
- Hietzinger Tor
- Prunkäume
- GRÜNBERGSTRASSE
- HIETZINGER HAUPTSTRASSE
- Schmetterlinghaus
- Palmenhaus
- Schlosspark
- Schöner Brunnen
- LAINZER STRASSE
- TRAUTMANNSDORFGASSE
- WATTMANNGASSE
- Botanischer Garten
- MAXINGSTRASSE
- Tiergarten
- Neptunbrunnen
- Römische Ruine
- Obelisk
- Swimming Baths
- Werkbundsiedlung
- Villa Skywa-Primavesi
- Tiroler Garten
- Gloriette
- Kleine Gloriette
- GLORIETTEGASSE
- Villa Schopp
- HIETZING
- MAXINGSTRASSE
- Friedhof Hietzing
- Barracks
- GASSMANNSTRASSE
- ELISABETHALLEE
- SCHÖNBRUNNER ALLEE
- FASANGARTENGASSE
- HETZENDORFERSTRASSE
- N
- 0   500m
- Lainnzer Tiergarten

Napoleon stayed at Schönbrunn in 1805 and 1809 – his eagles can still be seen on the main gates – and his son, the Duke of Reichstadt, lived out most of his brief life here, too. However, it wasn't until the reign of **Franz-Josef I** – who was born within the palace in 1830 and died here in 1916 – that Schönbrunn once more occupied centre stage in court life. In November 1918, the last of the Habsburgs, **Karl I**, signed away, in the palace's Blue Chinese Salon, all hopes of preserving the monarchy and thereafter the entire place became state property. Badly damaged in World War II, Schönbrunn served first as the Soviet, and then the British, army headquarters before being handed back to the state in 1947.

Visiting Schönbrunn

Surely this receptacle of abominations could not have existed in its present state during the reign of Maria Theresa. It is impossible to believe that one, whose days may be counted by the noble and beautiful works with which she adorned her empire, could have passed to her imperial creation at Schönbrunn within reach of this black and noxious stream, and suffered its unhallowed waters to flow between the wind and her regality.

The comments by Anthony Trollope's mother in 1838 on the foul-smelling River Wien, which flowed past the main gates of Schönbrunn, were not atypical of nineteenth-century tourists. Though the river no longer stinks like it once did, approaches to the palace now suffer from a different kind of plague: the roar of traffic from the nearby Linke Wienzeile and Schönbrunner Schlossstrasse. Consequently, the best way to **get there** is to head straight for the Meidlinger Tor on Grünbergstrasse from U-Bahn Schönbrunn, rather than struggle along the multi-lane freeway to the main gates. You could also continue one stop further on the U-Bahn to Hietzing, and dive into the park via the Hietzinger Tor on Hietzinger Hauptstrasse. This enables you to peek at the nearby Hofpavillon Hietzing, the imperial family's private U-Bahn station (see p.214).

If you're thinking of visiting the Prunkräume (State Rooms), you should head for the **ticket office** first, to book your place in the queue (see below). For **refreshments**, there's a reasonably priced *Beisl* near the Wagenburg, and a coffee shop beyond the ticket office in the palace itself. Whatever you do, don't be hoodwinked into going to the overpriced café-restaurant, on the east side of the main courtyard. In summer, tea and cakes are on offer in the wonderful surroundings of the Gloriette, and there are a fair few food stalls in the main courtyard. The Tiergarten has still more eating options, from *Wurst* stands to restaurants – you can even fix your own picnic from the food shop in the Tirolerhaus. Nevertheless, by far the cheapest and most convenient option is to bring your own supplies and find somewhere to relax in the park.

Prunkräume

Compared to the sterility of the Hofburg's state apartments, Schönbrunn's **Prunkräume** (State Rooms) are a positive visual feast. That said, not every room is worthy of close attention, so don't feel bad about walking briskly through some of them. Visits to the Prunkräume are carefully choreographed. First, you must make your way to the ticket office on the ground floor of the east wing. Here, you'll be allocated a visiting time; if the palace is busy, you may well have to wait several hours, in which case you should head off into the gardens, or visit one of Schönbrunn's other sights.

The Prunkräume are open April–Oct daily 8.30am– 5pm; Nov– March until 4.30pm.

There's a choice of two tours: the "Imperial Tour" (öS80), which takes in 22 state rooms, and the "Grand Tour" (öS110), which includes all 40 rooms open to the public. Even if you're no great fan of period interiors, it seems pointless to go on the "Imperial Tour", since it skips some of the palace's most magnificent Rococo delights. For both tours, you are given a hand-held audioguide in English; for the "Grand Tour", you also get the option of paying extra for an hour-long tour with a guide (öS140). The disadvantage of following a tour guide is that they give you the same, short space of time in each room, whether it's worth pausing in or not.

Emperor Franz-Josef I and Empress Elisabeth's apartments

Whichever tour you're on, the entrance is via the **Blauerstiege** (Blue Staircase) on the ground floor of the west wing. If you're on the "Imperial Tour", you'll miss the nine private apartments of Franz-Josef – no great loss, as anyone who's been to the Hofburg will tell you – entering at Elisabeth's Salon (see below).

For more on the Emperor Franz-Josef I, see p.81.

Visitors on the "Grand Tour", meanwhile, pass through the Guard Room into the **Billiard Room**, where, in Franz-Josef's day, those wishing an audience with the emperor were made to wait. While kicking their heels, they could admire the paintings, but sadly weren't invited actually to play billiards. Audiences with the emperor were given in the **Nussbaumzimmer** (Walnut Room) next door, named after the wood used for the chairs and gilded Rococo panelling; even the chandelier is carved from wood (painted over with pure gold). A nasty brown lines the walls of the emperor's gloomy **Study**, where Franz-Josef spent much of the day stood over his desk, pedantically reading and signing thousands of official documents; on the wall is a portrait of the Empress Elisabeth at sixteen, when she was betrothed to Franz-Josef. Next is the widower's **Bedroom**, with the simple iron bed on which the emperor died on November 21, 1916, at the age of 86. Beside it stands Franz Matsch's reverential rendition of the scene.

Passing through several tiny rooms, where the emperor did his ablutions, you come to the imperial couple's **Bedroom**, decorated in time for their nuptials in 1854 with matching blue Lyon silk upholstery, and twin rosewood beds. Elisabeth managed to avoid consum-

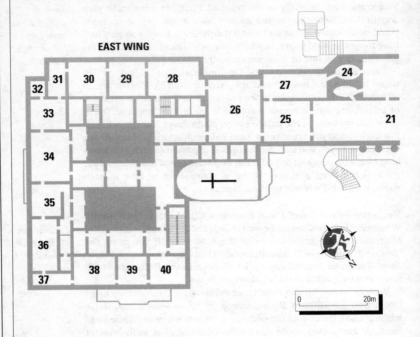

SCHÖNBRUNN: PRUNKRÄUME

EAST WING

32 31 30 29 28 27 24 26 25 21 33 34 35 36 37 38 39 40

0 — 20m

N

1. Guard Room
2. Billiard Room
3. Nussbaumzimmer
4. Franz-Josef's Study
5. Franz-Josef's Bedroom
6. West Terrace Cabinet
7. Stair Cabinet
8. Toilet Room
9. Joint Bedroom
10. Elisabeth's Salon

11. Marie-Antoinette Room
12. Nursery
13. Breakfast Room
14. Yellow Salon
15. Balcony Room
16. Spiegelsaal
17. Large Rosa Room
18. Small Rosa Room
19. Small Rosa Room
20. Lamp Room

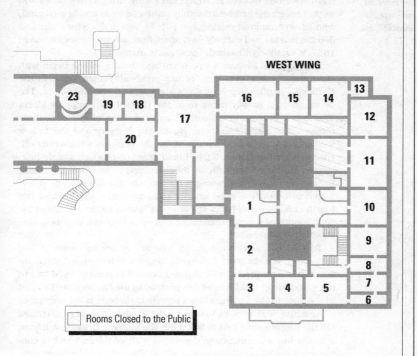

WEST WING

23	19 18	16 15 14 13
	17	12
	20	11
	1	10
	2	9 8
	3 4 5	7 6

Rooms Closed to the Public

21. Great Gallery
22. Little Gallery
23. Round Chinese Cabinet
24. Oval Chinese Cabinet
25. Carousel Room
26. Ceremonial Hall
27. Rössel Room
28. Blue Chinese Salon
29. Vieux-Laque Room
30. Napoleon Room

31. Porcelain Room
32. Miniatures Room
33. Millions Room
34. Gobelin Hall
35. Memorial Room
36. Red Salon
37. East Terrace Cabinet
38. Maria Theresa's Bedroom
39. Franz Karl's Study
40. Franz Karl's Salon

mating the marriage for the first two nights. The story goes that at family breakfast on the first morning, Elisabeth's crabby mother-in-law, the formidable Archduchess Sophie, asked her how well her son had performed in bed, at which the young bride broke down and wept. Though the empress dutifully produced a son and heir (Rudolf, who later committed suicide, see p.242), within five years, she had fled the marital bed entirely, and apart from a brief reconciliation in 1867, it's unlikely Elisabeth spent many nights here.

The Empress Elisabeth's personal apartments, which begin with her **Salon**, smack even less of her personality than those in the Hofburg – hardly surprising since she spent so little time here. The decor, in fact, mostly dates from the time of the Empress **Maria Theresa**, a century or so earlier, and the walls of the next three rooms – the Marie Antoinette Room, the Nursery and the Yellow Salon – are lined with portraits of the the empress's numerous off-spring. After her father, Karl VI, had failed to produce a male heir, leaving Maria Theresa with an uphill struggle to convince the rest of Europe she was "man" enough for the job, she herself was deter-mined to produce a good cropful of heirs – after the birth of her fourth child, she was heard to comment "I wish I were already in the sixth month of a new pregnancy". Out of her sixteen children, nine survived to adulthood.

Two of her sons went on to become emperors, Josef II and Leopold II, but the most famous of the lot was her youngest daugh-ter, **Marie Antoinette**, who married Louis XVI and followed him to the guillotine in 1793. Under her portrait in the Nursery, to the right of the door to the Empress Zita's private bathroom, is the only piece of furniture sent back to Vienna by the French after her execution. Off the Empire-style Yellow Salon lies the intimate **Breakfast Room**, a frothy Rococo concoction decorated with gilded cartouches con-taining floral silk embroidered by Maria Theresa and her daughters.

The state apartments

The first of the more elaborate state apartments is the **Spiegelsaal** (Mirror Hall), where, in 1762, the precocious seven-year-old Mozart performed a duet with his older sister Nannerl, in the presence of the Empress Maria Theresa and family, and famously "sprang on the lap of the empress, put his arms round her neck and vigorously kissed her", according to his father. From here you enter the **Large Rosa Room**, named for the idealized landscapes executed by the Polish court painter Josef Rosa in the 1760s, set into gilded frames on the walls.

The **Great Gallery** is, without doubt, the most splendid of all the rooms so far, a vast long hall, heavy with gilded stucco embellish-ments, lined with fluted pilasters sporting acanthus capitals and orig-inally lit by over 4000 candles. Of the three ceiling frescoes by Guglielmo Guglielmi glorifying the Habsburgs, the last – depicting

Austria's military prowess – was, ironically enough, destroyed by bomb damage in World War II, and is therefore a copy. Naturally, the hall was used for banquets during the Congress of Vienna in 1815, and it was here, in 1961, that J. F. Kennedy and Nikita Krushchev held their historic *détente* meeting.

It's worth venturing from here into the **Little Gallery**, which lies through the three arches to the south of the Great Gallery, to take a peek at the two *Chinoiserie* rooms – one round, one oval – to either side. The parquet flooring is sublime, but it's the oriental lacquer panels set into the wainscoting, and the numerous pieces of blue and white Chinese porcelain, that give the rooms their names. Of the two, the **Round Chinese Cabinet** is the most renowned, as this was where Maria Theresa used to hold her secret meetings with, among others, her chief adviser, Prince Kaunitz, whose apartments were linked to the room by a spiral staircase hidden behind one of the doors in the panelling. Another quirky feature of the room was the table designed to rise up through the floor, laden with food and drink, allowing the empress to dine without the need of servants, who might otherwise eavesdrop on matters of state. Kaunitz himself was particularly fond of food, and his table manners were legendary; on one memorable occasion, he "treated the company with the cleaning of his gums, a nauseous operation which lasted a prodigious long time and was accompanied with all manner of noises".

At the far end of the Great Gallery, you must pass through the **Carousel Room**, which gets its name from the painting of the special ladies' tournament held in the Winter Reitschule in 1743 (the sleighs used can be viewed in the Wagenburg). The final room for those on the "Imperial Tour" is the **Ceremonial Hall**, displaying five large paintings by pupils of the court painter, Martin van Meytens. The majority are concerned with recording the elaborate festivities which accompanied the wedding of Maria Theresa's eldest son, Josef II, to Isabella of Parma, in 1760. The magnifying glass, over one section of the painting of the wedding's opera performance, helps you pick out Mozart and his father from the crowd, though the family didn't, in fact, arrive in Vienna until two years after the event.

It was in the beautiful surroundings of the **Blue Chinese Salon**, on November 11, 1918, that the last Habsburg Emperor Karl I signed the document renouncing "all participation in the affairs of state". (He refused formally to abdicate or to renounce his claim to the throne, and made two unsuccessful attempts to regain the Hungarian half of his title in 1921, before dying in exile on Madeira the following year). As the name suggests, the room is another *Chinoiserie* affair – all the rage in the eighteenth century – lined with yellow wallpaper, hand-painted on rice paper, and inset with serene scenes of Chinese life on a deep blue background.

The audience rooms

The lightness of the Blue Chinese Room is in complete contrast to the oppressively opulent **Vieux-Laque Room**, with its black and gold lacquer panels, exquisite parquetry and walnut wainscoting. During his two sojourns at Schönbrunn, Napoleon is thought to have slept in the neighbouring walnut-panelled **Napoleon Room**, lined with Brussels tapestries depicting the Austrian army in Italy. It was also here that Maria Theresa is thought to have given birth to her brood, and that Napoleon's son by the Archduchess Marie Louise died in 1832, aged just 21 (see below).

Despite its name, only three items in the remarkable **Porcelain Room**, designed by Isabella of Parma, are actually genuine Meissen porcelain: the chandeliers, the clock and the wall bracket. The rest of the decor is carved from wood and painted over in blue and white to appear like porcelain. The delicate ink drawings set into the walls are signed works by Empress Maria Theresa's daughters, copied from French originals.

The most precious of all the rooms in Schönbrunn is the **Millions Room**, so called because it's estimated that Maria Theresa paid over a million silver florins to have it decorated. Unfortunately the most priceless items in the room – the miniature seventeenth-century Persian watercolours of life in the Moghul court – are somewhat overwhelmed by the surrounding, richly gilded cartouches set into the Caribbean rosewood panelling. Just off the Millions Room is the handy little breakfast room, known as the **Miniatures Room**, containing more works by the talented archduchesses. Next door in the **Gobelin Hall** are yet more Brussels tapestries, not only decorating the walls but also upholstering the six chairs, which depict the twelve months. Tapestries were a status symbol, partly because they were so labour-intensive, and therefore very expensive; the central tapestry in this room took eight people twelve years to complete.

The **Memorial Room** is dedicated to Napoleon's son, known variously as the Duke of Reichstadt, "King of Rome", or simply "L'Aiglon" (The Little Eagle). After the Emperor Napoleon's demise in 1815, the boy was kept a virtual prisoner in Schönbrunn, the stuffed skylark on the table among his few companions. Passing quickly through the Red Salon, and the East Terrace Cabinet, with its *trompe l'oeil* fresco of cherubs "in an azure firmament", as the brochure puts it, you reach **Maria Theresa's Bedroom**. The empress never actually slept in the red velvet and gold-embroidered four-poster bed, which was brought here from the Hofburg. Instead, the room was used exclusively for *levées* – a kind of official breakfast-in-bed – during her frequent pregnancies. This was also the modest little room in which Franz-Josef was born in 1830.

The last few rooms of the "Grand Tour" are those used by the **Archduke Franz Karl** (Franz-Josef's epileptic father), and his wife, the Archduchess Sophie, decked out in the usual red damask and

Empress Maria Theresa (1740–80)

In 1740, the Emperor Karl VI died suddenly, leaving no male heir. That the emperor's daughter, **Maria Theresa**, was able to ascend the throne was thanks to the Pragmatic Sanction of 1713 passed by her father granting her the right of inheritance. But as she herself put it, "I found myself without money, without credit, without an army, without experience and knowledge, even without counsel, because all my ministers were wholly occupied in trying to discover which way the cat was going to jump". Despite this inauspicious beginning, she surprised her male entourage by surviving against the odds, no thanks to her husband, Franz Stephan, who was good at fencing, hunting, shooting and womanizing, but unfortunately not much else.

Throughout Europe she was known as the "Virgin Empress", though with sixteen children to her name, she clearly wasn't in the literal sense. She was, however, out of step with the promiscuity of the period. Jesuit-educated and deeply pious, she insisted, much to her husband's discomfort, that they share a marital bed (this was by no means the usual custom). It was partly her husband's extra-marital activities that prompted her to set up the **Chastity Commission** in the autumn of 1747. Its commissioners were empowered to search houses, and to arrest any man found entertaining an opera singer, dancer or any other woman of presumed loose morals; offending ladies could be locked up in a convent or banished from the realm. Though in the end the commission fizzled out after just six months, it caused a certain amount of havoc – several acting troupes fell foul of the commission, as did Casanova himself, and one of the most celebrated sopranos of the day, Santini, who was escorted to the Venetian border.

Like her son, Josef II (see p.90), Maria Theresa was a keen reformer, establishing one of the best education systems in Europe at the time, with compulsory education for both sexes. However, she was no liberal, holding notoriously rabid anti-semitic views. Though Vienna had barely 500 Jews, the empress considered them to be an abomination, eventually expelling them all from the city in 1777, stating: "I know no worse public plague than this people, with their swindling, usury, and money-making, bringing people to beggary, practising all evil transactions which an honest man abhors; they are therefore to be kept away from here and avoided as far as possible." Normally, she would only communicate with them from behind a screen, though she happily used their money to help build Schönbrunn, and made an exception of the baptized Jew, Josef von Sonnenfels, who was one of her chief advisors.

Though Maria Theresa acquired a fun-loving reputation early in her reign, playing cards and dancing until all hours, her demeanour changed after the unexpected death of her husband on August 18, 1765. Thereafter she went into perpetual mourning, cutting her hair short, and wearing no jewellery or make-up. For the next thirty years, she is supposed to have heard Mass every day in the Kaisergruft at the foot of the sepulchre containing her dead husband, spending every 18th of the month and the whole of August in silent prayer. On Franz Stephan's death, she immediately appointed Josef co-regent, and pretty much left him to take over the day-to-day running of the state. In her old age, she grew so large she found it hard to walk and rarely left Schönbrunn at all. She had difficulty breathing, and would keep the windows at the palace constantly open, though the wind and rain which came in gave her terrible rheumatism, and prevented her from writing the sackful of letters she usually winged off to her children.

white panelling, and stuffed full of Habsburg portraits, including several by Martin van Meytens. The only items of note are the miniatures in Franz Karl's Study, to the right of the window, by Maria Christina – Maria Theresa's favourite daughter who was also the lover of Josef II's wife, Isabella of Parma. After Isabella's death from smallpox, Maria Christina went on to marry Albrecht of Saxony-Tetschen, with whom she helped found the Albertina (see p.96).

The outbuildings

With two exceptions (the Orangerie and the Wagenburg), the majority of the yellowy outbuildings that radiate from the main palace at Schönbrunn are closed to the public. A few, like the small Baroque **chapel** in the ground floor east wing close to the ticket office, have limited opening hours (Sun 9am–noon). The ornate **Schlosstheater**, built in 1747 by Pacassi on the west side of the main courtyard, is open only for summer performances of the Kammeroper and the Marionettentheater; pick up a leaflet in the main ticket office.

The vast **Orangerie**, to the east of the palace, is used for temporary exhibitions, usually on an appropriately imperial theme, for which there is an additional charge. Aside from this, by far the most rewarding of the outbuildings is the **Wagenburg**, housed in the former winter riding school to the west of the palace.

Wagenburg

The Wagenburg is open April–Oct daily 9am–6pm; Nov–March Tues–Sun 10am–4pm; öS30.

The main exhibition space of the **Wagenburg** is crowded with nineteenth-century carriages, which are of limited interest to the non-specialist. The best thing to do is pass quickly to the far end of the hall, where, below the gallery, there's an odd assortment of carriages and sleighs used to transport the imperial offspring. The most poignant is the *phaeton* designed for Napoleon's son, "L'Aiglon" (The Little Eagle), with mudguards in the shape of eagles' wings; the bees that decorate the sides of the carriage were the Bonaparte family symbol.

The highlights of the collection, though, lie beyond the gallery, where you'll find the Baroque and Rococo carriages of the Habsburgs. The most outrageous is the **coronation carriage of Franz Stephan**, Maria Theresa's husband, enormously long, dripping with gold-plating, and fitted with windows of Venetian glass. The painted panels were added in time for the coronation of Josef II as Holy Roman Emperor in 1764. The whole thing weighs an incredible 4000kg, every kilo of it taken to pieces and transported on several occasions for coronations in Budapest, Frankfurt and Milan. Check out the wonderful horses' harnesses, too, embroidered in red velvet and gold, and the horses' plumes of ostrich feathers.

The equally ornate carriage opposite, painted entirely in black, was used during oath fealty ceremonies for the new emperor, which coincided with periods of official mourning for the previous incumbent. The relatively modest **red-leather litter**, which stands close by, studded with over 11,000 gold-plated nails and buckles, is also worth a look. Originally built for long-distance travelling, to be carried by horses or mules, it was used, after 1705, solely for transporting the Archduke of Austria's hat from Klosterneuburg to Vienna and back for oath fealty ceremonies.

The richly carved, gold-plated carousel or **racing sleigh of Maria Theresa** is the sole survivor of a whole set built in the shape of giant scallops for the special ladies' tournament held in the Winter Reitschule in 1743; note the sleigh bells on the horses' mane decoration. Sleighs were frequently used during *Fasching* for rides in the parks and on the *glacis* outside the city walls. The wheels, on hand in case there was no snow, would be removed and the sleighs pulled by horses, steered by drivers who sat in the back seats and controlled the reins over the heads of the seated ladies.

The gallery is the place to head if you've a yen to see the Empress Elisabeth's horsewhip, with a photo of her husband set into the ivory handle, or the hoof of the horse used by the Emperor Franz-Josef I during his coronation as King of Hungary in 1867.

Schlosspark

Even if you've no interest at all in visiting the interior of Schönbrunn, it's worth coming out here to enjoy the glorious **Schlosspark**, concealed behind the palace. Like the Belvedere, the park is laid out across a sloping site ideal for the vistas and terraces beloved of Baroque landscape gardeners. Yet despite the formal French style of the gardens, originally executed in 1705 by Jean Trehetter to Fischer von Erlach's design, there are also plenty of winding paths in the woods on the slopes to give a hint of wildness, the result of modifications made under Josef II's co-regency by Adriaen van Steckhoven and later Johann Ferdinand Hetzendorf von Hohenberg. The latter was also responsible for the park's numerous architectural follies and features. Thanks to Josef II (see p.90), the Schlosspark was opened to the public as long ago as 1779.

The park is open daily 6am–dusk; free.

The lower park

The lower section of the Schlosspark is laid out in the formal French style, with closely cropped trees and yew hedges forming an intricate network of gravel paths. If you're approaching from the palace, however, the first thing that strikes you is the central axis of the **parterre**, decorated with carefully regimented flower beds, leading to the Neptunbrunnen and, beyond, to the triumphal colonnaded arch of the Gloriette. Along the edges are just some of the park's tally of stone statues, more of which lie concealed in the lower section of the park.

The theatrical **Neptunbrunnen** (Neptune Fountain) itself, erected in 1781 at the foot of the hill rising up to the Gloriette, is by no means upstaged by its grand setting. In it, the eponymous sea god presides over a vast array of wild sea creatures and writhing Tritons and naiads attempting to break in their sea-horses. Kneeling below Neptune, Thetis pleads with the sea god for calm seas to speed her son Achilles to Troy.

Hidden among the foliage to the east of the Neptunbrunnen are some of Hetzendorf's architectural follies. Particularly fine are the **Römische Ruine** (Roman Ruins), designed to tickle the imperial fancy of the Habsburgs. The idea was that these were the remains of some Corinthian palace – they were, in fact, taken from the Schloss Neugebäude (see p.236) – whose fallen stones now provide a watery retreat for a couple of river gods. The ruins were built as a stage set for open-air concerts and theatre, a tradition that continues to this day, in August and September. Close by the ruins is the outlet of the original **Schöner Brunnen**, a small grotto pavilion in which the nymph, Egeria, dispenses mineral water from a stone pitcher into a giant scallop basin.

Further east still stands an **Obelisk**, smothered in heiroglyphs glorifying the Habsburgs, topped by an eagle and an orb, and supported at the base by four, originally gilded, long-suffering turtles. Below the obelisk is a giant cascade of grottos, and a pond inhabited by yet more river gods. Up the hill, past Schönbrunn's municipal swimming baths, stands the **Kleine Gloriette** hidden among the trees. The imperial family used to breakfast here in fine weather, but despite its name, it's nothing like its larger namesake, and not worth bothering with.

The Gloriette

The Gloriette is open May–Oct daily 9am–5pm.

If you do nothing else in the Schlosspark, you should make the effort to climb up the zig-zag paths from the parterre to admire the triumphal **Gloriette**, and, of course, the view. Designed in Neoclassical style by Hetzendorf to celebrate the victory of the Habsburgs over the Prussians at the 1757 Battle of Kolín, the Gloriette stands at the focal point of the entire park, where Fischer von Erlach originally intended to build Schönbrunn itself. One eighteenth-century visitor found the whole thing a bit *de trop*, describing it as a "long portico-kind of building, as ugly as possible". It's certainly an overblown affair, its central arch flanked by open colonnades of almost equal stature, and surmounted by trophies and an enormous eagle, wings outstretched; yet more colossal trophies, guarded by lions, stand at either end of the colonnades. The central trio of arches have recently been enclosed to form a swanky café, from which – if you can get a window table – you can enjoy the view down to the palace. Alternatively, you can climb to the top of the colonnades and take in the scene from there.

Tiergarten

A substantial segment of the palace gardens is taken up by the **Tiergarten** (Zoo), which, originating in the royal menagerie founded by Franz Stephan back in 1752, is the world's oldest zoo. Here, the imperial couple would breakfast among the animals, in the octagonal pavilion designed for them by Jean-Nicholas Jadot, and decorated with frescoes by Guglielmi depicting Ovid's *Metamorphoses*. The pavilion has miraculously survived to this day – and is now a very good restaurant – along with several of the original Baroque animal houses, making this one of the most aesthetically pleasing zoos any captive animal could hope for.

There are three **entrances** to the Tiergarten: the main entrance closest to Hietzing; the Neptunbrunnen entrance and the Tirolergarten entrance up in the woods to the south. If you're thinking of going to either the Schmetterlinghaus or the Palmenhaus (described below), then it's worth forking out for a "KombiKarte" (öS140 for adults, and a bargain öS40 for kids).

Once inside, there are all the usual attractions – elephants, tigers, lions, giraffes, zebras, penguins, camels, monkeys – plus a few less common inhabitants such as beavers, wolves, polar bears and giant tortoises. Kids can get a bit closer to the more benign animals at the *Streichelzoo* (literally "stroking zoo"), but the nicest feature of the zoo, by far, is the **Tirolergarten**, on whose woody slopes perches a wonderfully large timber-framed farmhouse from the Tyrol. The original Tirolergarten was the dreamchild of the Archduke Johann, younger brother of Franz II, who was fond of the Alps, and commissioned two Tyrolean houses and an alpine garden, in which the imperial famliy could dispense with the formalities of court life and "get back to nature". Sheep, cows and horses occupy the lower floors of the farm, while upstairs there's an exhibition of the history of the building. If you're short of provisions, or just a glutton, check out the traditional Tyrolese soup, bread, cheese and cold meats in the farmhouse kitchen/shop.

Palmenhaus and Schmetterlinghaus

While its claim to be the largest greenhouse in the world, when it opened in 1882, may well be suspect, the Schönbrunn **Palmenhaus** is certainly one of the most handsome, with its gracefully undulating wrought-iron frame. Inside, three climate-controlled rooms each have a glorious canopy of palm trees and lots of rhododendrons, lilies, hydrangeas and begonias to provide a splash of colour below. The only disappointments are the lack of fauna (taped bird songs are broadcast from discreetly hidden speakers instead), and the fact that you can't climb the spiral staircases to the upper balconies.

A smaller greenhouse nearby provides a suitably steamy environment for the colourful tropical butterflies and moths of the **Schmetterlinghaus** (Butterfly House). Several giant cacti can be seen here, too, along with some very beautiful individual plants. Schönbrunn also boasts a small **Botanischer Garten** of its own, established by Franz Stephan to the west of the Tiergarten, tucked away between the zoo and Maxingstrasse, which is a beautiful place to escape the crowds.

Schönbrunn

The zoo is open May–Sept daily 9am–6.30pm; April until 6pm; March until 5.30pm; Feb & Oct until 5pm; Nov–Jan until 4.30pm; öS90.

The Palmenhaus is open May–Sept daily 9.30am–6pm; Oct–April until 5pm; the Schmetterlinghaus daily May–Sept 10am–5pm; Oct–April 10am–3.30pm (in good weather). Each costs öS40; combined ticket öS65.

Hietzing

With the imperial family in residence at Schönbrunn for much of the summer, the neighbouring quarter of **Hietzing** – now Vienna's thirteenth district – had become a very fashionable suburb by the nineteenth century. Over the years, it has remained a favourite with Vienna's wealthier denizens, and today boasts some of the city's finest villas, ranging from the Biedermeier summer residences beloved of the nobility, to the Jugendstil and modernist villas favoured by the more successful artists and businessmen of late-imperial Vienna. If you've a passing interest in the architecture, there are several villas within easy walking distance of Schönbrunn worth checking out. The incumbents of the local cemetery also reflect the area's cachet, and include the likes of Gustav Klimt and Otto Wagner. In the far west of the district is the **Lainzer Tiergarten**, the former imperial hunting ground that is now a vast woody retreat for the hoi polloi.

Hofpavillon Hietzing

The Hofpavillon is open Tues–Sun 9am–12.15pm & 1–4.30pm; öS25; the nearest U-Bahn is Hietzing.

One sight in Hietzing which you shouldn't miss is the newly restored **Hofpavillon Hietzing**, a one-off, Jugendstil pavilion built on the initiative of Otto Wagner in 1899 for the exclusive use of the imperial family and guests whenever they took the Stadtbahn (as the U-Bahn was then known). On the palace side of the gleaming white pavilion, Wagner provided a graceful wrought-iron canopy topped with miniature gilded crowns, underneath which the imperial carriage could shelter. At the centre of the building's rectangular groundplan is an octagonal waiting room, where, "in order to shorten the seconds spent waiting by the monarch with the sight of a work of art", Wagner commissioned a painting by Carl Moll, giving an eagle's eye-view of Vienna's Stadtbahn system. Wagner tried further to ingratiate himself with the Emperor Franz-Josef by decorating the interior with patterns formed out of the Empress Elisabeth's favourite plant, the split-leaved philodendron. Despite all Wagner's best efforts, however, the pavilion was used precisely twice by the emperor, who had a pathological distrust of all things modern. Now, looking well preserved, if a little forlorn beside the three-lane highway of Schönbrunner Schlossstrasse, the pavilion houses a small photographic exhibition of Wagner's other works (see p.124), and of the ornate *Kaiserzug* which the emperor used for his rides on the subway system.

Hietzinger Hauptstrasse

On the whole, Hietzing is just a sleepy little suburb now, with little to remind the visitor of the social whirl that was a feature of the place in the nineteenth century. The *Café Dommayer*, on the corner of

Hietzinger Hauptstrasse, is one of the few social institutions of the period to have survived (see p.285). It was here that Johann Strauss gave his first public concert in 1844, with a programme that included six of his own waltzes and one of his father's. Round the corner from the café, the enormous *Parkhotel Schönbrunn* (see p.271), built in 1907 for the emperor's personal guests, is another Hietzing landmark that's still going strong; the *Kaiserstöckl*, opposite, once the Foreign Minister's summer residence, is now the local post office.

Friedhof Hietzing

The **Friedhof Hietzing** can be a confusing place: not least because although it backs on to Schönbrunn's Schlosspark, the one and only entrance to the cemetery is on Maxingstrasse. And once you're inside, despite the map by the main gates, and the smallness of the graveyard, it's actually quite difficult to locate the tombs you want to see. Still, with perseverence, you should be able to find your way to Otto Wagner's rather pompous tomb from the early 1890s, designed by the architect himself, with some gloriously exuberant ironwork, but disappointingly devoid of even a hint of the Jugendstil motifs that became his later trademarks. Plans for a sarcophagus designed by Josef Hoffmann over Gustav Klimt's grave were never carried out, and a simple slab with gold lettering is all that marks the artist's resting place. Other notables buried here include Klimt's friend, the artist Kolo Moser; the Austro-fascist leader Englebert Dollfuss, murdered by the Nazis in 1934; Franz Grillparzer, Austria's greatest nineteenth-century playwright; Katharina Schratt, the Emperor Franz-Josef's mistress; and Alban Berg, the composer, who died in 1935 after an insect sting led to septicemia.

The cemetery is open March, April, Sept & Oct daily 8am–5pm; May–Aug until 6pm; Nov–Feb 9am–4pm; ten minutes' walk or two stops on bus #56B, #58B or #156B from Hietzing U-Bahn.

Hietzing's villas

A short stroll down Gloriettegasse immediately to the west of the Schlosspark gives a fair indication of the variety of architecture in Hietzing's villa-encrusted backstreets. Only fans of the international modern movement need continue their explorations further west to the Werkbundsiedlung; the rest can take tram #60 or #61 back to Hietzing U-Bahn, or continue west to the Lainzer Tiergarten.

Gloriettegasse

Your first port of call should be the modest Biedermeier villa at Gloriettegasse 9, with its delicate window pediments of necking swans, where Franz-Josef's mistress, the Burgtheater actress, **Katharina Schratt**, used to live. It was procured for Ms Schratt by the emperor himself, so that he could pop in for breakfast at around 7am, to enjoy a bit of chaste intimacy before continuing with his paperwork. "Do not get up too early tomorrow morning, I beg of you," he would write to her, "Allow me to come and sit on your bed. You know that nothing gives me greater pleasure." Afterwards they would go for a stroll in Schönbrunn, where onlookers would applaud the happy couple, who would regularly feed the remains of their imperial breakfast to the bears in the Tiergarten.

Turning right down Wattmanngasse to no. 29, brings you to an interesting terraced apartment block embellished by Ernst Lichtblau in 1914 with bands of majolica between the windows, depicting various quasi-medieval figures holding fruits and flowers. Back on Gloriettegasse, at no. 21, stands the **Villa Schopp**, a wonderful Jugendstil house designed in 1902 by Friedrich Ohmann, set back from the street behind curvaceous wrought-iron railings, and flanked by hefty gateposts topped by big, black-capped lamps. The house itself is in need of attention, but the stucco swags and floral flourishes on the facade are still impressive.

On the opposite side of the street, again set within its own grounds, is one of the most unusual of all Hietzing's villas, the **Villa Skywa-Primavesi**, at Gloriettegasse 14–16. Built in 1913–15 by Josef Hoffmann for the wealthy patrons of the Wiener Werkstätte, this is an almost obscenely large private house, designed in Neoclassical vein, with fluted pillars, and huge triangular pediments. Nude miniatures perch on shelves at the tops of the pillars, while two larger figures recline in the pediments. Unfortunately, from the street, there's no way of seeing the bizarre, modern Teetempelchen (Little Tea Temple) Hoffmann built in the garden, complete with pergola and pond.

Adolf Loos and the Werkbundsiedlung

"Loos swept clear the path before us. It was a Homeric cleansing: precise, philosophical, logical. He has influenced the architectural destiny of us all," Le Corbusier effused in the 1930s. The building authorities were less enthusiastic in 1912 when planning permission was sought for Adolf Loos's first Hietzing commission, **Haus Scheu**, at Larochegasse 3, on the other side of Lainzer Strasse from Gloriettegasse. As with the infamous Loos Haus in the old town (see p.56), the architect's almost religious aversion to ornament provoked a hostile reaction, as did the building's asymmetry, caused by the series of west-facing terraces that give the house its "stepped" look. Loos completed four other houses in Hietzing alone – Villa Strasser, Kupelwiesergasse 28, Villa Rufer, Schliessmanngasse 11, Haus Steiner, St-Veit-Gasse 10, and Haus Horner, Nothartgasse 7 – though they're widely dispersed across the district. The main frustration, however, when visiting Loos's houses is that it was in his use of the open-plan, and of in-built furniture, that Loos truly excelled – neither of which skills can be appreciated from his ornament-free exteriors.

A better bet for those in search of Bauhaus-style inspiration, is to head for the **Werkbundsiedlung**, a model housing estate of 70 houses, situated towards the west end of Veitingergasse. It was laid out between 1930 and 1932 by the Socialist city council for an exhibition of the *Deutscher Werkbund*, an association for the advancement of industrial design, who had constructed a similar housing estate at Stuttgart in 1927. Here, the emphasis was not on technical innovation, but on creating cheap, single family houses using minimal space. Josef Frank was in overall control, inviting an international posse of modernists, including Adolf Loos and Josef Hoffmann, to take part. Fortunately, many of the houses are still owned by the council and have recently been renovated, so the whole estate looks in good shape. The most surprising thing about the whole project is how small the houses are, with miniature roads to match. Within the estate, at Woinovichgasse 32 (designed by Frank himself) there's a small documentation centre with information on the estate.

The Werkbund-siedlung is a short walk up Jagdschloss-gasse from tram #61 and #62 terminus.

Egon Schiele in Hietzing

In 1912, the painter **Egon Schiele** rented a studio at Hietzinger Hauptstrasse 101, and, in between canvases, began flirting with the two respectable middle-class girls, Adele and Edith Harms, who lived opposite at no. 114. Edith and Schiele were ultimately married in 1915, and were expecting their first child when they were both killed in 1918 by the influenza that swept Europe following World War I, and which claimed more fatalities in Austria than had the war itself. Edith died first at their new studio flat at Wattmanngasse 6; Schiele succumbed three days later at his mother-in-law's house. Schiele is buried in the nearby **Friedhof Ober-St-Veit**, beneath a tombstone sculpted by the Hungarian Benjamin Ferenczy, commissioned by Schiele's friends on the tenth anniversary of his death.

To get to the cemetery, take bus #54B or #55B from Ober-St-Veit U-Bahn.

Lainzer Tiergarten

In the far west of Hietzing lies the former imperial hunting reserve of **Lainzer Tiergarten**, enclosed within a 25km-long wall by the Emperor Josef II. Since 1923, however, the reserve has been the wildest of Vienna's public parks. With virtually no traffic allowed within the park boundaries, and no formal gardens at all, this is the place to head for in the summer if you want to leave the urban sprawl far behind. It may not boast the views of Wienerwald, but you're more likely to spot wildlife here, including wild boar, wolves and, most easily, deer; in addition, the famous Lipizzaner horses of the Spanische Reitschule spend their summer holidays in the park.

The park's chief sight, the **Hermesvilla**, is just ten minutes' walk from the main gates of Lainzer Tor, at the end of Hermesstrasse. Unlike the rest of the park, this section of the Lainzer Tiergarten is open year round. Those with more energy might aim for the **Huburtuswarte**, an 18m-high lookout tower at the top of Kaltbrundlberg (508m), beyond the Hermesvilla in the centre of the park. **Refreshments** are available in the Hermesvilla restaurant, and

The Lainzer Tor is open Easter–Oct Wed–Sun 8am–dusk; free; tram #60 or #61 from Hietzing U-Bahn to Hofwiesen-gasse, then fif-teen minutes' walk or bus #60B down Hermesstrasse.

also from the *Rohrhaus* and the *Hirschgstemm*, both of which are signposted (with approximate walking times) from the Hermesvilla. Note that the St-Veiter Tor and the Adolfstor entrances, to the north of Lainzer Tor, are only open on Sundays and public holidays.

Hermesvilla

The Hermesvilla is open Wed–Sun 9am–4.30pm; öS50.

In 1882, in an effort to ingratiate himself with his estranged wife, the Emperor Franz-Josef decided to build Elisabeth an informal new residence, which she named **Hermesvilla** after her favourite Greek deity, the god of travel. Carl von Hasenauer was employed to design the building, and Gustav Klimt and Hans Makart among those commissioned to decorate the interior; there was even a purpose-built exercise room in which the empress could indulge in her daily gymnastics. In the end, though, the villa failed to entice Elisabeth back to Vienna, and she stayed there only very occasionally. The house is now used to host exhibitions put on by the Historisches Museum der

---

Empress Elisabeth (1837–98)

The **Empress Elisabeth** was born into the eccentric Wittelsbach dynasty that produced the likes of "Mad" King Ludwig II of Bavaria, one of Elisabeth's cousins. She enjoyed a carefree, sheltered upbringing, only to find herself engaged to the Habsburg Emperor Franz-Josef I – another cousin – at the age of just sixteen, after an entirely public, two-day courtship. In choosing Elisabeth instead of her older sister Hélène, Franz-Josef went against the wishes of his mother, the Archduchess Sophie, turning her against his new wife from the very start. Sophie took her revenge, preventing Elisabeth from fulfilling her role either as empress or mother to her children, by hand-picking her ladies-in-waiting, and having the children removed from her care as soon as they were born. Later, Elisabeth advised her daughter, "marriage is an absurd institution. At the age of fifteen you are sold, you make a vow you do not understand, and you regret for thirty years or more that you cannot break it".

By 1860, having dutifully produced a male heir, Elisabeth had given up on the marriage. She encouraged Franz-Josef to get a mistress, introducing him to the actress Katharina Schratt, "very much as a woman might put flowers into a room she felt to be dreary", as Rebecca West put it. Her sudden departure to Madeira, however, was more specifically a reaction to discovering that Franz-Josef had infected her with venereal disease. She sought solace in riding – she was reckoned to be one of the finest horsewomen in Europe – and spent much of her lonely life travelling around Europe, under the pseudonym of the Countess Hohenhelms. As she herself put it "When we cannot be happy in the way that we desire there is nothing for it but to fall in love with our sorrows".

The similarities between Elisabeth's life and that of Princess Di are difficult to ignore. Her marriage to Franz-Josef was the wedding of the century. The Emperor was marrying a virginal, "fairytale princess", whom he hardly knew, and, despite public appearances, the marriage was a disaster from the start. The issue of Franz-Josef and Sisi, like that of Charles and

---

Stadt Wien. Even if the particular show doesn't grab you, the well-preserved interior is rewarding in itself, though there's no information on the Hermesvilla's imperial days, nor anything specific on the Empress Elisabeth herself.

Less of a villa and more of a mini-chateau, the Hermesvilla is a rather sickly mixture of Renaissance and Baroque, surrounded by outbuildings linked by a wonderful parade of wrought-iron colonnades. Inside, the decor has that heavy, slightly sterile, strangely unweathered look common to Historicist architecture. Downstairs, the **Dining Hall** serves up rich helpings of marble and stucco, but the best stuff is preserved upstairs. Elisabeth's **Gym** is suitably decorated in Pompeiian style, with muscle men and lusty satyrs engaging in feats of strength. The **Empress's Bedroom** is smothered floor to ceiling in one of Makart's sumptuous *trompe l'oeil* frescoes depicting Elisabeth's favourite Shakespearean text, *A Midsummer Night's Dream*, with Titania and Oberon in a chariot pulled by leopards. The

---

Di, divided folk then, as it does historians and biographers now. Either Franz-Josef was a boorish, unimaginative prig, who visited brothels during their honeymoon, or Elisabeth was a frigid, neurotic, narcissistic brat, obsessed with her looks. Like Di, Elisabeth – or Sisi as she was and still is affectionately known – won over people's hearts with her beauty. Yet many Viennese grew to resent her absences from the capital, and were appalled at her pro-Hungarian sentiments.

In the 1870s, the growing insanity of her cousin, King Ludwig, spurred her to roam Europe in search of an elixir to cure madness. When Ludwig, and then her only son Rudolf, committed suicide within a few years of each other, she became convinced that she too was mentally unstable. From then on, she dressed only in black, and carried a black fan that she used to hide the wrinkles that were beginning to appear on her face. She criss-crossed Europe, never staying in one place for long, and went on interminable cruises – she had an anchor tattooed on her shoulder – alarming her companions by asking to be tied to the ship's mast during storms.

By 1897, Elisabeth's health began to deteriorate rapidly – a condition partly brought on by anorexia – to the extent that she could barely walk. Despite her poor health, and her obsession with madness and death, few would have predicted her final demise. On September 10, 1898, the empress was assassinated by an Italian anarchist, Luigi Luccheni, on Lake Geneva. A local newspaper had unwisely announced the arrival of the empress, who was attempting to travel incognito. As she was about to board a steamer to go to tea with Baroness Rothschild, Luccheni rushed up and stabbed her in the heart with a sharpened stiletto. Like the empress, Luccheni had also been wandering aimlessly around Europe, in his case looking for someone famous to kill. He was fixed on assassinating the Duke of Orléans, but when he failed to turn up in Geneva as planned, resolved to attack the Austrian empress instead. Naturally enough, thousands turned out for Sisi's funeral in Vienna; however unpopular she may have been, few would have wished her such a violent end. Over the years, her martyrdom has ensured that the myth and mystery around her life remain as compelling as ever.

Heitzing

four-poster bed, with its oppressive double-headed eagle over the headboard, would guarantee a disturbed night's sleep even in a more balanced individual than Elisabeth. The central chamber, the so-called **Kirchensaal**, is similarly overwrought, with gilded wood-panelling and a shallow oval dome.

Further afield

The sights in this section are widely dispersed across the great swathe of suburbs which stretch away north of Hietzing to the Wienerwald. The first of the bunch, the **Technisches Museum**, is within easy walking distance of Schönbrunn, but the others require careful route-planning on the Viennese transport system. Of these, the most rewarding destination is the **Kirche am Steinhof**, Otto Wagner's Jugendstil masterpiece, high up on Baumgartner Höhe. Two more Wagner villas can be admired in the leafy surroundings of neighbouring Hütteldorf. There's a more brutalist piece of early modern architecture by the spiritual godfather of post-modernism, Josip PleBnik, in the otherwise dour suburb of Ottakring. Further north still, in Pötzleinsdorf, the city's premier collection of Biedermeier furniture is housed in the peaceful **Geymüllerschlössl**.

Technisches Museum

The Museum finally reopened in March 1997; the nearest U-Bahn is Schönbrunn.

The **Technisches Museum**, on the opposite side of Auer-Welsbach-Park from the main gates of Schönbrunn, was conceived in the last decade of Habsburg rule, and opened in 1918. The whole place has been closed for some years, and was closed at the time of writing, so it's difficult to predict what the new museum will look like inside. However, the collection will undoubtedly continue to cover a wide range of subjects from the history of the postal system to atomic physics. The most popular exhibits, particularly with youngsters, are the steam locomotives, and primitive flying machines from the late nineteenth century. Vienna's **IMAX cinema**, next door, has daily showings of less-than-brilliant films, specially shot to show off the 180-degree projection system; tickets currently start at a hefty öS110 for an hour-long sitting.

Kirche am Steinhof

The Kirche am Steinhof is open for guided tours only Sat 3pm; öS30; bus #47A from Unter-St-Veit U-Bahn.

Despite its limited opening hours, anyone with even a passing interest in Jugendstil architecture should make the effort to visit the **Kirche am Steinhof**, completed in 1907 by Otto Wagner as a chapel for the city's main psychiatric hospital. The church occupies a fantastic site on the commanding heights of the Baumgartner Höhe, looming over the hospital's grid-plan streets below. In designing the building, Wagner clearly had the Karlskirche (see p.125) in the forefront of his mind: like the latter, the church is topped by a giant copper dome and lantern, both of which were originally gilded, and features two belfries capped with copper statues of seated saints; only Fischer von Erlach's columns are missing. Elements familiar from Wagner's other buildings are also evident, not least the marble veneer fixed onto the facade with copper bolts.

Inside, the church is deliberately organized on a north-south axis, rather than the usual east-west configuration, in order to allow more light to stream through the glorious mosaic windows, designed by Kolo Moser. Hygiene and safety were obviously a major concern: continuously running holy water in the fonts, no sharp edges to the pews, a raked floor to improve sightlines and facilitate cleaning, and special doors flanking the altar to allow hospital staff rapid access to the patients in emergencies. The interior decor is light and simple, focused very much on the main altar with its eye-catching, cage-like gilt baldachin, against a backdrop mosaic featuring St Leopold and sundry other saints. Sadly, the church is little used nowadays; it's too cold for services during the winter, and even in summer there are few takers among the patients. Guided tours are in German only, after which you're allowed a brief wander around.

Two Wagner villas

If you're fired with enthusiasm for Wagner's works, it's worth heading to the woody suburb of Hütteldorf, where two contrasting villas, built at either end of his career, stand side by side on Hüttelbergstrasse. **Villa Wagner I**, at no. 26, is an early work from 1888, designed in the style of a luxurious Palladian villa as the architect's very own out-of-town summer house. It's a grandiose building, typical of Wagner's Ringstrasse style (see p.106), with a central Ionic portico, flanked by two Doric pergolas. Badly damaged in World War II, the building was set to be destroyed by the council until, in 1968, a band of Austrian hippy artists, including Friedensreich Hundertwasser and Ernst Fuchs, protested by occupying the building. Fuchs, a purveyor of "fantasy-realism" from the *Judge Dredd* school of painting, eventually bought the property in 1972, and, since going into tax exile in Monaco, has turned it into the self-aggrandizing **Ernst-Fuchs-Museum**. Sadly, Wagner devotees come out of it worse off than Fuchs fans. The latter can lap up his lurid nudes and admire the rock 'n' roll decor; those hoping to see Wagner's work have to content themselves with the ceilings, and the left-hand pergola, which retains its vegetal, Jugendstil windows added in 1900. The psychedelic touches on the exterior, such as the multi-coloured cornice, are by Fuchs, though the wrought-ironwork is original. Fuchs is, naturally, responsible for the huge fertility goddess, with decorated mammaries, that fronts the building, and has also added his very own, Gaudit, not to say gaudy, style Nymphaeum fountain house in the garden.

To get to Wagner's villas, take tram #49 to its terminus, after which it's a ten-minute walk beside the Halterbach stream.

The Ernst-Fuchs-Museum is open by appointment Tues–Sat 10am–4pm; öS120; phone ☎914 85 75.

Providing a perfect contrast to its neighbour is the cube-shaped **Villa Wagner II**, at no. 28, into which Wagner moved in 1913. It was to be his last work, and, with its austere, ornament-free facade, and its use of reinforced concrete and aluminium, conforms to his later conversion to rationalism and modernism. The exterior decoration is limited to a distinctive band of indigo blue glass tiles alternating with aluminium bolts. Above the building's two entrances are the only other, gratuitous, decoration: the Kolo Moser glass and the series of colourful, mythological mosaics, which also feature under the side portico.

Schmelzer Pfarrkirche "Zum Heiligen Geist"

To get to the
Schmelzer
Pfarrkirche,
take tram #9
from
Schwegler-
strasse U-Bahn.

Don't be put off by the brutal, concrete classicism of its exterior: the **Schmelzer Pfarrkirche**, designed by the Slovene architect Josip Plebnik on Herbststrasse in 1913, is one of Vienna's hidden suburban gems. As the city's first-ever concrete church, it caused huge controversy, provoking the Archduke Franz Ferdinand to pronounce it a ridiculous mixture "of a temple to Venus, a Russian bath, and a stable or hayloft". Despite such confusion, the main body of the church is surprisingly light and modern, while Otto Holub's Jugendstil high altar is simply outstanding. A dove flanked by two angels, all in aluminium low-relief, are framed against a semi-circular golden sunburst, in turn set off against a luxuriant gold and purple wall mosaic featuring the seven levitating attributes of the Holy Spirit, from *Frömigheit* (Piety) to *Gotesfurcht* (Fear of God).

The church's *pièce de résistance*, however, is the concrete **crypt**, which you enter from stairs either side of the main altar; in order to see anything, you need to feed the light-meter with öS10. Several Jugendstil masterpieces brighten this gloomy underworld, with its low ceiling and trio of grottoes. On either side of the altar, murals feature Klimt-like celestial creatures: *Rachel Weeping for her Dead Children*, and *The Creation of Water*. Even more magical is the marble font, capped by a golden lid frothing with fish, out of which a heavenly figure rises up brandishing a cross.

Geymüllerschlössl

The museum is
open March–
Nov Thurs–
Sun 10am–
5pm; öS30;
take tram #41
to its terminus
from Volksoper
U-Bahn.

In the first decade of the early nineteenth century, the wealthy banker, Johann Heinrich von Geymüller, had a luxury summer house – known today as the **Geymüllerschlössl** – built in the sleepy village (now suburb) of Pötzleinsdorf. The Geymüllers were an archetypal wealthy Biedermeier family, *parvenu* business folk with bourgeois, artistic pretensions. Their house, so it was said, contained five grand pianos, one for each daughter; Franz Schubert and Franz Grillparzer were frequent visitors. It was at the Geymüllers' that Grillparzer fell in love with Katharina Fröhlich, a singer with "immense eyes, bottomless, really unfathomable"; they were engaged for a number of years, but in the end never married. Schubert, meanwhile, set one of Grillparzer's poems to music for a female quartet and alto solo, the serenade *Zögernd leise*, which was performed in the Geymüllers' garden one night as a surprise birthday treat for a friend of the family. Oddly, the house itself is no standard Biedermeier residence, but is, in fact, an exotic mixture of Gothic and Moorish elements executed by an unknown architect. It has the appeal of a garden folly, and the colour – white walls and green shutters – of an Italianate villa.

This building, so rich in Biedermeier associations, provides the best possible venue for the MAK's collection of **early nineteenth-century furniture**, and its temporary Biedermeier exhibitions, which are staged on the ground floor. A beautiful cantilever staircase leads up to the suite of first-floor rooms, which house the **collection of clocks** bequeathed, along with the house in 1965, by Dr Franz Sobek, former director of the Austrian National Printing Works. The clocks – fascinating though they are – are a side-show to the overall effect of the painstakingly restored **Biedermeier decor**. Though the term evokes a certain dull conventionality, the artistry of the period (1815–48) appeals to contemporary tastes with its subtle, almost minimalist, approach, and its emphasis on inlaid detail, sparing use of gilding, smooth, polished surfaces and *trompe l'oeil*. The most startling room is the **Salon mit Panoramatapete**, a drawing room equipped with period furniture made from ebony and gold and upholstered in deep blue, and dominated by the panoramic murals of idealized, Oriental landscapes.

Given that the Geymüllerschlössl is something of a trek, it might be worth bringing a picnic to have in the house's extensive gardens; alternatively, you could pop across the road into the local *Heuriger*. Those with children might consider combining a trip out here with a visit to the nearby **Pötzleinsdorfer Schlosspark**, by the tram terminus, which has a big playground, squirrel-infested woods, and a small farm with hens, goats, sheep and guinea fowl.

Döbling and the Wienerwald

Over the last century, **Döbling**, once a little village to the north of Vienna's *Linienwall*, has gradually been subsumed into the city, and now gives its name to the vast nineteenth district, which stretches right up into the **Wienerwald**, or Vienna Woods. Though built-up in parts, the district is still peppered with vineyards and the remnants of old villages, making it a unique mixture of city and countryside. Tourists and locals alike flock here in the summer to drink the local wine in one of the district's numerous *Heurigen*, or to get some fresh air during a walk in the hills. Nearer town, there are a couple of places of pilgrimage devoted to Beethoven, which draw a fair sprinkling of tourists, as does Vienna's most famous housing estate, which remains a symbol of both the success and failure of inter-war "Red Vienna".

For more on the district's Heurigen, *see p.291.*

Theodor Herzl (1860–1904)

Along with fascism, psychoanalysis and atonal music, Vienna can also be
said to be the birthplace of **Zionism**. Although he spent his childhood in
Budapest, **Theodor Herzl** – author of the seminal *Der Judenstaat* (The
Jewish State), and considered by many to be the father of the movement –
lived in the Austrian capital on and off for much of his adult life. He was
buried in the Jewish cemetery in Döbling until after World War II when he
was disinterred and reburied in Jerusalem. Yet despite his beatification by
the modern state of Israel, it's not at all clear what Herzl would have
thought about his current place of rest.

His family, though Jewish residents of Budapest, were thoroughly assimilated, politically liberal and culturally German. While at Vienna's university
studying law, Herzl himself was something of a dandy, "dark, slim, always
elegantly clothed", according to one contemporary. His true ambition was to
be a playwright, or at a push, "a member of the Prussian nobility". Having
failed on both counts, he became, instead, Paris correspondent of the *Neue
Freie Presse*. Herzl had experienced anti-semitism in Vienna, but nothing
prepared him for the bigotry aroused during the trial of the Jewish army officer, Alfred Dreyfus, in 1893–94. During this period, Herzl toyed with the
idea of challenging Vienna's leading anti-semites to a duel; his other, equally mad-cap scheme was to lead the Jews of Vienna into the Stephansdom for
a mass conversion to Roman Catholicism, with the approval of the Pope.

Ironically enough, it was a performance of Wagner's *Tannhäuser* – in
which the hero follows his heart rather than his head and returns to his spiritual homeland – that spurred Herzl into thinking about the creation of new
Jewish state, a utopian vision he later outlined in his most famous political
pamphlet, *Der Judenstaat*, in 1896. Yet Herzl's new state was more of a liberal utopia than a specifically Jewish one. The principal inducement for his fellow Jews was to be the new state's seven-hour day (one less than the Socialist
International promised to deliver); to drive the point home the flag was to feature seven gold stars. Yet he was no revolutionary, decrying "that a highly conservative people, like the Jews, have always been driven into the ranks of revolutionaries, is the most lamentable feature in the tragedy of our race".

Initially, he proposed that the European powers grant the Jews sovereignty over a slice of their colonial territories. He tried, but failed to elicit
the support of the likes of the Rothschilds; he even approached the Tsar,
the Pope, the German Kaiser and finally the Sultan, from whom he hoped
to secure Palestine. Failing that, Herzl, unlike most of his followers, was
prepared to accept a portion of Argentina or some central African colony.
Despite his rejection by most wealthy, assimilated Jews, and by the
Orthodox Jewry, Herzl's movement flourished, especially among the ghet-
tos of Eastern Europe. At the first World Zionist Congress in Basel in
1897, Herzl was hailed "King of the Jews", and by the time of his death in
1904, the Zionist bank in London boasted 135,000 shareholders, the
largest number financing any enterprise in the world.

Oberdöbling

Döbling used to be, in fact, two separate villages: Unterdöbling and
Oberdöbling. These lay just outside the *Linienwall* (now Gürtel),
and were popular summer retreats for the wealthier denizens of

Vienna in the days when they were surrounded by fields, gardens and vineyards. Nowadays, the two villages are mostly built-up, and only dedicated Beethoven fans will get much out of the district's chief sight, the **Eroicahaus**. If you're here at the weekend, however, it's worth paying a visit to the nearby **Villa Wertheimstein**, a rambling, *fin-de-siècle* house that once attracted the city's *literati* to its door.

Eroicahaus

In the summer of 1803, Beethoven took lodgings in a single-storey vintner's house – today's **Eroicahaus**, at Döblinger Hauptstrasse 92. Surrounded by gardens and vineyards, with a view across to Heiligenstadt, he grappled with the "heroic" concepts that would crystalize in his *Third Symphony*, the single most significant work of his entire life. Broadly speaking, until the emergence of this work, Beethoven was composing within the eighteenth-century tradition; with the *Third Symphony* Beethoven entered the age of Romantic complexity. The inspiration for the piece was clearly Napoleon, whom Beethoven hoped would liberate Europe from "bigotry, police control and Habsburg-worship", as one biographer put it. He intended to dedicate the work to Napoleon, but, shortly after completing it, received news that the former First Consul had crowned himself Emperor. Beethoven flew into a rage, tore up the dedication, and renamed the symphony, *Eroica*. In 1809, when Napoleon's artillery shelled Vienna, Beethoven hid under his kitchen table with a towel over his head, though this was probably less as a result of cowardice than in order to protect his poor hearing, which must have suffered terribly from the noise.

The Eroicahaus is open Tues–Sun 9am–12.15pm & 1–4.30pm; öS25; take tram #37 to Pokornygasse.

The rooms in which Beethoven lodged have been preserved, though the building's upper storey is a later addition. Despite the fact that the museum itself contains none of the composer's personal effects, you can get some idea of how the area looked in Beethoven's day from the contemporaneous maps and watercolours. All in all, notwithstanding the opportunity to listen to the *Eroica*, Beethoven fans would be better off visiting the composer's other memorial house in Heiligenstadt (see p.228).

Villa Wertheimstein

Two doors up the street from the Eroicahaus is a much more enjoyable house-museum, the **Villa Wertheimstein**, which serves as Döbling's district museum. Built in the 1830s by the silk manufacturer and patron of the arts, Rudolf Arthaber, it was bought in 1870 by the wealthy Jewish financier Leopold von Wertheimstein. While the latter spent most of his time in the family's town house, his young wife, Josephine, stayed at the Döbling villa, presiding over one of the most celebrated *salons* in Vienna, along with her only daughter, Franziska. The pianist Artur Rubinstein played there on more than

The museum is open Sat 3.30–6pm, Sun 10am–noon; closed July & Aug; öS25.

one occasion, while more frequent visitors included the artist Hans Makart, the philosopher Franz Brentano, the poets Eduard von Bauernfeld and Ferdinand von Saar, and the writer, Hugo von Hoffmannsthal. When Franziska died in 1907, the villa and its contents were bequeathed to the city. The house retains the same ramshackle quality it would have had in the *salon*'s heyday, and contains, among other things, commemorative rooms for the two poets and a small viticultural museum.

Heiligenstadt

Heiligenstadt is typical of Vienna's outlying suburbs, a combination of barracks-like housing and remnants of the old wine-making village. The latter became a fashionable spa retreat for the Viennese

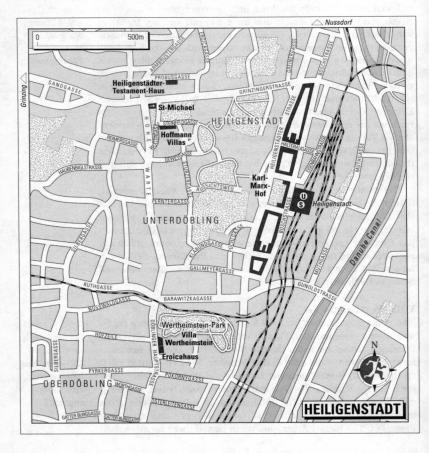

from 1784 onwards, thanks to the discovery of a curative mineral spring. Nowadays, the easiest way to get there is on the U-Bahn, from which you get one of the best views there is of Friedensreich Hundertwasser's funky **Fernwärme Wien**, his colourfully decorated paper incineration plant, which provides electricity for the surrounding district. Architecturally, it is, as one critic caustically dubbed it, merely "a painted shed", though it's certainly a lot more visually entertaining than most industrial plants, looking something like a psychedelic mosque.

Döbling and the Wienerwald

For more on Hundertwasser, see p.154.

Red Vienna

The bloody history and colourful, monumental exterior of Karl-Marx-Hof has made it a potent symbol of **Red Vienna**, the city's Austromarxist experiment in municipal socialism (1919–33). While other European socialist parties attempted piecemeal reforms, the Social Democratic Workers' Party (SDAP) developed a comprehensive proletarian counter-culture which was intended to serve as an alternative to both bourgeois culture and the Bolshevik experiment in Russia. Cheap tickets to the theatre and opera were provided for the workers, and workers' symphony concerts were held under the baton of one of Schönberg's pupils, Anton Webern. Perhaps the most powerful display of working-class/SDAP power took place during the International Worker Olympics in 1931, when 100,000 people marched through the city to take part in a mass festival held in the Prater Stadium (see p.189), watched by countless more thousands.

Though one cannot but be impressed by the ambition and scope of the SDAP's social and cultural programme, a large section of the working class remained untouched by either initiative. Throughout, the SDAP remained controlled and led by an oligarchy of party elite, who held a patronizing and deeply paternalistic view of the rank and file, and who by and large fulfilled a passive role in the whole process. The real achievements and failures of Red Vienna have become lost in the myths of time, but its legacy remains highly visible in the huge housing complexes that punctuate Vienna's outer suburbs. These workers' enclaves – purpose-built with communal laundries, bathhouses, kindergartens, libraries, meeting rooms, co-operative shops, and health clinics – were designed to help create the "neue Menschen" of the Socialist future. They may have failed in that lofty aim, but they continue to provide cheap and well-maintained housing for a populace who had, until then, been crowded into unsanitary tenements within the *Vorstädte*.

Karl-Marx-Hof may be the most famous of the Red Vienna housing complexes, but it is by no means the largest. Sandleiten-Hof and Friedrich-Engels-Hof are both larger; other biggies include Karl-Seitz-Hof and Raben-Hof. Though all are imposing, none are architecturally innovative, eschewing the modernist, avant-garde aesthetic of the inter-war era for a more traditional monumental architecture. If you're interested, there are guided tours organized by the city council, or you can visit them off your own bat. After Karl-Marx-Hof, the most impressive are Reumann-Hof, 5, Margaretengürtel (tram #6 or #8), and Raben-Hof, 3, Rabengasse (Kardinal-Nagl-Platz U-Bahn).

*The nearest
U-Bahn is
Heiligenstadt.*

Karl-Marx-Hof

If there is one housing complex that has come to symbolize the inter-war municipal socialism of "Red Vienna", it is the **Karl-Marx-Hof**, the kilometre-long, peach-and-salmon-coloured "people's palace", whose distinctive giant archways greet you as you exit from Heiligenstadt U-Bahn. Though right-wing critics charged that these housing complexes were built as fortresses by the socialists to protect their workers in case of civil war, their fragility was proved on February 12, 1934, when the World War I artillery of the Austro-fascist government reduced much of the Karl-Marx-Hof to rubble in a few hours. It took another four days for the government forces to flush the last defenders out, however. This is only the most famous of the battles of the civil war, which was fought just as keenly and bloodily in numerous other working-class housing estates in Vienna and other Austrian cities. Shortly after the battle, Edward VIII visited Vienna as Prince of Wales, and endeared himself to the Viennese socialists by asking to be taken to see the Karl-Marx-Hof – it would be difficult to think of a more unlikely political sympathizer.

Hohe Warte

*To get to the
Hohe Warte,
take tram #37
to its termi-
nus.*

In the first decade of this century, the architect Josef Hoffmann built five houses in the **Hohe Warte**, the high ground above the village church of Heiligenstadt. Hoffmann, a pupil of Otto Wagner, was one of the founders of the Secession (see p.120) and later of the Wiener Werkstätte (see p.133), but his architectural style, with its pared-down classicism and minimal decoration, is very much his own. The best preserved of the houses is the ivy-strewn **Villa Spitzer**, Steinfeldgasse 4, an idiosyncratic mixture of the classical and the medieval, completed in 1902. The **Villa Ast** (now the Saudi Arabian embassy), at no. 2, completed nearly a decade later at the height of Hoffmann's classical period, provides an interesting contrast. Earliest of the villas, the **Villa Moser-Moll I**, a couple of semi-detached houses built for his fellow Secession artists, Kolo Moser and Carl Moll, at no. 6 and no. 8 respectively, features decorative half-timbering similar to that of the Villa Spitzer.

Heiligenstädter-Testament-Haus

*The house is
open Tues–Sun
9am–12.15pm
& 1–4.30pm;
öS25; bus
#38A to Arm-
brustergasse
from U-Bahn
Heiligenstadt,
or a short walk
from tram #37
terminus.*

Beethoven moved out to the **Heiligenstädter-Testament-Haus**, Probusgasse 6, in 1802 on the advice of his doctor, who hoped the country air would improve his hearing. It was here he wrote his "Heiligenstadt Testament" – a facsimile of which is at the museum – addressed but never sent to his brothers. In it he apologizes for appearing "unfriendly, peevish, or even misanthropic", talks honestly about his deafness: "a sense which in me should be more perfectly developed than in other people", and the pain and embarrassment it brought him: "I was on the point of putting an end to my life – the only thing that held me back was my art". It reads like a will, though

Ludwig van Beethoven (1770–1827)

Born in 1770 in Bonn, **Ludwig van Beethoven** came to Vienna in 1787, but remained for just a few months due to his mother's illness. Her death, and his father's subsequent death from alcoholism in 1792, freed Beethoven to return to the Austrian capital, where he lived until his own demise in 1827. Like Mozart, who was fourteen years his senior, he was taught by his father, a singer in the *Hofkapelle*, and played piano in public at a very early age (though his father used to pretend he was two years younger than he actually was). Again like Mozart, Beethoven was a virtuoso pianist, yet their techniques couldn't have been more different: Mozart gliding over the keys with smooth fluency, Beethoven raising his hands above his head, and smashing the keys with such force that he regularly broke the strings. Unlike both Haydn and Mozart, Beethoven was never a slave to the aristocracy, but an independent artist, whose patrons clubbed together to pay him an annuity just to keep him in Vienna, and prevent him having to take up the post of *Kapellmeister* at Westphalia which was offered him in 1809.

Though recognized as a genius by Viennese high society, he was also regarded as something of a freak: unprepossessing, scruffily dressed, reeking of body odour and swearing like a trooper. Despite such shortcomings, he was clearly attractive to women, and was, in his own words, "generally involved in one entanglement or the other". However, while the names of the women he was involved with are well known, no one can be sure that his love was ever consummated or even fully reciprocated. The objects of his affections were almost invariably young, beautiful, educated, aristocratic, and occasionally even married – in other words, unobtainable. One theory put forward as to why Beethoven never married is that he had syphilis, hence why he frequently changed doctors, and talked in his letters of "a malady which I cannot change and which brings me gradually nearer to death" – some suggest it may even have been the cause of his deafness.

In 1815, Beethoven's brother, Karl, died at the age of just forty-one. Beethoven then made the fateful decision to adopt his nephew, also named Karl, no doubt hoping that Karl would be the son he never had. After a long drawn-out custody battle with his sister-in-law, Beethoven succeeded in removing the boy from his mother in 1820, only to send him to boarding school. Beethoven proved totally unsuitable as a father, and Karl's misery reached such a pitch that in 1826, the fifteen-year-old tried unsuccessfully to shoot himself. He was immediately removed from Beethoven's care, at which the composer fell into despair, eventually dying of pneumonia in March 1827. His funeral, in contrast to Mozart's, attracted a crowd of 20,000 to the Trinity Church of the Minorites on Alserstrasse, with Austria's chief poet, Franz Grillparzer, composing the funeral oration. He was buried in Währinger Friedhof, but now rests in the Zentralfriedhof (see p.234).

it was more of a confession, the cathartic soliloquy of someone who had reached rock bottom.

After the onset of his deafness, Beethoven kept a Conversation Book and a pencil with him at all times. He would offer the book and pencil to whoever he was trying to communicate with, though he himself rarely wrote in them, simply bellowing his replies to his companions. By the time of his death in 1827 there were 400 "conversations", 136 of which have survived (and are kept in the Royal Library in Berlin). Despite his personal distress, while resident at Probusgasse Beethoven completed his joyful *Second Symphony*, "brought home right from the meadows of Heiligenstadt, so full is it of summer air and summer flowers" – a keen antidote to the simplistic theory of trying to fit the works to the composer's mood each day.

Beethoven changed addresses more times even than Mozart (see p.46), and spent a further four summers at various addresses in Heiligenstadt. The house in Probusgasse is one of the best preserved of all Beethoven's many residences, and probably the most rewarding of the city's three memorial museums to the composer. Confusingly, there are, in fact, two museums situated here. The official municipal one, on the far side of the shady, cobbled courtyard, occupies the rooms rented by Beethoven, and contains a lock of the composer's hair, his death mask, and the original doorhandle and lock from the Schwarzspanierhaus (now demolished), in which he died in 1827.

The Beethoven Ausstellung is open Tues, Thurs & Sat 10am–noon & 1–4.30pm; öS10; at other times, enquire at no. 5.

On the opposite side of the courtyard is the rival **Beethoven Ausstellung**, run by the elderly lady who lives at no. 5, on behalf of the Beethoven Society. There's more of an attempt at a bit of period atmosphere here, and an information sheet in English detailing the exhibits. However, there's still little to get excited about, beyond a few woodcuts by turn-of-the-century artist Carl Moll.

Nussdorf and Grinzing

Nussdorf is accessible on tram #D.

Nussdorf has less going for it than Heiligenstadt, though devotees of Otto Wagner might be persuaded to take a trip out here to see the architect's monumental **Nussdorfer Wehr- und Schleusenanlage** (weir and lock), completed in 1898 as part of Wagner's regulation of the Danube Canal. The most distinctive feature of the design are the pylons topped by a pair of fine bronze lions. Nussdorf's other claim to fame is that from 1932 the composer, Franz Lehár, lived in the small Baroque palace at Hackofergasse 18, previously home to the musical maestro Emanuel Schikaneder. The building, known as the **Lehár Schlössl**, is now a memorial museum, open to groups only.

The cemetery is open May–Aug daily 7am– 7pm; March, April, Sept & Oct until 6pm; Nov–Feb 8am– 5pm; tram #38 terminus is close by.

Further inland, up the slopes towards the Wienerwald, is the village of **Grinzing**, by far the most famous of the wine-making districts, whose *Heurigen* are mobbed by tour groups throughout the summer. To find a more authentic *Heuriger*, you're better off in any of the less well-known neighbouring districts, but devotees of the composer Gustav Mahler might consider a trip to **Grinzinger Friedhof**. The composer was buried here in 1911, having converted to Catholicism earlier in his career in order to make himself more acceptable to the anti-semitic Viennese establishment that ran the opera house. His modernist tombstone, designed by Josef Hoffmann, was commissioned by his widow, Alma Mahler-Werfel, who lies close by. Other notable corpses include the one-armed pianist Paul Wittgenstein (brother of philosopher Ludwig), and the writer Heimito von Doderer.

Wienerwald

The forested hills of the **Wienerwald** (Vienna Woods) stretch from the northern tip of the city limits to the foothills of the Alps, away to the southwest. The peaks you can see to the north and west of Vienna are an uplifting sight – few other capitals can boast such an impressive green belt on their doorstep. In the eighteenth century, the wealthier folk used to move out into the villages on the vine-clad slopes of the Wienerwald for the duration of the summer. With the arrival of public transport, even those without such means could just hop on a tram to the end of the line, and enjoy a day in the countryside. Still today, the Wienerwald remains a popular weekend jaunt, and throughout the summer, the wine-gardens of the local *Heurigen* are filled not only with tour groups, pumped on the Wienerwald nostalgia industry, but also the Viennese themselves, who come here to sample the new wine.

For more on the district's numerous Heurigen, *see p.291.*

Approaching the Wienerwald

There are several ways of **approaching the Wienerwald**. Tram #38 deposits you in the centre of Grinzing. If you walk up Cobenzlgasse, turn right up Krapfenwaldgasse and then go straight on at the cross-roads, up Mukenthalerweg, you'll find yourself on the right path to Kahlenberg (see below). To avoid the worst of the crowds and the traffic, though, it's probably better to start walking from the terminus of tram #D in Nussdorf, following Beethovengang past the Beethoven memorial, then going up Kahlenberger Strasse. Either way, it's a good 3km uphill to Kahlenberg itself. The shortest, stiffest climb is from Kahlenbergerdorf S-Bahn station up Nasen Weg, a kilometre-long path of tight switchbacks that takes you to the top of Leopoldsberg.

The lower reaches of the Wienerwald are no longer the rural idyll they once were, partly due to the winding *corniche*, known as the Höhenstrasse, which was built in the 1930s, allowing traffic access to both Kahlenberg and Leopoldsberg. Bus #38A from Heiligenstadt U-Bahn will take you all the way to Kahlenberg, Cobenzl and (less frequently) Leopoldsberg. If you want to lose the traffic altogether, the best plan is to take the bus to one of the above places, and start walking from there. If you haven't got it together to bring your own picnic, all the above have several restaurants and cafés.

Kahlenberg, Leopoldsberg and around

One of the most popular places from which to admire the view over Vienna is **Kahlenberg** (484m), the higher of the two hills that rise to the north of Vienna, close by the Danube. There's a café, with a magnificent terrace and a viewing platform, but the whole place is literally mobbed at the weekend. According to tradition, this was where the papal legate, Marco d'Aviano, and the Polish king, Jan Sobieski, celebrated mass in 1683, before Sobieski led the Polish army down the mountain to relieve the city from the Turks. The Baroque Josefskirche, in which the event is supposed to have taken place, is now run by the Poles, and the church's Sobieski Chapel is a Polish national shrine. The most striking thing about the plain interior is the hundreds of rosaries, pendants and lucky Madonna and Child talismen, which hang on the walls from floor to ceiling.

Tradition notwithstanding, it has been proved fairly conclusively that the aforementioned mass actually took place on the neighbouring peak of **Leopoldsberg** (425m), just over 1km by road east of Kahlenberg. To confuse matters further, the two hills swopped names after the Leopoldskirche was built on what is now Leopoldsberg in 1693. This is certainly a more beguiling spot in which to relax and enjoy the view. There's a much more pleasant courtyard and café, shaded by pine trees, and a more dramatic view from the restored ramparts, originally built by the Babenbergs in 1135. The main lookout point doubles as a memorial for the Austrian POWs who were finally allowed home from the Soviet Union in the 1950s. The church itself is also better looking than the one on Kahlenberg, and has a historical display of prints and documents relating to the Turkish siege.

If you're planning a longer walk in the woods, you're probably better off getting off bus #38A in the big car park at **Am Cobenzl**, which gives better access to some of the other peaks in this part of the Wienerwald. Cobenzl itself offers a variety of eating and drinking options, from the posh *Schlossrestaurant Cobenzl* to the more modest *Café Cobenzl*, both of which enjoy extensive views over Vienna. From Cobenzl, it's around 3km via Bei der Kreuzeiche and Jägerkreuz to the lookout tower on **Hermannskogel** (542m). Alternatively, you can enjoy the view while walking downhill from Am Cobenzl via the **Bellevuehöhe** (388m), where a plaque erected in 1977 records that "Here, on July 24, 1895, the secret of dreams revealed itself to Dr Sigm. Freud". At the bottom of the hill, you can catch bus #39A to Oberdöbling.

For more on the Wienerwald, see Chapter Nine, "Out of the City".

Zentralfriedhof

In a city where some people still keep a separate savings account in order to ensure an appropriately lavish funeral, it comes as little surprise that the **Zentralfriedhof** (Central Cemetery) is one of the biggest cemeteries in Europe. Larger than the entire Innere Stadt, and with a much greater population – 2.5 million – than the whole city, it's so big it even has its own bus service to help mourners get about. It was opened in 1874, at the height of Viennese funereal fetishism, when having *eine schöne Leich* (a beautiful corpse) was

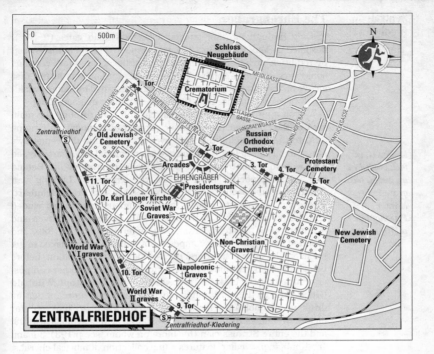

something to aspire to. Today, it's still very much a working grave-yard, and is particularly busy on Sundays, and on religious holidays, most notably All Saints' Day (November 1), when up to a million Viennese make the trip out here and virtually every grave is left with a candle burning in remembrance.

Visiting the cemetery

The most obvious way to **reach the Zentralfriedhof** is on tram #71 from Schwarzenbergplatz or on #72 from Schlachthausgasse U-Bahn. Take note, however, that the cemetery has three separate tram stops on Simmeringer Hauptstrasse: the 1. Tor, the first stop, deposits you outside the old Jewish section; the second stop, the 2. Tor, serves as the main entrance; the third stop (and the terminus for tram #72) is the 3. Tor, close to the entrance to the Protestant sec-tion, and within easy walking distance of the new Jewish section. In addition to the tram stops on Simmeringer Hauptstrasse, there are two S-Bahn stations along the southwest wall of the cemetery: Zentralfriedhof, a short walk from the 11. Tor and 12. Tor, and Zentralfriedhof-Kledering by the 9. Tor. Both stations are on the S7 line which calls at Wien-Nord, Wien-Mitte and Rennweg. The *Rundkurs* bus does a circuit of the graveyard every thirty minutes.

The cemetery is open May–Aug daily 7am–7pm; March, April, Sept & Oct until 6pm; Nov–Feb 8am–5pm.

The Ehrengräber

Passing through the monumental Jugendstil main gates (2. Tor),
designed by Max Hegele in 1905, you come to a semi-circular sweep
of red-brick arcades, which, though a little uncared-for, contains
some very elaborate tombs. The most extraordinary is in the first
alcove on the left: a mock-up mine entrance guarded by lantern-wield-
ing dwarves commemorating the Austrian mining magnate Zang.

As you approach the central church, you pass through the main
area of the so-called **Ehrengräber** (Tombs of Honour). In Gruppe
32A, to the left, facing the main avenue, you'll find the cemetery's

*Mozart is, in
fact, buried in
an unmarked
grave in St-
Marxer
Friedhof (see
p.170).*

most famous musicians. Centrestage is a memorial to Mozart, topped
by a woman trying to stop a load of books from falling off. Behind
him, at a respectful distance, lie the graves of **Ludwig van
Beethoven**, emblazoned with a busy gilded bee, and **Franz Schubert**,
whose bust is about to receive the posthumous honour that eluded
him during his lifetime in the shape of a garland. Beethoven and
Schubert were disinterred from Währinger Friedhof in 1889, and
reburied here – and fellow composer Anton Bruckner managed to get
his hands on both composers' corpses during the operation, before
being physically restrained by the officials present. Another composer reburied nearby is Maria Theresa's favourite, **Christoph Willibald
Gluck**, who died in 1779 after refusing his doctor's orders that he
drink no alcohol after dinner. Other composers to look out for
include **Johannes Brahms, Hugo Wolf**, who died of syphilis in 1903,
and the entire **Strauss** clan (for more on whom, see p.193); Johann
Jr's tomb, in particular, features a fine collection of musical cherubs.

The Ehrengräber on the opposite side of the main avenue, in
Gruppe 14A, are the more eye-catching tombs of *fin-de-siècle*
Vienna's wealthier denizens; most of the names mean little to non-
Austrians, with the possible exception of Ringstrasse architect
Theophil Hansen and artist **Hans Makart**, another victim of
syphilis. One of the most magnificent is that of the former mayor of
Vienna, **Dr Johann Prix**, which features a pompous copper bal-
dachin. Continuing towards the church, you come to a sort of sunken
roundabout surrounded by shrubs; this is the illustrious
Prezidentsgruft, containing the remains of the presidents of the
Second Republic, only one of whom, **Dr Karl Renner**, has any great
claim to fame, as the first postwar president.

To the right of the presidents, in Gruppe 14C, are several other
notable politicians, including the former chancellors Julius Raab and
Leopold Figl; the architect, **Josef Hoffmann**, is also buried here. To the
left of the presidents, in Gruppe 32C, you'll find more intriguing incumbents like the sculptor, **Fritz Wotruba**, who lies under a self-designed
tombstone. He also provided the highly appropriate cuboid tombstone
for the atonal composer, **Arnold Schönberg**, who died in Los Angeles
in 1951. Adjacent to Schönberg, and more universally mourned by the
Viennese, is **Bruno Kreisky**, the popular Austrian chancellor

(1970–83). Nearby lie the graves of the writer **Franz Werfel**, the composer **Alexander Zemlinsky**, Schönberg's mentor, who died in exile in
the USA in 1942, and the architect **Adolf Loos**, whose tomb is a typically ornament-free block of stone. Loos designed a similarly minimalist tombstone for his friend, the poet **Peter Altenberg**, who is buried in
Gruppe O, by the wall to the left of the main gates.

**Zentral-
friedhof**

Dr Karl Lueger-Kirche and beyond

The focal point of the cemetery is the garagantuan **Dr Karl Lueger-
Kirche**, completed by Max Hegele, a pupil of Otto Wagner, in 1910.
Initially at least, this domed church – badly in need of renovation –
resembles Wagner's Jugendstil Kirche am Steinhof (see p.220), but
on closer inspection, it's clear that Hegele has taken a more austere
Neoclassical approach. There are guided tours of the church on the
first Sunday of the month after mass (9.45am); otherwise you'll just
have to peep in from the vestibule. The chief vault in the church is
that of the anti-semitic city mayor, Karl Lueger (see p.110).

Few tourists venture further than the Ehrengräber and the Lueger-
Kirche, but there are plenty of other points of interest, if you've got
the legs for it. Directly behind the church a large **Soviet war cemetery** contains the graves of those who fell during the 1945 liberation
of Vienna, centred on a statue of two Red Army soldiers, flags downcast, with patriotic quotes from Stalin around the plinth. Continuing
down the central avenue, the path terminates at Anton Hanak's
despairing memorial to those who fell in **World War I**; behind it, in
Gruppe 91, is a semi-circular green field, its soft turf studded with
small graves. To the southeast, in Gruppe 88, are the graves of
Napoleonic troops who died during the 1809 French occupation of
Vienna, the majority inscribed with the words "Français non identi-
fié". Over 7000 Austrians who died fighting in the Nazi *Wehrmacht*
in **World War II** are commemorated by a field of black crosses to the
southwest in Gruppe 97.

Those who died fighting for the freedom of their country from
1934 to 1945 have their own memorial – a big heroic bronze man
accompanied by two mourning women – at the giant intersection to
the southeast of the Lueger-Kirche. Nearby are the uniform graves of
those who died in the riot outside the Justitzpalast on July 15, 1927
(see p.113), and a memorial to war victims from the Czechoslovak
section of the Austrian Communist Party. To the east, in Gruppe 28,
the victims of the civil war of February 1934 (see p.324), those who
died under the Austro-fascists, and martyrs of the Spanish Civil War,
have their own memorial. Further east still, the **Social Democrats**
have their own Ehrengräber featuring their early leaders, among
them Otto Bauer, Viktor Adler, and the latter's brother, Friedrich
Adler, who assassinated the prime minister Count Karl von Stürgkh
in 1916 (see p.49). Opposite, the casualties of the 1848 revolution
are commemorated by a simple obelisk.

Zentral-friedhof

Several non-Catholic denominations share the Zentralfriedhof: there's a Protestant section, accessible from 4. Tor, a growing Islamic section in Gruppe 26 and 36, and a small Russian Orthodox section around the onion-domed church in Gruppe 21, to the left of the main gates. By far the largest non-Catholic sections, however, are the two large **Jewish cemeteries**. The old Jewish section, founded in 1863 and accessible from 1. Tor, was desecrated by the Nazis on *Kristallnacht*, though some 60,000 graves are still standing, and work is finally being undertaken to try and stop the whole place from falling into rack and ruin. Among those buried here are the Viennese branch of the Rothschild family and the playwright Arthur Schnitzler. The Jewish section, accessible from 5. Tor, on the other side of the Zentralfriedhof, was inaugurated in 1917, and, despite being damaged during *Kristallnacht*, still functions today. The sheer size of these two graveyards is a testament to the pre-war magnitude of Vienna's Jewish community – testament also to the several generations systematically wiped out in the Holocaust.

The Crematorium and the Friedhof der Namenlosen

The cremator-ium is open the same hours as the Zentral-friedhof.

For the terminally obsessed, the city's **Crematorium** is but a short stroll from the main gates (2. Tor) of the Zentralfriedhof; take the underpass to the other side of Simmeringer Hauptstrasse, and walk in a northwesterly direction. The Roman Catholic church forbids cremation, which was championed by the anti-clerical Social Democrats between the wars as a secular alternative. The Viennese have never been entirely convinced by this ecologically sound form of burial, however, and a mere eighteen percent opt for it even today. Nevertheless, the central complex of buildings is worth checking out, a startling work designed in the early 1920s by Clemens Holzmeister. The central courtyard, with its arcade of Gothic lancet arches, is the most impressive section, along with the zig-zag roofline of the cre-matorium itself, all smothered in smooth grey, rendered concrete. The crenellated perimeter walls of the crematorium date back to the **Schloss Neugebäude**, built as a magnificent Mannerist palace by the Emperor Maximilian II. What remains of the palace can be seen at the far end of the Garden of Rest, behind the crematorium building. There are plans afoot to reconstruct the building, though by the looks of the place right now, there's some way to go yet.

Last, and probably least, is the **Friedhof der Namenlosen** (Cemetery of the Nameless Ones), to the east of the Zentralfriedhof at Alberner Hafen, containing the graves of the poor souls fished out the Danube each year. Some of the corpses are later identified, and are therefore no longer "nameless", but the majority are not, and the over-riding feeling is one of melancholy. To get there, you have to study the timetable of bus #6A very carefully; it leaves from the terminus of tram #71, but only occasionally makes it as far the cemetery.

Chapter 9

Out of the City

Thanks to Austria's efficient public transport system, day trips from Vienna are easy; the elegant spa town of **Baden** even has its own tram link with the capital. Though no longer the fashionable holiday retreat it once was, the town is still a good base from which to make a brief foray into the neighbouring Wienerwald (Vienna Woods). Another possible day trip is to **Eisenstadt**, a sleepy provincial town near the Hungarian border that's associated with the

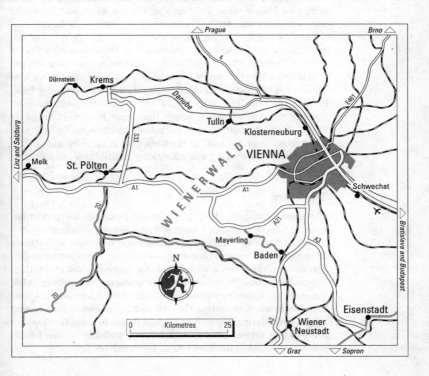

composer Josef Haydn, who worked for the Esterházy family most of his life, and is now buried in his very own mausoleum.

Heading up the River Danube is another popular way of daytripping from the capital. The first place of interest is the glorious monastery of **Klosterneuburg**, barely beyond the northern limits of the city. Slightly further afield is the town of **Tulln**, birthplace of the artist Egon Schiele, and first stop for boats heading upriver from Vienna (see p.252). Of all Austrian towns on the Danube, though, there are few as beguiling as **Krems**, with its medieval counterpart, Stein. Beyond lies the **Wachau**, a tortuously winding stretch of the Danube where vine-bearing, ruin-encrusted hills roll down to the river on both sides. Marking the upstream end of the Wachau is **Melk**, arguably Austria's finest monastery, a stunning Baroque confection that towers over the town and river below.

Baden bei Wien

Just 25km south of Vienna, the spa town of **BADEN** is an easy day trip from the capital, accessible either by train or via its very own slow-stopping tram link. It's a compact little town, peppered with attractive Neoclassical buildings, in varying shades of magnolia and ochre. Its distinctive Biedermeier appearance is largely the result of a building frenzy – much of it under the direction of the architect, Josef Kornhäusel – prompted by the devastating fire of 1812. Arriving hot foot from Vienna, Baden comes across as deeply provincial, a haven of peace for its elderly spa patients. But back in the eighteenth and nineteenth centuries, this was *the* most fashionable spa town in the Habsburg empire, the favourite summer holiday retreat of none other than the Emperor Franz II (1792–1835) himself. A swim in Baden's hot thermal baths is still highly recommended and, as the town lies on the very edge of the Wienerwald, the walking and picnicking possibilities are a further enticement

The town

The small, triangular **Hauptplatz**, at the centre of the pedestrian zone, is typical of Baden's modest scale. Almost dwarfing the surrounding buildings, including Kornhäusel's Neoclassical **Rathaus** from 1815, is the central plague column erected a hundred years earlier, and crowned with a gilded sunburst. Even the last of the Holy Roman Emperors, Franz II, chose an unassuming three-storey building – now the **Kaiserhaus**, on the east side of the square – as his summer residence. The last of the Habsburgs, Emperor Karl I, also stayed here, during World War I, when Baden became the Austrian Army headquarters. (Baden later reached its nadir in the 1950s, when it was used as the Soviet Army headquarters.)

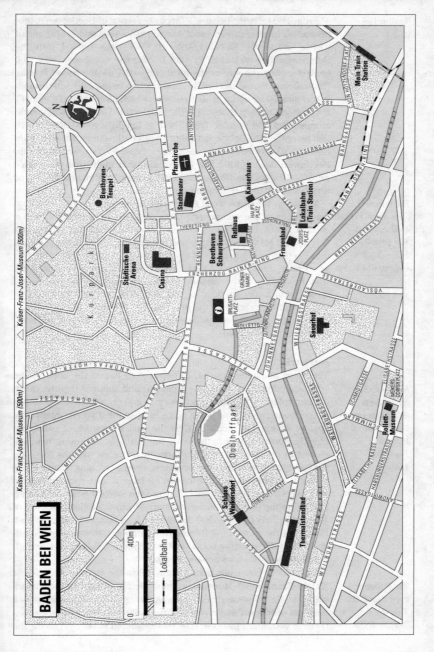

BADEN BEI WIEN

Kaiser-Franz-Josef-Museum (500m) △

Kaiser-Franz-Josef-Museum (500m) △

0   400m

Lokalbahn

Beethoven-Tempel

Städtische Arena

Casino

Pfarrkirche

Stadttheater

Kaiserhaus

Beethoven Schauräume

Rathaus

Frauenbad

Lokalbahn (Train Station)

Josefs-Platz

Brusatti-Platz

Sauerhof

Rollett-Museum

Doblhoffpark

Schloss Weikersdorf

Thermalstrandbad

Main Train Station

WELLERGASSE

KAISER FRANZ RING

ANTONSGASSE

ANNAGASSE

STRARRGASSE

GRABENGASSE

WASSERGASSE

HILDEGARDGASSE

VON HOTTENDORF-PLATZ

STRASSERNGASSE

BAHNGASSE

THERESIENG.

BAHNGASSE

BRENGASSE

BRETT

HAUPT PLATZ

RATHAUSGASSE

ERZHERZOG RAINER-RING

GRÜNER MARKT

ROLLETTG.

JOHANNESGASSE

ROTTOR-WIRTH

WEILBURGSTRASSE

BIEGERTH

KAISER FRANZ JOSEF-RING

BRAITNERSTRASSE

VÖSLAUERSTRASSE

ANDREAS-HOFER-ZEILE

HOCHSTRASSE

MOZARTSTRASSE

MITTERBERGSTRASSE

MARCHETSTRASSE

PERGASSE

SCHLOSSGASSE

DOBLHOFFGASSE

HELENENSTRASSE

SCHIMMER

SCHMIDGASSE

ELISABETHSTRASSE

HABSBURGERSTRASSE

ELISABETHSTRASSE

WEILBURGSTRASSE

WEILBURGSTRASSE

SANDWIGGASSE

MEIEREI DOBNER-PLATZ

N

From 1804, Baden became a favourite retreat of Beethoven's, too; he made a total of fifteen visits, staying at various addresses, one of which, at nearby Rathausgasse 10, has been turned into the **Beethoven Schauräume**. In the 1820s, the composer was well known around the spa as the local eccentric, as one friend recalls, "his hair was coarse and bristly . . . and when he put his hand through it, it remained standing in all directions which often looked comical". He even got himself arrested in the nearby town of Wiener Neustadt, after a local had been so frightened by his dishevelled appearance that she called the police. On being arrested, the composer said "I am Beethoven", to which the constable replied "You are a tramp, Beethoven doesn't look like that". Later that night that the town's musical director was finally called out to identify him, and the mayor sent him back to Baden in the state coach.

The museum is open Tues–Fri 4–6pm, Sat & Sun 9am–11am & 4–6pm; öS25.

Woefully, the three small rooms Beethoven rented out contain no mementoes of the composer's three sojourns here (there's even a section about later, lesser-known Badenites, including Katharina Schratt and Max Reinhardt, to pad things out). It was in these rooms that Beethoven wrote parts of his *Missa Solemnis* in 1821, and, two years later, finished his *Ninth Symphony*, though he had to get a friend to persuade the landlord to take him back on the promise of good conduct. The landlord agreed on condition that Beethoven pay for a set of new shutters (the previous set, on which Beethoven had made financial and musical calculations, had been sold by the landlord for a piece of gold).

Kurpark

The focus of Baden the spa, as opposed to Baden the town, is the ochre-coloured Kurhaus (now a casino) and summer theatre, north of Hauptplatz by the **Kurpark**, which is laid out on the steep slopes of the Wienerwald. This is the place to head for if you're intent on a spot of walking or picnicking, as the park's network of paths can quickly transport you high above the town. In its lowest reaches, closest to the town, the park is formally arranged with the focus on the bandstand and the **Udinebrunnen**, an eye-catching fountain featuring a gilded water sprite emerging from a vast rockery replete with oversized frogs, serpents, fish and the sprite's giant stepfather. Higher up the park, monuments emerge from the foliage: statues of Johann Strauss and his rival Josef Lanner, a temple to Mozart and, biggest of the bunch, the **Beethoven-Tempel**, a Neoclassical rotunda from 1927, sporting some dubious modern frescoes and graffiti, but with the best views across the spa.

In fine weather, concerts take place in the bandstand May–Sept Tues–Sun 4.30pm.

The museum is open April–Oct Tues–Sun 1–7pm; öS30.

For a more physically taxing walk, follow the signs to the off-beat **Kaiser-Franz-Josef-Museum**, roughly half an hour from the bandstand, in a northwesterly direction. Although it advertises itself as a museum of folk art and craftwork, the collection is a lot more eclectic than you might imagine. The reconstructed smithy is par for the course, but the mousetrap from the room in which Albrecht von Waldstein was murdered in 1634 is rather more unusual. In addition, there's a whole collection of arms and uniforms from the seventeenth to the twentieth century, bank notes, Habsburg memorabilia, a paper theatre, cake moulds and two penny farthings, to mention but a few.

The Rollett-Museum and Doblhoffpark

The museum is open daily except Tues 3–6pm; öS20.

An even more bizarre collection of exhibits fills the **Rollett-Museum**, ten minutes' walk southwest of Hauptplatz on Weikersdorfer Platz. It's worth coming out here for the building alone, designed in extravagant neo-Renaissance style in 1905 as the town hall for Weikersdorf, only to become redundant seven years later when Weikersdorf was subsumed into Baden. The most fascinating section is the array of skulls, busts, brains and death masks – plus a wax model of Marie Antoinette's hand, and a plaster cast of Goethe's – amassed by Franz-Josef Gall (1758–1828), the founder of phrenology, a pseudo-science which claimed a person's talents could be traced to areas of the brain. The rest of the museum is a hotchpotch: some crystals, an Egyptian sarcophagus and a cabinet of curios from the world tour of local nineteenth-century bigwig Josef von Doblhoff.

If you'd prefer something less mentally taxing, head for the vast hot thermal **open-air swimming pool complex**, which hides behind the 1920s facade of the *Thermalstrandbad* on Helenenstrasse. After your dip, you can relax in the nearby **Doblhoffpark**, a lovely mix of formal gardens and English park, with a large rosarium, a pergola and a huge, bushy plane tree at the centre. To the north is the sixteenth-century Schloss Weikersdorf, seat of the Doblhoff family

---

S&M in Baden

The staid spa town of Baden is the unlikely setting for *Venus im Pelze* (Venus in Furs), an account of sexual slavery written by **Count Leopold von Sacher-Masoch (1836–95)**. The count willingly signed his freedom away to the "Baroness Bogdanoff" (real name Fanny Pistor), becoming her manservant, taking the name of Gregor, and embarking upon "a liaison, marked materially by a prodigality in which furs and foreign travel were to be conspicuous". She agreed to wear furs "as often as possible, especially when in a cruel mood", while he agreed to "comply unreservedly with everyone of her desires and commands". After six months of slavery, including an extensive tour of Italy in which Fanny managed to ensnare a third party for their games, the two parted company. We have the count to thank for the term "sado-masochism", though he himself never coined the phrase. That was left to one of Freud's early mentors, Richard von Krafft-Ebing (1840–1902), who first used the term – with reference to Sacher-Masoch's writings – in his *Psychopathia sexualis*, published in Latin in 1886 (but later translated into seven languages), about which the Emperor Franz-Josef I once quipped, "it's about time someone brought out a decent book on Latin grammar".

The Mayerling Tragedy

Mystery still surrounds the motives behind the suspected double suicide of
Crown Prince Rudolf (1858–89), eldest son of the Emperor Franz-Josef I and
heir to the throne, and his half-Greek, seventeen-year-old mistress, Baroness
Maria Vetsera. The tragedy took place in the early hours of the morning on
January 29, 1889, at Rudolf's hunting lodge at Mayerling, 15km northwest of
Baden. It's an event which has captured the popular imagination for over a
hundred years – even though Franz-Josef had the entire lodge demolished
shortly after the incident, and a Carmelite nunnery erected in its place, folk still
flock to the site, and as recently as 1988, an Austrian businessman confessed
to having stolen Maria's coffin after becoming obsessed with Mayerling.

Numerous theories continue to be put forward as to why Rudolf chose to
take his life. The Viennese, who love to sentimentalize the tragedy, tend to
claim it was all for love, yet Rudolf was a notoriously fickle womanizer, and
Maria Vetsera was just one in a long line of pretty mistresses. The plot thick-
ens when we discover that the previous summer, Rudolf had proposed a suicide pact to another of his mistresses, Mizzi Caspar, but was turned down.
On the very night before his suicide, Rudolf spent the evening with Mizzi,
before leaving to meet Maria at Mayerling. It's true that his marriage to
Princess Stephanie of Belgium – arranged by his father for political reasons
– was a dismal failure, but it wasn't enough to drive him to suicide, and certainly didn't prevent him from keeping bachelor digs at the Hofburg where
he could receive his numerous mistresses. One plausible theory is that, at the
beginning of 1887, he contracted a venereal disease which he believed to be
incurable. Worse still, it's thought that he had infected Stephanie, causing
her to become infertile, having failed to provide a male heir to the throne.

Others contend that it was a political act, born of frustration with his lack
of any part in the decision-making process of government. Franz-Josef allowed
his son very little real power, and, in any case, disagreed with him on most
issues. Rudolf, who was never close to his father, tended to mix with liberals
opposed to his father's ministers' policies, and even wrote anonymous, critical
articles to the liberal *Neues Wiener Tagblatt*. There were even rumours at the
time that Rudolf had been assassinated by his political opponents, a version of
events upheld by the Empress Zita as recently as 1982. Another possible
explanation is that Rudolf, having written to the Pope to seek an annulment of
his marriage, had been snubbed by the pontiff, who had returned the petition
directly to Franz-Josef. We do know that on January 26, 1889, Rudolf and his
father had a fierce argument – what it was about remains a mystery.

Four days later, Rudolf and Maria's bodies were discovered by Rudolf's
hunting partner, Count Hoyos, who had got no answer when he called in at
Mayerling. The first official version of events was that Rudolf had died of
apoplexy, but after the post-mortem it was admitted that he had shot himself. As suicides were denied a Christian burial, the pathologists in charge
were wise enough to suggest that "the act was committed in a moment of
psychological unbalance", thus allowing the Catholic authorities an escape
clause. Rudolf's request to be buried in the nearby village of Alland alongside
his mistress was denied, and he was buried in the Kaisergruft amid much
pomp and circumstance. Maria Vetsera's presence at Mayerling was never
acknowledged by the Habsburgs, though rumours abounded. Some 36 hours
after the incident, her fully clothed corpse, in the first stages of rigor-mortis,
was wedged upright in a carriage between her two uncles, transported by
carriage to Heiligenkreuz and secretly buried in the cemetery there.

from 1741 until 1966 (it's now a hotel, but you should be able to sneak a look at the arcaded courtyard). Finally, if you've time to spare, check out the contemporary art in the low-slung **Frauenbad** (Tues–Sun 10am–noon & 3–7pm) on Josefplatz.

Practicalities

The quickest way to **get to Baden** is by train or S-Bahn from Vienna's Südbahnhof (every 30min; 20min) to Baden's main train station, ten minutes' walk southeast of the town centre. You could also jump on the special *Lokalbahn* trams – distinguishable from Vienna's other trams by their Prussian blue and cream livery – which run from the section of the Ringstrasse by the Staatsoper to Josefsplatz (every 15min; 1hr 10min). Baden's **tourist office** is attractively ensconced in the Leopoldsbad, a magnolia-coloured Biedermeier building on Brusattiplatz. The *Café Central*, on Hauptplatz, is a big traditional *Kaffeehaus*, and a great place for watching life go by. If the weather's fine, you're best off packing a picnic and heading off into the woods, but if you've no provisions, the *Central* offers reasonably priced food, as does *Café Damals*, Rathausgasse 3.

The tourist office is open Mon–Sat 9am–12.30pm & 2–6pm, Sun 9am–noon.

Eisenstadt

Some 50km southeast of Vienna, on the edge of a ridge of hills that slopes down gently to the Hungarian plain, **EISENSTADT** is known, above all, for its associations with the composer Josef Haydn, who was in the employ of the local bigwigs, the Esterházys, for most of his adult life. Haydn may be the main draw nowadays, but the town also has a well-preserved Jewish ghetto and an excellent new Jewish museum. It also possesses a rather unusual history, having been the Hungarian town of Kismarton for much of its history, only becoming the capital of Burgenland by default in 1921, when the province changed hands from Hungary to Austria, but for the old regional capital, Sopron (Ödenburg), which remained in Hungary.

The town

For a provincial capital – albeit of Austria's smallest Land – Eisenstadt is tiny little place, its old town made up of just three streets. **Domplatz**, the southernmost of the three, is open to traffic and used primarily as the local bus station; its fifteenth-century Domkirche was only given cathedral status in 1960 and, apart from its gilded pulpit and organ, is nothing special. **Hauptstrasse**, the pedestrianized main street, is prettier, particularly the Rathaus, with its shapely Baroque gables, three oriel windows and lively folk paintings of the seven virtues.

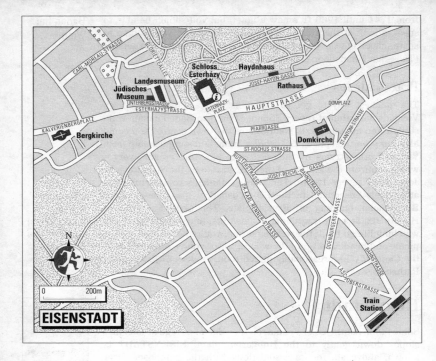

EISENSTADT

Schloss Esterházy

Guided tours of the Schloss set off hourly May–Oct Tues–Sun 9am–5pm; Nov–April Tues–Fri only; öS50.

Nothing in the town's modest little houses prepares you for the sheer scale of the **Schloss Esterházy**, which presides over Esterházy-Platz, at the western end of Hauptstrasse. It's a strange, slightly heavy building, a sort of oversized French country chateau, daubed in a fresh coat of imperial yellow paint with smart green shutters to match. All of which is hardly surprising, given that the Schloss was originally built as a medieval quadrilateral fortress with bulky corner towers, later received a Baroque conversion, and was finally redesigned in Neoclassical style (though you can't actually see the fancy, colonnaded north facade overlooking the gardens). Most of the rooms are now used as offices by the provincial government, but a few are open for hour-long guided tours; these are usually in German, so ask for the English notes.

Frankly, the only room worth seeing is the one which kicks off the guided tour, the **Haydnsaal**, whose coved ceiling is smothered with over thirty colourful frescoes, and whose walls are lined with painted roundels of Hungarian heroes. The acoustics are tremendous, and Haydn himself conducted numerous performances of his own music here. If you can catch a live performance, do – it'll also save you having to endure the second half of the guided tour. This takes you round the **Esterházy-Museum**, which contains Esterházy treasures, and traces the history of the family, who still own the Schloss, and who remain one of the wealthiest landowners in the country. At the end of this endurance test, you emerge in another fine concert hall, the **Empiresaal**, which takes its name from the Neoclassical pastel greens, blues and brown *trompe l'oeil* decor.

Unterberg

A hundred metres or so west of the Schloss lies the old Jewish quarter of **Unterberg**, established as a walled ghetto back in medieval times, and for centuries home to a comparatively large Jewish population. All 446 of the town's Jews were deported to the camps shortly after the Anschluss in 1938 – today there are just two families left in Eisenstadt – though Unterberg has since been repopulated. The remarkable thing about the district, however, is that despite the human destruction that was wrought on the community, the ghetto itself – made up of five streets and two cemeteries to the north of Esterházystrasse – remains more or less physically intact. As you enter the ghetto's main street of Unterbergstrasse, you can even see one of the two stone piers, between which a chain was placed on the Jewish Sabbath (a practice that was continued right up until 1938).

Österreichisches Jüdisches Museum

Further up Unterbergstrasse on the right, at no. 6, is the **Österreichisches Jüdisches Museum** (Austrian Jewish Museum), in the house that once belonged to Samson Wertheimer (1658–1724). Wertheimer was chief administrator of financial affairs to three successive Habsburg emperors, became first rabbi of Eisenstadt, and was eventually appointed *Landesrabbiner* (Chief Rabbi) of the Hungarian Jewry in 1693 by the Emperor Karl VI.

The museum is open May–Oct Tues–Sun 10am–5pm; öS50.

The museum stages temporary exhibitions on the ground floor, while the **permanent exhibition** on the first floor is a fairly standard rundown on Judaism, with a few models of (now demolished) synagogues from Vienna and of the old ghetto. Captions are exclusively in German, with the only English-language information in the museum's pricey catalogue. All the more reason, then, to head for the **multimedia catalogue** room, which has two televisual presentations in German and English. The first is a history of Jews in Burgenland, while the second describes the horrors of the Nazi period, and catalogues recent neo-Nazi attacks on the region's surviving Jewish cemeteries. Also on the first floor is the **Wertheimer'sche Schul**, Wertheimer's private synagogue, built in the early eighteenth century, but whose current *trompe l'oeil* decor dates from the early nineteenth. It was one of the few in the Third Reich to survive *Kristallnacht*, perhaps because by then Eisenstadt had already been cleared of Jews, and was used in the decade after World War II by Jewish soldiers of the Red Army.

Burgenländisches Landesmuseum

Another wealthy Jewish burgher's former home – the rather attractive house with the corner oriel at the junction of Unterbergstrasse and Museumgasse – has been converted into the **Landesmuseum**. As usual, there's no information in English, but the building itself is a lovely, rambling mansion, with a plant-filled rooftop loggia, and, in the cellar, a whole series of impressive Roman mosaics, the largest of which features Bellerophontes killing the lion Ceres. The local history section on the first floor is particularly strong on the territorial dispute after World War I, with propaganda posters from the period: Death in a Hungarian costume depicted playing the fiddle over Ödenburg (now Sopron). Finally, you shouldn't miss Franz Liszt's plushly furnished *Blauer Salon*, transferred here in its entirety from the Schottenhof in Vienna, where the Hungarian composer stayed on and off from 1869 to 1886.

The Landesmuseum is open Tues– Sun 9am– noon & 1–5pm; öS30.

Haydn's Eisenstadt

The house that Haydn bought in Eisenstadt, where he kept chickens, two horses and probably a cow, is now the **Haydnhaus**, on Josef-Haydn-Gasse. This was the composer's home, on and off, from 1766 to 1788, but there's no attempt to recreate his abode in any way. With no information at all in English (unless you buy the pricey catalogue) and only a few battered sections of one of the composer's own organs to look at, this is one for all but the most fanatical to skip.

The Hadynhaus is open Easter– Oct daily 9am–noon & 1–5pm; öS20.

A better way of paying your respects to Haydn is to head for the squat Baroque **Bergkirche**, which, as its name suggests, is located on raised ground 500m west of the Schloss, on the other side of Unterberg. The church itself is a *trompe l'oeil* fantasy in pinks and greys, but the reason most folk come here is to visit the purpose-built **Haydn-Mausoleum**, erected by the Esterházys at the west end of the church in 1932 in order to receive Haydn's decapitated corpse (his head had been stolen shortly after his burial in 1809). Twenty-four years later, his head was finally reunited with his body, and the whole of Haydn now lies in the marble tomb mourned over by four lounging cherubs.

The Bergkirche is open April– Oct daily 9am–noon & 1–5pm; Nov–Feb by appointment only; öS20; ☎02682/ 626 38.

The Bergkirche's other star attraction (covered by the same ticket) is the **Kalvarienberg**, accessible from the eastern exterior of the church. Here, steps lead up to a small chapel, beside which a turnstile lets you into a labyrinth of mini-chapels begun in 1701, depicting the story of the Passion in theatrical tableaux of full-size statues. First, you enter a subterranean grotto, then you wind your way round the outside up to the Crucifixion tableau on top of the church (great views over Burgenland), and finally back down to the Entombment on the other side.

Josef Haydn (1732–1809)

Of the big three classical composers, **Josef Haydn** is seen as coming a poor third to Mozart and Beethoven, despite the fact that his music is in many ways just as radical as theirs. Part of the problem undoubtedly lies in the ordinariness of both Haydn's character and his life – during his lifetime he acquired the nickname "Papa Joe" for his generally amiable personality (notwithstanding his boorish behaviour towards his wife).

Haydn was born in 1732 to a master wheelwright in the Lower Austrian village of Rohrau. His father, who played the harp, recognized his son's musical talents, and sent him off at the age of eight to join the choir of the Stephansdom in Vienna, where he was a pupil for nine years. When Haydn's voice broke in 1749, he was kicked out of the choir, and his little brother Michael became the new star pupil. Haydn then suffered a difficult poverty-stricken decade as a freelance musician, which ended with his appointment in 1758 as music director for Count von Morzin. Two years later Haydn made the biggest mistake of his life, as he later saw it, and married Maria Keller, the daughter of a hairdresser, with whom he could neither get on nor conceive children.

In 1761, Haydn was appointed assistant *Kapellmeister* to the Esterházy family at Eisenstadt. Haydn's patron, Prince Paul Anton Esterházy was a keen music lover, but he died the following year; luckily he was succeeded by Prince Nikolaus "the Magnificent", another music fan and a lavish entertainer. After a visit to Versailles in 1764, Prince Nikolaus decided to establish his own version of the palace on the other side of the Neusiedler See from Eisenstadt. By 1766 the complex – named Esterháza – was ready for occupation, with a new theatre, opera house and a marionette theatre. Although Esterháza was intended only as a summer residence, it became a more or less permanent home for the prince and for Haydn, now the family's chief *Kapellmeister*, who was glad of the chance to escape his wife and sleep with his mistress.

In 1790, Prince Nikolaus died; his successor, Anton, was less interested in music (and had less money). The family's court orchestra was disbanded, but as a sign of the family's respect for his loyalty, the Esterházys continued to pay Haydn's salary and allowed him to keep his title. He immediately moved to Vienna, embarked on two long tours of England, and enjoyed late, but great acclaim, letting his hair down and earning himself a great deal of money at the same time. His final years were plagued by illness and he died in Vienna in 1809 (see p.173).

Practicalities

The fastest and most direct **trains** from Vienna to Eisenstadt leave from the suburban station of Wien-Meidling (U-Bahn Meidling Philadelphiabrücke); the journey takes just over an hour with trains leaving hourly during the week, less frequently at weekends. You could also catch one of the trains from Vienna's Südbahnhof, which run hourly throughout the week, but this entails changing at Neusiedl am See.

Eisenstadt's **train station** is just ten minutes' walk southeast of the town centre, and you'll find the **tourist office** (daily 9am–5pm) in the east wing of the Schloss. A nice place to **eat or drink** *al fresco*, and enjoy a view of the Schloss, is the reasonably priced *Schlossrestaurant*, directly opposite in the former stables on Esterházy-Platz. Alternatively, *Zum Silberfuchs*, near the Bergkirche on Kalvarienbergplatz, offers a good range of Austrian dishes and daily specials for around öS75.

Klosterneuburg

Just north of the city limits, hidden behind the hills of the Wienerwald, the village of **KLOSTERNEUBURG** is one of the easiest day trips from Vienna. Chief attraction is its imposing Augustinian monastery, the oldest and richest in Austria, whose Baroque domes and neo-Gothic spires soar above the right bank of the Danube. It was founded in the twelfth century by the Babenberg Leopold III, who, so the story goes, vowed to build an abbey on the spot where he found his wife's veil, which had been carried off by the wind from a nearby castle. Leopold was canonized in 1485, and later became the patron saint of Austria, making Klosterneuburg a popular place of pilgrimage. Having withstood the Turkish siege of 1683, Klosterneuburg enjoyed a second golden age under the Emperor Karl VI (1711–40), who planned a vast imperial palace here, along the lines of the Escorial in Spain. The project was never fully realized, but the one wing that was completed gives some idea of Karl's grandiose plans.

Practicalities

The easiest way to get to Klosterneuburg is on S-Bahn line S40. If you already have a travelcard (see p.30), show it when buying your ticket. Trains to Klosterneuburg-Kierling (the nearest station to the monastery) depart from Franz-Josefs Bahnhof (every 30min; 12 min). To reach the monastery, which is clearly visible from the train station, head up Hundskehle, and then take the steps to your left.

Guided monastery tours in German only; minimum 5 people, Mon–Sat hourly 9–11am & 1.30–4.30pm, Sun 11am & 1.30–4.30pm; Nov–March no 9am tour; öS50.

To visit the monastery, you must sign up for a **guided tour**. The ticket office is right by the entrance to the monastery at Rathausplatz 20. If you're peckish, or have time to kill before your tour departs, the *Stiftscafé* (daily 9am–6pm), next door, offers reasonable **food**, and a chance to sample the local **wine**. The pricier *Stiftskeller* restaurant is open all day, though the *Keller* itself is only open from 5pm. On November 15, St Leopold's Day, the whole town indulges in a spot of barrel-sliding, using a giant wine cask made in 1704, and estimated to hold 56,000 litres.

The monastery

The tour starts with the **church**, which still hints at its origins as a Romanesque basilica, despite over-zealous nineteenth-century restoration. Neo-Gothic finials and other details obscure the west front, but the south door, with its blind arcading, is still much as it would have been in the Babenbergs' day. Inside, the church is a riot of seventeenth-century early Baroque, replete with frescoes and mountains of stuccowork. The most impressive craftsmanship is in the chancel: the richly gilded choirstalls, exuberant high altar, and, above all, Johann Michael Rottmayr's *Assumption*, without doubt the pick of the frescoes.

To the north of the church are the **medieval cloisters**, built in the late thirteenth century. The central courtyard is encroached upon, in the southwest corner, by the little L-shaped Gothic Freisinger chapel, containing the episcopal tomb of its namesake, who died in 1410. More intriguing is the polygonal wellhouse, which juts out into the courtyard from the eastern cloister, and boasts some fine tracery over the portal; the highlight is the magnificent, giant bronze candalabra, crafted in Verona in the twelfth century.

The monastery's most outstanding treasure by far, though, is the **Verduner Altar**, in the Leopoldskapelle to the east of the cloisters. This stunning winged altar, completed in 1181 by Nikolaus of Verdun, is made up of over fifty gilded enamel plaques, depicting Biblical scenes from both testaments. Sadly, you can't get close enough to appreciate the detail, but the overall effect is dazzling. The top half of Saint Leopold is buried in the Wiener Werkstätte casket underneath the altar; his legs are beneath the nearby wrought-iron grille.

You can get some idea of the Spanish-bred Emperor Karl VI's big plans for Klosterneuburg from the **Residenztrakt**, to the east of the medieval buildings. Plans were drawn up in 1730 for a vast imperial edifice, enclosing four inner courtyards, in deliberate imitation of the Escorial in Spain, which the Habsburgs had recently lost to the Bourbons. The building was to sprout numerous domes, which were to be capped by crowns, each one representing one of the Habsburg lands. In the end, the money ran out even before the completion of the first courtyard, and the roof sports just two domes, one capped with the imperial crown, the other with the archducal hat of Lower Austria. The showpiece of the Baroque wing is the **Marmorsaal** (Marble Hall), with its giant oval dome, supported by coupled composite columns, and decorated with frescoes by Daniel Gran glorifying the Habsburg dynasty.

The rest of the monastery and Kierling

After the tour, it's worth taking a stroll round the outlying monastic buildings, particularly those surrounding the **Leopoldhof**, a secluded little cobbled courtyard to the northwest of the monastery church, with an attractive, late-Gothic oriel window on one side. The main courtyard, Stiftsplatz, to the south of the church, centres on a lovely

**Klosterneu-
burg**

*The Kafka-
Gedenkraum
is open
Mon–Sat
8am–noon &
1–5pm; öS15.*

Gothic **Lichtssäule** (Lighted Column), once a common sight in Austrian towns, now a rare, surviving example.

While you're in the vicinity, you might be interested to know that the Prague-born writer Franz Kafka died of tuberculosis in Dr Hoffmann's sanatorium, in the nearby village of **Kierling** on June 3, 1924, at the age of forty. Die-hard devotees can catch a bus from outside the train station to Hauptstrasse 187, and visit the second-floor room, now known as the Kafka-Gedenkraum, in which he spent the last few weeks of his life, correcting proofs of his collection of short stories, published as *The Hunger Artist*.

Tulln

Another easy day trip, slightly further up the River Danube, is the little town of TULLN, situated in the fertile plain roughly 25km northwest of Vienna. The town has an ancient history, beginning its life as the Roman naval fort of Comagena, but its main claim to fame today is as the birthplace of the painter Egon Schiele (1890–1918), who was born above Tulln's main train station, where his father was stationmaster.

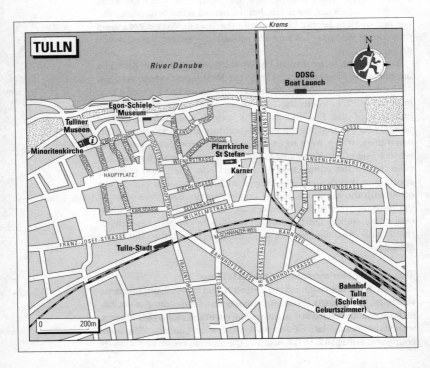

The town

On the 100th anniversary of the artist's birth, Tulln finally honoured its most famous son by opening an **Egon-Schiele-Museum** in the town's former prison by the banks of the River Danube. Before touring the museum, be sure to pick up the free booklet in English from the ticket desk. The ground floor, filled with reproductions of his works, and photos from his brief life, also features a cell transformed to represent the Neulengbach cell in which Schiele was incarcerated for 24 days in 1912. He was charged with displaying erotic drawings in a room open to children, and sentenced to three days in prison (by a judge who was himself a collector of pornography); since he had already served more than that in the course of his remand, he was immediately released. On the walls are reproductions of the watercolours he executed while imprisoned here, mostly angst-ridden self-portraits and interiors of his tiny cell.

The museum is open Tues–Sun 9am–noon & 2–6pm; öS40.

The museum's modest collection of Schiele originals is displayed on the first floor. There's a goodly selection of pencil sketches, among them numerous nudes, a ghostly *Madonna and Child* in chalk and an early oil painting from 1908 of *Trieste Harbour*, a favourite destination of the artist, who, due to his father's occupation, benefitted from cheap train tickets. In the attic, you'll find one of the artist's sketchbooks and the energetic *Ruined Mill at Mühling*, painted in oil in 1916, when Schiele was employed as a clerk in a POW camp for Russian officers.

The town's brand new museum complex, the **Tullner Museen**, housed in the former Minorite monastery, three blocks west down Albrechtsgasse, is, despite its stylish new premises, a bit of a disappointment. The main courtyard, sporting an elegant glass roof, houses the town's collection of historic fire engines from the horse-drawn carts of the eighteenth century to the diesel monsters of the 1970s. Other displays tell the story of the town's uneventful history, while the basement is given over to the less-than-impressive archeological finds dug up during the renovation of the cloisters.

The Tullner Museen are open Wed–Fri 3–6pm, Sat 2–6pm, Sun 10am–6pm; öS30.

All in all, you'd probably get more out of a quick peek inside the adjacent Baroque **Minoritenkirche**, which has been lovingly restored and is positively gleaming with white and gold paint. Be sure to check out the church's sacristy, with its cabinets of inlaid wood and Rococo ceiling decoration, and the brick-built Loretto chapel, a mock-up of Mary's house in Nazareth, complete with obligatory Black Madonna and Child, surrounded by cherubs.

Also worth a once-over is the **Pfarrkirche St Stefan**, two blocks east of the main square of Hauptplatz. Underneath this bulky Baroque church, the original Romanesque basilica can still be seen at ground level. Particularly fine is the west portal, which boasts thirteenth-century mug shots of the apostles. Best of all, though, is the old charnel house to the east of the church, one of the best preserved Romanesque buildings in Austria, dating back to 1250. The hexago-

> **Boats up the Danube**
>
> On Saturdays and Sundays, from April to October, the *Donaudamfschiff-ahrtsgesellschaft* (*DDSG*) run a daily boat up the Danube from Vienna to Dürnstein. The boat leaves from Vienna's Reichsbrücke at 9am, calling at Tulln at 11.45am and Krems at 2.10pm. In the opposite direction, it calls in at Krems on the way back downstream at 4.35pm, reaching Tulln at 6.20pm, and arriving two hours later in Vienna. *DDSG* also runs four daily sailings along the most picturesque section of the river between Krems and Melk; with some careful organization, you could feasibly take the train to Krems in time to catch the first sailing at 10am, arriving in Melk at 12.50pm in time to wander round the monastery and still get back to Vienna before nightfall. These were the correct times at the time of going to print, however, you should check with the Vienna tourist office before setting out.

nal rib vaulting looks clumsily restored, but the series of weird and wonderful animals and beasts that decorate the walls, above the blind arcading, are fantastic, as are the devilish characters with outsized ears and noses that accompany them.

If you've time to kill while waiting for the train back to Vienna, you may as well visit **Egon Schieles Geburtszimmer**, occupying two rooms on the first floor of the main train station (Bahnhof Tulln), which has changed very little since Schiele's childhood. However, there's not a great deal to see beyond a reconstruction of the bedroom in which the artist was born, a small model railway – understandably, trains were a major feature of Schiele's childhood, and reproductions of a few of his early drawings (of trains).

The Geburtszimmer is open Tues–Sun 10am–noon & 3–5pm; öS20.

Practicalities

Fast *Regionalbahn* **trains** run from Vienna's Franz-Josefs Bahnhof to Bahnhof Tulln, the main station, some fifteen minutes' walk southeast of the town centre (hourly; 25min). S40 S-Bahn trains depart more frequently from Franz-Josefs Bahnhof, taking 45 minutes, but terminating at Tulln-Stadt, less than five minutes' walk south of the centre. Tulln's **tourist office** (Mon–Fri 9am–noon & 2–6pm, Sat & Sun 1–6pm), on the east side of Minoritenplatz, will furnish you with a free map and any other information you might need. The best place for no-nonsense Austrian **food** is the *Albrechtsstuben*, Albrechtsgasse 24, east of Minoritenplatz.

Krems

Some 75km northwest of Vienna, **KREMS** sits prettily on the terraced, vine-clad slopes of the left bank of the Danube. Site of a twelfth-century Babenberg mint, over the following century Krems became a wealthy provincial wine-growing town. The architectural fruits of this boom period, which lasted until the seventeenth century, are clearly visible in the town's narrow streets. In 1995, Krems' 1000th anniversary prompted a frenzy of much-needed restoration and culminated in the building of a swanky new arts centre and a post-graduate university, which together look set to enhance the town's cultural life.

Krems town

Present-day Krems is actually made up of three previously separate settlements: Krems, Und and Stein, giving rise to the side-splitting local joke, "Krems Und Stein sind drei Städte" (Krems and Stein are three towns). Most people restrict their wandering to Krems proper, but, in many ways, it's Stein which has most successfully retained its medieval character.

Krems's main thoroughfare, **Landstrasse**, three blocks north of the train station, is a busy, pedestrianized shopping street studded with old buildings. The finest of these is the **Bürgerspitalskirche**, originally built in 1470 on the site of the old Jewish ghetto as the town's hospital chapel. Over the doorway is the A.E.I.O.U. motto of the Emperor Friedrich III (see p.41), while inside the little church boasts some wonderful lierne vaulting. On the opposite side of the street stands the sixteenth-century **Rathaus**, whose Renaissance origins are only visible in the corner oriel window facing onto Kirchengasse. Further west along the main street, at Obere Landstrasse 10, it's worth peeping into the exquisite arcaded court-yard of **Fellnerhof**, which features Tuscan columns from 1618.

To the north of Landstrasse, the hilly cobbled streets and squares successfully preserve their late-medieval character. The largest of the squares, Pfarrplatz, is dominated by the **Pfarrkirche**, originally a late-Romanesque church, enlarged at the end of the seventeenth century – you can see this most clearly in the tower. The interior is a perfect example of High Baroque drama, with *trompe l'oeil* masonry and gold covering just about everything, including the entire pulpit and the high altar – an explosion of gilded saints and cherubs set against the background of an enormous sunburst. The ceiling frescoes are by local-born Baroque artist Johann Martin Schmidt, known as "Kremser Schmidt", whose works can be found in churches and museums all over town.

A covered stairway known as the Piaristen Stiege, on the far side of Pfarrplatz, leads up to the imposing late-Gothic **Piaristenkirche**, whose tower doubled as the town's lookout post for many centuries. The church boasts some fine stellar vaulting, and several Baroque altarpieces by Kremser Schmidt, but it's worth the climb, above all, for the stupendous view across town. From here, you can descend via **Hoher Markt**, perhaps the prettiest of Krems's cobbled squares, which slopes down to the wonderfully scruffy-looking **Palais Gozzo**, a honey-coloured medieval palace with a ground-floor loggia. Round the corner, at Margarethenstrasse 5, the **Sgraffitohaus**, as its name

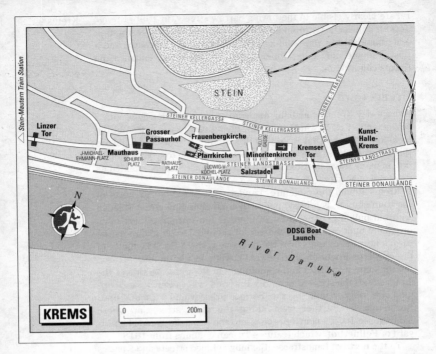

The museum is
open
March–Nov
Tues
9am–6pm,
Wed–Sun
1–6pm; öS40.

suggests, is smothered in sixteenth-century *sgraffito* depicting medieval folk frolicking and feasting.

West of Pfarrplatz lies the town's recently overhauled **Weinstadt Museum**, atmospherically located in the former Dominican monastery on Körnermarkt. Most of the museum amounts to little more than a mildly diverting trot through Krems's history and its viti-culture. However, you do get the chance to look around the thir-teenth-century monastery, whose cloisters feature unusual zig-zag, trefoil arcading, and whose church – now used for temporary exhibi-tions – is refreshingly free of Baroque clutter, and boasts the rem-nants of its original medieval frescoes. The museum also allows you the opportunity of a closer look at some of Kremser Schmidt's art-works and sculptures. There's something dark and tortured about Schmidt's work which makes it compulsive viewing. Born in nearby Grafenwörth in 1718, he trained under local artisans and set up his own workshop in Krems, eschewing the cosmopolitan art scene of the capital; it's this attachment to provincial roots that sets his work apart from the more academic painters of the Austrian Baroque.

Landstrasse, and the old medieval town of Krems, officially termi-nate at the strangely hybrid **Steiner Tor**, a monstrously belfried fif-teenth-century town gate, flanked by two cone-capped bastions.

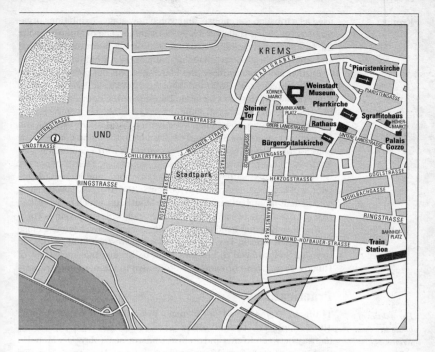

Appropriately enough, the district of **Und** links Krems, in the east, with Stein, to the west. There's no reason to pause in Und, unless you wish to visit the town's tourist office (see below), housed in the former Capuchin monastery. And if you're keen to sample some of the region's wines, you can sign up for a wine-tasting tour of the monastery's cellars (daily 11am–7pm; öS130).

Stein

It's the **Kremsor Tor**, ten minutes' walk west of the Steinertor, that, confusingly, signals the beginning of Stein. As you approach the gateway, it's difficult to miss the **Kunst-Halle-Krems**, the town's vast new arts venue, which hosts major modern art exhibitions, stages shows in the nearby Minoritenkirche (see below) and puts on a whole series of events on Friday and Saturday evenings.

The Kunst-Halle-Krems is open Tues–Sun 10am–6pm; öS70.

Stein itself is much quieter than Krems, its narrow main street, **Steiner Landstrasse**, a sequence of Renaissance town houses and crumbling old facades, opening out every hundred metres or so into small cobbled squares facing onto the River Danube. The first church you come to is the impressive thirteenth-century shell of the **Minoritenkirche**, whose high vaulted, late-Romanesque interior was used as a tobacco warehouse, and which now stages exhibitions organized by the Kunst-Halle-Krems. At the southern end of Minoritenplatz the two sixteenth-century **Salzstadl** (salt barns) sport distinctive red and white quoins, characteristic of many of Stein's old buildings.

Further along Landstrasse, the Pfarrhof stands out owing to its rich Rococo stuccowork, followed shortly afterwards by the Gothic **Pfarrkirche** which sports a classic Baroque onion dome. Steps round the east end of the church climb sharply to the fourteenth-century **Frauenbergkirche**, now a chapel to Austrian war dead. From here, you get a great view across Stein and the Danube to the onion domes of the hilltop monastery of Göttweig to the south. It's worth continuing a little further along Steiner Landstrasse to appreciate Stein's two other winsome squares, Rathausplatz and Schürerplatz, and its remarkable parade of Renaissance houses: in particular, the **Grosser Passauerhof**, with its half-moon battlements, and the **Mauthaus**, which boasts faded *trompe l'oeil* frescoes and a lovely false oriel, with ribbed supports.

Kremser Schmidt lived in the prettily gabled Baroque house close by the squat **Linzer Tor**, which marks the western limit of the old town of Stein. If you're heading back to Krems, the backstreet of Hintere Fahrstrasse provides an alternative to Steiner Landstrasse.

Practicalities

For details of boats to Krems, see p.252.

Trains to Krems leave from Vienna's Franz-Josefs Bahnhof (hourly; 1hr 10min). The **tourist office** is in the former Und monastery, halfway between Krems and Stein at Undstrasse 6 (May–Oct Mon–Fri 9am–6pm, Sat & Sun 10am–noon & 1–6pm; Nov–April Mon–Fri 8.30am–noon & 1.30–5pm). A convenient place to **eat** in town is *Gozzoburg zu den 3 Raben*, at the bottom of Hoher Markt (closed Tues); at the more upmarket *Graffito*, Margarethenstrasse 5, it's worth trying the house *Nudeln*, while *Halil*, Pfarrplatz 8, has decent pizza and pasta. If you're en route from Krems to Stein, the swanky café-restaurant in the Kunst-Halle-Krems is convenient.

Melk

Strategically situated at the western entrance to the Wachau, some 40km upstream from Krems, the town of **MELK** boasts by far the most spectacular Baroque monastery in Austria. Dramatically perched on a high granite bluff overlooking the Danube, the palatial mustard-yellow abbey dominates the landscape from whichever direction you approach, dwarfing the town into insignificance. Initially a Roman border post and later a tenth-century Babenberg fortress, the site was handed to the Benedictines in 1089. Very little of the medieval structure survives, and what draws in a staggering half a million tourists a year is the flamboyant Baroque pile built in the first half of the eighteenth century.

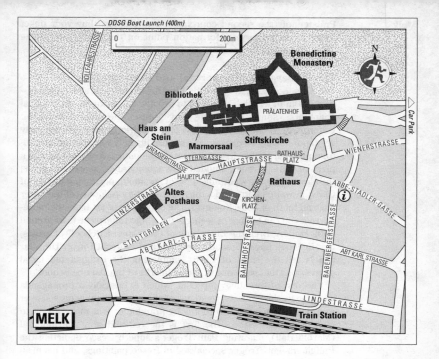

The monastery

Melk's early renown was based on its medieval scholarship (discussed in some detail in Umberto Eco's monastic detective story *The Name of the Rose*), and its possession of some very valuable relics, including the body of the Irish missionary Saint Koloman, who was revered for his powers of healing. The medieval abbey was gutted by fire during the Turkish invasion of 1683, and lay in ruins until Melk's ambitious abbot Berthold Dietmayer commissioned local architect Jakob Prandtauer to design a brand new showpiece monastery. The project was so overblown that Dietmayer faced a rebellion by his own monks, dismayed by the affront to their asceticism, and the abbot had to prove that the monastery could afford the work before building could recommence. The abbey continues to function today, with around 34 monks (half of whom are resident); the monastery school, containing some 700 boys and girls, remains one of Austria's most prestigious academic institutions.

Access to the monastery is via the main gates to the east. You can walk through several of the courtyards and peek at the abbey church without paying, but to see inside the monastery, you must buy a ticket at the top of the Kaiserstiege in the southwest corner of

The monastery is open daily Palm Sunday–early Nov 9am–5pm; May–Sept until 6pm; early Nov– Palm Sunday guided tours only 11am & 2pm; öS50 without a guide; öS65 with a tour.

Prälatenhof (the second courtyard). You can also buy your ticket from the monastery's information point on the south side of the Vorhof (the first courtyard).

The Kaisergang, Marmorsaal and Bibliothek

The **Kaisergang**, at the the top of the Kaiserstiege, is a vast gallery – over 190m in length – designed to provide access to the 88 imperial chambers, some of which now house the abbey museum. Unfortunately, the abbey 's most precious trio of treasures are only very sporadically on display, and are usually only represented by photographs: the Melker Kreuz, a fourteenth-century cross, containing a piece of Christ's cross, studded with aquamarines, pearls and gems; the eleventh-century portable altar of Swanhild, portraying the life of Christ in walrus horn; and a thirteenth-century reliquary of the lower jaw and tooth of Saint Koloman. The only work of art from the museum that you can be sure of seeing is the winged altarpiece from around 1502 by Jörg Breu the Elder, one of the "Danube School" of artists, that included Lucas Cranach the Elder and Albrecht Dürer. The altar panels tell the story of Christ, employing the exaggerated facial expressions that were one of the hallmarks of the Danube School.

The rest of the abbey museum, which is basically a propaganda exercise by the monastery and its school, can be happily passed over in order to reach the two rooms by Prandtauer that make a visit to Melk worth the effort. The first is the red and grey **Marmorsaal** (Marble Hall), featuring Paul Troger's superb fresco depicting the Enlightenment. Troger specialized in fresco paintings, and his masterly handling of perspective makes the ceiling appear much higher than it really is. Despite its name, the only furnishings in the hall made from real marble are the doorframes. To get to Prandtauer's **Bibliothek** (Library), you must first take a stroll outside across the curvaceous terrace, from whose balcony you can admire the the town below and the Danube in the distance. The library's ancient tomes – rebound in matching eighteenth-century leather and gold leaf – are stacked up to the ceiling in beautifully carved shelves of aspen, walnut and oak. Despite having never been restored, Troger's colourful fresco – a cherub-infested allegory on Faith – has kept its original hue, thanks to the library's lack of lighting and heating. From the library, you descend a cantilevered spiral staircase to the Stiftskirche.

Stiftskirche

The **Stiftskirche**, designed by Jakob Prandtauer in 1702 and completed in 1738 after his death, occupies centre stage at Melk, dominating the monastery complex with its fanciful symmetrical towers and octagonal dome. From the balconies above the side altars to the acanthus leaf-capitals of the church's fluted pilasters, the red stucco interior literally drips with gold paint. The Galli da Bibiena family of Italian theatrical designers are responsible for the stunning all-gold pulpit, and the design of the awesome high altar with its gilded papal crown suspended above the church's patron saints, Peter and Paul. The airy frescoes and side altar paintings are mostly by Johann Michael Rottmayr, who, along with Troger, was responsible for importing High Baroque art to Austria from Italy.

It's impossible not to notice the grisly reliquaries in the church's side altars, some of them featuring skeletons reposing in glittering garments. The most hallowed bones, those of Saint Koloman (presumably not including his jaw) are hidden away from the public gaze inside the sarcophagus in the north transept. Beyond this lies the entrance to the **Babenbergergruft**, where the remains of Babenberg rulers were traditionally thought to have been buried. In 1969, however, the remains were exhumed and examined, after which it was concluded that only Adalbert (1018–55), Ernst (1055–75) and possibly Heinrich I (994–1018) were actually interred here.

The town

The town of Melk itself is hardly much bigger than the monastery, and, inevitably, with such enormous numbers of tourists passing through, it does suffer from overcrowding. However, there are a few good-looking houses that repay a stroll around the town. Pretty painted shutters adorn the chemist's, next door to the Rathaus, and there are a couple of dinky turrets on the old bakery at the corner of Sterngasse, but the single most attractive building is the **Altes Posthaus**, built in 1792 at Linzerstrasse 3–5. The facade features stucco reliefs of horses' heads, agricultural tools, an eagle holding a post horn in its beak and so on, while the roof balustrade is peppered with urns spouting golden cacti, and, as its centrepiece, a double-headed crowned eagle. For a glimpse of old Melk that few tourists get to see, seek out the vine-covered **Haus am Stein**, set back in its own courtyard behind Kremser Strasse.

Practicalities

Fast **trains** from Vienna's Westbahnhof take an hour to get to Melk, but only a few actually stop there, as is obvious by the thunderous noise of through-trains that regularly shakes the town. The more frequent slower service stretches the journey time from Vienna to two hours, unless you take the fast train to St Pölten and change there, in which case you should be able to cut it down to an hour and ten minutes. Melk's **train station** is at the head of Bahnhofstrasse, which leads directly into the old town.

For details of boats to Melk, see p.252.

The **tourist office** is on Abbe-Stadler-Gasse (April–Oct Mon–Sat 9am–7pm, Sun 10am–2pm; Nov–March Mon–Fri 9am–noon & 1–4pm). For **eating**, *Gasthaus Melferstüberl*, Wienerstrasse 7, is a good local place, slightly off the tourist track, with a reasonable three-course daily lunchtime menu. Another good bet is the *Goldener Stern*, Sterngasse 17, which has a pleasant terrace.

Listings

Dialogs

Chapter 10

Accommodation

As you might expect, Vienna has some of the most opulent, historic **hotels** in Europe, with mesospheric prices to match. However, reasonably priced, central accommodation can be found, especially in the numerous **pensions**. These are not necessarily inferior in quality or price to hotels – in fact some are a whole lot better. The distinction is purely technical: pensions occupy one or more floors, but not the whole, of a building; to be a hotel, the entire block must be occupied.

Vienna also has plenty of **hostel** space in official HI and independent hostels, although these can be booked up months in advance, so try to ring ahead and make a reservation before you leave. Inveterate **campers** have a wide choice of peripheral sites.

The **high season** for accommodation in Vienna is from April to October, and for the two weeks over Christmas and New Year (during which there is sometimes a surcharge). That said, some hotels drop their rates in July and August, as the opera house and the theatres are all on vacation during this period. If you're arriving during the peak season, it's best to plan ahead in order to guarantee yourself a room (we've given fax numbers where possible, after the telephone numbers). If you arrive without a booking, any of the tourist offices mentioned on p.30 can make a reservation for you, for which they charge around öS35.

Hotels and pensions

Hotels and pensions in Vienna tend to adhere to the standards of efficiency, modernity and cleanliness you'd expect in Austria. Although you can stay right in the centre of Vienna, in the **Innere Stadt**, without breaking an arm and a leg, the cheapest places tend to be in the districts beyond the Ringstrasse. This is no bad thing, as areas like **Neubau** and **Josefstadt** have a wider choice of restaurants and bars than the central tourist zone.

Breakfast is included in the price at most of the hotels and pensions, though what it actually amounts to can differ enormously. "Continental breakfast" means coffee and a couple of rolls; "full continental breakfast" means you should get a bit of choice, perhaps cold meats and cheeses, and if you're really lucky a hot egg-based snack; and "buffet" means you can gorge yourself on as much cereal, muesli, eggs, bread, rolls, cheese and meats as you can eat.

Before you commit yourself, it's always worthwhile having a look at the room, as **natural light** is in short supply in some buildings in Vienna. Many old blocks of flats retain their beautiful antique **lifts**, some of which are so ancient they only carry passengers up and not down, and can only be operated by placing an öS1 coin in the slot.

INNERE STADT

The Innere Stadt is Vienna's old town and its commercial centre, and is there-

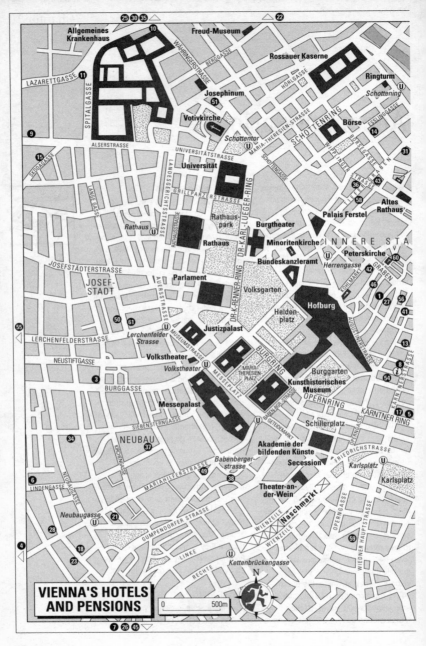

VIENNA'S HOTELS AND PENSIONS

0   500m

Allgemeines Krankenhaus

Freud-Museum

Rossauer Kaserne

Ringturm

Schottening

Josephinum

Börse

Votivkirche

Schottentor

Universität

Rathaus-park

Altes Rathaus'

Palais Ferstel

Burgtheater

Minoritenkirche

INNERE STA

Rathaus

Peterskirche

Bundeskanzleramt

Herrengasse

Parlament

Volksgarten

Hofburg

Helden-platz

Josef-stadt

Justizpalast

Lerchenfelder Strasse

BURGRING

Volkstheater

Volkstheater

MARIA THERESIEN PLATZ

Burggarten

Kunsthistorisches Museum

Messepalast

OPERNRING

Schillerplatz

KARNTNER RING

Akademie der bildenden Künste

Secession

Karlsplatz

Neubaugasse

Theater-an-der-Wien

Karlsplatz

Babenberger-strasse

NEUBAU

Naschmarkt

Kettenbrückengasse

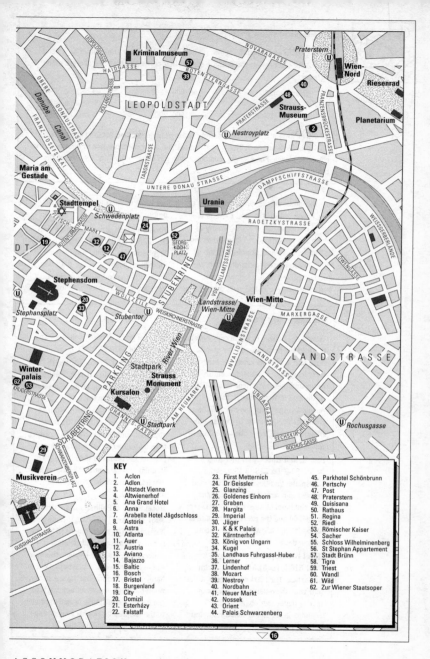

KEY

1. Aclon
2. Adlon
3. Altstadt Vienna
4. Altwienerhof
5. Ana Grand Hotel
6. Anna
7. Arabella Hotel Jägdschloss
8. Astoria
9. Astra
10. Atlanta
11. Auer
12. Austria
13. Aviano
14. Bajazzo
15. Baltic
16. Bosch
17. Bristol
18. Burgenland
19. City
20. Domizil
21. Esterházy
22. Falstaff

23. Fürst Metternich
24. Dr Geissler
25. Glanzing
26. Goldenes Einhorn
27. Graben
28. Hargita
29. Imperial
30. Jäger
31. K & K Palais
32. Kärntnerhof
33. König von Ungarn
34. Kugel
35. Landhaus Fuhrgassl-Huber
36. Lerner
37. Lindenhof
38. Mozart
39. Nestroy
40. Nordbahn
41. Neuer Markt
42. Nossek
43. Orient
44. Palais Schwarzenberg

45. Parkhotel Schönbrunn
46. Pertschy
47. Post
48. Praterstern
49. Quisisana
50. Rathaus
51. Regina
52. Riedl
53. Römischer Kaiser
54. Sacher
55. Schloss Wilhelminenberg
56. St Stephan Appartement
57. Stadt Brünn
58. Tigra
59. Triest
60. Wandl
61. Wild
62. Zur Wiener Staatsoper

Accommodation

Accommodation Prices

All the hotels and pensions below are listed in alphabetical order under area headings. After each review you'll find a symbol that corresponds to one of eight **price categories**:

① under öS500
② öS500–750
③ öS750–1000
④ öS1000–1250
⑤ öS1250–1500
⑥ öS1500–2000
⑦ öS2000–2500
⑧ öS2500–3000
⑨ over öS3000

All prices are for the cheapest **double room** available in high season (April–Oct, Christmas & New Year). This may mean without a private bathroom or shower in the cheapest places. For a single room, expect to pay between half and two-thirds the price of a double.

fore the place where everyone wants to stay. Prices reflect this, and there is a surfeit of upper-range hotels (many of which we haven't even bothered listing below), and a corresponding dearth of inexpensive places (most of which we *have* listed). As all the following hotels and pensions are in the city's first district, we have omitted to put the district code before the address.

Pension Aclon, Dorotheergasse 6–8 ☎512 79 40-0; fax 513 87 51; U-Bahn Stephansplatz. Family-run pension in an incredible location on the third floor, next door to the wonderful *Café Hawelka*, with an ancient up-only lift (öS1). Nicely

---

Vienna's Big Four

Vienna specializes in big **luxury hotels**, but four big Ringstrasse piles stand head and shoulders above the others for their heavy late nineteenth-century decor and their historical associations. At the end of World War II, the Americans took over the *Bristol*, the Russians occupied the *Grand* and the *Imperial*, while the British holed up in the *Sacher*.

Ana Grand Hotel, Kärntner Ring 9 ☎515 80-0; fax 515 13 13; U-Bahn Karlsplatz. Faultlessly luxurious, modernized reincarnation of the famous imperial hotel on this site. Rooms start at öS4500 and the presidential suite is öS35,000, but it's worth asking about special deals. ⑨.

Hotel Bristol, Kärntner Ring 1 ☎51 516-0; fax 51 516-550; U-Bahn Karlsplatz. The least remarkable of the four from the outside, but a feast of marble inside, with barley-sugar columns in the *Korso* restaurant, and opulent repro decor in all the rooms

(doubles go for öS3000; suites for anything up to öS12,900). ⑨.

Hotel Imperial, Kärntner Ring 16 ☎501 10-0; fax 501 10-410; U-Bahn Karlsplatz. Incredibly lavish converted palace, built for the Duke of Würtemberg, and later the "favourite hostelry of crowned heads, their heirs-apparent, and ambassadors" according to one observer in 1877. Hitler stayed here on his return to the city in 1938. Doubles start at a mere öS4600; suites reach the stratospheric heights of öS39,000. ⑨.

Hotel Sacher, Philharmonikerstrasse 4 ☎51 456; fax 51 457-810; U-Bahn Karlsplatz. The most famous of the lot, not only because of its legendary *Sachertorte*, but also because this was where the aristocratic playboys used to hang out in the imperial days. A heavy, wood-panelled, red velvet approach to the decor and stiflingly formal approach to the hospitality. Double rooms range between öS3800 and öS5400. ⑨.

furnished rooms, some without shower or toilet. ③.

Hotel Astoria, Kärntnerstrasse 32–34 ☎515 77-0; fax 515 77-82; U-Bahn Karlsplatz. Grandiose flagship of the *Austropa* hotel chain and preferred pad of visiting opera stars owing to its proximity to the Staatsoper. The entrance is on Fürichgasse. ⑦.

Hotel Austria, Wolfengasse 3 ☎515 23; fax 515 23-506; U-Bahn Schwedenplatz. Plush family-run hotel, somewhat characterless but pleasantly located in a quiet cul-de-sac off Fleischmarkt. ④.

Pension Aviano, Marco d'Avianogasse 1 ☎512 83 30; fax 512 83 30-6; U-Bahn Karlsplatz. Part of *Pertschy* pension chain, squeezed onto the top floor of a building just off Kärntnerstrasse. Low ceilings, but roomy rooms, all en suite, with TV and fluffy, floral decor. ④.

Hotel Bajazzo, Esslinggasse 7 ☎533 89 03; fax 535 39 97; U-Bahn Schottenring. Popular, modern hotel with just twelve en suite rooms. ⑥.

Pension City, Bauernmarkt 10 ☎533 95 21; fax 535 52 16; U-Bahn Stephansplatz. On the second floor of a wonderful late nineteenth-century building and run by a friendly woman proprietor. Tastefully decorated rooms, all en suite. ④.

Pension Domizil, Schulerstrasse 14 ☎513 31 99-0; fax 512 34 84; U-Bahn Stephansplatz. Small rooms, clean modern furnishings, friendly staff and big breakfasts. ⑥.

Pension Dr Geissler, Postgasse 14 ☎533 28 03; fax 533 26 35; U-Bahn Schwedenplatz. Anonymous modern pension on the eighth floor; all rooms with satellite TV, some en suite. ②.

Graben Hotel, Dorotheergasse 3 ☎512 15 31-0; fax 512 15 31-20; U-Bahn Stephansplatz. The foyer is suitably lugubrious, with heavy velvet drapery, but all the rooms are modernized and smart, with en suite shower and toilet and the location is great. ⑤.

K & K Palais Hotel, Rudolfsplatz 11 ☎533 13 53; fax 533 13 53-70; U-Bahn Schwedenplatz. Built in 1890 and once the town house of Franz-Josef's mistress Katharina Schratt, the *K & K* retains an appropriately imperial ambience in the lobby. The rooms have been modernized and are fully en suite. ⑦.

Hotel Kärntnerhof, Grashofgasse 4 ☎512 19 23; fax 513 22 28-33; U-Bahn Schwedenplatz/Stephansplatz. Characterful rooms, though some are a bit dingy, so check first. Rooms without en suite facilities are cheaper. ③.

Hotel König von Ungarn, Schulerstrasse 10 ☎515 84-0; fax 515 848; U-Bahn Stephansplatz. Tastefully modernized hotel with a remarkable wooden-panelled, covered courtyard bar/lounge. Pleasantly decorated rooms equipped throughout with air-conditioning, satellite TV, and en suite shower and toilet. ⑥.

Pension Lerner, Wipplingerstrasse 23 ☎533 52 19; fax 533 56 78; U-Bahn Schottentor/Herrengasse. Bright, plain rooms with shower, toilet, satellite TV, plus nice high ceilings and fans. Big buffet breakfasts served until 11am. ③.

Pension Neuer Markt, Seilergasse 9 ☎512 23 16; fax 513 91 05; U-Bahn Stephansplatz. Very popular pension on the second floor of a lovely old patrician building. All rooms with bath or shower, some with views over Neuermarkt. ④.

Pension Nossek, Graben 17 ☎533 70 41-0; fax 535 36 46; U-Bahn Stephansplatz. Large pension on three floors of an old building on the Graben; book in advance. ④.

Hotel Orient, Tiefer Graben 30 ☎533 73 07; fax 535 03 40; U-Bahn Herrengasse. Vienna's equivalent of a Tokyo "love hotel", with rooms rented by the hour and per night. Couples come for the mind-boggling exotic decor, and the wide range of themed rooms from inexpensive to more than öS2000. ③.

Pension Pertschy, Habsburgergasse 5 ☎534 49; fax 534 49 49; U-Bahn Stephansplatz. Flagship of the *Pertschy* chain, with rooms off a series of plant-strewn balconies looking onto a lovely

Accommodation

Accommodation

old courtyard – all have high ceilings, tasteful furnishings and TVs. ④.

Hotel Post, Fleischmarkt 24 ☎515 83-0; fax 515 83-808; U-Bahn Schwedenplatz. Civilized, central hotel with big old rooms and modern furnishings, some without shower and toilet. ③.

Pension Riedl, Georg-Coch-Platz 3 ☎512 79 19; fax 512 79 19; U-Bahn Schwedenplatz/Wien Mitte. Bright, cheerful pension on the fourth floor of a wonderful *fin-de-siècle* building overlooking the Postsparkasse. The rooms are small, but all have shower and toilet, and you get breakfast in bed. ③.

Hotel Römischer Kaiser, Annagasse 16 ☎512 77 51-0; fax 512 77 51-13; U-Bahn Karlsplatz. Turn-of-the-century family-run hotel on a delightfully narrow side street off Kärntnerstrasse. New furnishings are successfully combined with the originals, though some rooms feature plainer modern decor. Cable TV and en suite throughout. ⑦.

St Stephan Appartement-Pension, Spiegelgasse 1 ☎512 29 90–0; fax 512 29 90-20. Incredible location in the Braun building overlooking Graben. An antique lift takes you up to the fourth floor, where there are just six doubles, each furnished in keeping with the period, with creaky parquet flooring. All have TV, shower, toilet and cooking facilities. No breakfast. ④.

Hotel Tigra, Tiefer Graben 14–20 ☎533 96 41; fax 533 96 45; U-Bahn Herrengasse. Thoroughly modernized, if characterless, chain hotel, with satellite TV and en suite facilities. Good big breakfasts. ⑤.

Hotel Wandl, Petersplatz 9 ☎534 55–0; fax 534 55-77; U-Bahn Stephansplatz. Modernized nineteenth-century hotel with uniformed staff and some period fittings in the grandiose dining room and in the high-ceilinged rooms. ④.

Hotel zur Wiener Staatsoper, Krugerstrasse 11 ☎513 12 74; fax 513 12 74-15; U-Bahn Karlsplatz. Flamboyant late nineteenth-century facade and foyer, but much plainer rooms, all en suite and with TV. ⑤.

LANDSTRASSE, WIEDEN AND MARGARETEN

Parts of Landstrasse (3rd district) are eminently avoidable, though the area around the Belvedere is a much more desirable locale. Wieden (4th district) and Margareten (5th district) are quieter, residential districts, to the south of Karlsplatz and the Naschmarkt.

Pension Bosch, 3, Keilgasse 13 ☎798 61 79; fax 799 17 18; S-Bahn Rennweg or tram #0. Decent pension near the Südbahnhof, in a quiet backstreet behind the Belvedere, an easy tram ride into town. ②.

Hotel Goldenes Einhorn, 5, Am Hundsturm 5 ☎544 47 55; U-Bahn Margaretengürtel. Inexpensive family-run place with just fourteen rooms. In a residential area just within the Gürtel but well connected to the centre. Booking essential. ①.

Hotel im Palais Schwarzenberg, 3, Schwarzenbergplatz 9 ☎798 45 15; fax 798 47 14; tram #D. Hidden behind the Soviet War Memorial, this is *the* hotel to go for if money's no object – a Baroque palace designed by Hildebrandt and Fischer von Erlach, with period furnishings courtesy of, among others, Rubens, Meissen and Gobelins. ⑨.

Das Triest, 4, Wiedner Hauptstrasse 12 ☎589 18-0; fax 589 18-18; U-Bahn Karlsplatz. Inspired by what Phillippe Starck did for the *Paramount* in New York, Terence Conran has lent his designer touch to Vienna's *Das Triest*. Rooms are en suite, boasting all mod cons; those on the top floor have great views across the city skyline. ⑧.

MARIAHILF, NEUBAU AND JOSEFSTADT

The 6th, 7th and 8th districts are home to some of Vienna's liveliest bars and choicest restaurants, and therefore ideal areas in which to be based. Neubau includes the lively Spittelberg area, while Josefstadt is more studenty.

Altstadt Vienna, 7, Kirchengasse 41; ☎526 33 99-0; fax 523 69 89-55; U-Bahn Volkstheater. A cut above most other pensions, with laid-back staff, relaxing lounge and full-on buffet breakfast. Beautifully decorated en suite rooms, with high ceilings, and a great location, near Spittelberg and within easy walking distance of the Ring. ⑥.

Altwienerhof, 15, Herklotzgasse 6 ☎892 60 00; fax 892 60 00-8; U-Bahn Gumpendorfer Strasse. Just across the Gürtel from Mariahilf, and close to the Westbahnhof. Popular for its excellent restaurant, and the opulent furnishings. Doubles with sink are a bargain. ③.

Pension Anna, 7, Zieglergasse 18 ☎523 01 60; fax 523 01 60-39; U-Bahn Webgasse. First-floor pension run by a friendly couple. The startling light-blue decor doesn't extend into the fourteen bedrooms, all of which have en suite shower and toilet. ④.

Pension Astra, 8, Alserstrasse 32 ☎402 43 54; fax 402 46 62-46; U-Bahn Alserstrasse. Mid-sized pension on the mezzanine of an old patrician building. Friendly staff and a range of modernized rooms from simple doubles without shower or toilet to roomy apartments. ③.

Pension Baltic, 8, Skodagasse 15 ☎405 01 73; U-Bahn Alserstrasse. Variable rooms, all of them large, with endearing creaky parquet floors and crudely added showers. ②.

Hotel Burgenland, 6, Esterházygasse 26 ☎587 03 81; U-Bahn Neubaugasse. Just off Mariahilferstrasse, and a bit gloomy inside, but fairly spacious rooms all with en suite shower and toilet. ②.

Pension Esterházy, 6, Nelkengasse 3 ☎587 51 59; U-Bahn Neubaugasse. Basic rooms, but clean and close to Mariahilferstrasse. There's no reception as such and no breakfast – it's simply a place to crash. ①.

Fürst Metternich Hotel, 6, Esterházygasse 33 ☎588 70; U-Bahn Neubaugasse. Incredible pink late nineteenth-century hotel with ornate marble foyer. Much plainer rooms, all en suite. ⑥.

Pension Hargita, 7, Andreasgasse 1 ☎526 19 28; fax 526 04 92; U-Bahn Neubaugasse. Nice old building with bright cheerful rooms looking out onto Mariahilferstrasse, and decked out in peasant-style pine. Not for lie-ins, owing to the bustle and noise on the streets below. ②.

Hotel Kugel, 7, Siebensterngasse 43 ☎523 33 55; fax 523 16 78; U-Bahn Neubaugasse. Jovial ownership and good location within spitting distance of Spittelberg's numerous restaurants and bars. Plain rooms, and continental breakfast only in the *gemütlich* peasant-style breakfast room. ③.

Pension Lindenhof, 7, Lindengasse 4 ☎523 04 98; fax 523 73 62; U-Bahn Neubaugasse. On the first floor of a turn-of-the-century building at the Spittelberg end of this long street. Lovely, up-only lift (öS1) and appealing rooms with creaky parquet flooring. ②.

Pension Mozart, 6, Theobaldgasse 15 ☎ & fax 587 85 05; U-Bahn Neubaugasse/Babenbergerstrasse. No frills pension on the mezzanine of a Jugendstil building, handy for Mariahilferstrasse and the Westbahnhof. ②.

Pension Quisisana, 6, Windmühlgasse 6 ☎587 33 41; fax 587 33 41; U-Bahn Neubaugasse/Babenbergerstrasse. Wonderful late nineteenth-century pension, a short stroll from the Kunsthistorisches, run by a friendly old couple. Rooms are small but clean, and there's continental breakfast in the adjoining café. ②.

Hotel Rathaus, 8, Lange Gasse 13 ☎406 01 23; fax 408 42 72; U-Bahn Lerchenfelder Strasse. Clean, comfortable and quiet hotel a few blocks west of the Rathaus, with some cheap singles without en suite bathroom. ④.

Pension Wild, 8, Lange Gasse 10 ☎406 51 74; fax 402 21 68; U-Bahn Lerchenfelder Strasse. Backpackers' favourite, a short walk from the Ring in a student district behind the university. Booking essential. ②.

Accommodation

Accommodation

ALSERGRUND

Separated from the rest of the *Vorstädte* by the giant city hospital, the ninth district has a life of its own, with a good selection of trendy cafés, bars and restaurants, and frequent tram connections to the centre.

Hotel Atlanta, 9, Währinger Strasse 33 ☎405 12 39; fax 405 53 75; tram #37, #38, #40, #41 or #42. Plush Alsergrund hotel within easy walking distance of the district's best bars and restaurants. All rooms are en suite with cable TV. Prices drop significantly in low season. ⑤.

Pension Auer, 9, Lazarettgasse 3 ☎406 21 21; fax 406 21 21-4; tram #5 or #33. Not the prettiest of spots, but pleasant enough inside and a real bargain, within walking distance of Josefstadt. ②.

Pension Falstaff, 9, Müllnergasse 5 ☎317 91 27; fax 317 91 864; tram #D. Highly regarded, comfortable pension with plain rooms, in a late nineteenth-century building. ②.

Hotel Regina, 9, Rooseveltplatz 15 ☎404 46-0; fax 408 83 92; U-Bahn Schottentor. Huge Ringstrasse hotel next door to the Votivkirche, with gloriously heavy Viennese decor in the public areas and in some of the rooms. ⑥.

LEOPOLDSTADT

Separated from the Innere Stadt by the Danube Canal, Leopoldstadt, Vienna's 2nd district, is quiet and slightly dowdy, seldom visited by tourists. Yet the area lies just a couple of tram stops from the central district and the greenery of the Prater. The backstreets near Wien-Nord train station double as a red-light district, but the atmosphere is rarely intimidating.

Hotel Adlon, 2, Hofenedergasse 4 ☎216 67 88; fax 216 67 88-116; U-Bahn Nestroyplatz. Next to a brothel, but within easy walking distance of the Prater. Though the decor is a bit tacky, the hotel itself is in no way seedy. All en suite. ③.

Hotel Nestroy, 2, Rotensterngasse 12 ☎211 40-0; fax 211 40-7; U-Bahn Nestroyplatz. Modern decor, something of an acquired taste in the foyer and

covered courtyard, but a little easier on the eye in the rooms, all of which have en suite facilities and satellite TV. Also a sauna and gym. ⑥.

Hotel Nordbahn, 2, Praterstrasse 72 ☎211 30-0; fax 211 30-72; U-Bahn Nestroyplatz/Praterstern. Birthplace of Max Steiner, composer of film music to *Gone with the Wind* and *Casablanca*, and now a large, pleasantly modernized hotel with shower, toilet and TVs in all rooms. ③.

Hotel Praterstern, 2, Mayergasse 6 ☎214 01 23; fax 214 78 80; U-Bahn Nestroyplatz. Turn-of-the-century hotel with a few nice period touches and a pleasant outdoor courtyard. Simply furnished rooms with shower and toilet. ②.

Hotel Stadt Brünn, 2, Rotensterngasse 7a ☎24 63 22; fax 246 32 27; U-Bahn Nestroyplatz. Late nineteenth-century hotel with nice period feel. Shower, toilet and cable TV throughout; pleasant *Beisl* decor in the breakfast room. ④.

THE SUBURBS

Arabella Hotel Jagdschloss, 13, Jagdschlossgasse 79 ☎804 35 08; fax 804 35 00-10; tram #61 from U-Bahn Hietzing. Convenient for Schönbrunn and the Lainzer Tiergarten, with a hunting lodge theme to the breakfast room and an outdoor pool. All rooms have shower or bath, toilet and TV. ④.

Gartenhotel Glanzing, 19, Glanzinggasse 23 ☎470 42 72-0; fax 470 42 72-14; tram #41. Classic inter-war modernist villa in the northern suburbs with amazing views over Vienna from some rooms. TVs and en suite bathrooms throughout, lovely shady garden, plus sauna and solarium. ⑤.

Hotel Jäger, 17, Hernalser Hauptstrasse 187 ☎486 66 20-0; fax 486 66 208; tram #37. Friendly family-run palatial hotel set back off a busy shopping street. ⑤.

Landhaus Fuhrgassl-Huber, 19, Rathstrasse 24 ☎440 30 33; fax 440 27 14; bus #35A from U-Bahn Nussdorferstrasse. A real *gemütlich* country hotel right out in the wine villages at the foot of the Wienerwald. Not easy to get to by public transport. ⑤.

Parkhotel Schönbrunn, 13, Hietzinger Hauptstrasse 10–20 ☎87 804; fax 87 804-3220; U-Bahn Hietzing. Vienna's largest hotel, built in 1907 right by Schönbrunn to house the imperial guests. Lots of over-the-top touches from those days, plus mod cons like an indoor pool and sauna. ⑤.

Schloss Wilhelminenberg, 16, Savoyenstrasse 2 ☎485 85 03-0; fax 485 48 76; bus #146B or #46B from S-Bahn Ottakring or tram #J terminus. Impressive Neoclassical pile, with incredible views over Vienna. Not a good idea if you want to sample the nightlife. ④.

Hostels, student halls, private rooms and camping

Vienna's official **Hostelling International** *Jugendherbergen* (youth hostels) are efficient, clean, and, occasionally, even friendly. However, with just one exception, they are all a long way from the centre. Most of the beds are in segregated dorms, but some do have bunk-bed doubles. Prices vary, but are around öS150 a night (including a simple continental breakfast). Nowadays, you can join Hostelling International on the spot at any of the hostels listed below (if you're already a YHA member, you're automatically in the HI). Last, but by no means least, you should make an **advance reservation** as soon as you know when you might be arriving, as places can be booked out months in advance; at the very least, you should ring before turning up on spec.

The biggest practical drawback to the official hostels is that they throw you out each day at the ungodly hour of 9am in order to clean, and won't let you back in until 3 or 4pm. There are also **curfews**, though these are not that rigidly adhered to in those hostels with 24hr receptions (in any case, you'd be mad to go to bed later than 1am, given that you have to be up early). The lure of the **independent hostel**, then, is that while the prices are much the same as the HI hostels, there is generally no curfew and no lock-out. However, the places do tend to be a bit more run-down and cramped.

From July to September, there are dorm beds, doubles and even single rooms available in *Studentenheime* or **student halls** of residence. Prices tend to be a little higher than in the hostels (and breakfast is often not included), but then there's no curfew or lock-out.

The city's tourist offices (see p.30) can book **private rooms** for upwards of öS300 per person per night (with a minimum of three nights' stay) for a small commission. The *Mittwohnzentrale*, 8, Laudongasse 7 (☎402 60 61; Mon–Fri 10am–6pm) charges slightly less, and can arrange longer-term accommodation. Another agency to try is the nearby youth travel specialists, *ÖKISTA*, 9, Türkengasse 8 (☎401 48; Mon–Wed & Fri 9.30am–4pm, Thurs 9.30am–5.30pm).

Finally, Vienna's **campsites** are all out on the perimeters of the city and for committed campers only. Pitches cost around öS60, plus a fee of around öS60 per person.

OFFICIAL HI HOSTELS

Jugendgästehaus Brigittenau, 20, Friedrich-Engels-Platz 24 ☎332 82 940; fax 330 83 79; tram #N from U-Bahn Schwedenplatz or Dresdner Strasse. Huge modern hostel in a dour working-class suburb, with dorms and en suite bunk-bed doubles. 1am curfew (24hr reception). ①.

Jugendgästehaus Hütteldorf-Hacking, 13, Schlossberggasse 8 ☎877 02 63; fax 877 02 63-2; S- and U-Bahn Hütteldorf. A 271-bed dorm-only hostel way out in the sticks, but convenient for those who wish to explore the wilds of the Lainzer Tiergarten and Schönbrunn. Nightlife is somewhat curtailed by the 11.45pm curfew. ①.

Kolpingfamilie Wien-Meidling, 12, Bendlgasse 10–12 ☎83 54 87; fax 81 22 130; U-Bahn Niederhofstrasse. Modern hostel easily reached by U-Bahn from the centre. Beds in the big dorms go for under öS100 (without breakfast). 1am curfew (24hr reception). ①.

Jugendherberge Myrthengasse/ Neustiftgasse, 7, Myrthengasse 7/Neustiftgasse 85 ☎523 63 16;

Accommodation

Accommodation

fax 523 58 49; bus #48A or ten minutes' walk from U-Bahn Volkstheater. The most central of all the official hostels, with 243 dorm beds divided between two addresses, round the corner from each other. Book well in advance and go to the Myrthengasse reception on arrival. 1am curfew. ①.

Schlossherberge am Wilhelminenberg, 16, Savoyenstrasse 2 ☎45 85 03-7000; fax 45 85 03-702; bus #146B or #46B from S-Bahn Ottakring or tram #J terminus. 164 beds in a beautiful location next to a Neoclassical mansion in the Vienna Woods, but not a great base from which to sample the nightlife. 11.45pm curfew. Dorm beds ①; doubles ③.

INDEPENDENT HOSTELS

Hostel Ruthensteiner, 15, Robert-Hamerling-Gasse 24 ☎83 46 93; U-Bahn Westbahnhof. In easy walking distance of the Westbahnhof with dorm beds, singles and doubles (discounts for HI members). Open all year. No curfew. ①.

Turmherberge "Don Bosco", 3, Lechnerstrasse 12 ☎713 14 94; U-Bahn Kardinal-Nagl-Platz. Without doubt the cheapest beds in town (öS70 without breakfast), in a church tower in the back end of Landstrasse. Open March–Nov. 11.25pm curfew. ①.

Hostel Zöhrer, 8, Skodagasse 26 ☎43 07 30; fax 40 80 409; U-Bahn Josefstädter Strasse or tram #5 and #33. Small private hostel centrally located with dorms and bunk-bed doubles. Open all year. No curfew/no lock-out. ①.

STUDENT ROOMS

Auersperg, 8, Auerspergstrasse 9 ☎432 54 90; U-Bahn Lerchenfelder Strasse. Excellent central location, just off the Ring. Singles and doubles with or without shower and toilet. ②.

Haus Döbling, 19, Gymnasiumstrasse 85 ☎34 76 31-16; tram #38. Prices vary slightly according to whether you want "hotel service" or not. ①.

Josefstadt, 8, Buchfeldgasse 16 ☎406 52 11; U-Bahn Rathaus. Tucked behind the Rathaus in a quiet backstreet. All rooms have en suite shower. ②.

Porzellaneum, 9, Porzellangasse 30 ☎317 72 82; tram #D. Functional singles, doubles and quads per öS175 per head, popular with backpackers. No breakfast, but showers, courtyard, and lounge with TV. ①.

Campsites

Aktiv Camping Neue Donau, 22, Am Kleehäufel ☎220 93 10; S-Bahn Lobau or bus #91A from U-Bahn Kaisermühlen-VIC. Not a first choice, as it's squeezed between the *Autobahn* and the railway lines on the east bank of the Danube. Open mid-May to mid-Sept.

Camping Rodaun, 23, An der Au 2 ☎88 41 54; tram #60 from U-Bahn Hietzing to its terminus, then five minutes' walk. Nice location by a stream in the very southwestern outskirts of Vienna, near the Wienerwald. Open April to mid-Nov.

Campingplatz Schloss Laxenburg, Münchendorfer Strasse ☎02236/713 33; bus from Wien-Mitte, or train (R61) from Südbahnhof to Laxenburg-Biedermannsdorf, followed by a 1.5km walk. Nice location, just outside Vienna, with adjacent outdoor pool and the huge grounds of Laxenburg to explore, but inconvenient without your own transport. Open May–Oct.

Wien Süd, 23, Breitenfurter Strasse 269 ☎865 92 18; bus #62A from U-Bahn Meidling. Noisy locaion by the River Liesing, and a bit of a bother to get to. Open Aug only.

Wien West I, 14, Hüttelbergstrasse 40 ☎914 23 14; bus #151 from U-Bahn Hütteldorf or a fifteen-minute walk from tram #49 terminus. In the plush, far western suburbs of Vienna, close to the Wienerwald. Open mid-July to Aug.

Wien-West II, 14, Hüttelbergstrasse 80 ☎914 23 14; bus #151 from U-Bahn Hütteldorf or a fifteen-minute walk from tram #49 terminus. Just one bus stop on from Wien West I, but much larger, and with bungalows to rent (April–Oct; öS400; sleep four people). Closed Feb.

Chapter 11

Cafés and Restaurants

Like nowhere else in Austria, Vienna has a huge variety of places to eat and drink, most of them taking great care over the preparation and presentation of their food. You can snack on a toasted baguette, stuff yourself with hearty Austrian fare or try one of the capital's numerous ethnic restaurants, mostly Chinese and Italian, but also ranging from Mongolian to South Indian. Though there are few budget options, outside the most exclusive restaurants prices are fairly reasonable – and fairly uniform, though Innere Stadt places tend to be more expensive – whether you eat in a traditional *Kaffeehaus*, a studenty café or a pizzeria.

For visitors the most annoying discovery is the dearth of good-value eating places around Stephansplatz, the Hofburg, Karlsplatz and the Belvedere, where they spend much of their time. The **Spittelberg** area (see p.173) has the highest concentration of good cafés and restaurants, and there are further options dispersed more widely throughout the surrounding district of **Neubau**, and in neighbouring **Josefstadt**

The listings in this chapter are split into five sections: self-service and city-wide ventures, where you can snack on as much or as little as you like, more often than not on the hoof; *Mensen* or student canteens, for those on a budget, which offer no frills sit-down fare, primarily aimed at the city's students, but open to the public; *Kaffeehäuser* or cafés, which usually offer lunches as well as coffee, cakes and snacks; *Beisln*

and restaurants, the former being the Viennese version of the local pub where you can either order a meal or simply go to drink beer or wine; and lastly Vienna's innumerable *Heurigen*, or wine taverns, mostly located in the wine-growing suburbs, though there are some in the centre of town. These come into their own in the summer, when a night out at one is just about obligatory. Although the primary reason to go to a *Heuriger* is to drink the local wine, there's usually plenty of traditional Viennese food on offer, too.

Viennese cuisine

Vienna's cuisine is more varied than your average German-speaking city, reflecting the multi-ethnic origins of the old empire. However, fundamentally, it most closely resembles the cuisine of Bohemia, whence the majority of Vienna's inhabitants (and certainly its cooks) once came. In other words, it's hearty stuff, with a heavy meat quotient – usually pork or beef – accompanied by dumplings or potatoes and cabbage.

One culinary highpoint is soup (*Suppe*), served mainly at lunchtimes, and the starting point of most menus. Be sure to ask for some of the country's delicious bread to go with it. Austrian bread comes in a bewildering variety of loaves, though the standard loaf or *Hausbrot* is a mixture of wheat and rye flour.

FOOD GLOSSARY

Basics

Brot	bread	*Öl*	oil
Semmel	bread roll	*Auflauf*	omelette
Frühstuck	breakfast	*Spätzle* or *Nockerl*	pasta
Butter	butter	*Gebäck*	pastries
Käse	cheese	*Pfeffer*	pepper
Tasse	cup	*Teller*	plate
Nachspeise	dessert	*Topfen*	quark
Knödel	dumplings	*Reis*	rice
Ei	egg	*Salat*	salad
Gabel	fork	*Salz*	salt
Glas	glass	*Beilagen*	side dishes
Honig	honey	*Suppe*	soup
Kren	horseradish	*Löffel*	spoon
Messer	knife	*Vorspeise*	starter
Mittagessen	lunch	*Zucker*	sugar
Hauptgericht	main course	*Abendessen*	supper/dinner
Senf	mustard		

Vegetables (*Gemüse*)

Blaukraut	red cabbage	*Lauch*	leek
Bohnen	beans	*Maiskolben*	corn on the cob
Champignons	button mushrooms	*Paprika*	green or red peppers
Erbsen	beans	*Paradeiser*	tomatoes
Erdäpfel	potatoes	*Kohlsprossen*	brussel sprouts
Fisolen	green beans	*rote Rübe*	beetroot
G'röste	fried grated potatoes	*Paradeiser*	tomato
		Pilze	mushrooms
Gurke	gherkin/cucumber	*Pommes Frites*	chips/French fries
Karfiol	cauliflower	*Sauerkraut*	pickled cabbage
Karotten	carrots	*Spargel*	asparagus
Knoblauch	garlic	*Spinat*	spinach
Kohl	cabbage	*Zwiebeln*	onions

Meat (*Fleisch*) and Poultry (*Geflügel*)

Anten	duck	*Kalbfleisch*	veal
Eisbein	pig's trotters	*Kuttelfleck*	tripe
Ente	duck	*Lamm*	lamb
Fasan	pheasant	*Leber*	liver
Gans	goose	*Nieren*	kidneys
Hackfleisch	mincemeat	*Puter*	turkey
Hammelfleisch	mutton	*Rindfleisch*	beef
Hase	hare	*Schinken*	ham
Hirn	brains	*Schweinefleisch*	pork
Hirsch	venison	*Speck*	bacon
Huhn	chicken	*Taube*	pigeon
Innereien	innards	*Zunge*	tongue

Fish (*Fisch*)

Aal	eel	*Lachs*	salmon
Fogosch	pike-perch	*Makrele*	mackerel
Forelle	trout	*Matjes*	herring
Hecht	pike	*Muscheln*	mussels
Hummer	lobster	*Scholle*	plaice
Karpfen	carp	*Seezunge*	sole
Krabben	prawns	*Thunfisch*	tuna
Krebs	crab	*Tintenfisch*	squid

Cafés and
Restaurants

Common terms

Am Spiess	on the spit	*Gegrillt*	grilled
Blau	rare	*Gekocht*	cooked
Eingelegte	pickled	*Hausgemacht*	home-made
Frisch	fresh	*Heiss*	hot
Gebacken	fried in bread-crumbs	*Kalt*	cold
		Kümmelbraten	roast with caraway seeds
Gebraten	roasted		
Gedämpft	steamed	*Powidl*	plum sauce
Gefüllt	stuffed	*Räucher*	smoked

Fruit (*Obst*)

Ananas	pineapple	*Marillen*	apricots
Apfel	apple	*Pampelmuse*	grapefruit
Banane	banana	*Pflaumen*	plums
Birne	pear	*Pfirsiche*	peaches
Brombeeren	blackberries	*Ribisel*	redcurrants
Erdbeeren	strawberries	*Rosinen*	raisins
Heidelbeeren	bilberries	*Trauben*	grapes
Himbeeren	raspberries	*Zwetschen*	plums
Kirschen	cherries		

Desserts

Beiser	meringue	*Mohr im Hemd*	chocolate steamed pudding with ice cream
Bienenstich	honey and almond tart		
Buchtelm	sweet dumplings	*Palatschinken*	pancakes
Käsekuchen	cheesecake		

Austrian specialities

Backhendl	chicken fried in bread-crumbs	*Grammelknödel*	pork dumplings
		Schinken-fleckerln	ham with noodles
Bauernschmaus	platter of pork and ham	*Stelze*	leg of veal or pork
Beuschel	chopped lung		
Debreziner	paprika-spiced sausage	*Tafelspitz*	boiled beef
		Wiener Schnitzel	breaded veal

For a glossary of **coffee** and **cakes** see p.280

Cafés and Restaurants

A little known fact: Vienna is the home of the bagel and the croissant; the former is, of course, of Jewish origin, but is said to have been popularized here after a Jewish baker presented one to Jan Sobieski after the lifting of the 1683 siege of Vienna; the croissant also arose from this historical period, its shape said to represent the half-cresent moon on the Turkish flags (Maria Thersa's daughter, Marie Antoinette, is responsible for exporting the croissant to France when she married Louis XVI).

The capital's most famous dish is, of course, *Wiener Schnitzel*, traditionally deep-fried breaded veal, but also made from chicken or pork, normally accompanied by *Erdäpfelsalat*, a potato salad in a sweet dill dressing. The Emperor Franz-Josef's favourite dish (and that of many of his subjects) was *Tafelspitz*, thick slices of boiled beef, usually served with *G'röste* (grated fried potato). Another popular meat dish is *Backhendl*, a young chicken, breaded and deep fried, and for the adventurous, there's the likes of *Beuschel* (veal lung stew) to chew on.

On a healthier note, look out for *Eierschwammerl*, chanterelle mushrooms that appear in various guises on menus in the autumn. The prevalence of *Gulyas* (goulash) is a Hungarian legacy, while the Italians make their presence known with dishes featuring *Nockerl*, the Austrians' heavy version of pasta; *Schinkenfleckerl*, flecks of ham baked in pasta, is especially popular.

Obviously in a country with such a famous sweet tooth, there's no shortage of rich puddings on most menus. Apart from the ubiquitous *Apfelstrudel*, *Palatschinken* (pancakes), filled with jam and/or curd cheese, are a regular feature. Look out, too, for *Marillonknödel*, sweet apricot dumplings, and the politically incorrect *Mohr im Hemd* – literally "Moor in a shirt" – a chocolate pudding

with hot chocolate sauce and whipped cream.

In the last ten years or so, there has been something of a culinary reaction to the traditional protein-heavy national food. This *Neue Wiener Küche*, as it's known, is the Viennese version of *nouvelle cuisine*, using fresh produce to come up with a new, slightly Mediterranean bent on traditional dishes. It has had a widespread influence not only in the top-class restaurants, but also in some of the more modern cafés, and even in the odd traditional *Kaffeehaus*.

Lastly, it's as well to remember that the *Mittagessen* or midday meal is traditionally considered the main meal of the day. The *Nachtmahl* or evening supper would normally be simply a cold meal eaten at home. Obviously not everyone follows this pattern, and restaurants, in particular, consider the evening slot just as important as the lunchtime one.

Alcohol

Austrians tend to drink a lot more beer than wine, though in Vienna it's **wine** that holds a special place in the capital's history and geography. It's a place literally surrounded by vineyards, many of which lie within the city boundaries – some suggest that the city's name is itself derives from the word "wine".

The best place to try the local vintage is, of course, in a *Heuriger* or wine tavern (see p.291). Wine is drunk by the *Viertel* (a 25cl mug) or the *Achterl* (a 12.5cl glass). The majority of wine produced in Austria is white, the dry, fruity *Grüner Veltliner* being the most popular. Look out, too, for *Sturm*, the half-fermented young wine which hits the streets and bars in autumn. Most red wine hails from Burgenland, where *Blaufränkisch* is the most sought after. Burgenland is also famous, of course, for the great anti-freeze scandal of 1985, when several local wine growers were convicted of adulterating their wine.

Most Austrians defer to the Czechs when it comes to **beer**, and you should be able to find Bohemian *Budvar* and

Drinks Glossary

Apfelsaft	apple juice	*Mineralwasser*	mineral water
Bier	beer	*Orangensaft*	orange juice
Flasche	bottle	*Obstler*	fruit schnapps
Gespritzer	white wine with soda	*Rotwein*	red wine
		Roséwein	rosé
Glühwein	mulled wine	*Sauermilch*	sour milk
Grog	hot water with rum and sugar	*Sekt*	sparkling wine
		Schnapps	spirit
Kaffee	coffee	*Sturm*	new wine
Kakao	cocoa	*Tee*	tea
Kir	white wine with blackcurrant	*Traubensaft*	grape juice
		Trocken	dry
Korn	rye spirit	*Wasser*	water
Kräutertee	herbal tea	*Weisswein*	white wine
Milch	milk	*Zitronentee*	tea with lemon

Pilsener Urquell in quite a few bars and restaurants. The most common Austrian beers are the local-brewed *Gold Fassl* from the suburb of Ottakring, and *Gösser*, from Styria. Those with a keen interest in beer should check out the following micro-breweries: *Siebenstern Bräu*, 7, Siebensterngasse 19 (see p.290) and *Fischer Bräu*, 19, Billrothstrasse 17 (see p.291).

Beer is generally drunk by the half litre or *Krügerl*, but you can also ask for a third of a litre or *Seidl*, an eighth of a litre or *Pfiff*, and occasionally a *Mass* or litre jug. Draught beer is *Bier vom Fass*, and you can occasionally get *dunkel* (dark) as opposed to *hell* (light) beer. Bottled *Weissbier* (wheat beer) is worth trying: it's extremely fizzy, and you must pour it extremely slowly to avoid creating a vast head.

Austrians are also extraordinarily fond of spirits, particularly *Schnaps*, made in a variety of delicate fruit flavours, and occasionally known as *Brand*.

Snacks, self-service and city-wide ventures

The most obvious snack in Vienna is, of course, a *Wurst* (hot sausage) – *Hasse* in the local dialect – from one of the ubiquitous *Würstelstand* around town. There are numerous varieties available:

the *Bratwurst* (fried sausage) or *Burenwurst* (boiled sausage) are the most common, but you could also try a *Debreziner*, a spicy Hungarian sausage, a *Currywurst*, which speaks for itself, or a *Tirolerwurst*, a smoked variety. To accompany your sausage, you usually get a roll and some *Senf* (mustard), which can be either *scharf* (hot) or *süss* (sweet).

At the following places (not all of them chains) you'll get fast and efficient service and filling snacks, occasionally even full meals, but in most cases, they are not places to idle away several hours.

Aida, branches at 1, Stock-im-Eisen-Platz 2; 1, Bognergasse 3; 1, Rotenturmstrasse 24 (all U-Bahn Stephansplatz). The largest Viennese *Konditorei* chain serving a staggering selection of calorific cakes and coffee in rather dodgy decor. Varied hours but usually *Mon–Sat 7am–8pm, Sun 9am–8pm*.

Anker (Treff zum Nestroy), 1, Bräunerstrasse 4–6; U-Bahn Stephansplatz (hundreds of branches across Vienna). *Anker* are the largest bakery chain in the country, producing excellent bread, rolls and pastries. This branch also does hot food: breakfast until 11am, full Austrian cuisine there-after. *Mon–Fri 7.30am–6pm*.

Cafés and
Restaurants

Breakfast

Most Viennese rise so early that they don't really bother with anything other than a gulp of coffee or tea and a bread roll. As a result, the whole concept of *Frühstuck* or breakfast is alien to the Viennese. At most hotels and pensions, however, breakfast is included in the price of the room, and will consist of anything from tea or coffee and a roll to an all-you-can-eat buffet with muesli, rolls and bread, cheese, cold meats, boiled eggs, yoghurt and fruit. If breakfast is not included, however, and you want to have a proper sit-down, then you basically need to go to one of the city's trendier cafés, described in greater detail later in this chapter:

Berg; see p.285. Breakfast Mon–Fri 10am–2pm, Sat & Sun 10am–3pm.

Daun; see p.284. Breakfast Mon–Sat 9–11.30am.

Europa; see p.284. Breakfast Mon–Fri 9–11.30am, Sat & Sun all day.

Lux; see p.284. Breakfast daily 10am–3pm.

Stein; see p.285. Breakfast daily 7am–8pm.

Tunnel; see p.284. Breakfast daily 9–11am.

Bizi, 1, Rotenturmstrasse 4; U-Bahn Stephansplatz. Devise your own pizza toppings, assemble your own salad, or choose one of the main dishes and/or roasted vegetables. Take-away or sit-down. *Daily 11am–midnight.*

Demel vis-à-vis, Kohlmarkt 11; U-Bahn Herrengasse. Opposite the *Demel Kaffee-Konditorei*, this is a sort of *k.u.k.* version of *Nordsee* (see below) with all kinds of fresh seafood to eat in or take away. *Daily 11am–10pm.*

Hopferl, 1, Naglergasse 13; U-Bahn Herrengasse. Cave-like beer bar, with a large selection of cold and hot snacks and, of course, beers. *Mon–Fri 11am–11pm, Sat 11am–3pm.*

Lukullus-Bar, 1, Graben 19; U-Bahn Stephansplatz. Stand-up buffet at the rear of the flagship outlet of the Julius Meinl delicatessen/supermarket chain, where you can eat traditional hot dishes and lighter snacks. *Mon–Sat 8am–5pm.*

Makrokosmos, 1, Fleischmarkt 16; U-Bahn Schwedenplatz. Organic veggie health food shop that does take-away soup and snacks, which you then devour in the leafy courtyard. *Mon, Wed & Thurs 10am–6pm, Tues & Fri 10am–6.30pm, Sat 10am–1pm.*

Naschmarkt, branches at 1, Schottengasse 1 (U-Bahn Schottentor); 1, Schwarzenbergplatz 16 (U-Bahn Karlsplatz); 6, Mariahilferstrasse 85 (U-Bahn Neubaugasse). Perfectly decent self-service Austrian restaurant chain, where you can eat as much or little as you like. Varied hours but Schwarzenbergplatz branch is *Mon–Fri 6.30am–9pm, Sat & Sun 9am–9pm.*

Nordsee, branches at 1, Kärntnerstrasse 25; 1, Kohlmarkt 6 (both U-Bahn Stephansplatz). Fish and seafood self-service restaurant, with everything from rollmop rolls to fish and chips, lobster and salad – you name it. Take-away or eat-in. Varied hours; Kärntnerstrasse branch is *daily 9am–11pm.*

Rosenberger Markt, 1, Meysedergasse 2; U-Bahn Karlsplatz. Self-service basement buffet just off Kärntnerstrasse, where you can fill youself for under öS100. *Daily 11am–11pm.*

Trześniewski, 1, Dorotheergasse 1; U-Bahn Stephansplatz. Minimalist sandwich bar that's a veritable Viennese institution, serving mouth-watering slices of rye bread (*Brötchen*) topped with fishy, eggy and meaty spreads – wash it all down with a *Pfiff*. Stand-up tables and a few seats. *Mon–Fri 8.30am–7.30pm, Sat 9am–1pm.*

Wild, 1, Neuer Markt 16; U-Bahn Stephansplatz. Very upmarket, long-established deli with a stand-up buffet;

full meals or snacks washed down with alcohol. *Mon–Fri 8.30am–6.30pm, Sat 8am–12.30pm.*

Zum schwarzen Kameel, 1, Bognergasse 5; U-Bahn Herrengasse. A terribly smart, convivial deli that's yet another Viennese institution, with stand-up tables only. *Mon–Sat 9am–7pm.*

Mensen

If you're on a tight budget, then it's worth considering using the city's numerous university canteens or **Mensen**, which are open to the general public (you get an extra discount with student ID). It might not be cordon bleu, but the food is generally perfectly decent, traditional Viennese fare, and you usually get a couple of courses for under öS45 – about half what you'd pay in a restaurant.

Afro-Asiatisches Institut, 9, Türkenstrasse 3; U-Bahn Schottentor. Vienna's most multi-ethnic clientele, but not great for veggies; situated on the ground floor through the archway. *Mon–Fri 11.30am–2pm.*

Katholische Hochschulgemeinde, 1, Ebendorferstrasse 8. Two choices of set menu (occasionally veggie). *Mon–Fri 11.30am–2pm. Closed Easter & Aug to mid-Sept.*

Musikakademie, 1, Johannesgasse 8. Small central Mensa with a pleasant summer courtyard; not great for veggies. *Mon–Fri 7.30am–2pm.*

Neues Institutsgebäude, 1, Universitätsstrasse 7; U-Bahn Schottentor. This is the main university Mensa; take the dumb-waiter lift to floor 6 and then walk up another flight of stairs – nice view over to the Votivkirche. *Mon–Fri 8am–7pm.*

Technische Universität, 4, Wiedner Hauptstrasse 8–10; U-Bahn Karlsplatz. Big Mensa on the first floor (follow the yellow B signs) of the building behind the main university block on Karlsplatz. *Mon–Fri 11am–2.30pm.*

Kaffeehäuser (cafés)

You have troubles of one sort or another – to the COFFEEHOUSE!
She can't come to you for some reason no matter how plausible – to the COFFEEHOUSE!
You have holes in your shoes – the COFFEEHOUSE!
You have a salary of 400 crowns and spend 500 – THE COFFEEHOUSE!
You are frugal and permit yourself nothing – THE COFFEEHOUSE!
You find no woman who suits you – THE COFFEEHOUSE!
You are SPIRITUALLY on the threshold of suicide – THE COFFEEHOUSE!
You hate and disdain people and yet cannot do without them – THE COFFEEHOUSE!
Nobody extends you any more credit anywhere – THE COFFEEHOUSE!

The Coffeehouse
Peter Altenberg (1859–1919)

Paris may have more of them, but Vienna is the spiritual home of the *Kaffeehaus* or café. Legend has it that coffee was first introduced to Vienna by a certain Georg Franz Koltschitzky, an Austrian spy who regularly penetrated the Turkish camp during the siege of 1683. When the siege was finally lifted, Koltschitzky was asked what he wanted in return for his services. He requested to be given the "camel fodder" – in actual fact sacks of coffee beans – left behind by the hastily departed Turks, and went on to open the first coffeehouse in Vienna the same year.

Whatever the truth of this story, by the late nineteenth century the *Kaffeehaus* had become the city's most important social institution. It was described by writer Stefan Zweig as "a sort of democratic club to which admission costs the small price of a cup of coffee. Upon payment of this mite, every guest can sit for hours on end, discuss,

Cafés and
Restaurants

Cafés and
Restaurants

COFFEE AND CAKES

COFFEE

On average, the Austrians drink almost twice as much coffee as beer (over a pint a day per head of the population). When ordering a coffee, few Viennese ever actually ask for a straight coffee, or *Kaffee*. First you need to choose what type of coffee you want, perhaps prefixing it with the word *kleiner* (small) or *grosser* (large). The varieties of coffee are legion, but whatever you order, if you're in a traditional *Kaffeehaus*, it will come on a little silver tray, accompanied by a glass of water.

Brauner Black coffee with a small amount of milk.

Einspänner The traditional Viennese coffee, served in a glass and topped with whipped cream (*Schlagobers*).

Eiskaffee Iced coffee with ice cream and whipped cream.

Fiaker A coffee with a shot of rum.

Kaffee Crème Coffee served with a little jug of milk.

Kapuziner Viennese version of a capuccino.

Konsul Black coffee with a spot of cream.

Kurz Viennese version of an espresso.

Mazagran Coffee served with an ice cube and laced with rum.

Mélange (pronounced like the French) Coffee with equal measures of frothed milk and coffee.

Mokka Black coffee flavoured slightly with mocha.

Pharisäer Coffee in a glass topped with whipped cream, served with a small glass of rum on the side.

Schwarzer Black coffee.

Türkische Brewed with the grains and sugar and served in a copper pouring pot.

Verlängerten Slightly weaker than normal coffee.

CAKES

In most cafés, the *Torten* or cakes will be piled up in a display cabinet, in whcih case you can simply point to whichever takes your fancy. The best cafés still bake their own cakes, and all can be served with helping of *Schlagobers*. The following are some of the more common:

Apfelstrudel Apple and raisins wrapped in pastry and sprinkled with icing sugar.

Dobostorte A rich Hungarian cake made up of alternate layers of biscuit sponge and chocolate icing sugar.

Esterházytorte Several layers of cream and sponge coated in white icing with a feather design on top.

Guglhupf Freud's favourite, at its most basic a simple sponge cake baked in a fluted ring mould and cut into slices.

Linzertorte A jam tart made with almond pastry.

Mohnstrudel A bread-like roly-poly pudding with a poppy seed and raisin filling.

Sachertorte The most famous of the Viennese cakes, and in some ways the least interesting. It's really just a chocolate sponge cake coated in chocolate. Most also have a layer of apricot jam beneath the chocolate coating.

Topfenstrudel Like an *Apfelstrudel*, but with a sweet curd cheese filling.

write, play cards, receive his mail, and above all, can go through an unlimited number of newspapers and magazines". The *Kaffeehaus* became an informal

office for its *Stammgäste* or regulars, where they could work, relax and receive clients in warmth and comfort. At certain cafés, the head waiter or *Herr Ober* could direct each customer to a certain table or *Stammtisch* depending on what subject he (or less frequently she) wished to debate.

The Viennese coffeehouse is no longer what it once was, not least because much of its most loyal clientele was to be found among the city's Jewish intellectuals, who either fled or perished in the Holocaust. Nevertheless, there is still something unique about the institution even today. While the rest of the world queues up for fast food, the Viennese *Kaffeehaus* implores you to slow down, or, as the sign in one such café says, "sorry, we do not cater for people in a hurry". For the price of a small coffee, you can still sit for as long as you like without being asked to move on or buy another drink. Understandably, then, the price of this first drink is astronomical and will regularly set you back around öS35.

The meal most closely associated with the *Kaffeehaus* at the turn of the century was the *Jause* or afternoon snack eaten around 3pm, consisting of coffee and a pastry. This explains why even those *Kaffeehäuser* that don't serve hot meals will always have at least a selection of cakes. Nowadays, cafés tend to make more fuss over the midday meal, and some will put aside a number of tables for those customers who wish to eat. The food is generally traditional Austrian fare, inexpensive and tasty.

As well as the traditional *Kaffeehaus* – the smoky type, with a wide range of newspapers to read, and a waiter in a tuxedo – there's also the *Kaffee-Konditorei*, where the coffee is a mere side-show to the establishment's cakes and pastries (see box below). We've listed both the above café types under "**Traditional**". In the last decade or so, there's been something of a café revival, with new modern variants on the old *Kaffeehaus* appearing, particularly in the Vorstädte. These places generally eschew the tuxedoes, heavy Viennese cooking and *Torten*, and consequently attract a younger crowd. We've listed them

under "**Szene**", the German term for a trendy hangout.

Lastly, some cafés have what is known as a *Schanigarten* – named after the assistant waiter or *Schani*, whose job it is to set out the tables and chairs – don't get too excited, however, as this is rarely much of a garden, simply a few tables *al fresco*.

Cafés and
Restaurants

Innere Stadt

Traditional

Alt Wien, 1, Bäckerstrasse 9; U-Bahn Stephansplatz. Bohemian *Kaffeehaus* with *Beisl* decor, posters on nicotine-stained walls, and a dark, smoky atmosphere even on the sunniest day. *Daily 10am–3am.*

Bräunerhof, 1, Stallburggasse 2; U-Bahn Herrengasse. A real *Kaffeehaus* atmosphere: nicotine-coloured walls, slightly snooty tuxedoed waiters and decent food, too. Live music on the weekend from 3 to 6pm. *Mon–Fri 7.30am–8.30pm, Sat 7.30am–6pm, Sun 10am–6pm.*

Central, 1, Herrengasse 14; U-Bahn Herrengasse. The most famous of all Viennese cafés, resurrected in the 1980s and still the most architecturally interesting (see p.58). Trotsky was once a regular. Piano music 4 to 7pm. *Mon–Sat 9am–8pm.*

Demel, 1, Kohlmarkt 14; U-Bahn Herrengasse. The king of the *Kaffee-Konditorei* – and one of the priciest. The cake display is a work of art, as is the interior. *Daily 10am–6pm.*

Diglas, 1, Wollzeile 10; U-Bahn Stephansplatz. Smoky old *Kaffeehaus* – once Franz Lehár's favourite haunt – with burgundy upholstery and piles of cakes and papers to choose from. *Mon–Sat 7am–11.30pm, Sun 10am–11.30pm.*

Engländer, 1, Postgasse 2; U-Bahn Stubentor. Stylish minimalist *Kaffeehaus* with a long pedigree – viz the erstwhile Jewish maitresse on the wall – serving *Neue Wiener Küche* at reasonable prices. *Daily 8am–2am.*

**Cafés and
Restaurants**

Frauenhuber, 1, Himmelpfortgasse 6; U-Bahn Stephansplatz. One of the oldest *Kaffeehäuser* in Vienna – Beethoven was a regular – with vaulted ceiling, deep burgundy upholstery and an excellent menu. *Mon–Fri 8am–11pm, Sat 8am–4pm.*

Griensteidl, 1, Michaelerplatz 2; U-Bahn Herrengasse. Recently resurrected (at least in name) literary café which is perfectly OK, but not what it was in 1897 (see p.57). *Daily 8am–midnight.*

Haag, 1, Schottengasse 2; U-Bahn Schottentor/Herrengasse. Simple cream-coloured vaulted café, with tables outside in the lovely Schottenstift courtyard in the summer. *Mon–Thurs 7.30am–10pm, Fri 7.30am–8pm, Sat & Sun 10am–8pm.*

Hawelka, 1, Dorotheergasse 6; U-Bahn Stephansplatz. Small, smoky bohemian café run by the same couple since it opened shortly after World War II; you'll have to fight for a table. *Mon–Sat 8am–2am & Sun 4pm–2am.*

Heiner, 1, Wollzeile 9 & Kärntnerstrasse 21–23. You don't come here for the ambience or the newspapers, but for the top-class Viennese patisserie. *Mon–Sat 8am–7.30pm, Sun 10am–7.30pm.*

Korb, 1, Brandstätte 9; U-Bahn Stephansplatz. Traditional 1950s' style *Kaffeehaus* tucked in the backstreets of the Innere Stadt. *Mon–Sat 7am–midnight, Sun noon–9pm.*

Krugerhof, 1, Krugerstrasse 8; U-Bahn Karlsplatz. A plain, but classic *Kaffeehaus* just off Kärntnerstrasse, with coat-stands, newspapers, billiards, food and comfy booths. *Mon–Sat 7am–10pm.*

Lehmann, 1, Graben 12; U-Bahn Stephansplatz. Former *k.u.k. Konditorei* with outstanding cake and pastry selection. *Mon–Sat 8.30am–7pm.*

Szene

Aera, 1, Gonzagagasse 11; U-Bahn Schwedenplatz. Big high-ceilinged, L-shaped café/bar with great music,

huge pizzas and lots of veggie snacks. *Daily 10am–2am.*

Kleines Café, 1, Franziskanerplatz 3; U-Bahn Stephansplatz. Cosy little café, one of the first of the cross-overs between the new and the traditional *Kaffeehaus*, designed by the Viennese architect Hermann Czech in the 1970s. *Mon–Sat 10am–2am, Sun 1pm–2am.*

Virtuality Café, 1, Postpassage; U-Bahn Schwedenplatz. Not everyone's idea of a relaxing cybercafé, with more virtual-reality games than internet consoles. *Mon–Sat noon–11pm, Sun 3–11pm.*

Ringstrasse

Traditional

Am Heumarkt, 3, Am Heumarkt 15; U-Bahn Stadtpark. Real traditional *Kaffeehaus*, with billiards, cards and chess and typical hearty fare. *Mon–Fri 9am–11pm; closed Aug.*

Eiles, 8, Josefstädter Strasse 2; U-Bahn Rathaus. Very traditional *Kaffeehaus* set back from the Ringstrasse, behind the Rathaus. Decor dates from the 1930s when the café was the meeting point for the Nazis who assassinated the Austro-fascist leader, Englebert Dollfuss. *Mon–Fri 7am–10pm, Sat & Sun 8am–10pm.*

Landtmann, 1, Dr-Karl-Lueger-Ring 4; U-Bahn Herrengasse. One of the poshest of the *Kaffeehäuser* – and a favourite with Freud – with impeccably attired waiters, and a high quota of politicians and Burgtheater actors. *Daily 8am–midnight.*

Ministerium, 1, Georg-Coch-Platz 4; U-Bahn Stubentor. Not quite a classic *Kaffeehaus* – the streaked yellow paint-work and musak put paid to that – but the lunchtime cooking is excellent. *Mon–Sat 7am–11pm.*

Museum, 1, Friedrichstrasse 6; U-Bahn Karlsplatz. Adolf Loos designed this L-shaped café way back in 1899 and it was a favourite haunt of Klimt, Kokoschka and Schiele, among others. It's changed a lot since then, but remains endearingly well worn and is still popular with art students. *Daily 7am–11pm.*

Prückel, 1, Stubenring 24; U-Bahn Stubentor. The *Prückel* has lost its ornate interior, but the dowdy 1950s' refurbishment looks appealingly dated now, and still draws in lots of elderly shoppers and dog-owners from the nearby Stadtpark. *Daily 9am–10pm.*

Raimund, 1, Museumstrasse 6. Not exactly a classic, but very convenient for the Kunsthistorisches – food's not bad either. *Mon–Fri 7am–midnight, Sat & Sun 9am–midnight.*

Sacher, 1, Philharmonikerstrasse 4; U-Bahn Karlsplatz. For all its fame (see p.117), the *Sacher* is a bit of a let-down. The decor is imperial red and gold, but the room is small and the *Sachertorte* overrated – practically the only folk who come here nowadays are tourists. *Daily 6am–midnight.*

Schottenring, 1, Schottenring; U-Bahn Schottentor/Schottenring. Situated on the corner of Börsegasse, this L-shaped *Kaffeehaus*, with its high stuccoed ceiling, is an oasis of calm on the Ringstrasse. *Daily 8am–11pm.*

Schwarzenberg, 1, Kärntner Ring 17; U-Bahn Karlsplatz. Opulent café with rich marble, ceramic and wood-panelled decor, plus huge mirrors and a great cake cabinet. Live music Tues–Fri 8–10pm, Sat & Sun 4–7pm & 8–10pm. *Daily 7am–midnight.*

Sluka, 1, Rathausplatz 8; U-Bahn Rathaus. Lovely little *Kaffee-Konditorei* tucked under the arches by the Rathaus. White wood gilded panelling,

mirrors and chandeliers – a Ringstrasse classic. *Mon–Fri 8am–7pm, Sat 8am–5.30pm.*

Szene

MAK Café, 1, Stubenring 5; U-Bahn Stubentor. Not strictly speaking a traditional *Kaffeehaus*, but it does have a wonderfully high coffered ceiling. This is a trendy hangout, as you might expect from the MAK (see p.131). The food is pricey, with a Mediterranean edge. *Tues–Sun 10am–2am.*

Landstrasse

Traditional

Zartl, 3, Rasumofskygasse 7; tram #N. An unusual find in these parts, a real local corner *Kaffeehaus*, with cream and green decor, billiards, booths and lots of ice cream sundaes. *Mon–Fri 8am–midnight, Sat 9am–6pm; closed Aug.*

Szene

KunstHaus, 3, Weissgerberlände 14; tram #N. Round the corner from the Hundertwasserhaus (see p.152), a wonky, colourful café designed by the man himself. *Daily noon–midnight.*

Mariahilf, Neubau and Josefstadt

Traditional

Drechsler, 6, Linke Wienzeile 22; U-Bahn Kettenbrückengasse. Laid-back, scruffy *Kaffeehaus* by the Naschmarkt, popular with the younger generation of Viennese,

Cafés and
Restaurants

*All the cafés on
the Ringstrasse
can be reached
by tram #1 or
#2.*

Vegetarians

Vegetarianism has not caught on in a big way in Vienna – and there are remarkably few vegetarian restaurants. The key phrases are *Ich bin vegeterianisch(e)* (I'm vegetarian) and *Ist das ohne Fleisch* (literally "Is that without meat?"). There are a few traditional vegetarian dishes on most menus: *Gebackener Emmenthaler* (or some other kind of cheese), which is breaded and deep fried; *Knödel mit Ei*, (dumplings with scrambled egg); *Spinatnockerl* (spinach pasta).

The following are the best of Vienna's exclusively vegetarian restaurants:

Lecker; see p.288.   **Vega**; see p.290.
Légume; see p.291.   **Wrenkh**; see p.288.
Siddharta; see p.288.

Cafés and Restaurants

especially clubbers attracted by the early opening hours. *Mon–Fri 3.30am–8pm, Sat 3.30am–6pm.*

Hummel, 8, Albertgasse 27; U-Bahn Josefstädter Strasse. Bustling local *Kaffeehaus*, doing a brisk lunchtime trade, with tables looking out on the nearby square. *Mon–Sat 7am–2am, Sun 8am–2am.*

Jelinek, 6, Otto-Bauer-Gasse 5; U-Bahn Webgasse. Family-run *Kaffeehaus* tucked away in the backstreets south of Mariahilferstrasse, this is a rare survivor, still serving an exclusively local clientele. *Mon–Fri 8am–10pm, Sat 8am–8pm.*

Ritter, 6, Mariahilferstrasse 73; U-Bahn Neubaugasse. Vast, high-ceilinged V-shaped café popular with veteran card players and shoppers. *Mon–Sat 7am–11pm, Sun 8am–11pm.*

Rüdigerhof, 5, Hamburger Strasse 20; U-Bahn Kettenbrückengasse. Wonderful Jugendstil building on the outside, less soothing on the eye inside, but still a *Kaffeehaus* in the traditional style. Food is cheap and filling, but the riverside terrace is marred by the nearby busy road. *Daily except Sat 9am–2am.*

Savoy, 6, Linke Wienzeile 36; U-Bahn Kettenbrückengasse. Wonderfully scruffy, but ornate *fin-de-siècle* decor, packed with bohemian bargain-hunters during the Saturday flea market. *Mon–Fri 5pm–2am, Sat 9am–6pm, Sun 9pm–2am.*

Sperl, 6, Gumpendorfer Strasse 11; U-Bahn Karlsplatz/Babenbergerstrasse. One of the classics of the *Kaffeehaus* scene, L-shaped, billiard tables and still a hint of shabbiness despite its renovation. *Mon–Sat 7am–11pm, Sun 3–11pm.*

Westend, 7, Mariahilferstrasse 128; U-Bahn Westbahnhof. Conveniently located directly opposite Westbahnhof, this traditional *Kaffeehaus* – once frequented by Hitler – is the best possible introduction to Vienna for those who've just arrived by train. *Daily 7am–11pm.*

Szene

Benno, 8, Alserstrasse 67; U-Bahn Alserstrasse. Very popular studenty café

with groovy music, half a 2CV sticking out of the wall, lots of board games and a menu of toasted baguette munchies for under öS75. *Daily 11.30am–2am.*

Blue Box, 7, Richtergasse 8; U-Bahn Neubaugasse. Café with stripped-down decor, serving breakfasts and baguette snacks all day. In the evening, it becomes more of a *Musikcafé*, with projected images on the wall and a resident DJ to keep the groove going. *Mon 6pm–2am, Tues–Thurs 10am–2am, Fri & Sat 10am–4am.*

Daun, 8, Skodagasse 25; tram #43 or #44. Friendly minimalist *Kaffeehaus* near the university, serving breakfasts until 11.30am, and öS70 daily specials the rest of the day. *Mon–Sat 9am–1am, Sun 3pm–1am.*

Europa, 7, Zollergasse 8; U-Bahn Neubaugasse. Lively, spacious café that attracts a trendy crowd, who love the posey window booths. Food is a tasty mixture of Viennese and Italian. *Daily 9am–4am.*

Das Käuzchen, 7, Gardegasse 8; U-Bahn Volkstheater. Spittelberg café with zany decor, toasted snacks and more substantial fare. *Daily 8am–2am.*

Lux, 7, Spittelberggasse 3; U-Bahn Volkstheater. Pared-down modern version of a *Kaffeehaus*, with a friendly bistro feel and an eclectic menu featuring tofu-based dishes, pizzas, pancakes. *Daily 10am–2am.*

Merkur, 8, Florianigasse 18; tram #5 or bus 13A. Welcoming Josefstadt *Kaffeehaus* that attracts a studenty clientele. *Daily 9am–2am.*

Nil, 7, Siebensterngasse 39; tram #49. Trendy Egyptian café hung with lanterns, offering simple Arab dishes and backgammon. *Mon–Thurs 10am–midnight, Fri 10am–2am, Sat 5pm–2am, Sun 5pm–midnight.*

Tunnel, 8, Florianigasse 39; tram #5. Popular clean-living student café with good food, filling breakfasts until 11am; live music in the basement of an evening. *Daily 9am–2am.*

Alsergrund

Traditional

Stadlmann, 9, Währinger Strasse 26; U-Bahn Schottentor. Sepia-coloured *Kaffeehaus*, with unrenovated red velvet alcoves, brass chandeliers and mirrors. *Mon–Fri 8am–9pm; closed Aug.*

Weimar, 9, Währinger Strasse 68; tram #40, #41 and #42. Renovated L-shaped *Kaffeehaus* with a high ceiling, chandeliers, tuxedoed waiters and snug booths. Good-value öS85 lunchtime menu. *Mon–Thus 9am–2am, Fri & Sat 9am–4am.*

Szene

Berg, 9, Berggasse 8; U-Bahn Schottentor. Relaxed modern mixed gay/straight café with an attractive assortment of chairs and great *Neue Wiener Küche*. *Daily 10am–1am.*

Luxor, 9, Grünentorgasse 19; tram #D. Lively neighbourhood café/bar with lugubrious decor, a column of water on the bar, an aquarium and the odd pinball machine. *Mon–Thurs 9am–2am, Fri & Sat 9am–4am.*

Stein, 9, Währingerstrasse 6; U-Bahn Schottentor. The king of the new generation of posey designer cafés, on the corner of Kolingasse, with minimalist decor, funky music, on-line facilities, trendy loos, baguettes, veggie food and breakfasts served until 8pm. *Mon–Sat 7am–1am, Sun 9am–1am.*

Leopoldstadt

Traditional

Rotunde, 2, Ausstellungstrasse/Mölkereistrasse; tram #21. Real neighbourhood *Kaffeehaus*, deeply untrendy but a great escape from the nearby Volksprater, two stops from Praterstern. *Mon–Sat 7.30am–2am.*

The suburbs

Traditional

Dommayer, 13, Dommayergasse 1; U-Bahn Hietzing. Historic *Kaffeehaus* where Johann Strauss Junior made his première.

Tuxedoed waiters, comfy alcoves, occasional live music and lots of coffee and cakes. A good rest stop after a hard day at Schönbrunn. *Daily 5pm–midnight.*

Beisln and restaurants

You can, of course, eat lunch or dinner at most of the cafés listed earlier; the establishments reviewed below are special enough to make a night of it. Phone numbers have been given only for those restaurants where it's advisable to **book a table**.

We've given each restaurant a price category (see p.286), which reflects the cost of the majority of main course dishes on the menu. These are only a guideline: obviously if you choose the most expensive item on the menu, you're going to exceed our estimate; equally if you choose the cheapest item on the menu, you'll probably end up eating for much less. Don't forget, however, that we have not included the price of starters or puddings, since the main dish alone is often filling enough, nor the price of any drinks.

Tipping is usually done in a *Beisl* by simply rounding up to the nearest öS10, so when the waiter gives you a bill for, say öS134, you say öS140 as you hand over the cash (few, if any, *Beisl* will take plastic). In restaurants, add fifteen percent to the bill unless it's already been done for you. To keep the price of meals to a minimum, look for the set *Tagesmenu* (especially at lunchtime), which usually gives you two courses for under öS100.

Lastly, a quick word on the *Wiener Beisl*, the city's main eating and drinking establishment. These are unpretentious wood-panelled pubs, where you're more than likely to share a table with other customers. The best are still family-run and as much about drinking (beer usually) as they are about eating hearty home cooking.

Innere Stadt

a Tavola, 1, Weihburggasse 3 ☎512 79 55; U-Bahn Stephansplatz. Designer Italian *osteria* with a stylish, cave-like inte-

Cafés and Restaurants

Cafés and Restaurants

rior and some excellent innovative cuisine. *Daily 11.30am–midnight. Moderate.*

Achilleus, 1, Köllnerhofgasse 3; U-Bahn Schwedenplatz. Strangely Austrian-looking, excellent Greek restaurant. *Daily 11.30am–3pm & 5.30pm–12.30am. Moderate.*

Amur, 1, Franz-Josefs-Kai 49; U-Bahn Schwedenplatz. Ornate Chinese restaurant offering, among other things, tasty *dim sum* snacks. *Daily 11.30am–11.30pm. Moderate.*

Arche Noah, 1, Seitenstettengasse 2; U-Bahn Schwedenplatz. Vienna's most central kosher restaurant with solid Jewish specialities, and of course, *gefilte Fisch. Daily 11.30am–3.30pm & 6.30–11pm. Moderate.*

Asiana Sushi Bar, 1, Hoher Markt; U-Bahn Stephansplatz. Simple sushi café. *Mon–Sat 10.30am–10.30pm. Moderate.*

Bastei Beisl, 1, Stubenbastei 10; U-Bahn Stubentor. Perfectly ordinary *Beisl* with little booths and small *Schanigarten.* Good value lunchtime menus. *Mon–Fri 11am–11pm; closed July & Aug. Inexpensive.*

Beim Czaak, 1, Postgasse 15; U-Bahn Schwedenplatz. Garish exterior, but excellent *Wiener Beisl* feel and food inside. *Mon–Fri 8.30am–midnight, Sat 6pm–midnight. Inexpensive.*

Brezlg'wölb, 1, Ledererhof 9; U-Bahn Herrengasse. Wonderful candle-lit cave-like restaurant with deliberately zany decor. Hidden in a cobbled street off Drahtgasse, it serves the usual Austrian favourites plus specials like Greek salad. *Daily 11.30am–1am. Moderate.*

Da Capo, 1, Schulerstrasse 183; U-Bahn Stephansplatz. Popular Italian place with

a huge variety of pizzas, great salads and lots of pricier fresh fish dishes. *Daily 11.30am–midnight. Inexpensive–Moderate.*

Danieli, 1, Himmelpfortgasse 3 ☎513 79 13; U-Bahn Stephansplatz. Italian joint with a bare bricks Pompeii look and a nice big conservatory at the back. Huge pizzas, fresh fish and meat dishes too. *Daily 9am–2am. Moderate.*

DO & CO, 1, Stephansplatz 12 ☎535 39 69-18; U-Bahn Stephansplatz. Yuppie designer restaurant on the top of the Haas Haus (see p.36) specializing in Thai food and fish dishes. *Mon–Sat noon–3pm & 6pm–midnight. Expensive.*

El Pulpo, 1, Hafnersteig 6; U-Bahn Schwedenplatz. Grotto-like Spanish restaurant specializing in fish and seafood. *Mon–Sat 6pm–1am. Inexpensive–Moderate.*

Figlmüller, 1, Wollzeile 5; U-Bahn Stephansplatz. The place to eat *Wiener Schnitzel*, though they're not cheap at öS145 a go. Wash it down with wine (there's no beer). *Daily 8am–10.30pm, Sat 8am–3pm; closed Aug. Moderate.*

George and the Dragon, 1, Rotenturmstrasse 24; U-bahn Schwedenplatz. A Viennese version of a "traditional English pub" with waiter service and no English beer, just Guinness at öS48 a *Seidl. Mon–Sat 10am–1am. Moderate.*

Gösser Bierklinik, 1, Steindlgasse 4; U-Bahn Stephansplatz. Ancient inn with wooden booths for drinking, and a more formal backroom restaurant serving traditional Austrian food. *Mon–Sat 10am–midnight. Moderate.*

Griechenbeisl, 1, Fleischmarkt 11 ☎ 533 19 77; U-Bahn Schwedenplatz. Possibly the most ancient of all Vienna's inns (see p.71), frequented by the likes of Beethoven, Schubert and Brahms, something which it predictably milks in order to draw in the tourists. *Daily 11am–1am. Moderate–Expensive.*

Gulasch-Museum, 1, Schulerstrasse 20; U-Bahn Stubentor. Not a museum at all just a *Beisl* specializing in goulash. *Daily 9am–midnight. Inexpensive.*

Ilona-Stüberl, 1, Bräunerstrasse 2; U-Bahn Stephansplatz. Gypsy-music free Hungarian restaurant with lashings of goulash on offer. *Mon–Sat noon–3pm & 6–11pm. Inexpensive–Moderate.*

Inigo, 1, Bäckerstrasse 18; U-Bahn Stibentor. Designer *Beisl* overlooking the Jesuit Church, with an interesting menu including a fair proportion of soya-based veggie dishes. *Mon–Thurs 8am–midnight, Fri 8am–1am, Sat 10am–8pm, Sun 10am–midnight. Inexpensive.*

Jelinek, 1, Franz-Josefs-Kai 65; U-Bahn Schottenring. Cheap no-nonsense *Beisl* with plenty of meat and veggie choices. *Mon–Fri 8am–10pm. Inexpensive.*

K2, 1, Rotgasse 8; U-Bahn Schwedenplatz. Designer sushi bar attached to *Kiang* restaurant (see below). *Mon–Sat 11.30am–3pm & 6pm–midnight. Moderate.*

Kiang, 1, Rotgasse 8; U-Bahn Schwedenplatz. Vienna's best known designer Chinese restaurant decked out in loud primary colours with huge fishbowl windows. The food is freshly prepared right in front of your nose. *Mon–Sat 11.30am–2pm & 6pm–1am. Moderate.*

Kolar, 1, Kleeblattgasse 5; U-Bahn Stephansplatz. Stylish, cavernous bar/restaurant hidden away in the backstreets of the Innere Stadt, serving traditional favourites with a fresh approach. *Daily 1pm–2am. Inexpensive.*

Korso, Mahlerstrasse 2 ☎ 51 51 65 46; U-Bahn Karlsplatz. *Hotel Bristol's* incredibly opulent gourmet restaurant serving international food for those with plenty of Schillings; call to reserve. *Mon–Fri & Sun noon–3pm & 7pm–midnight; closed Aug. Expensive.*

Kuckuck, 1, Himmelpfortgasse 15 ☎ 512 84 70; U-Bahn Stephansplatz. Tiny vaulted restaurant, with lots of cuckoo clocks (hence the name), antique furniture, and regional cookery. Good value lunch menu (öS190 for two) but otherwise more than double that. *Daily 6–1am. Expensive.*

Lale, 1, Franz-Josefs-Kai/Rabensteig; U-Bahn Schwedenplatz. Stylish Turkish place on the edge of the Bermuda Triangle. *Mon–Thurs & Sun 11.30am–midnight, Fri & Sat until 1am. Moderate.*

La Lanterna, 1, Schönlanterngasse 4; U-Bahn Stephansplatz/Schwedenplatz. Long-established family-run Italian place serving pizzas, pasta and more substantial Italian dishes *Mon–Sat 11.30am–2.30pm & 6–11.30pm. Inexpensive.*

Mongolian Barbecue, 1, Fleischmarkt 4; U-Bahn Schwedenplatz. All-you-can-eat buffet grill of beef, lamb, pork, turkey and horsemeat for öS220. *Daily noon–2.30pm & 5.30pm–midnight. Expensive.*

Oswald und Kalb, 1, Bäckerstrasse 14 ☎ 512 69 92; U-Bahn Stephansplatz. Wondeful dimly lit *Gasthaus* specializing in Styrian dishes. *Daily 6pm–midnight. Moderate.*

Palatschinkenkuchl-Milchbar, 1, Köllnerhofgasse 4; U-Bahn Schwedenplatz. Informal restaurant popular with kids and adults alike for its savoury and sweet pancakes and milkshakes. *Mon–Sat 8am–midnight, Sun 3pm–midnight. Inexpensive.*

S'Palatschinkengartl, 1, Salzgasse 8; U-Bahn Schwedenplatz. Plain pancake place serving savoury and sweet varieties on the edge of the Bermuda Triangle. *Daily 11am–midnight. Inexpensive.*

Salzamt, 1, Ruprechtsplatz 1; U-Bahn Schwedenplatz. Typical of Vienna's mod-

Cafés and Restaurants

Cafés and Restaurants

ern *Beisln*: popular, minimalist and serving up excellent traditonal Viennese food in a nouveau way. Tables outside in the summer. *Daily 5pm–4am. Moderate.*

Siddhartha, 1, Fleischmarkt 16 ☎ 513 11 97; U-Bahn Schwedenplatz. Strangely normal decor for this Buddhist vegetarian restaurant that has a cheap weekday lunch menu. *Daily 11.30am–3pm & 6–11pm. Moderate.*

Wrenkh, 1, Bauernmarkt 10 ☎ 533 15 26; U-Bahn Stephansplatz. Very fashionable designer vegetarian restaurant. *Mon–Sat 11am–1am. Moderate.*

Zu den drei Hacken, 1, Singerstrasse 28; U-Bahn Stephansplatz. Old-style *Beisl* with cheap fare with a Styrian bent – quite a boon in this part of town. *Mon–Sat noon–midnight; closed Aug. Inexpensive.*

Zu den drei Husaren, 1, Weihburggasse 4 ☎ 512 10 92; U-Bahn Stephansplatz. Very formal Viennese restaurant that appeals to locals and visitors yearning for the days of the Habsburgs. *Mon–Sat noon–2pm & 6.30–11.30pm; closed July & Aug. Expensive.*

Zum Scherer, 1, Judenplatz 7; U-Bahn Stephansplatz. Traditional wood-panelled *Beisl*, popular with locals and tourists, with the usual Viennese menu (brains etc). *Mon–Sat 11am–midnight. Moderate.*

Ringstrasse

Glacisbeisl, 7, Messeplatz 1; U-Bahn Volkstheater. Hidden in the entrails of the Messepalast, this is a popular venue in summer. Good vegetarian selections. *March & April Mon–Sat 10am–midnight; May–Dec daily. Moderate.*

Noodles, 1, Karlsplatz 5 ☎ 505 38 39; U-Bahn Karlsplatz. Ignore the sickly snogging couple on the advertising, this is a decent Italian restaurant that does brisk trade before and after theatre/concert performances. Live piano after 9am. *Mon–Fri & Sun 11am–3pm & 6pm–4am, Sat 6pm–4am. Inexpensive–Moderate.*

Palais Schwarzenberg, 3, Schwarzenbergplatz 9 ☎ 78 45 15-600; tram #D. Idyllic setting in the glorious Baroque palace hidden behind the Soviet war memorial (see p.130) with views across the private gardens; call to reserve a terrace table. *Daily noon–3pm & 6–11pm. Expensive.*

Rathauskeller, 1, Rathausplatz 1 ☎ 42 12 19; U-Bahn Rathaus. Formal gourmet Viennese restaurant deep in the vast neo-Gothic cellars of the Rathaus; can get booked out with groups, but can be fun; call to reserve. *Mon–Sat 11.30am–3pm & 6–11.30pm. Moderate–Expensive.*

Zwillingsgwölb, 1, Universitätsstrasse 5; U-Bahn Schottentor. Popular, unpretentious, smoky student *Beisl*, just down from the university. *Mon–Fri 9am–1am. Inexpensive.*

Landstrasse

Lecker, 3, Ungargasse 57; tram #0. Excellent vegetarian Taiwanese restaurant, with lots of meat and fish on the menu, all of them ingenious soya imitations; very cheap three-course menu. *Daily 11.30am–2.30pm & 5.30–11.45pm. Inexpensive.*

Schwarzes Café, 3, Bechardgasse 23; tram #N or #0. The thinking anarchist's café/pub, suitably decorated and offering a cheap and cheerful selection of snacks and full meals, with lots of veggie choices, and *Palatschinken* to finish with. *Daily 5pm–2am. Inexpensive.*

Steiereck, 3, Rasumofskygasse 2 ☎ 713 31 68; tram #N. The discerning diplomats' favourite gourmet restaurant and arguably Vienna's finest with a Styrian flavour to much of the food (hence the name). *Mon–Fri noon–2pm & 7pm–midnight. Expensive.*

Weinhaus Wild, 3, Radetzkyplatz 1; tram #N or #0. Nice traditional *Beisl* near the Hundertwasserhaus, with a *Schanigarten* on the square. *Daily 8am–11pm. Inexpensive–Moderate.*

Mariahilf and around Naschmarkt

Altwienerhof, 15, Herklotzgasse 6 ☎ 892 60 00; U-Bahn Westbahnhof. Not strictly speaking in Mariahilf, but only the other side of the Gürtel. This hotel restaurant serves outstanding French food and wines. *Mon–Fri noon–2pm & 6.30–11pm, Sat 6.30–11pm. Expensive.*

Apadana, 5, Hamburgerstrasse 1; U-Bahn Kettenbrückengasse. Persian restaurant popular with Vienna's exile community, offering kebabs and an assortment of rice dishes. *Tues–Sun noon–3pm & 6–11pm.*

Hunger-Künstler, 5, Gumpfendorferstrasse 48 ☎587 92 10; U-Bahn Kettenbrückengasse. Candle-lit but unpretentious restaurant serving Voralberg specialities and plenty of veggie options. *Daily 6pm–1am. Inexpensive.*

Salz und Pfeffer, 6, Joanelligasse 8; U-Bahn Kettenbrückengasse. This place's chief virtue is its all-night hours. *Daily 6pm–8am. Inexpensive.*

Schlossgasse 21, 5, Schlossgasse 21; tram #62 or bus #13A. Local nouveau *Beisl* just south of Naschmarkt, popular with the professionals of Margareten. Good-value midday menu. *Mon–Fri noon–2am, Sat & Sun 6pm–2am. Moderate.*

Neubau/Josefstadt

Amerlingbeisl, 7, Stiftgasse 8; U-Bahn Volkstheater. Spacious modern Beisl that's a popular drinking hole with Vienna's younger generation. Good range of veggie food and salads; breakfast served from 9am. Shady courtyard and occasional live music. *Daily 9am–2am. Inexpensive.*

Alte Backstube, Lange Gasse 34 ☎43 11 01; U-Bahn Rathaus. Café in the front room, ancient preserved bakery beyond, and excellent restaurant in the back room, serving imaginative Austrian food. *Tues–Sat 9am–midnight, Sun 2pm–midnight; closed Aug. Moderate.*

Bombay, 7, Neustiftgasse 65; bus 13A and 48A. Friendly south Indian restaurant (a rarity in Vienna) with veggie or meat thalis for öS110. *Daily 11am–3pm & 6pm–midnight. Moderate.*

Ilija, 8, Piaristengasse 36; tram #J or bus 13A. Croatian restaurant that serves up delicious fried squid, grilled kebabs and the like. *Mon–Sat 11am–3pm & 6pm–1am. Inexpensive.*

Kiang II, 8, Lederergasse 14; tram #5 or bus #13A. Suburban branch of successful designer Chinese restaurant chain (see p.287). *Mon–Fri & Sun 11.30am–3pm & 6pm–1am, Sat 6pm–1am. Moderate.*

Küche & Keller, 7, Zollergasse 14 ☎523 24 80; U-Bahn Neubaugasse. Elegant and excellent Viennese cooking. *Mon–Sat 6pm–midnight. Moderate.*

Orlando, 8, Florianigasse 20; U-Bahn Rathaus, tram #5 or bus #13A. Nice little Italian place with nautical decor, plenty of fish and great pasta (no pizza), and Italian muzak for authenticity. *Daily noon–11pm. Inexpensive.*

Pedro's, 7, Siebensterngasse 5; U-Bahn Volkstheater. Spanish restaurant offering a great blow-out paella for öS290 for two. *Mon–Sat 6pm–1am. Inexpensive–Moderate.*

Phönixhof, 7, Neustiftgasse 55; bus #13A and #48A. Relaxed, evening-only *Beisl* that's a real favourite with the locals. *Daily 6pm–2am. Moderate.*

Plutzer Bräu, Schrankgasse 2; U-Bahn Volkstheater. Spacious designer beer bar in Spittelberg, good for a quiet lunch, or a much more boisterous evening drink. *Daily 11am–2am. Inexpensive.*

Pontoni, 7, Burggasse/Halbgasse; tram #5 or bus #48A. A modish crowd frequent this nouveau stripped-down *Beisl*; the food is traditional but imaginatively presented and freshly prepared. *Daily 11am–2pm & 5pm–1am. Inexpensive.*

Sasso, 8, Florianigasse 36 ☎403 90 71; tram #5 or bus #13A. Popular, flashy candle-lit Italian *enoteca* offering great pasta and seafood (no pizza). *Mon–Sat 6pm–2am. Moderate.*

Schnattl, 8, Lange Gasse 40 ☎405 34 00; U-Bahn Rathaus. Innovative *Neue Wiener Küche* cooked by Herr Schnattl himself; call to reserve a table in the

Cafés and Restaurants

See p.286 for an explanation of the price categories we've used in the restaurant reviews.

Cafés and Restaurants

courtyard. *Mon–Sat 11.30am–2.30pm & 6pm–midnight, Sun 6pm–midnight. Expensive.*

Schnitzelwirt, 7, Neubaugasse 52; tram #49. After *Figlmüller* (see p.286), the place to eat *Wiener Schnitzel* – they're just as humungous and cheaper too. It's very popular with backpackers. *Mon–Fri 10am–10pm, Sat & Sun 10am–2.30pm & 5–10pm. Inexpensive.*

Siebenstern Bräu, 7, Siebensterngasse 19; tram #49. Popular modern *Bierkeller* which brews its own beer, and serves a range of others on tap. The food is solid Viennese; the pan-fried dishes come with the pan, the black bread is delicious. *Mon–Sat 4pm–1am, Sun 11am–midnight. Inexpensive.*

Sobieski, 7, Burggasse 85–87; bus #13A or #48A. Lots of Polish favourites – *pierogi, golabki* and *bigos* – plus the standard Viennese dishes. *Mon–Fri 11am–2.30pm & 6–11pm. Moderate.*

Spatzennest, 7, Ulrichsplatz 1; bus #13A and #48A. Traditional *Wiener Beisl* with a good "salad and vegetable lovers' menu". *Daily except Fri & Sat 10am–midnight. Inexpensive.*

Spittelberg, 7, Spittelberggasse 12; U-Bahn Volkstheater. A chic brasserie with some veggie options and delicious crepes for dessert. *Daily from 6pm–late. Moderate.*

Stiftkeller, 7, Stiftgasse 11; U-Bahn Neubaugasse. Real home cooking in this traditional *Beisl* off Mariahilferstrasse. *Mon–Fri 7am–midnight, Sat & Sun 10am–11pm. Inexpensive–Moderate.*

Ungar-Grill, 7, Burggasse 97; bus #13A or #48A. Lively Hungarian restaurant popular with émigrés. Live Hungarian gypsy music of an evening. *Mon–Sat 6pm–1am. Moderate.*

Vega, 7, Neubaugasse 81; tram #46. Strangely sterile vegetarian restaurant serving Viennese dishes redone with soya, a few Indian staples and draught Budvar. *Tues–Sun 11.30am–3pm & 6–11pm. Moderate.*

Wegenstein, 7, Lerchenfelder Strasse 73 ☎526 78 72; tram #46. Three generations of owners make this a real local family-run *Wiener Beisl*, no messing. *Mon–Fri 8am–midnight, Sat 9am–2pm. Inexpensive.*

Witwe Bolte, 7, Gutenberggasse 13; U-Bahn Volkstheater. Long-established *Wiener Beisl* in the charming backstreets of Spittelberg, famous for having been visited by Josef II *incognito* in the eighteenth century. Lovely summer garden. *Daily 11am–midnight. Moderate.*

Wratschko & Schmid, 7, Neustiftgasse 51; bus #13A and #48A. Lively wood-panelled café/restaurant with lovely etched glass partitions and a good range of food. *Daily 5pm–1am. Inexpensive.*

Yeti, 7, Fassziehergasse 1; U-Bahn Volkstheater. Nepalese curries and stews, plus exotica like potato and bamboo soup. *Mon–Sat 5pm–2am. Inexpensive.*

Alsergrund

Allegro, 9, Währinger Strasse 67; U-Bahn Währinger Strasse/Volksoper. Bosnian bistro with loud decor that does brisk business with its *burek* before and after the opera opposite. *Daily noon–11pm. Inexpensive–Moderate.*

Bier Oase, 9, Liechtensteinstrasse 108; tram #5, #47 or #48. Friendly little *Beisl* with ten beers on tap and numerous exotic bottled beers. Simple pub food available too. *Summer Mon–Fri 11am–midnight, Sat 7pm–midnight; winter Mon–Fri from 5pm only. Inexpensive.*

Francesco, 9, Währinger Strasse 66; tram #40, #41 or #42. Smart atmospheric Italian joint serving cheap pizzas and pasta, plus pricier meat, fish and seafood. *Daily noon–11pm. Inexpensive–Moderate.*

Feuervogel, 9, Alserbachstrasse 21 ☎341 03 92; tram #5 or tram #D. Long-established Ukrainian restaurant that's a social focal point for the émigré community. *Daily 7pm–2am; closed Aug. Moderate–Expensive.*

Gasthaus Wickerl, 9, Porzellangasse 24; tram #D. Good neighbourhood *Beisl. Mon–Fri 9am–midnight, Sat & Sun 10am–2pm. Inexpensive.*

Légume, 9, Währinger Strasse 57; tram #40, #41 or #42. Plain lunch time only vegetarian diner attached to a health-food shop of the same name; set three-course menu for around öS100. *Mon–Fri 11.30am–2.30pm. Inexpensive.*

Rasta Masr, 9, Grünentorgasse 19; tram #D. Pleasant Egyptian restaurant opposite the Servitenkirche offering a short menu with plenty of veggie options. *Daily 11am–10pm. Inexpensive.*

Sacromonte, 9, Währinger Strasse 26; tram £40, #41 or #42. Lovely bare brick-vaulted Spanish restaurant with great *tapas. Daily noon–midnight. Inexpensive.*

Skopje-Grill, 9, Liechtenstein Strasse 33; tram #D. No frills Macedonian grills. *Mon–Fri 10.30am–11.30pm, Sat & Sun 11.30am–11.30pm. Inexpensive.*

Stadtbeisl, 9, Währinger Strasse 59; tram #40, #41 or #42. Funky arty *Beisl* in the trendy w.u.k. arts complex with a varied menu, half veggie, half organic meat dishes. *Daily 11am–2am. Inexpensive.*

Leopoldstadt

Altes Jägerhaus, 2, Aspernallee, Prater; bus #77A. Lively *Beisl* at the far end of the Hauptallee serving typical hearty fare washed down with *Budvar* beer. *Wed–Sun 10am–11pm. Moderate.*

Leopold, 2, Grosser Pfarrgasse 11; tram #N or #21. Chic modern designer *Beisl,* with high ceiling, pine furniture, imaginative *Neue Wiener Küche;* a real oasis in Leopoldstadt. *Daily Mon–Sat 5pm–2am, Sun 11am–2am. Moderate.*

Lusthaus, 2, Hauptallee, Prater ☎728 95 65; bus #77A. Eighteenth-century rotunda at the far end of Hauptallee that makes a perfect food halt while exploring the Prater. *May–Sept Mon–Fri noon–11pm, Sat & Sun noon–6pm; shorter hours in winter and closed Wed. Moderate.*

Schweizerhaus, 2, Strasse des 1 Mai 116; U-Bahn Praterstern. Czech-owned in the Prater. Known for its draught beer and Czech specialities such as tripe soup and roast pork. *March–Oct daily 10am–11pm. Inexpensive.*

Suburbs

Fischer Bräu, 19, Billrothstrasse 17; U-Bahn Nussdorferstrasse. Very civilized micro-brewery pub, which produces a great, lemony, misty beer. Lots of tasty snacks and more substantial pub fare to be consumed in the bare boards interior or the shady courtyard. Worth the trek. *Daily 4pm–1am. Inexpensive.*

Heurigen

Heurigen are the wine taverns found predominantly in the former villages of the city's outer suburbs, to the north and west of the centre on the slopes of the Wienerwald. The word *heurig* means "this year's", as it was here that the vintner would encourage tastings in order to try and sell a few bottles of his (exclusively white) wine. As an instituion they are as old as the city itself, but came into their own during the Biedermeier period (1815–48). In the good old days, people used to bring their own picnics to consume sat on wooden benches in the vintner's garden while drinking the wine, but nowadays, most *Heurigen* provide a self-service buffet of traditional Viennese fare.

According to the Emperor Josef II's 1784 law, real *Heurigen* are only permitted to open for 300 days in any one year, and may only sell wine and food produced on the premises. If the *Heuriger* is open, the custom is to display a *Buschen* or bunch of evergreen boughs over the entrance and a sign telling you it's *ausg'stekt* (hung out). Those that still abide by the strict *Heurigen* laws generally have a sign saying *Buschenschank,* though it has to be said that some have now got themselves restaurant licences in order to open all year round.

Cafés and
Restaurants

Cafés and Restaurants

Traditionally a visit to a *Heuriger* is accompanied by *Schrammelmusik*, sentimental fiddle, guitar and accordion music, though today such music only features at the more touristy ventures. In addition to the *Heurigen* in the outer suburbs, there are a handful of wine taverns known as *Stadtheurigen* located closer to the centre of town, usually in the cellars of the city's monasteries. These are not real *Heurigen* at all, but are still great places to drink wine and eat the local cuisine.

In the listings below, only *Stadtheurigen* are specifically detailed. For the villages, there are no specific listings, as the opening times of most *Heurigen* are unpredictable (most don't open until mid-afternoon). Part of the fun of visiting a *Heuriger* is to simply set off to one of the districts and take pot luck. A display board at the centre of each village lists those *Heurigen* that are open.

Stadtheurigen

Augustinerkeller, 1, Augustinerstrasse 1; U-Bahn Karlsplatz. Vast array of green and black striped booths in the cellars underneath the Albertina. Fast service and hearty Viennese food; a tad touristy, but fun – prices are cheaper in the day. *Schrammelmusik* from 6.30pm. *Daily 11am–midnight.*

Esterházykeller, 1, Haarhof 1; U-Bahn Herrengasse. Snug, brick-vaulted wine cellar with a limited range of hot and cold snacks. Situated off Naglergasse. *Mon–Sat 11am–10pm. Inexpensive.*

Gigerl, 1, Rauhensteingasse 3; U-Bahn Stephansplatz. Relatively new *Stadtheuriger* with a self-service buffet. *Daily noon–1am. Inexpensive.*

Melker Stiftskeller, 1, Schottengasse 3; U-Bahn Schottentor. Vast, high ceilinged wine cellar owned by the famous Melk monks. *Mon–Sat 5pm–midnight. Moderate.*

Piaristenkeller, 8, Piaristengasse 45; tram #J or bus #13A. Traditional Viennese food in an atmospheric wine cellar. *Mon–Sat 6pm–1am, Sun 11am–2pm & 6pm–1am. Moderate.*

Specht, 1, Bäckerstrasse 12; U-Bahn Stephansplatz. Smart new *Stadtheuriger* with a self-service counter for food and a long wine list. *Daily 4pm–late. Inexpensive–Moderate.*

Selected Heurigen

Grinzing is the most famous of the *Heuriger* villages, and consequently the most touristy. There are numerous *Heurigen* on the main street of Sandgasse, but to avoid the worst of the crowds head further up Cobenzlgasse. The next most popular villages are the nearby **Heiligenstadt** and **Nussdorf**. Less touristy alternatives include Sievering and Neustift am Walde. Another option is to cross over the Danube and head for the village of Stammersdorf, and its immediate neighbour Strebersdorf. The single recommendations below are meant as a sort of starting point for each district.

Grinzing
Altes Presshaus, 19, Cobenzlgasse 15; tram #38 to the end terminus.

Nussdorf
Schübel-Auer, 19, Kahlenberger Strasse 22; tram #D to the end terminus.

Heiligenstadt
Mayer am Pfarrplatz, 19, Pfarrplatz 2: bus #38A from U-Bahn Heiligenstadt.

Neustift am Walde
Huber, 19, Rathstrasse 15: bus #35A from U-Bahn Nussdorfer Strasse.

Sievering
Haslinger, 19, Agnesgasse ; bus #39A from U-Bahn Heiligenstadt to the end stop.

Stammersdorf
Wieninger, 21, Stammersdorfer Strasse 78; tram #31 to the end terminus.

Thomaskeller, 1, Postgasse 2; U-Bahn Stubentor. Good daily specials served up in the atmospheric red-brick cellars of a Dominican monastery. *Mon–Sat 6pm–midnight. Inexpensive–Moderate.*

Urbani-Keller, 1, Am Hof 12; U-Bahn Herrengasse. Well-known slightly pricey *Heuriger* with live *Schrammelmusik. Daily 6pm–1am. Moderate–Expensive.*

Wein-Comptoir, 1, Bäckerstrasse 6; U-Bahn Stephansplatz. Beuatiful wood-panelled *Beisl on several levels with bottles stacked up on the walls. Mon–Sat 5pm–2am. Moderate.*

Zwölf-Apostelkeller, 1, Sonnenfelsgasse 3; U-Bahn Stephansplatz. An attractive seventeenth-century building with bars housed in three levels of cellars. *The place to drink wine, but often difficult to find a space; cold food only. Daily 4.30pm–midnight; closed July. Inexpensive.*

Cafés and
Restaurants

Chapter 12

Bars, Clubs and Live Venues

Surveys have shown that the vast majority of the Viennese are safely tucked up in bed by as early as 10pm. Meanwhile, however, a hard core stay up until early in the morning – in fact it's quite possible to keep drinking round the clock.

Vienna's late-night **bars** are concentrated in three main areas, the most famous of which is the so-called **Bermuda Triangle** or *Bermuda Dreieck*, where, the idea is, you could get lost forever. This area is focused on Rabensteig, Seitenstettengasse, Ruprechtsplatz and the streets around. During the day, the area is pretty quiet, frequented mostly by tourists come to visit the city's only surviving pre-war synagogue. After work, though, the bars begin to fill up, and by midnight, the place is heaving. And so it has been since the 1980s, when the emergence of the Bermuda Triangle helped kick-start Vienna's nightlife out of its stupor. Sadly, though, the area has become a victim of its own success: prices have gone up and more moneyed punters now predominate. That said, such is the variety packed into these few streets that you're bound to find somewhere that appeals.

The dives in the streets around **Kärntnerstrasse** are mostly worth avoiding. It's here you'll find the more "respectable", more expensive hostess bars – though not all of them fall into that category, they set the tone rather. Lastly, there's the much larger area

stretching from the **Naschmarkt** – where late-night licences abound – north into Neubau. In Neubau, the **Spittelberg** area – the narrow streets between Burggasse and Siebensterngasse, behind Messepalast – has the highest concentration of late-night places, though many are restaurants and cafés rather than simply drinking holes as such.

Vienna's **club** scene is very small indeed for a city of 1.5 million. Dance culture, such as one would find in, say, London, is restricted to just a few venues. Aside from discos, the majority of Vienna's clubs are, in fact, bars, which either occasionally, or regularly, have live bands. The other, more interesting phenomenon peculiar to Vienna is the *Musikcafé*, where resident DJs spin discs (both danceable and non-danceable) while the punters simply chill out and drink. As it's so difficult to differentiate between what is a bar, what's a club and what's a live venue, we've simply organized the listings by area. To find out what's on at Vienna's clubs, check out the *Musik-U* section in the weekly listings tabloid *Falter*.

Drink prices are relatively high – bars in the Bermuda Triangle tend to charge öS40 and upwards for a *Krügerl* (half litre) – but in those clubs where there is an admission charge, it's rarely more than öS100–150. As for how to get home in the wee small hours, there's details on the city's nightbuses on p.32. Nightbuses leave from Schwedenplatz

Lesbian and Gay Nightlife

Vienna's lesbian and gay scene is pretty limited for your average western European capital, perhaps reflecting the conservatism inherent in the country at large. Only the merest handful of bars and clubs, scattered across the city, are at all open about their existence. The traditional "gay district" around Naschmarkt is a mixture of old-style closet clubs, where you have to ring the bell to gain entry, and more relaxed venues.

Bars, Clubs and Live Venues

The social and political heart of the gay community is focused on the **Rosa-Lila Villa**, 6, Linke Wienzeile 102 (U-Bahn Pilgramgasse) which proudly flies the rainbow flag and proclaims itself as a *Lesben und Schwulen Haus*. In early September, there's usually a week-long Gay Film Festival staged at the Filmcasino, 5, Margaretenstrasse 78 (U-Bahn Pilgramgasse).

The best gay clubs are the one-nighters like the mixed gay/lesbian *Kinky Disco*, every Saturday at *Volksgarten*, 1, Burgring 1, and *Heaven* every Thursday at *U4*, 12, Schönbrunner Strasse 222. In addition, check out the following:

Alfi's Goldener Spiegel, 6, Linke Wienzeile 46; U-Bahn Kettenbrückengasse. Naff but popular gay men's bar with a bar and restaurant; entrance is on Stiegengasse. *Daily except Tues 9pm–4am.*

Alte Lampe, 4, Heumühlgasse 13; U-Bahn Kettenbrückengasse. Long-established gay bar south of the Naschmarkt, with live piano and lots of Viennese schmaltz. *Daily 9pm–4am.*

Café Berg, 9, Berggasse 8; U-Bahn Schottentor (also reviewed on p.000). Cool café with mixed gay/straight clientele, especially during the day. The food's good, and you can pick up flyers about up-and-coming gay events. *Daily 10am–1am.*

Café Savoy, 6, Linke Wienzeile 36; U-Bahn Kettenbrückengasse (also reviewed on p.000). Even more than the

Berg, this scruffy *fin-de-siècle* café is by no means exclusively gay, but things pick up in the evening. *Mon–Fri 5pm–2am, Sat 9am–6pm, Sun 9pm–2am.*

Café Willendorf, 6, Linke Wienzeile 102; U-Bahn Pilgramgasse. Café/restaurant inside the Rosa-Lila Villa with a nice leafy courtyard. Another good place to pick up info about the latest events. *Daily 7pm–2am.*

Eagle Bar, 6, Blümelgasse 1; U-Bahn Neubaugasse. Vienna's cruisy leather bar for gay men. *Daily 9pm–4am.*

Frauencafé, 8, Lange Gasse 11; U-Bahn Lerchenfelder Strasse. Vienna's only permanent women-only space is a small, but friendly café. *Mon–Sat 8pm–1am.*

Why Not?, 1, Tiefergraben 22. Late-night gay/lesbian bar and disco. *Wed–Sun 11pm–5am.*

and usually do a circuit of the Ring before heading off to their destination – pick up a leaflet from the tourist office or one of the transport offices (see p.31).

The Bermuda Triangle

Casablanca, 1, Rabensteig. Small, crowded bar with a minute stage and live bands every night; sets at 8pm & 11pm. *Daily 7pm–late.*

Excess, 1, Rabensteig. Soft metal and MTV in the upstairs bar; karaoke in the

concrete catacombs; expensive beer. *Daily 6pm–4am.*

First Floor, 1, Seitenstettengasse 1. As the name suggests, an upstairs bar, with a vast array of aquariums and packed with a well-dressed, moneyed crowd. *Mon–Sat 7pm–4am, Sun 11pm–4am.*

Jazzland, 1, Franz-Josefs-Kai 29. Vienna's main trad-jazz venue, just below the Ruprechtskirche. *Tues–Sat 7pm–2am, occasionally Sun & Mon.*

The nearest U-Bahn to the Bermuda Triangle is Schwedenplatz.

Bars, Clubs and Live Venues

Kaktus, 1, Seitenstettengasse 5. Very loud and very packed. *Daily 6pm–2am, Fri & Sat until 4am.*

Krah Krah, 1, Rabensteig 8. Crowded bar known for its excellent selection of draught beers; snacks also on offer, and occasional live jazz. *Daily 11am–2am.*

Ma Pitom, 1, Seitenstettengasse 5. Swish Italian late-night bar/restaurant that's chic, minimalist and popular. *Mon–Thurs 11.30am–3pm & 5.30pm–1am, Sat until 2am, Sun 5.30pm–1am.*

Roter Engel, 1, Rabensteig 5. Stylish café/bar designed by deconstructionist mob, Coop Himmelblau, in 1979. Live music most nights; sets at 9.30pm (Fri & Sat at midnight, too). *Mon–Wed 3pm–2am, Thurs–Sat 3pm–4am, Sun 5pm–2am.*

Steh-Achterl, 1, Sterngasse 3. A loud young crowd fill this black UV and candle-lit cellar that features a male stripper on Wednesdays. *Daily 6pm–2am, Fri & Sat until 4am.*

The rest of the Innere Stadt

Aera, 1, Gonzagagasse 11; U-Bahn Schwedenplatz. Relaxing café upstairs and dimly lit cellar downstairs where live bands perform. *Daily 10am–2am.*

American Bar (Kärntner Bar), 1, Kärntner Durchgang; U-Bahn Stephensplatz. Small, dark late-night bar off Kärntnerstrasse with surprisingly rich interior by Adolf Loos. Shame about the strip club next door. *Daily noon–4am; June–Aug from 6pm only.*

Benjamin, 1, Salzgries 11; U-Bahn Schwedenplatz. Good alternative to the Triangle, with loud music and darts. *Daily 7pm–2am, Fri & Sat until 4am.*

Bierhof, 1, Naglergasse 13; U-Bahn Herrengasse. Smart beer bar at the far end of Graben, with leafy courtyard, lots of draught beers, cocktails and pub snacks. *Mon–Sat 4pm–2am.*

Flex, 1, Donaukanal/Augartenbrücke; U-Bahn Schottenring. Hip-hop bar down by the canal, overlooking Wagner's Schützenhaus, with music from 9pm. *Daily 3pm–late.*

Kix, 1, Bäckerstrasse 4; U-Bahn Stephansplatz. Slightly overwhelming design in primary colours, with lots of aluminium and hour-glass shaped tables. *Daily 8pm–2am.*

Krebitz, 1, Salzgries 9; U-Bahn Schwedenplatz. A small slice of post-industrial cool, with the occasional live band, low-key DJ, table football and pin-ball. *Daily 6pm–2am.*

Lindbergh, 1, Mahlerstrasse 11; U-Bahn Karlsplatz. Soul, retro and house at this clubby venue. *Daily 9pm–4am.*

Molly D'Arcy's Irish Pub, 1, Teinfaltstrasse 6; U-Bahn Herrengasse. Fair approximation of an Irish pub, with none too cheap *Guinness* and *Kilkenny* on tap. *Daily 6pm–2am.*

P1, 1, Rotgasse 9; U-Bahn Stephansplatz. Big city-centre disco playing commercial dance music to a youngish crowd. *Daily 9pm–4am, Fri & Sat until 6am.*

Porgy & Bess, 1, Spiegelgasse 2; U-Bahn Stephansplatz. Venue for up-and-coming jazz bands. *Mon–Fri 7pm–2am, Sat & Sun 8pm–4am.*

Reiss-Bar, 1, Marco-d'Aviano Gasse 1; U-Bahn Stephansplatz. Expensive champagne bar that's another Coop Himmelblau design, and not a place to go to on a budget. *Daily until 3am.*

Schwimmende Pyramida, 1, Seilerstätte 3a; U-Bahn Stubentor. Rowdy late-night beer bar with huge range of beers. *Daily 4pm–4am.*

X-s, 1, Kärntnerstrasse 61; U-Bahn Karlsplatz. Bewildering variety of nights from "neofolk" to loudasfuck metal evenings. *Mon & Wed–Sat 9pm–late.*

Wunder-Bar, Schönlanterngasse 8; U-Bahn Schwedenplatz. Hermann Czech-designed bar from the 1970s that has a post-modern feel; an older crowd tend to sink into the brown leather seats. *Daily 4pm–2am.*

Ringstrasse

Atrium, 4, Schwarzenbergplatz 10; U-Bahn Karlsplatz. Austria's longest-established disco, young and studenty. *Thurs*

LATE-NIGHT CAFÉS, PUBS AND RESTAURANTS

Check out the following cafés, pubs and restaurants, all of which are open until at least 2am; they're all reviewed in the previous chapter.

Bars, Clubs and Live Venues

Innere Stadt
Alt Wien, 1, Bäckerstrasse 9 (see p.281)
Engländer, 1, Postgasse 2 (see p.281)
Hawelka, 1, Dorotheergasse 6 (see p.282)
Kleines Café, 1, Franziskanerplatz 3 (see p.282)
MAK Café, 1, Stubenring 5 (see p.283)
Noodles, 1, Karlsplatz 5 (see p.288)
Salzamt, 1, Ruprechtsplatz 1 (see p.287)

Naschmarkt to Josefstadt
Amerlingbeisl, 7, Stiftgasse 8 (see p.289)
Benno, 8, Alserstrasse 67 (see p.284)
Drechsler, 6, Linke Wienzeile 22 (see p.283)
Europa, 7, Zollergasse 8 (see p.284)
Das Käuzchen, 7, Gardegasse 8 (see p.284)

Lux, 7, Spittelberggasse 3 (see p.284)
Merkur, 8, Florianigasse 18 (see p.284)
Hummel, 8, Albertgasse 27 (see p.284)
Phönixhof, 7, Neustiftgasse 55 (see p.289)
Plutzer Bräu, Schrankgasse 2 (see p.289)
Rüdigerhof, 5, Hamburger Strasse 20 (see p.284)
Savoy, 6, Linke Wienzeile 36 (see p.284)

Alsergrund
Luxor, 9, Grünentorgasse 19 (see p.285)
Stadtbeisl, 9, Währinger Strasse 59 (see p.291)
Weimar, 9, Währinger Strasse 68 (see p.285)

Leopoldstadt
Leopold, 2, Grosser Pfarrgasse 11 (see p.291)

& *Sun 8.30pm–2am, Fri & Sat 8.30pm–4am.*

Papa's Tapas, 4, Schwarzenbergplatz 10; U-Bahn Karlsplatz. Good tapas and live music, situated above *Atrium* (see above). *Mon–Thurs & Sun 8pm–2am, Fri & Sat until 4am.*

Pavillon, 1, Burgring 1; U-Bahn Volkstheater. Strange location right by the Hofburg for this trendy garden café which attracts clubbers heading for the *Volksgarten* (see below). *Daily 8pm–2am.*

Tiffany, 1, Robert-Stolz-Platz 4; U-Bahn Karlsplatz. New addition to the club and live music scene, specializing in techno and trance. *Mon–Sat 9pm–4am, Sun 5pm–midnight.*

Volksgarten, 1, Burgring 1; U-Bahn Volkstheater. Situated in the park of the same name, Vienna's trendiest club and

a firm favourite with the dance crowd; the outdoor dance floor is a summertime treat. *Daily 8pm–5am.*

Naschmarkt and Mariahilf

Jazzclub Sixth, 6, Gumpendorferstrasse 9; U-Bahn Babenbergerstrasse. Live jazz venue just south of Mariahilferstrasse. *Daily 9pm–2am, Fri & Sat until 4am.*

Jazzpelunke, 6, Dürergasse 3; U-Bahn Kettenbrückengasse. Newish jazz venue with live acts from trad to modern, located near the Naschmarkt. *Mon–Fri 6pm–2am, Sat & Sun 11am–2am.*

Nachtasyl, 6, Stumpergasse 53–55; U-Bahn Westbahnhof. Darkened beer hall managed by an expatriate Czech, and the odd live music. *Daily 8pm–4am.*

Stehbeisl, 6, Windmühlgasse 6; U-Bahn Babenbergerstrasse. Small amiable

**Bars, Clubs and
Live Venues**

rock/folk bar off Mariahilferstrasse with occasional live music and cheap pub snacks. *Mon–Thurs & Sun 6pm–2am, Fri & Sat 6pm–4am.*

Neubau and Josefstadt

Blue Box, 7, Richtergasse 8. *Musikcafé* with resident DJs and a good snack menu (see cafés). Live music from 8pm. *Mon 6pm–2am, Tues–Thurs 10am–2am, Fri & Sat 10am–4am.*

Chelsea, 8, U-Bahnbögen 29–31, Lerchenfelder Gürtel; U-Bahn Thaliastrasse. Punky anglophile haunt with regular live music; situated underneath the U-Bahn. *Mon–Sat 7pm–4am, Sun 4pm–4am.*

Donau Bar, K. Schweighofergasse 10; U-Bahn Neubaugasse. Ambient/jungle *Musikcafé* with in-house DJ and strange monochrome projections on the walls. *Daily 9pm–4am.*

Hokus Pokus, 7, Burggasse/Stuckgasse; bus #13A or #48A. Friendly neighbourhood jazz bar with darts. *Daily 7pm–late.*

Holzwurm, 7, Ulrichsplatz 5. Draught beer and jazz. *Daily 5pm–2am, Sat & Sun 7pm–2am.*

La Colombie, 8, Laudongasse 57; U-Bahn Josefstädter Strasse. Latin American club in the basement of restaurant of the same name. Good when there's a crowd or a popular live act visiting. *Daily 7pm–2am.*

Miles Smiles, 8, Lange Gasse 51; U-Bahn Rathaus. Helps if you're a devotee of the trumpeter, though this mellow café does have the occasional live jazz act. *Daily 8pm–2am, Fri & Sat until 4am.*

Tunnel, 8, Florianigasse 39; tram #5. Large, clean-living student establishment with café upstairs and frequent live bands down in the cellar. *Daily 9am–2am.*

Alsergrund

w.u.k., 9, Währingers Strasse 59; tram #40, #41 or #42. Formerly squatted old red-brick school, now legitimate arts venue with a great café and a wide programme of events, including live music; check the *Falter* listings. *Daily 11am–2am.*

Leopoldstadt

Bricks, 2, Taborstrasse 38; tram #N or #21. Small brick-built cellar bar with resident DJ and the odd live act. Music from 9pm. *Mon–Wed & Sun 8pm–4am, Thurs–Sat 8pm–6am.*

Woodquarter, 2, Leopoldsgasse 17; bus #5A. Beaten-up *Beisl*-look and a young clientele who satisfy their appetites with *Erdäpfelpuffer* and toasted sandwiches. *Daily 5pm–2am.*

Suburbs

Arena, 3, Baumgasse 80; U-Bahn Erdberg. It's a long trek out to this former slaughterhouse on the corner of Franzosengraben, but a real variety of stuff goes on here – all-night raves, outdoor concerts, films – so check the listings before setting out. *Daily 7pm–late.*

B.A.C.H., 16, Bachgasse 21; tram #46 from U-Bahn Thaliastrasse. A favourite of the alternative crowd, but a way out; DJs and occasional live bands. *Daily 8pm–2am, Fri & Sat until 4am.*

Blues Man, 19, Glatzgasse 4; U-Bahn Nussdorfer Strasse. Reasonably-priced, relaxed blues and jazz café just the other side of the Gürtel from Alsergrund; live music most nights from 9pm. *Mon–Sat 6pm–2am.*

Szene Wien, 11, Hauffgasse 26; tram #71 from Schwarzenbergplatz. Live music venue run by a radical bunch from Simmering. *Daily 6pm–late*

U4, 12, Schönbrunnerstrasse 222; U-Bahn Meidling-Hauptstrasse. Dark, cavernous disco, mostly rock/indie, with frequent gigs; a mecca of the alternative crowd. Gay/lesbian night Thurs. *Mon & Tues 11pm–4am, Wed–Sun until 5am.*

Chapter 13

The Arts

Vienna prides itself on its musical associations, and classical music and opera, in particular, are heavily subsidized by the Austrian state. The season runs from September to June, though smaller concerts are held throughout the year in the city's churches and palaces. The chief cultural festival – featuring opera, music and theatre – is the **Wiener Festwochen**, which lasts from early May until mid-June. The city's film festival or **Viennale** and the **Wien Modern** festival of contemporary classical music both take place towards the end of October. But by far the busiest time of the year is **Fasching**, Vienna's ball season, when it can be difficult to find a room on spec.

To find out **what's on**, pick up the tourist board's free monthly listings booklet *Programm*, which gives the programmes of the big opera and concert houses, plus a day-by-day concert guide, ball calendar and details of the current art exhibitions. The weekly listings tabloid *Falter* also lists classical concerts under its *Musik-E* section.

Tickets

Ticket **prices** vary enormously in Vienna: the Staatsoper is a case in point with seats ranging from öS50 to öS2300. For some events – most notably the Vienna Boys' Choir and the New Year's Day Concert – it's not so much the price as the availability that's problem. However, the big state venues offer cheap *Stehplätzen* on the day of the performance (see box below), and some offer unsold tickets at a

discount to students, around an hour or thirty minutes before the show starts.

The cheapest way of **buying tickets** is to go to the venue's own box office. You can buy direct from the big four state theatres – Staatsoper, Volksoper, Burgtheater and Akademietheater – which also have a central box office, the *Bundestheaterkassen*, by the Staatsoper at 1, Hanuschgasse 3 (☎514 44-2955; Mon–Fri 9am–5pm, Sat & Sun 9am–noon; U-Bahn Karlsplatz; www.austria-info.at/kultur/wswv/index.html). There's also a box office on the Kärntnerstrasse side of the Staatsoper, which sells half-price tickets for musicals and for other events, and several on the Kärtner Ring such as *Flamm*, 1, Kärntner Ring 3 (☎512 42 25).

Rock, pop and jazz venues are covered in the previous chapter.

> ### Stehplätze
>
> Vienna may be an expensive place, but its top opera houses and concert halls are open to even the poorest music student thanks to the system of *Stehplätze* or **standing-room tickets** which can cost as little as öS20 each. *Stehplätzen* are limited to one per person and usually go on sale one hour before the performance (for very popular concerts, you may find that tickets go on sale somewhat earlier, so check first). It's standard practice, once you've got into the auditorium, to tie a scarf to the railings to reserve your standing place.

The Arts

Opera and classical music

Vienna has a musical pedigree second to none. Josef Haydn, Wolfgang Mozart and Ludwig Beethoven spent much of their time here, as did local-born Franz Schubert. Johannes Brahms and Anton Bruckner followed in their wake, and coincided with the great waltz fever generated by the Strauss family and Josef Lanner. At the turn of the century, the Vienna opera house was under the baton of Gustav Mahler, while its concert halls resounded to the atonal music of Arnold Schönberg, Anton Webern and Alban Berg.

Though Vienna no longer produces world-class composers, it does still boast one of Europe's top opera houses in the **Staatsoper**, served by one of its finest orchestras, the **Wiener Philharmoniker** (which only allowed women into its ranks after a long struggle in 1996). The orchestra's New Year's Day Concert (*Silvesterkonzert*) in the Musikverein is broadcast across the globe; to obtain tickets you must contact the box office on January 2 for the following year's concert (☎712 12 11; fax 712 28 71). If you don't have a ticket, don't despair, not only is the concert broadcast live on Austrian TV, it's also relayed live on an enormous screen in front of the Rathaus at midday and again at 5pm. When the big state theatres are closed in July and August, opera and classical music concerts captured on film are also shown for free every evening outside the Rathaus.

The most famous musical institution in the city is, of course, the **Wiener Sängerknaben** or Vienna Boys' Choir, who perform Mass at the Burgkapelle in the Hofburg every Sunday from mid-September to June at 9.15am. Tickets for the Mass (öS60–280) are sold out weeks in advance, though some are held over each week and go on sale on Fridays between 4 and 6pm (you need to be there at least half an hour before the box office opens). To book in advance write to Hofburgkapelle, Hofburg, A-1010 Wien, Austria, stating which Sunday Mass you wish to attend, and you will be sent back a reservation slip to take to the box office on arrival in Vienna. The other option is to settle for a *Stehplatz* ticket which is free and goes on sale before Mass; get there for 8.30am to be sure of a ticket.

Mostly opera and operetta

Kammeroper, 1, Fleischmarkt 24 ☎513 08 51; U-Bahn Schwedenplatz. Vienna's smallest opera house, hidden in the backstreets of the Innere Stadt and performing a variety of works from Rossini to Britten. In July and August, when the theatre is closed, the Kammeroper stages Mozart operas in Schönbrunn (see p.210).

Staatsoper, 1, Opernring 2 ☎514 44-2955; U-Bahn Karlsplatz. Vienna's largest opera house stages around forty operas a season played in rep. It's a conservative place, but attracts the top names, and has the benefit of the Wiener Philharmoniker in the pit. With over 500 *Stehplätze* a night it is also one of the most accessible opera houses in the world.

Volksoper, 9, Währinger Strasse 78 ☎514 44-2955; U-Bahn Volksoper or tram #40, #41 or #42. Vienna's number two opera house, which specializes in operetta, but also branches out into JanáBek, Shostakovitch and the late Romantics; over 100 *Stehplätze* a night.

Mostly music

Bösendorfer Saal, 4, Graf Starhemberg-Gasse 14 ☎504 66 51; U-Bahn Taubstummengasse. Chamber music concert hall belonging to the famous Austrian piano manufacturers.

Konzerthaus, 3, Lothringerstrasse 20 ☎712 12 11; U-Bahn Karlsplatz. Early twentieth-century concert hall designed by Viennese duo Helmer & Fellner. Three separate halls: the Grosser Saal, Mozart-Saal and Schubert-Saal. The Wiener Sängerknaben perform here in the summer (excluding July & Aug).

If you yearn to hear schmaltzy Viennese songs sung live, check out Café Schmid Hansl, 18, Schulgasse 31 (☎43 36 58; U-Bahn Volksoper; Tues–Sat 9pm–4am).

Fasching

Though clearly analogous with Mardi Gras and Carnival, Vienna's **Fasching** lasts much longer, with the first balls taking place on November 11, and continuing – mostly on Saturdays and Sundays – until Ash Wednesday the following year. Traditionally the most famous ball is the *Kaiserball*, held in the Hofburg and in days gone by presided over by the emperor himself. Its place at the top of the hierarchy is now challenged by the *Opernball*, held on the Thursday before Ash Wednesday in the Staatsoper, and pictured in many a tourist brochure, with the débutantes all in white. The other 300 or so balls are a hotchpotch held by various associations – everything from the *Drogistenball* to the *Ball der Burgenländischen Kroaten* – in Vienna's top hotels and palaces; those followed by the word *Gschnas* are masked. To find out what's on in Fasching, pick up a *Wiener Ballkalender* from the tourist office in the months leading up to and during Fasching. If you're worried about your dancing ability, there are numerous dance classes held during the season; ask the tourist board for details.

The Arts

Kursalon, 1, Johannesgasse 33 ☎713 21 81; U-Bahn Stadtpark. The best place to hear Strauss and other popular tunes. *April–Oct* only.

Musikverein, 1, Bösendorferstrasse 12 ☎505 81 90; U-Bahn Karlsplatz. Two ornate concert halls in one buidling, gilded from top to bottom inside. The larger of the two, the Grosser Saal, has the best acoustics in the country, while the smaller hall, the Brahms-Saal, is used mainly for chamber concerts; *Stehplätze* available for the Grosser Saal.

Theatre

Obviously for the non-German speaker, most of Vienna's theatres and satirical cabarets have limited appeal. However, there are a couple of English-speaking theatre groups: *International Theatre*, 9, Porzellangasse 8 (☎319 62 72; tram #D), and *Vienna's English Theatre*, 8, Josefsgasse 12 (☎402 12 60; U-Bahn Lerchenfelderstrasse), a few theatres that specialize in musicals, and the Burgtheater, whose interior alone is worth the price of a ticket.

Straight theatres

Akademietheater, 3, Lisztstrasse 1 ☎514 44-0; U-Bahn Karlsplatz. Number two to the Burgtheater, using the same pool of actors.

Burgtheater, 1, Dr-Karl-Lueger-Ring 2 ☎514 44-0; U-Bahn Herrengasse. Vienna's most prestigious theatrical stage puts on serious drama in rep. The foyer and staircases are spectacular; the auditorium was modernized after bomb damage in 1945.

Kammerspiele, 1, Rotenturmstrasse 20 ☎533 28 33; U-Bahn Schwedenplatz. Contemporary comedies, satires and farces.

Theater-in-der-Josefstadt, 8, Josefstädter Strasse 24–26 ☎402 51 27; U-Bahn Rathaus or tram #J. Beautiful early nineteenth-century theatre that puts on a variety of serious drama from classics to contemporary.

Volkstheater, 7, Neustiftgasse 1 ☎523 27 76; U-Bahn Volkstheater. Modern plays and classics and even the odd operetta.

Mostly musicals

Raimund Theater, 6, Wallgasse 18 ☎599 77-27; U-Bahn Westbahnhof. Late-nineteenth-century theatre where *Beauty and the Beast* was enjoying a long run at the time of going to press.

Ronacher, 1 Seilerstätte 9 ☎514 02; U-Bahn Stephansplatz. Beautifully refur-

The Arts

bished turn-of-the-century music hall that puts on a variety of dance shows and musicals.

Theater-an-der-Wien, 6, Linke Wienzeile 6 ☎ 588 85; U-Bahn Karlsplatz/Kettenbrückengasse. Historic early nineteenth-century theatre (see p.128), specializing in musicals.

Puppet theatre and mime

Lilarum, 14, Phillipsgasse 8 ☎ 894 21 03; U-Bahn Hietzing. Puppet theatre opposite Schönbrunn, with several performances a day, Fri–Sun.

Schönbrunner Schloss-Marionettentheater, 13, Schloss Schönbrunn, Hofratsktrakt ☎ 817 32 47. String puppet theatre in Schönbrunn specializing in over-long Mozart operas – try and catch a different show if you can. Performances Wed–Sun 4 & 8pm.

Serapionstheater im Odeon, 2, Taborstrasse 10 ☎ 214 55 62; tram #N or #21. Top-class mime.

Cinema

Austrian cinema is not really up there with the greats, and unless your German is up to scratch, you're best off sticking to British and American films. One film that's fun to see, and regularly gets a screening here, is *The Third Man* (Der Dritte Mann), set amid the rubble of post-war Vienna and starring Orson Welles. The best place to check out the week's cinema listings is *Falter*, the city's weekly tabloid. *OF* means it's in the original (without subtitles), *Omengu* means it's in the original with English subtitles, *OmU* means it's in the original with German subtitles, but should not be confused with *OmÜ*, which means it's in the original, but has a live voice-over German translation, and finally *dF* means it's dubbed into German.

Burg-Kino, 1, Opernring 19; U-Bahn Babenbergerstrasse. Cinema on the Ringstrasse that regularly shows films in the original.

De France, 1, Schottenring 5; U-Bahn Schottenring. Another Ringstrasse cinema that shows films in the original.

Filmhaus Stöbergasse, 5, Stöbergasse 11–15; bus #12A or #14A. Art house cinema south of the Naschmarkt.

Filmmuseum, 1, Augustinerstrasse 1; U-Bahn Karlsplatz. Vienna's main art house cinema, on the ground floor of the Albertina, with a very esoteric programme.

Imax Filmtheater, 14, Mariahilferstrasse 212; U-Bahn Schönbrunn or tram #52 and #58. Specially made films to show off the 400-square-metre wrap-round screen's awesome scope.

Star-Kino, 7, Burggasse 71; bus #48A. Art house cinema specializing in old black and white movies.

Top Kino Center, 6, Rahlgasse 1; U-Bahn Babenbergerstrasse. Specializes in original language films.

Votiv-Kino, 9, Währinger Strasse 12; U-Bahn Schottentor. Popular, central, two-screen art house cinema.

Visual arts

In addition to its vast permanent collections of art, Vienna has a large number of galleries that host temporary exhibitions. To check out the latest shows and opening times, consult the tourist board's free monthly booklet *Programm*.

Architektur Zentrum Wien, 7, Museumsquartier, Messepalast; U-Bahn Babenbergerstrasse/Volksoper. In the courtyard of the vast Messespalast complex, and specializing in contemporary architectural exhibitions. *Daily 11am–7pm*.

EA-Generali Foundation, 4, Wiedner Hauptstrasse 15; tram #62 or #65 from Karlsplatz. Interesting contemporary art gallery. *Tues, Wed & Fri 11am–6pm, Thurs until 8pm, Sat & Sun until 4pm*.

Kunstforum, 1, Freyung 8; U-Bahn Herrengasse. Major venue for visiting foreign exhibitions of fine art sponsored by the Bank of Austria. *Daily 10am–6pm, Wed until 9pm*.

Kunsthalle Wien, 4, Treitlstrasse 2; U-Bahn Karlsplatz. Adolf Krsichanitz's corrugated carbuncle on the face of Karlsplatz is a "temporary" venue for big contemporary art exhibitions. *Mon & Wed–Sun 10am–6pm, Thurs until 8pm.*

KunstHausWien, 3, Untere Weissergerberstrasse 13; tram #N. Friedensreich Hundertwasser's gallery, with a permanent show of his works and visiting exhibitions of fellow travellers. *Daily 10am–7pm.*

Künstlerhaus, 1, Karlsplatz 5; U-Bahn Karlsplatz. Major retrospectives in painting, sculpture and photography, in the building next door to the Musikverein. *Daily 10am–6pm, Thurs until 9pm.*

Palais Harrach, 1, Freyung 3; U-Bahn Herrengasse. Temporary space used by the Kunsthistorisches Museum for its special exhibitions. *Daily except Tues 10am–6pm.*

Secession, 1, Friedrichstrasse 12; U-Bahn Karlsplatz. The famous Jugendstil exhibition space, with Klimt's Beethoven Frieze in the basement (see p.120), continues to host provocative modern art shows and installations. *Tues–Fri 10am–6pm, Sat & Sun 10am–4pm.*

The Arts

Chapter 14

Shopping

Few people come to Vienna to shop, but the city does have some excellent browsing opportunities, especially along Kärntnerstrasse, Graben and Kohlmarkt. In the backstreets of the Innere Stadt, you'll also find numerous excellent bookstalls and little antique shops. The streets of Neubau, to the north of Marahilferstrasse are also good for browsing.

For a capital, Vienna has very few large supermarkets, with just the small *Billa* stores and the odd *Julius Meinl* store scattered across the capital. Mariahilferstrasse remains the main shopping drag for department stores and mainstream shops. Viennese with cars head off to *Shopping-Center-Süd*, Austria's biggest shopping complex, some way south of the city limits at Vösendorf. The easiest way to get there on public transport is on the *Lokalbahn* to Baden, which departs from the tram stop opposite the Staatsoper.

Arts, crafts and antiques

The only place you'll find anything remotely resembling a bargain when it comes to antiques/bric-a-brac is at the flea market by the Naschmarkt; the Spittelberg market is also worth a browse (see p.173).

Augarten, 1 Stock-im-Eisen-Platz 3–4; U-Bahn Stephansplatz. Vienna's very own hand-painted china manufacturers have an outlet here, though you can also visit and buy direct (including some seconds) from the factory (see p.194).

Dorotheum, 1, Dorotheergasse 17; U-bahn Stephansplatz. "Aunt Dorothy's", as it's known, is one of the world's leading auction houses, with daily sales and a fixed-price shop; there's even a café for posing in.

Galerie Holzer, 7, Siebensterngasse 39; tram #49. Antique shop specializing in

---

Opening Times

Shopping hours in Vienna are still strictly controlled by the state. Until recently virtually all shops were only permitted to open from 8 or 9am until 5 or 6pm Monday to Friday, and from 8 or 9am until noon or 1pm on Saturday. On the first Saturday of the month – the so-called *langer Samstag* – shops stayed open until 5 or 6pm. Only very recently, the government changed the Saturday restrictions, allowing all shops to open

until 5 or 6pm on Saturdays. However, how many shops will do so remains to be seen. No shops, except those at the main railway stations, are open on Sundays. In the city centre and the main suburban shopping streets, most shops have no weekday lunch break or *Mittagssperre*, but in the quieter streets and the sleepier suburbs, this custom is still followed, usually between noon and 2pm.

Art Deco and Jugendstil furniture and fittings.

J. & L. Lobmeyr, 1, Kärntnerstrasse 26; U-Bahn Stephansplatz. Famous glass manufacturers, and a lovely shop, with a museum on the top floor (see p.48). You can buy glass designed by Adolf Loos and Josef Hoffmann as well as more modern pieces.

MAK-Design, 1, Weiskirchnerstrasse 3; U-Bahn Stubentor. Museum shop selling wacky modern furniture and accoutrements by the designers of the School of Applied Arts.

H. Seemann, 1, Seilergasse 19; U-Bahn Stephansplatz. Old photos, prints and postcards.

Wiener Interieur, 1, Dorotheergasse 14; U-Bahn Stephansplatz. Antique shop famed for its selection of Jugendstil *objets d'art*.

Woratsch, 1, Wipplingerstrasse 20; U-Bahn Herrengasse. Antique shop specializing in Biedermeier-era furniture and furnishings.

Bookshops

Though Vienna has a staggering number of bookshops, most of them in the Innere Stadt, only a handful are English-language. Nevertheless, many of the stores below stock a wide choice of English-language volumes. Be warned, however, that the Austrians slap tax on books, and prices are consequently much higher than elsewhere in Europe.

American Discount, 4, Rechte Wienzeile 5; U-Bahn Karlsplatz. Trash literature, crime, pulp fiction and lots of dodgy comics and US gun magazines.

British Bookshop, 1, Weihburggasse 24–26; U-Bahn Stephansplatz. A fair selection of novels and biographies in English, with half the shop given over to teaching materials.

Freytag & Berndt, 1 Kohlmarkt 9; U-Bahn Stephansplatz. Flagship store of Austria's most prestigious map makers, with loads of maps, as well as guides

on Vienna and the rest of the world in English, including a large selection of Rough Guides.

Heger Bücher, 1, Wollzeile 4; U-Bahn Stephansplatz. Fine choice of art and architectural monographs, posters and literary postcards.

Heidrich, 21 Plankengasse 7; U-Bahn Stephansplatz. Second-hand and anti-quarian books, some of them in English.

Hintermayer, 7, Neubaugasse 29; tram #49. Lots of second-hand and antiquarian books, including a small English-language selection.

Morawa, 1 Wollzeile 11; U-Bahn Stubentor. Huge bookshop stretching right back to Bäckerstrasse: the English section is on the first floor; guides and a huge choice of English magazines and newspapers at the back.

Prachner, 1, Kärntnerstrasse 30; U-Bahn Stephansplatz. Bookish place with shelves stacked high. Great architecture section and a selective English section with guides on Vienna, novels and some history.

Sallmayer'sche Buchhandlung, 1 Neuer Markt; U-Bahn Stephansplatz. Great art and photography sections, lots on hobbies – anything from trains to Barbie dolls – plus a selection of Red Army watches.

Satyr-Filmwelt, 1, Vorlaufstrasse 9–13; U-Bahn Schwedenplatz. Loads of books in German, French and English (mostly the latter) on movies and music. Good selection of art house videos and posters and CD soundtracks, too.

Shakespeare & Co, 1 Sterngasse 2; U-Bahn Schwedenplatz. Ramshackle, friendly English-language bookstore with a great selection of novels, art books and magazines.

Clothes

Vienna has all the usual designer label stores you'd find in most European capitals. The shops listed below concentrate on retro clothes shops and clubbing gear. There are also a few places listed

Shopping

Shopping

where you can buy *Tracht*, the traditional Alpine costume of *Dirndl* dresses and blouses for women and *Walker* (jackets) or *Loden* (capes) for men.

Absolut Hödl, 1, Tuchlauben 27; U-Bahn Stephansplatz. Great 1960s retro and repro for men and women.

Derby Handschuhe, 1, Plankengasse 5; U-Bahn Stephansplatz. A veritable quality glove-fest in suede and leather.

Helford Jersey, 1, Franz-Josefs-Kai 19; U-Bahn Schwedenplatz. Model cars, baseball caps, Vienna T-shirts, and reasonably priced *Trachten* clothes for the kids.

Lanz, 1, Kärntnerstrasse 10; U-Bahn Stephansplatz. The full Austrian *Trachten* monty – *Dirndl, Lederhosen, Walkjanker* – at a price.

Tostmann, 1, Schottengasse 3a; U-Bahn Schottentor. The place to fix yourself up head to toe in *Tracht.*

Turek Workshop, 6, Mariahilferstrasse 115; U-Bahn Zieglergasse. Driving force behind clubbing fashion in Vienna, with designer labels, own brand gear and flyers for up-and-coming raves.

Wow, 7, Neustiftgasse 23; U-Bahn Volkstheater. Lots of 1960s and 1970s retro gear for women, including some serious platforms.

Department stores

Gerngross, 7, Mariahilferstrasse 38–48; U-Bahn Neubaugasse. Vienna's most down-to-earth department store with prices to match.

Herzmansky, 7, Mariahilferstrasse 38–48; U-Bahn Neubaugasse. Big department store with lots of food outlets including a branch of *Trześniewski* (see p.278).

Steffl, 1, Kärntnerstrasse 19; U-Bahn Stephansplatz. Classic deparment store – the only one in the Innere Stadt – with perfume and jewellery on the ground floor, books on the top floor (along with a memorial to Mozart, who died in a building on the same site). No café though.

Food and wine

For cheap fruit and veg, you really have to go to the Naschmarkt (see box opposite). With such small supermarkets, the gap is filled, in part, by the city's flash quality delis.

Altmann & Kühne, 1 Graben 30; U-bahn Stephansplatz. The swishest chocolate shop in the city.

Anker, 1, Bräunerstrasse 4–6; U-Bahn Stephansplatz (plus hundreds of branches across Vienna). The largest bakery chain in the country, producing excellent bread, rolls and pastries.

Böhle, 1, Wollzeile 30; U-Bahn Stubentor. Top-notch Austrian deli with a huge range of beer, wine, vinegar, fruit and salads, plus a daily take-away menu.

Burton's, 1, Naglergasse 17; U-Bahn Herrengasse. Dubious assortment of British food for ex-pats missing curry powder, crisps, Boddingtons and Cadbury's chocolate.

Da Conte, 1, Judenplatz 1; U-Bahn Stephansplatz. Expensive Italian *alimentari* with marinaded olives and artichokes, Parma ham, Italian sweets and wines.

Demel vis-à-vis, 1, Kohlmarkt 11; U-Bahn Herrengasse. Deli opposite the famous *Demel Kaffee-Konditorei*, selling chocolates and fresh seafood to eat in or take away.

Demmer's Teehaus, 1, Mölkerbastei 5; U-Bahn Herrengasse. Tea addicts' paradise, with Indian and Chinese teas sold loose, and a café upstairs.

Gettingers Wien Kabinett, 1, Tuchlauben 17; U-Bahn Stephansplatz. Reasonably priced, friendly little wine shop with lots of Austrian plonk.

Arthur Grimm, 1, Kurrentgasse 10; U-Bahn Stephansplatz. Wonderful bakery with a vast range of fresh bread and pastries. Serves coffee, too.

Julius Meinl, 1, Graben 19; U-Bahn Stephansplatz. Flagship outlet of the long-established deli/supermarket chain.

Sacher, 1, Philharmoniker Strasse 4; U-

Bahn Karlsplatz. The only place to get the authentic *Sachertorte* (see p.280), sold in a variety of sizes, smartly boxed for export.

Schönbichler, 1, Wollzeile 4; U-Bahn Stephansplatz. Amazing selection of over 100 teas, plus china teapots, brandies, *kirsch* and marmalade.

Unger & Klein, 1, Gölsdorfgasse 2; U-Bahn Schwedenplatz. Trendy Eichinger oder Knecht designed wine shop where you can buy a glass to drink or a bottle to take away.

Wild, 1, Neuer Markt 16; U-Bahn Stephansplatz. Very upmarket, long-established deli with a stand-up buffet and sales counter.

Zum Schwarzen Kameel, 1, Bognergasse 5; U-Bahn Herrengasse. Terribly smart deli that's yet another Viennese institution, eat in or take-away food and lots of very fancy wine too.

Music

Arcadia, 1, Kärntnerstrasse 40; U-Bahn Karlsplatz. Bookshop beneath the arcades of the Staatsoper and full of things to do with opera. A great place to mug up on the plot before you go and see a show.

EMI Austria, 1, Kärntnerstrasse 30; U-Bahn Stephansplatz. Big jazz, rock, world music and classical CD collection with lots of listening stations.

Gramola, 1, Graben 16; U-Bahn Stephansplatz. Excellent selection of cheap classical CDs in this tiny stuccoed store.

Katzenmusik, 1, Hafnersteig 10; U-Bahn Schwedenplatz. Modern classical and world music specialists.

Sing Sing, 7, Neustiftgasse 23; U-Bahn Volkstheater. Second-hand mostly rock/pop LPs, CDs and casettes.

Virgin Megastore, 6, Mariahilferstrasse 37; U-Bahn Babenbergerstrasse. Vienna – and Austria's – biggest music store, with a vast collection of rock, pop, folk, soul, roots, rave and classical; plenty of listening posts too.

Why Not, 7, Kirchengasse 3; U-Bahn Neubaugasse. Indie, hip-hop and hard-core plus lots of 12″ discs.

Toys and accessories

Hobby-Sommer, 7, Neubaugasse 26; U-Bahn Neubaugasse. Model railways from

Shopping

Markets

Antikmarkt, 1, Am Hof; U-Bahn Herrengasse. Bargain-free art and antique market. *March–Christmas Eve Fri & Sat.*

Brunnenmarkt, 16, Brunnengasse; U-Bahn Thaliastrasse. Fruit and veg market that stretches for something like a kilometre along Brunnengasse. *Mon–Sat.*

Christkindlmarkt, 1, Rathausplatz; U-Bahn Rathaus or tram #1 and #2. Christmas market held in front of the Rathaus, selling gifts and food. *Daily late Nov–Christmas Eve.*

Kunstmarkt, 1, Heiligenkreuzhof; U-Bahn Schwedenplatz. Art and crafts market held in a picturesque monastic courtyard. *April–Sept first Sat & Sun*

of the month; also on the four week-ends before Christmas.

Naschmarkt, 6 & 7, Linke & Rechte Wienzeile; U-Bahn Karlsplatz/Kettenbrückengasse. Vienna's most exotic fruit and veg market, with Turkish, Balkan, Chinese, Middle Eastern and Austrian produce, take-away stalls plus clothes and sundries. On Saturday mornings, there's a flea market (*Flohmarkt*) extension west of Kettenbrückengase U-Bahn. *Mon–Sat.*

Spittelberg, 7, Spittlebergasse; U-bahn Volkstheater. Artsy, craftsy market in the narrow streets of the Spittelberg area. *April–June, Sept & Oct every third weekend; Aug & Dec daily.*

Shopping

around the world, and models of the Airfix variety.

Piatnik, 7, Kandlgasse/Kaiserstrasse; U-Bahn Burggasse-Stadthalle. Famous Austrian firm that makes playing cards, and also sells Zippo lighters, pipes and games.

Rudolf Waniek,
1, Hohermarkt/Tuchlauben; U-Bahn Schwedenplatz. Former court suppliers of glassware and metalware: salt cellars,

decanters, coffee-making machines and quality domestic utensils.

Spielzeugschachtel,
1, Rauhensteingasse 5; U-Bahn Stephansplatz. The "Toy Box" contains a feast of jigsaws, games, wooden toys and children's books.

Stahlwaren, 7, Siebensterngasse 39; tram #49. Amazing selection of knives, scissors, daggers and swords by top manufacturers (at a price).

Chapter 15

Directory

Airlines Air Canada 1, Krugerstrasse 11 ☎515 55 31; Air France 1, Kärntnerstrasse 49 ☎514 18 18; Alitalia 1, Kärntner Ring 2 ☎505 17 07; Austrian Airlines 1, Kärntner Ring 18 ☎505 57 57; British Airways 1, Kärntner Ring 10 ☎505 76 91; Delta 1, Kärntner Ring 17 ☎512 66 46; Lauda Air 1, Opernring 6 ☎514 77; Qantas 1, Opernring 1 ☎587 77 71; South African Airways 1, Opernring 1 ☎587 14 89; TWA 1, Opernring 1 ☎587 68 68. The nearest U-Bahn for all the above airlines is Karlsplatz.

American Express 1, Kärntnerstrasse 21–23; U-Bahn Stephansplatz.

Children Children are generally neither seen nor heard in Vienna. You won't see too many of them in the cafés and restaurants around town; hotels and pensions tend to be slightly more accommodating. The obvious attractions for children are the Tiergarten (zoo) and Schmetterlinghaus (Butterfly House), for which see p.212. The Prater (see p.186) can also be fun, and most children love to ride on the trams. Museums that might appeal to kids include the Strassenbahnmuseum (Tram Museum) described on p.171, the Puppen- and Spielzeug-Museum (Doll and Toy Museum), on p.64, and Haus des Meeres (Aquarium) on p.173.

Embassies and Consulates
Australia 4, Mattiellistrasse 2–4 ☎512 85 80.
Canada 1, Laurenzberg 2 ☎531 38.
Czech Republic 14, Penzinger Strasse 11–13 ☎894 37 41.

Hungary 1, Bankgasse 4–6 ☎533 26 31.
Ireland 3, *Hotel Hilton*, Landstrasse Hauptstrasse 2 ☎715 42 46.
Slovakia 19, Armbrustergasse 24 ☎318 90 55.
Slovenia 1, Niebelungengasse 13 ☎586 13 04.
South Africa 19, Sandgasse 33 ☎326 49 30.
UK 3, Jauresgasse 12 ☎713 15 75.
USA 9, Bolzmanngasse 16 ☎313 39.

Horse Racing From September to June trotting races take place in the Prater at the Krieau Trabrennbahn, 2, Nordportalstrasse 247 (tram #N to its terminus); flat racing takes place from April to November at the Freudenau Rennbahn, 2, Rennbahnstrasse 65 (bus #77A from U-Bahn Schlachthausgasse).

Hospital *Allgemeines Krankenhaus*, 9, Währinger Gürtel 18–20; U-Bahn Michelbeuern-AKH.

Language Schools *International House*, 1, Schwedenplatz 2 (U-Bahn Schwedenplatz).

Laundries 8, Josefstädter Strasse 59 (tram #J or bus #13A); 9, Nussdorferstrasse 80 (tram #37 or #38).

Libraries *Amerika Haus*, 1, Friedrich Schmidt Platz 2 (U-Bahn Rathaus); *British Council* 1, Schenkenstrasse 4 (U-Bahn Herrengasse).

Lost Property *Fundamt*, 9, Wasagasse 22 (Mon–Fri 8am–noon); lost on public transport, phone ☎79 09-105; lost on

Directory

Austrian Railways, phone ☎ 58 00-32996 or 58 00-35656.

Religious Services *Anglican* 3, Jauresgasse 12; *Baptist* 6, Mollardgasse 35; *Inter-denominational* 1, Dorotheergasse 16; *Methodist* 15, Sechshauser Strasse 56; *Orthodox Jewish* 1, Seittenstettengasse 4; *Progressive Jewish* 2, Schüttelstrasse 19a (door 3); *Roman Catholic* 9, Votivkirche, Schottentor.

Soccer Vienna's top soccer team, *SK Rapid*, play at the Gerhard Hanappi Stadion on Kaisslergasse in Hütteldorf (U-Bahn Hütteldorf); *FK Austria*, their main rivals, play at the Franz Horr Stadion in Favoriten; big international games are played at the Prater (aka Wiener) Stadion in the Prater (U-Bahn Praterstern).

Swimming The *Amalienbad*, 10, Reumannplatz 23 (U-Bahn Reumannplatz) has a wonderful Art Deco interior, particularly the sauna; the *Jörgerbad*, 17, Jörgerstrasse 42–44 (tram #43) is also very beautiful inside. The *Krapfenwaldbad*, 19, Krapfenwaldlgasse 65–73 (bus #38A) is an outdoor pool up in the foothills of the Wienerwald (May–Sept) with great views, so too the *Schafbergbad*, 18, Josef-Redl-Gasse (bus #42B).

Time Austria is generally one hour ahead of Britain, and six hours ahead of EST, with the clocks going forward in April and back again in October – the exact date changes from year to year.

Contexts

A History of Vienna

These two tribes crashed through the Danubian frontier in 169 AD only to be beaten back by the Emperor Marcus Aurelius, who died in Vindobona in 180 AD.

The Babenbergs

The Romans finally abandoned Vindobona to the Huns in 433 AD, and the city, like the rest of Europe, entered the Dark Ages. However, it's interesting to note that even at this early stage in its history, during the great migrations that followed the collapse of Roman power, the area of modern-day Vienna stood on one of the main ethnic crossroads of Europe: pressed from the east by first the Huns, later the Avars, from the north and south by the Slavs, and from the west by the Germanic tribes.

The coronation of Charlemagne as Holy Roman Emperor in 800 marked the end of the Dark Ages in Europe. Parts of modern-day Austria, meanwhile, became a military colony – referred to by nineteenth-century historians as the "Ostmark" – of Charlemagne's Frankish Empire. With the collapse of the empire in 888, it was the Saxon king, Otto the Great, who succeeded in subduing the German lands. His successor, Otto II, went on to hand the "Ostmark" to the Babenberg dynasty in 976 whose job it was to protect the empire's eastern frontiers, once more formed by the Danube. The Babenberg dynasty ruled the territory for the next 270 years, first as margraves and later as dukes.

In their search for some kind of official birthday for their country, many Austrian scholars have latched on to the first known mention of the name *Ostarrîchi*, which appears in a Latin parchment from around 996. However, throughout the Middle Ages, the region was mostly referred to either simply as *provincia orientalis* or else named after its first ruler, the Margrave Leopold I (976–94). To begin with, the Babenberg Margravate was confined to a small stretch of the Danube centred most probably on Melk, but gradually it expanded eastwards as far as the River Leitha and northwards as far as the River Thaya. Successive Babenbergs founded a number of monasteries in the region, in particular

The Romans

People have lived in the area of modern-day Vienna for many thousands of years, due to its geographical position at the point where the ancient trade route or amber route crossed the Danube. Following on from early Bronze and Iron Age settlements, a Celtic tribe known as the Boii occupied the hills above Vienna probably from as early as 500 BC, but were driven from the area in around 50 BC by the short-lived Dacian kingdom. Vienna was then swallowed up by the neighbouring Celtic kingdom of Noricum.

In 15 BC, the Romans under the Emperor Augustus advanced into Noricum as far as the Danube and the area was absorbed into the Roman province of Pannonia. For the next four centuries, the river was used as a natural military border or *Limes* by the Romans, further strengthened by a series of forts along its banks. The main Roman camp along this stretch of the Danube was at Carnuntum, to the east, with Vienna – or Vindobona as it was then called – as a subsidiary fort.

The Roman Forum is thought to have been somewhere around the Hoher Markt (see p.68) in today's Innere Stadt. In the first century AD, Vindobona became the base for the 10th legion, whose job it was to fend off attacks from the neighbouring Germanic tribes to the north and east, particularly the Marcomanni and the Quadi.

Leopold III (1095–1136), who was later canonized for his good works, and became the country's patron saint.

In 1156, during the reign of Heinrich II Jasomirgott (1141–77), the Babenbergs' Margravate was at last elevated to a Duchy, with its new capital at Vienna and the ducal palace situated in Am Hof (see p.63). However, in 1246 the Babenberg male line came to an end with the death of Duke Friedrich II (1230–46) on the battlefield. The dispute over who should rule over the Duchy of Austria and Styria, as it was now known, dragged on for the next thirty years. In 1251, the future Bohemian king, Otakar II, took up residence in Vienna and claimed the duchy for himself, shoring up his claim by marrying Friedrich II's widow.

The early Habsburgs

While Otakar was laying claim to the Babenbergs' inheritance, he was also putting himself forward as a candidate for the throne of the Holy Roman Empire. In the end, though, the throne was handed in 1273 to Rudolf of Habsburg, a little known count whose ancestral home was the castle of Habichtsburg (hence Habsburg) above the River Reuss in modern-day Switzerland. In 1278 Otakar was defeated (and killed) by Rudolf's forces at the Battle of Marchfeld, to the east of Vienna, allowing Rudolf to lay claim to the Duchy of Austria. The Viennese, who had backed Otakar, were less than pleased about the outcome of the battle, and weren't easily placated by Rudolf's son, Albrecht, who had been given the duchy by his father.

The Habsburgs, though, were here to stay, their dynasty destined to rule over Austria for the next 640 years. Initially, however, Vienna only sporadically served as the dynastic capital. Rudolf IV (1356–65) was one of the few to treat it as such, founding the university and laying the foundation stone of what is now the Stephansdom, before dying at the age of just 26. Rudolf's endeavours earned him the nickname "The Founder", but he failed in securing a bishopric for Vienna.

For that the city had to wait until the reign of Friedrich III (1440–93). Despite numerous setbacks – he was besieged in the Hofburg by one of his own family in 1462 and briefly lost control of Vienna to the Hungarian King Matthias Corvinus in 1485 – it was Friedrich who was responsible for consolidating the Habsburgs' power base. In 1452, he became the last Holy Roman Emperor to be crowned in Rome, and the following year elevated the family's dukedom to an archdukedom. The Holy Roman Empire, famously dismissed by Matthias Corvinus as "neither holy, Roman, nor an empire", was something of a fantasy, whose emperor, theoretically at least, ruled over all the German-speaking lands. Though this was far from reality, the Habsburgs persisted with its imperial pretensions, passing the title down the male line, until its eventual dissolution in 1806 (see p.317).

In the meantime, the Habsburgs continued to add to their dynastic inheritance through a series of judicious marriages by Maximilian II (1564–76) and his offspring, prompting the oft-quoted maxim, adapted from Ovid: "let others wage war; you, happy Austria, marry." By the time the Emperor Karl V came to the throne in 1519, the Habsburgs ruled over an empire on which, it was said, the sun never set, with lands stretching from its Spanish possessions in South America to Vienna itself – bolstered in 1526 by the addition of the kingdoms of Bohemia and Hungary. Vienna remained just one of several imperial residences, its development constantly hampered by the threat posed by the Ottoman army of Süleyman the Magnificent who had been advancing steadily westwards across Europe throughout the fourteenth century.

The Turkish sieges

In 1526, the Turks scored a decisive victory at the Battle of Mohács against the Hungarians, and began to advance into Habsburg territory. In the summer of 1529 they captured Budapest, and by September the Sultan's vast army were camped outside Vienna, the "city of the golden apple" as they called it. Although it is the later siege of 1683 (see opposite) that captured the imagination of historians, the 1529 siege was a much closer-run thing. The Ottoman Empire was at its zenith and Vienna was defended only by a small garrison under Count Salm. However, having shelled the city and killed some 1500 Viennese, the Turks suddenly withdrew – whether because of bad weather or some other reason, no one knows – back to Hungary in October. It seems almost as if Vienna simply wasn't worth the effort, despite the fact that the city was there for the taking.

In a defiant gesture, Ferdinand I (1521–64) subsequently established Vienna as his permanent base, building the zig-zag fortifications that were to surround the city for the next 300 years or more. With the retreat of the Turks, Ferdinand's troubles were by no means over, however, for Lutheranism was spreading at an alarming rate among the German-speaking lands. By the middle of the century it's estimated that Vienna was 80 percent Protestant. To combat this new plague, Ferdinand called in the fiercely proselytizing Jesuits in 1556. Nevertheless, the new creed flourished under the relatively liberal reign of Maximilian II (1564–76), and it was only after Rudolf II (1576–1612) moved the capital to Prague, leaving the Archduke Ernst in charge of Vienna, that the tide began to turn due to the repressive measures introduced.

By the outbreak of the Thirty Years' War in 1618, Vienna was well on the way to becoming a Catholic city, thanks partly to the Jesuits' stranglehold on the education system. By the time of the Peace of Westphalia in 1648, Vienna, which had emerged from the war relatively unscathed, was firmly under the grip of the Counter-Reformation, and those Viennese who would not renounce their Protestantism were forced to go into exile.

The siege of 1683

The fact that the city managed to survive the 1683 siege was no thanks to its emperor, Leopold I (1658–1705), a profligate, bigoted man whose reign marked the beginning of the Baroque era in Vienna. Under Leopold, a whole new wing of the Hofburg was built, but the emperor is best known for his operatic extravaganzas – he himself was a keen composer – in particular the four-hour long equestrian ballet he staged (see p.75), just one of some 400 theatrical events put on during his reign.

While Leopold was busy working out ways of spending more of the state's coffers, the priest Abraham a Santa Clara was busy preaching against such indulgences, not to mention against the Protestant, the Jew and the Turk, "an Epicurean piece of excrement" as he put it in one of his fiery sermons. In 1679, a plague claimed the lives of an estimated 70,000 Viennese, and four years later, Vienna was to face the worst crisis in its history as the town was forced to endure its second siege by the Ottoman army.

Naturally enough, at the approach of the Turks, Leopold, and anyone else who had the money, fled to the safety of Linz and Passau.

If anything, Vienna had more chance of surviving the siege of 1683 than it had in 1529. The Turks were no longer at the zenith of their power and the city was properly fortified this time – in addition, there was a relief force on its way albeit rather slowly. Nevertheless, the city was still confronted with an army of over 200,000, made up of 100,000 infantry, 50,000 cavalry, plus a harem of over 1500 concubines guarded by 700 black eunuchs, a contingent of clowns, and numerous poets trained in bawdy songs. The Viennese, protected by a garrison of just 10,000 men, were understandably ready to make peace with the Grand Vizier, Kara Mustafa.

The Grand Vizier's crucial mistake was that he was over-confident. Loath to share the booty among his army (which would be inevitable if they took the city by force), he orchestrated a two-month siege of Vienna. By September, however, a relief force of Poles, under their king Jan Sobieski, and sundry German troops under the Duke of Lorraine, finally came to the aid of the city. On September 12, the papal legate Marco d'Aviano conducted a mass on the hills above the city and though outnumbered, the imperial forces managed to rout the Turks, in the process capturing 20,000 buffaloes, bullocks, camels and mules, 10,000 sheep, corn and flour, sugar, oil and most famously, coffee (see p.279). Diamonds, rubies, sapphires and pearls, silver and gold, and "the most beautiful sable furs in the world", belonging to Kara Mustafa, fell into the grateful hands of King Sobieski. The Grand Vizier was discovered to have decapitated his favourite wife and his pet ostrich, rather than have them fall into the hands of the infidels, and, as was the custom in humiliating cases of defeat, he effected his own execution by allowing an emissary to strangle him with a silken cord in Belgrade on Christmas Day later that year.

The eighteenth century

Following the siege of 1683, Vienna could finally establish itself as the Habsburgs' permanent *Residenzstadt* or *Kaiserstadt*. Over the following years, Baroque art and architecture really took off, as extensive rebuilding of damaged churches, monasteries and palaces took place within the Innere Stadt. The Viennese aristocracy could also now at last build in the suburbs without fear of attack. Most famously the palace of Schönbrunn began to evolve, while Prince Eugène of Savoy (see p.161), who took command of the imperial forces and drove the Turks out of Hungary, built the Belvedere.

In keeping with the spirit of the age, the Emperor Karl VI (1711–40) proved as spendthrift as his father Leopold, adding the magnificent Prunksaal library and the Winter Reitschule to the Hofburg, and erecting Vienna's finest Baroque church, the Karlskirche (see p.125). The one area in which Karl VI singularly failed was in producing a male heir to the throne. In the end, the emperor had to accept the fact that his eldest daughter, Maria Theresa, was going to have to take over when he died. In an attempt to smooth her accession, Karl introduced the so-called Pragmatic Sanction in 1713, which allowed for female succession, and got all the states nominally within the Holy Roman Empire to promise to recognize his daughter's right to the Habsburgs' hereditary lands. Naturally enough, everyone agreed with the emperor while he was alive, and as soon as he died immediately went back on their word.

Maria Theresa (1740–80)

So it was that Maria Theresa (see p.209) found herself forced to fight the War of the Austrian Succession (1740–48) as soon as she took over from her father. For a while, she was even forced to hand over the imperial title to Karl of Bavaria in an attempt to pacify him, though it was eventually regained, and handed to her husband, Franz Stephan of Lorraine (she herself, as a woman, could not become Holy Roman Emperor). At the end of the war in 1748, Maria Theresa was forced to cede Silesia to Prussia,and despite an attempt to win it back during the Seven Years' War (1756–63), it remained, for the most part, in Prussian hands.

On the domestic front, Maria Theresa's reign signalled the beginning of the era of reform, influenced by the ideas of the Enlightenment. To push through her reforms the empress created a formidable centralized bureaucracy, taking power away from the provincial Diets. When the pope abolished the Jesuit order in 1773, Maria Theresa took the opportunity of introducing a state education system. In 1776 she abolished torture, and passed de facto abolition of the death penalty

(though hard labour usually killed the convict within a year in any case). Despite her reforms, it would be wrong to get the impression that the empress was some free-thinking democrat. She believed wholeheartedly in absolutism, and, as a devout Cathlic, ensured Catholic supremacy within the empire with yet more anti-Protestant edicts.

Josef II (1780–90)

With the death of her husband in 1765, Maria Theresa appointed her eldest son, Josef, as co-regent. But it wasn't until after the empress's death in 1780 that Josef's reforming zeal could come into its own (see p.90). His most significant edict was the 1781 *Toleranzpatent*, which allowed freedom of worship to Lutherans, Calvinists and Greek Orthodox. Like his mother, he was himself a devout Catholic, but was even more determined to curtail church – and particularly papal – power. To this end, he dissolved four hundred contemplative or "idle" monasteries, and, as many saw it, was bent on "nationalizing" the church.

Under Josef II all religious processions (previously a daily occurence on the streets of Vienna) were banned except the Corpus Christi procession. The blessed sacrament was no longer carried through the streets, causing the faithful to fall to their knees. Pope Pius VI was so concerned he came to Vienna in person in 1782 to try to change the emperor's mind, but to no avail. With the best of intentions, Josef interfered in every aspect of his citizens' lives, causing widespread resentment. For – again like his mother – despite his enlightened policies, Josef was very much the despot. He was, above all, responsible for creating the Habsburgs' secret police force, which was to become so infamous in the nineteenth century.

The Napoleonic era

The Emperor Leopold II, who unenthusiastically succeeded Josef II in 1790, died suddenly of a stroke after a reign of less than two years. As a result, Leopold's eldest son became the Emperor Franz II (1792–1835). No great military man – his troops had been fighting the French for two years before he bothered to show himself at the front line – Franz was an unlikely candidate to become one of Napoleon's great adversaries.

In his first Italian campaign, Napoleon succeeded in humiliating the Habsburg forces at

Mantua, and was within a hundred miles of Vienna when the emperor sued for peace. It was a scenario that was repeated again in 1800 when Napoleon's forces were once more marching on Vienna. By 1803, the Habsburgs had lost the Netherlands plus several territories in northern Italy to the French. Napoleon then added insult to injury by declaring himself emperor the following year, with the clear intention of re-establishing the Holy Roman Empire under French hegemony. In retaliation, Franz declared himself Emperor Franz I of Austria (a hitherto non-existent title), though the gesture looked more like an admission of defeat, since Franz was already Holy Roman Emperor.

The 1805 occupation of Vienna

In 1805, in alliance with Russia and Britain, Austria decided to take on Napoleon again, only to suffer a crushing defeat at Ulm. Unable to stop the advance of the *Grande Armée*, the allies decided to regroup further east, leaving Napoleon free to march on Vienna, where he arrived on November 13, 1805. The imperial family had already taken flight to Hungary carrying the contents of the Hofburg with them. Though there was no fighting, having 34,000 French troops billeted in the city put an enormous strain on the place and supplies quickly ran short. The French stayed on until January 12, 1806, having exacted taxes, war reparations and appropriated many works of art, including 400 paintings from the Belvedere. Four days later, Franz returned to Vienna amid much rejoicing, though, in political terms, there was little to rejoice about. The Treaty of Pressburg, concluded after the defeat at Austerlitz in December, left the Habsburgs without their Italian possessions, the Tyrol and the Voralberg. Further humiliation followed in 1806 when Napoleon established the Confederation of the Rhine and Franz was forced to call it a day by relinquishing his title of Holy Roman Emperor.

The 1809 occupation of Vienna

For the next few years, there was no hope of the Austrians exacting any revenge. But in the spring of 1809, with Napoleon encountering problems fighting Wellington in Spain, the Austrians decided to sieze the moment to reopen hostilities. Although they were once more defeated at Ratisbon, the Austrian forces under the emperor's brother, the Archduke Karl, managed to regroup

to the east of Vienna. Once more Napoleon was free to march on Vienna. As usual the imperial famliy had taken flight to Hungary, but this time the city tried to defend itself. Napoleon reached the outskirts of the city on May 10, 1809 and sent two emissaries to negotiate. They were promptly lynched by the Viennese; the French bombardment started the following evening. It was an uneven battle – "our batteries shot off a few shots; they were ineffective" as one eye-witness stated; the French, for their part, fired some 1600 shells, and killed 23 civilians. The next day, the city capitulated, its 16,000-strong garrison no match for the 100,000 French troops.

Despite taking Vienna, Napoleon's *Grande Armée* went on to suffer its first major defeat ten days later at Aspern, just east of Vienna. However, the Archduke Karl failed to press home his advantage, and Napoleon succeeded in holding on to Vienna, going on to defeat the Austrians decisively six weeks later at nearby Wagram, when the Austrians threw in the towel. The city was forced to celebrate the new Emperor's birthday on August 13, and in the peace, signed on October 14, the Austrians were forced to give up Galicia and Croatia. Two days later Napoleon left Vienna, but without leaving instruction for his French engineers to blow up the city's defences. On October 29, the French held a farewell ball, and towards the end of the following month, the Emperor Franz crept back incognito into the Hofburg.

Clemenz Metternich became the chief minister of Austria, and began to pursue a policy of rapprochement. His greatest coup in this direction was getting Napoleon to marry the Emperor Franz's eighteen-year-old daughter, Marie Louise, in March 1810 (see p.95). By 1813, with the tide turning against Napoleon, Metternich even managed to persuade his reluctant emperor to join the latest anti-French grand alliance.

1815 Congress of Vienna

Vienna missed out on the rest of the Napoleonic wars, but it was centre stage when it came to the peace. Following the defeat of Napoleon at Leipzig and his exile to Elba, the victorious powers met for the Congress of Vienna in the autumn of 1814. If nothing else, the congress was a great social success (see p.61), or as one participant famously put it *"le congrès danse, mais il ne marche pas"*. The most public celebration took place on the anniversary of the Battle of Leipzig, when some 20,000 war veterans were wined and dined *al fresco* in the Prater (see p.190). All of Vienna was agog at the spectacle, but by New Year, most of the foreigners had outstayed their welcome. The congress was costing the emperor a fortune that even he could not afford, forcing him to raise taxes, while many of the participants were living on credit notes. Nevertheless, it dragged on until after Napoleon escaped from Elba, finally winding itself up in May 1815, just twelve days before the Battle of Waterloo.

Despite the shenanigans, the congress did, in fact, manage fairly successfully to establish a status quo in Europe. Many of the borders agreed upon in Vienna were to endure for over a century. In the peace deal, Austria won back much of North Italy and Galicia, Croatia, Salzburg, the Tyrol and the Voralberg, but on Metternich's advice, claims over the Netherlands, and other far-flung territories that would be hard to defend, were relinquished. The congress also pledged itself to further regular meetings between the heads of the victorious states – meetings at which it was agreed that in order to maintain international peace, they would combine to suppress any further revolutionary uprisings within Europe.

Biedermeier Vienna

Following the congress, Vienna enjoyed more than thirty years of peace and stability, a period known retrospectively as the *Vormärz* – literally "pre-March" – because it preceded the March 1848 revolution. The same stretch of time is also known throughout the German-speaking lands as the Biedermeier era (for more on the origin of the term, see p.338). In later years, the Viennese would look back on this period through rose-tinted spectacles as a time of introspective domesticity, played out to the tunes of Johann Strauss the Elder and the melodies of Franz Schubert.

As ever, there is more than a grain of truth in the myth, as there is in the counter-myth that this was one of the most oppressive regimes in the history of the Habsburgs. The man most closely associated with the conservative and reactionary politics of the Biedermeier era was Metternich. Under him, and his "poodle" the chief of police Count Josef Sedlnitzky, the vast machinery of the Josephine civil service which had been designed to help push through reforms, was now used to thwart any further reforms. Censorship and the

activities of the secret police and its informers did so much to stifle intellectual life that by 1848 the playwright Franz Grillparzer reflected miserably "despotism has destroyed my life, at least my literary life".

With the death of the Emperor Franz I in 1835, the Habsburgs faced something of a crisis, as the heir to the throne, Ferdinand I – a victim of Habsburg in-breeding – was, in the vocabulary of the day, an "imbecile", nicknamed *Nandl der Trottel* (Ferdy the Dotty). He was, in fact, nothing of the sort: he could be perfectly coherent, but suffered badly from epilepsy, which affected his short-term memory. To combat the latter's deficiencies, a Regency Council was established, with Ferdinand as chair – or in his absence his brother the Archduke Ludiwg – and his brother Franz Karl, Count Kolowrat and Metternich as permanent members. Within the council Metternich had to struggle to maintain his influence.

The 1848 revolution

With the deposition of the French King and the outbreak of revolution in Paris in late February, 1848, it was only a question of time before matters came to a head in the other European capitals. Vienna, now a city of 400,000, suffered from chronic overcrowding (though this was nothing new), and sporadic food shortages, yet it still came as some surprise when it became the first city to follow in the footsteps of the French. On March 13, the Estates of Lower Austria, consisting of nobles and senior clergy, were due to meet in the Landhaus on Herrengasse (see p.58). They were pressing for various reforms including the freedom of the press, but top of the agenda was the removal of Metternich. In the morning a crowd gathered outside the Landhaus, and, after listening to a German translation of the inflammatory speech given recently by the Hungarian revolutionary Lajos Kossuth in the Hungarian Diet, forced their way into the building. At around 1pm, a detachment of Italian grenadiers fired into the crowd, killing around 30 unarmed protesters, mostly students, and sparking off a revolution.

That evening, after playing for time, Metternich finally resigned and fled from the capital (disguised as a washerwoman according to popular legend). The emperor – who when told of the outbreak of revolution had apparently said "but do they have permission?" – immediately made a rapid retreat, declaring "tell the people I agree to everything". A National Guard was formed – with Johann Strauss the Younger as *Kapellmeister* – augmented by an academic legion of armed students, with whom they were to man the city in place of the despised imperial troops. In addition a constitution was promised, and a "Responsible Ministry" of bureaucrats formed to produce it. On April 25, a constitutional monarchy was proposed, with two chambers elected by limited franchise based on property. Not surprisingly, the ide was rejected and rioting, in favour of a single chamber parliament elected by universal suffrage, ensued on May 15. Barricades were erected around the city, and the emperor and his entourage quickly fled to Innsbruck in a stagecoach.

Elections were duly held throughout the empire (with the exception of Italy and Hungary which were busy with their own revolutions) and the first parliament in Habsburg history met in the unlikely surroundings of the Hofburg's Winter Reitschule (see p.89) on July 22. The deputies were by no means revolutionaries, the majority coming from the educated middle classes, with close to a third of peasant origin. Hampered throughout by disputes between the various nationalities, the assembly did manage to pass one lasting piece of legislation, the emancipation of the peasantry. By August, the court felt secure enough to return to Vienna, bolstered by General Radetzky's military victory over the rebels in Italy and the recapture of Prague by General Windischgrätz.

The spark that lit the final fuse of the Viennese revolution took place on October 6. A battalion, due to be sent to fight against Kossuth's Hungarian revolutionaries, mutinied and joined forces with radicals in the National Guard. Civil war then broke out as some within the National Guard fired on the radicals. In the confusion, the War Minister, General Latour, was lynched by the mob (see p.64) and the imperial family removed themselves once more, this time to Olomouc in Moravia. As Windischgrätz marched his troops towards the capital, the radicals among the academic legion and the National Guard erected barricades and awaited the final showdown. Their only hope lay in the possibility of a Hungarian relief force, which in the event arrived too late. After several days' bombardment and around 2000 casualties, Windischgrätz flushed out the last of the rebels on October 31.

The reign of Franz-Josef I

Meanwhile, back in Olomouc, the Emperor Ferdinand (and his brother Franz Karl) was coerced by the imperial family into renouncing the throne in favour of the latter's eighteen-year-old nephew, Franz-Josef (see p.81). A new government was formed under the leadership of the arch-conservative Prince Felix Schwarzenberg, while the assembly continued to meet in the nearby Moravian town of Kroměříž to try to thrash out a new constitution. Then, to the astonishment of the assembly, on February 28, 1849, Schwarzenberg announced that as the emperor had himself formulated a new constitution, their services were no longer required. Although the new constitution granted equal rights to all, it was anything but liberal, granting the emperor the power of veto over all legislation, the power to dissolve parliament and rule by decree and the power to dismiss and appoint ministers as he saw fit. Meanwhile in Hungary, the Austrians were forced to swallow their pride and enlist the help of the Russians in order to defeat Kossuth's Hungarian revolutionaries once and for all.

In the immediate aftermath of the revolution, it was decided to strengthen the fortifications of the city. Eventually, though, the tide of opinion in the government shifted in favour of tearing down the walls, to prevent a repeat of October 1848 when the revolutionaries had managed to resist the forces of law and order. Finally, in 1857, the emperor decreed that the walls were to come down, and in their place a Ringstrasse, lined with noble institutions, was to be constructed (see p.103). This wide boulevard remains the most significant architectural legacy of Franz-Josef's, though it wasn't until the last decade of the emperor's reign that the final sections were completed.

1866 and all that

After some ten years of relative peace, Franz-Josef suffered his first of many embarassing military setbacks at the Battle of Solferino in 1859. It was not so much the resultant loss of Lombardy that was the problem, but the opportunity it gave the Hungarians to demand their independence once more. In an attempt to placate them, Franz-Josef agreed in 1861 to establish a two-chamber parliament in Vienna. The Hungarians remained unimpressed and failed to send delegates to fill any of their 85 alloted seats in the lower house.

Five years later, the empire was rocked by an even greater crisis with its army's humiliating defeat at the Battle of Königgrätz in the Austro-Prussian War. Not only did the Habsburgs lose forever the battle for hegemony over the rest of Germany, but they were finally forced to strike a deal with the Hungarians (while studiously ignoring the demands of the empire's other nationalities).

With the 1867 Ausgleich or Compromise the so-called Dual Monarchy of Austria-Hungary was established. According to this new arrangement, Franz-Josef was to be crowned King of Hungary (he was already Emperor of Austria), and the Hungarians were to get their own parliament in Budapest, with autonomy over everything except defence, foreign affairs and the overall imperial budget. Everything within Hungary was to be prefaced with a k. for königlich, everything in the rest of the empire was to be prefaced with the initials k.k. or kaiserlich-königlich (imperial-royal), while everything Austro-Hungarian was prefaced with k.u.k. or kaiserlich-und-königlich.

Meanwhile delegates from the "Austrian" half of the empire met in Vienna's parliament (see p.112). Among the delegates were Czechs, Poles, Croats, Slovenes, Italians and German-speakers from every corner of the empire, who spent most of their time arguing over language issues and abusing each other both verbally and physically. The number of people eligible to vote increased gradually until universal male suffrage was finally introduced in 1907, but in reality, the emperor still ruled supreme since he and his ministers could pass any laws they wanted as "emergency measures", not to mention dissolve parliament and rule by decree (which they did on numerous occasions).

To make matters worse, the economy suffered its worst financial crisis ever in the crash of May 1873, shortly after the opening of Vienna's Weltausstellung or World Exhibition in the Prater (see p.186). The 72 banks in Vienna were reduced to 8 in the decade following the crash; construction of the Ring was halted and the big projects – the Parliament, Rathaus, Burgtheater and Universität – were only completed in the 1880s. The empire's industrialization was also affected, with railway construction reaching an annual low of 75km of new track in 1880, which had a severe knock-on effect in the other heavy industries.

Fin-de-siècle Vienna

From 1860 to the turn of the century, Vienna more than trebled in size, its population topping two million. Like most industrialized cities of the period, it was a city of enormous contrasts. Wealth and power were in the hands of the upper aristocracy, who alone had an entrée into court society, and exercised enormous influence over the careers of individuals through the system of Protektion or patronage. Meanwhile, the bulk of the population, many of them recently arrived immigrants from other parts of the empire, were packed like sardines in the Mietkaserne (rent barracks) of the newly built suburbs. At the bottom of the heap were the nocturnal Bettgeher, the five percent of the population who could afford only to rent someone else's bed from them during the day.

A significant proportion of the new immigrants were Jews from the empire's rural Shtetls – by the turn of the century they made up nearly ten percent of the population. In some walks of life, they comprised an even greater percentage: more than half of the all the city's doctors and lawyers were Jews, as were most of its journalists and bankers. The Jew had long been a stock Viennese scapegoat (see p.66). Now with the 1873 crash – the fault, it was said, of Jewish financiers – and the continuing influx of orthodox Jews into the city, anti-semitism began to flourish. It found a spokesman in the figure of the pan-German nationalist Georg von Schönerer, whose fanatical followers used to wear the effigy of a hanged Jew on their watch chains. Schönerer's political career faltered, however, after 1888 when he was sent to prison for breaking into the offices of the Jewish-owned newspaper, the Neues Wiener Tagblatt.

Anti-semitism was given a more respectable, populist twist by Karl Lueger (see p.110). This Vienna-born politician became leader of the Christian Social Party, whose combination of Catholicism, anti-semitism and municipal socialism, went down alarmingly well with the Viennese electorate. In 1897, Lueger became Mayor of Vienna, and the crowd that turned out for his funeral in 1910 was the largest the city had ever seen – among the mourners was the young Adolf Hitler (see p.119).

Most middle-class Jews, understandably, gravitated towards the other side of the political spectrum, dominating the upper echelons of the

Social Democratic Workers' Party (SDAP), after it was founded in 1889. The party's chief ideologue before World War I was the Prague-born Jew Viktor Adler, whose peculiar brand of Austro-Marxism was to dominate the party's thinking for the next half century. As far as Adler was concerned capitalism was doomed to failure, so the party could afford to adopt a peaceful approach to politics until the time was right for revolution.

In among all the tensions between Right and Left, Jew and gentile, rich and poor, *fin-de-siècle* Vienna also succeeded in nurturing intellectual and artistic creativity such as the city had never known, much of it inspired by the city's assimilated Jews. In music, Arnold Schönberg, and his followers Alban Berg and Anton Webern, changed the face of classical music with their atonal – or as Schönberg preferred "pantonal" – revolution (see p.125). Gustav Mahler, meanwhile, turned heads both as a composer and as boss of the Staatsoper. In medicine, Sigmund Freud (see p.178) coined the term "psychoanalysis", and expounded on the new discipline in his seminal *Interpretation of Dreams*. In 1897 the artist Gustav Klimt led a revolt against the artistic establishment, known as the Secession (see p.120); following in his footsteps were the likes of Egon Schiele and Oskar Kokoschka. Otto Wagner left the most visible legacy of this period, in the Jugendstil and early modernist buildings which can still be seen on the streets of Vienna today.

World War I

On July 28, 1914, the heir to the throne, the Archduke Franz Ferdinand and his wife, Sophie, were assassinated in Sarajevo by Bosnian Serbs, with weapons supplied by the chief of Serbia's army intelligence. There was little genuine sadness in court circles, for as Stefan Zweig bluntly put it "the archduke Franz Ferdinand lacked everything that counts for real popularity in Austria; amiability, personal charm and easygoingness". Even his uncle, the Emperor Franz-Josef, was more relieved than anything else, as the two got on famously badly.

To begin with, there was also very little action by Austria on the diplomatic front, but eventually on July 23 Franz-Josef and his ministers sent an ultimatum to Serbia, with an impossible set of conditions and a 48-hour time limit. As Serbia could not agree to all the conditions, Austria-Hungary declared war on her, without consulting its German or Italian allies. The Russians immediately mobilized to defend their Slav brothers, with Britain and France, Russia's allies, following suit. By August 12, the major European powers were at war.

Perhaps surprisingly, the outbreak of war brought patriotic crowds on to the streets of Vienna, and other cities around the empire, with Left and Right alike rallying round the Habsburg cause. Of course, everyone thought the war would be over by Christmas; it was only after several years of military defeats, huge casualties and food shortages, that the population began to turn against the war. On October 21, 1916, Viktor Adler's son, Friedrich, took matters into his own hands and assassinated the Austrian Prime Minister, Count Karl Stürgkh (see p.49). At his trial in May the following year, Friedrich Adler gave such a damning indictment of the war that his execution was postponed so as not to boost the anti-war cause further. On November 21 1916, Franz-Josef finally died at the age of 86, leaving the throne to his 29-year-old great-nephew Karl.

The Emperor Karl I is perhaps best known for his bungled attempt at negotiating a separate peace for his empire with the western allies in March 1917. The approach was rebuffed at the time and a year later became public knowledge, causing huge embarrassment to all concerned. Only victory on the battlefield could now save the dynasty – it was not to come.

In October 1918, the empire began to crumble from within, with national committees taking over in the empire's regional capitals. In Vienna, the Social Democrats, who were in favour of self-determination for the empire's various nationalities, set up a provisional government under Karl Renner. On November 2, 1918, with the end of the war in sight, the Hungarian battalion guarding Schönbrunn upped and left, leaving the imperial family and their servants unguarded. The next day an armistice was signed, and eight days later, the Emperor Karl I agreed to sign away his powers (see p.207), withdrawing first to Eckartsau outside Vienna, and eventually, in 1919, going into exile in Switzerland.

The First Republic

The Austrian Republic – or more correctly *Deutsch-Österreich* or "German Austria" – was

0 300km
Austria-Hungary
Post 1918 Borders
GERMANY
POLAND
SOVIET UNION
CZECHOSLOVAKIA
Prague
Kraków
Vienna
Danube
SWITZERLAND
AUSTRIA
Budapest
HUNGARY
ROMANIA
Trieste
Zagreb
Belgrade
Bucharest
Danube
YUGOSLAVIA
Adriatic Sea
MONTENEGRO
SERBIA
BULGARIA
Black Sea
ITALY
N

THE BREAK-UP OF THE AUSTRO-HUNGARIAN EMPIRE 1918

proclaimed from the steps of Vienna's parliament on November 12, 1918 (see p.112); the colours chosen for the national flag – red, white, red – were those of the Babenbergs. At first, however, there was precious little enthusiasm for the new country among its people. The Christian Socials wanted a constitutional monarchy, the Pan-Germans wanted Anschluss with Germany, while the Socialists wanted Anschluss with a Socialist Germany. In the proclamation of November 12, the country was even described as "a constituent part of the German Republic". In the regions, both the Tyrol and Salzburg voted overwhelmingly in favour of Anschluss with Germany, while the Voralberg even voted to join the Swiss.

In February 1919, the first national elections took place, creating a coalition government of the SDAP and the Christian Socials under the chancellorship of Social Democrat Karl Renner. Nevertheless a political vacuum continued until the end of the year, with soldiers' and workers' councils threatening to follow the revolutionary soviet example of neighbouring Bavaria and Hungary. There were even two unsuccessful attempts by the newly formed Austrian Communist Party (KPÖ) to stage a putsch, in April and June 1919.

The new government's foremost task was to feed the population, particularly that of Vienna. Deprived of its former territories, and hampered by a bad harvest, they managed it only with the help of the Allied Famine Relief programme. The government's next most arduous job was to negotiate the Treaty of St-Germain with the victorious allies. Many in the delegation still hoped for Anschluss with Germany, but it was not to be. The Austrians (along with the Hungarians) were branded an "enemy state", while the rest of the so-called "successor states" like Czechoslovakia, were not, and were expressly forbidden ever to undertake Anschluss with Germany. With his oft-quoted remark, Georges Clemenceau summed up the Austrians' lack of a bargaining position when he pointed to the map and said "What's left is Austria".

Red Vienna

Vienna began the war with an ethnically diverse population of 2.1 million, imperial capital of a multi-national empire of 52 million; by the end of the war, the city's population was down to 1.8 million, head of a country of just 6.4 million. Only two significant minorities remained: Czechs and Jews, who together made up around 20 percent of the total population. The Czechs, who now had their own independent motherland, enjoyed the status of a protected minority, leaving the Jews to serve once more as the chief scapegoat.

This situation was exacerbated by the very visible presence of around 25,000 Jewish refugees from Galicia, an army of poverty-stricken peddlars whose Orthodox garb made them all the more conspicuous. At the same time, the much larger, assimilated Jewish population, who were prominent in the arts, the media and the SDAP, became the target of a vicious, anti-semitic campaign led by the Christian Social and Pan-German parties. The cleric Ignaz Seipel, head of the Christian Socials, was one of the most vociferous anti-semites, who flirted with the idea of re-ghettoizing the Jews. This sort of rhetoric was a permanent feature of the First Republic, and one which the SDAP consistently failed to tackle head on.

In the municipal elections of May 1919, the Social Democrats won 54 percent of the vote, and Vienna got its first Socialist mayor, Jakob Reumann. The party held power in the capital for nearly fifteen years, a period which has gone down in history as *Rotes Wien* or Red Vienna (see p.227). Their social reforms have since become legendary, but their most visible legacy is the huge housing estates like the Karl-Marx-Hof (see p.228) that ring the city.

Meanwhile, in the national elections of June 1920, the SDAP-Christian Social coalition broke down, and in fresh elections in October that year, the latter came out as the biggest single party. The two parties remained at loggerheads throughout the 1920s, with the extremist Pan-German Greater German People's Party a further destabilizing element.

Paramilitary politics

For most of the First Republic, then, the country remained split between the heavily industrialized Social Democrat capital of Vienna, where some thirty percent of the population lived, and the deeply conservative Catholic rural *Länder* where the Christian Socials dominated. What made this policial polarization all the more dangerous was that by the mid-1920s both sides were backed up by paramilitary organizations, as if the country were at civil war. The right-wing *Heimwehr*, on the one hand, had their origins in armed groups which defended Austria's borders in the chaotic early days of the republic. Based on individual *Länder* and each with their own leader, the *Heimwehr* organizations didn't share a political platform but were united in their opposition to the Left.

The Social Democrats, on the other hand, had created the republic's first ad hoc army, the *Volkswehr*, in the last weeks of the war. They continued to dominate the *Volkswehr* until it was replaced by the establishment of the official Austrian army or *Bundeswehr*. As a result, the SDAP eventually formed its own armed division, the *Schutzband* in 1923. Throughout the 1920s the party mouthed the rhetoric of class war, while pursuing moderate, social democratic policies. In 1926, the party went even further and declared itself ready to use force if necessary to protect the interests of the workers. The bourgeois press interpreted this as a call for revolution, though the slogan coined by Otto Bauer was "democratic as long as we can be; dictatorship only if we are forced to it, and insofar as we are forced". To the dismay of many on the left, the SDAP proved itself much less willing to resort to violence than its right-wing foes.

On July 14, 1927, three right-wing activists were acquitted of murdering a socialist man and boy. The following day several thousand workers spontaneously descended on the Justizpalast (see p.113) and set fire to it. Taken by surprise by the size of the demonstration, the mounted police panicked and fired point-blank into the crowd. In the ensuing chaos, 89 people were killed, and up 1000 wounded, and the Justizpalast burned to the ground. The SDAP called an indefinite national strike, but refused to call out the *Schutzband*. With the heavily armed *Heimwehr* acting as strike breakers, the general strike was easily crushed and civil war was postponed for a few more years.

Austro-fascism

The onset of the Great Depression further destabilized what was already a fragile democracy.

In the elections of November 1930, the *Heimwehr*, under Prince Starhemberg, won its first parliamentary seats for its newly formed political wing the *Heimatblock*. The Social Democrats, meanwhile, emerged for the first time since 1919 as the largest single party, with 41 percent of the vote, but once more it was the Christian Socials who went on to form a series of weak coalition governments. The last of these was formed in May 1932 under the chancellorship of Engelbert Dollfuss, with a parliamentary majority of just one.

On March 4, 1933, in an attempt to break a tied vote in parliament, the Social Democrat Karl Renner resigned as speaker in order to free himself to vote. When Renner's two deputy speakers from the Christian Social and Pan-German parties both followed suit, Dollfuss siezed the opportunity to dissolve parliament, claiming it could no longer function properly. The same weekend, Adolf Hitler won an absolute majority in the German parliament. The onset of Nazism had a sobering effect on the majority of Austrians, particularly the SDAP, which immediately dropped their call for Anschluss.

On March 15, Dollfuss sent the police in to prevent parliament from reconvening. In response, the SDAP leadership procrastinated and held back from calling in the *Schutzband*; two weeks' later the latter was outlawed. Dollfuss was determined to combat the threat from Nazi Germany, but instead of agreeing to an anti-Nazi alliance with the SDAP, the chancellor threw in his lot with Mussolini, holding the first of many meetings with the Italian dictator in April. On May 21, no doubt prompted by Mussolini, Dollfuss established the Austro-fascist Fatherland Front (VF), under the slogan "Austria Awake!".

In May the Communist Party was banned and in July the Austrian Nazi Party was outlawed. A violent showdown with the Social Democrats, who still controlled the Vienna city council, followed in February 1934. The first incident took place in Linz, where the local *Schutzband* on their own intiative opened fire on police. A three-day battle ensued, with the bloodiest set-to in Vienna's Karl-Marx-Hof housing estate, which Dollfuss eventually ordered the army to bomb into submission. The SDAP had stumbled into civil war and it was soundly beaten. The party was swiftly outlawed, and its leaders fled abroad or were imprisoned.

Just as it appeared he had successfully established an Austro-fascist state, Dollfuss was assassinated on July 25, 1934 (see p.60), during an abortive putsch staged by Austrian Nazis, apparently without the knowledge of Hitler. His successor, Kurt Schuschnigg, was forced to rely ever more heavily on Mussolini for support. As a foreign policy this proved disastrous for in 1935 Hitler and Mussolini began to patch up their differences, and suddenly Schuschnigg found himself being urged by Mussolini to come to an agreement with Hitler. Schuschnigg did just that in the Austro-German agreement of July 11, 1936. In return for Hitler's recognition of Austria's "full sovereignty", Schuschnigg agreed to an amnesty of all Nazi prisoners, and the appointment of various "prominent nationalists" – not Nazis, but fellow travellers – to his government.

In January 1938, the Austrian police raided the apartment of Leopold Tavs, one of Schuschnigg's deputies, and discovered a plan to overthrow the government with German help. As tension between the two countries mounted, the Nazi ambassador, Franz von Papen, suggested Schuschnigg should visit Hitler at his mountain retreat at Berchtesgaden by the Austrian border. At this meeting, Schuschnigg was given one of Hitler's command performances in which he ranted and raved and eventually demanded, among other things, that Schuschnigg hand over yet more key governmental posts to the Austrian Nazi Party. Schuschnigg acquiesced and agreed to appoint the Nazi Dr Arthur Seyss-Inquart Interior Minister.

As the Austrian Nazis increased their activities, Schuschnigg decided to chance his arm with a plebiscite to decide the country's future, reckoning (probably correctly) that the majority would vote against the Anschluss. Hitler was certainly not prepared to risk electoral defeat and swiftly demanded the resignation of Schuschnigg and his entire government. Schuschnigg announced his resignation over the radio, in order to avoid "spilling German blood", and Seyss-Inquart took over the chancellorship. President Wilhelm Miklas refused to agree to the latter's appointment and resigned, and Seyss-Inquart wasted no time in inviting the German army into the country on the pretext of preventing civil war.

Anschluss and World War II

In the event, there was no bloodshed: German troops crossed the border into Austria on March 12, 1938, and encountered no resistance what-

soever. Hitler himself began his slow and triumphant journey to the capital in the wake of his
troops. First he visited his birthplace of Braunau-
am-Inn, then he moved on to his "home town"
of Linz, where he was received with such enthusiasm by the locals that he decided there and
then to immediately incorporate Austria into the
Greater German Reich, rather than pursue the
more conciliatory path of preserving Austrian
autonomy. Eventually on March 15, Hitler
appeared on the balcony of the Hofburg before
thousands of jubilant Viennese.

As a propaganda exercise, Hitler also decided
to go ahead with Schuschnigg's plebiscite, which
took place on April 10. The 99 percent "Yes" vote
in favour of the Anschluss came as no surprise,
with less than two thousand Viennese voting
"No". To be fair, those known to be opposed to
the Nazis, including Schuschnigg and his followers, had already been arrested – some 76,000 by
the time Hitler arrived in Vienna – while Jews and
other "undesirables" were barred from voting. On
the other hand, many whom one would expect
to have opposed the Anschluss, publicly declared
themselves in favour, including the Archbishop of
Vienna, Cardinal Theodor Innitzer, and the Social
Democrat, Karl Renner.

Although the Treaty of St-Germain precluded
any Anschluss with Germany, only the Soviet
Union and Mexico lodged any formal international protest against the invasion. Meanwhile,
the very name of Austria was wiped off the map,
initially replaced by the term "Ostmark", but eventually simply divided into seven *Gaue* or districts,
ruled by Nazi *Gauleiter*.

The fate of Vienna's Jews

The Anschluss unleashed a "volcanic outburst of
popular anti-semitism", in the words of eye-witness George Clare. Jews were dragged out into
the street, physically assaulted and humiliated,
and then forced to scrub the Schuschnigg slogans off the walls. In one instance in the well-to-
do suburb of Währing, a group of Nazis urinated
on local Jewish women as they forced them to
scrub the streets in front of cheering onlookers. A
large number of the city's most prominent Jews
were arrested immediately, and either sent to the
camps, or released with orders to leave the
country.

In May, without warning, 2000 Jews were
arrested and shipped off to Dachau, primarily to

encourage still more Jews to emigrate. On the
night of November 10–11 – dubbed *Kristallnacht*
or "Crystal Night" – the majority of synagogues in
the Reich were torched, and numerous Jewish
premises ransacked. Another 7800 Jews were
arrested that night, 4600 of whom were sent to
Dachau. By the outbreak of World War II, more
than half of Vienna's Jews had emigrated.

Once the Nazis had invaded Poland, their policy towards the Jews changed, with deportation
to the camps favoured over forced emigration.
The deportations began in earnest in February
1941, while emigration came to a complete
standstill in November 1941. Of the 57,000 Jews
now left in Austria, more than half had been sent
to the death camps by June 1942. By the end of
the war, around 200 or so Austrian Jews had
managed to survive in hiding, with just over 2000
returning after the war.

Collaboration and resistance

Seyss-Inquart was initially appointed
Reichsstatthalter (governor) of Vienna, but was
transferred to Poland after the outbreak of the
war, and eventually ended up in control of the
Netherlands, where as *Reichskommissar* he oversaw countless atrocities for which he was
hanged at the Nürnberg war trials. Control of
Vienna was eventually handed over to the dashing young German lieutenant, Baldur von
Schirach, whose artistic pretensions – he wrote
poetry – were considered highly suitable for
Viennese sensibilities. Schirach made the most of
his position, moving into the sumptuous governmental offices on Ballhausplatz, employing no
fewer than 17 chambermaids, and entertaining
official visitors in lavish style in the Hofburg.

Although Hitler preferred to import German
Nazis to many positions within Austrian Nazi
hierarchy, the Austrians themselves provided
more than their ten percent population ratio of
concentration camp guards. The Linz-born Nazi
Adolf Eichmann, who ran Vienna's "Central Office
for Jewish Emigration" (see p.167) and was one
of the architects of the "Final Solution", is probably the most infamous, though *Schindler's List*
has also increased the infamy of the Vienna-born
camp commandant Amon Goeth. Another Linz-
born Nazi, Ernst Kaltenbrunner, rose to number
two in the SS to Heinrich Himmler, while the
Carinthian Odilo Globocnik, with ninety other fellow Austrians on his staff, supervised the death

of some two million Jews in the extermination camps of Sobibor, Treblinka and Belzec.

Organized resistance to Hitler was, it has to be said, extraordinarily difficult for anti-Nazi Austrians, given the level of collaboration among their fellow citizens, and the efficient way in which the Nazis had wiped out the potential leadership. Aside from individual acts of heroism, there was very little significant non-Communist resistance within Austria. Partisan activity was restricted to a few remote alpine areas, and it wasn't until the spring of 1944 that an organized home resistance, codenamed 05, began to emerge.

Unlike every other Nazi-occupied country, however, the Austrians had no official government-in-exile. Exiled Austrian politicians spent their time bickering, split between an unlikely alliance between the son of the last emperor, Otto von Habsburg, and the Communists, and the two mainstream political parties. The most positive diplomatic step took place in November 1943, when the Allied powers published the Moscow Declaration stating that Austria was a "victim" of Nazi aggression and that it should be re-established as a "free and democratic state".

The liberation of Vienna

Vienna itself remained relatively free from direct contact with the war until 1944, when Allied bombing raids intensified. Over the next fourteen months, they were responsible for the deaths of some 9000 Viennese civilians. Among the most important buildings hit were the Staatsoper, the Belvedere, the Burgtheater, Schönbrunn, the Rathaus, Parlament and the Universität; Stephansdom fell victim to Soviet artillery in the last few days of the city's liberation.

By April 5, 1945, the Red Army had reached the very outskirts of the city. The 05 leadership under Major Szokoll had planned to initiate an uprising against the Nazis the very next day, but were betrayed by a junior officer, Lieutenant Walter Hanslick. Several of the 05 leaders were arrested, tortured and publicly hung. The revolt had failed and it took the Russians another three days to reach the Gürtel, and another five days' street fighting to finally win control of the city.

The commander-in-chief of the Russian troops in Austria, Marshal Tolbukhin, gave his assurances that the Soviets would liberate the country, respect the social order and refrain from appropriating any territory. In reality, Soviet troops spent much of the next few months raping Austrian women and stealing anything they could find. The actions of the Red Army during this period gave rise to the grim Viennese joke that Austria could probably survive a third world war, but it could never endure a second liberation.

Allied Occupation (1945–55)

On April 27, the Soviets sponsored the formation of a provisional government under the veteran Social Democrat Karl Renner, causing widespread alarm about Soviet intentions among the western Allies. Although Renner's cabinet was made up, for the most part, of Socialists and members of the newly founded right-wing People's Party or VPÖ, the Communists were given three posts, including the key positions of Interior Minister and Education and Information Minister. As a form of protest at this unilateral action, the western Allies refused to recognize the Renner government.

Meanwhile, there was continuing confusion over the occupation zones. Although the Moscow Declaration had stated that Austria was a victim of Nazi aggression, the country was nevertheless to be divided just like Germany, with Vienna, like Berlin, lying deep within the Russian sector. However, controversy over the exact zoning of Vienna helped delay the arrival of western troops in the capital until late August. The Russians took the opportunity of fleecing the capital and eastern Austria of all they could. Vienna, it was agreed, was to be divided between the four Allies, with the Innere Stadt preserved as an international sector, patrolled by one representative of each of the occupying powers. This comical sight on the streets of Vienna became the hallmark of the so-called "four-in-a-jeep" period – and the setting for the famous film The Third Man – when, as Karl Renner put it, Vienna was a like a small rowing boat in which four elephants sat at the oars pulling in various directions.

Elections and de-Nazification

In October the western Allies finally recognized the Renner government, and the Russians, for their part, agreed to free elections. However, whatever hopes they might have had of the Communists gaining power in Austria were

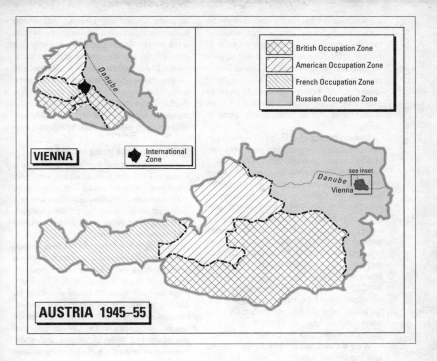

Legend:
- British Occupation Zone
- American Occupation Zone
- French Occupation Zone
- Russian Occupation Zone

VIENNA — International Zone

Danube

see inset
Danube
Vienna

AUSTRIA 1945–55

dashed by the results of the November 1945 elections. The Communists won a derisory 5.4 percent of the vote, up from their previous high of 1.9 percent in 1932, but earning them just four seats in the 165-seat parliament, and the consolation prize of the Ministry of Electrification. In an almost exact repeat of the election results of the 1920s, the country remained split down the middle between Left and Right. Although the ÖVP won almost fifty percent of the vote, it was Renner who headed the new coalition government of the Socialist Party (SPÖ) and the ÖVP.

One of the most pressing and controversial tasks of the postwar era was the de-Nazification process. Initially, this was the responsibility of the Allied powers: the Americans and the British busied themselves by handing out forms in which the respondents were invited to confess; the French, with collaborators of their own back home, were less keen to get involved; the Russians, predictably, were the most assiduous,

though they were as concerned to remove political opponents as ex-Nazis. Of the half a million Austrians who were Nazi party members, only a handful were executed at Nürnberg (for crimes committed outside of Austria); Schirach was given twenty years. Back in Austria itself, the government took over the de-Nazification process, condemning 38 Nazis to death, and depriving the rest of their civil rights for a brief period before an amnesty was agreed in 1948. Some attempt was made to rid the state bureaucracy of its ex-Nazis, but inevitably many – including Eichmann himself who fled to South America – slipped through the net.

Communist agitation

When the Red Army liberated Vienna in April 1945, few people thought that the city and the country would remain under Allied occupation for ten years. However, the Soviets were keen to pay back the Austrians for their mass participation in the Nazi armed forces. At the postwar Potsdam conference, the Soviets were granted, instead of cash reparations for war damage, the right to all external German assets in eastern Austria. Over the next ten years, the Russians took this as a *carte blanche* to asset-strip the entire region of eastern Austria, transporting factories piece by piece back to the Soviet Union, and all in all reaping some half a billion dollars' worth of assets.

Soviet control of eastern Austria – the country's agricultural heartland – also gave them considerable political leverage. With the entire country suffering chronic food shortages, the Soviets deliberately hoarded supplies from their sector, supplying them direct to workers in Soviet-run industries. This won them considerable support in the eastern zone, and increased unrest in the western zones. For despite the Communists' electoral setback, the Russians still had hopes of taking control of Austria. The winter of 1946–47 was particularly harsh, and the Communists took advantage of this by fomenting food riots in May 1947. The rioters besieged the Austrian chancellery and called for a national strike. In the end, the putsch failed, because the Socialist trade union leaders refused to support the strike, and the Russians held back from using military force.

While Marshall Plan aid from the west helped ease conditions throughout Austria from the summer of 1947 onwards, the Communist coup in Czechoslovakia in February 1948 and the Berlin blockade (June 1948–May 1949) only increased political tensions. Despite their recent setbacks, the Communists had high hopes for the national elections of October 1949. However, though the ruling coalition lost ground, it wasn't to the Communists, who remained on a derisory 5 percent, but to the newly formed extreme right-wing Union of Independents (VdU), who scored 11.6 percent of the vote, attracting the support of the majority of ex-Nazi Party members, who had recently been given back their voting rights.

In the autumn of 1950, Marshall Plan aid was cut back drastically. With the Austrian government forced to increase sharply the price of food, coal and electricity, strikes broke out among workers in cities across Austria. Seizing the moment, the Communists staged their second and most serious coup attempt. Once again, it began with a Communist-inspired mass demonstration outside the chancellery, after which barricades were erected, roads blocked, tram tracks

cemented up and bus windows broken. The Russians stopped police reinforcements in their sector from being called up, and it was only with great difficulty that the situation was kept under control. In the end, however, the Socialist trade unions and the government took sufficient steps to stem the tide, and the general strike held on October 4, though heeded by large numbers of workers in the Russian sectors of the city and eastern Austria, was called off the following day.

The Austrian State Treaty of 1955

The withdrawal of the four Allied powers from Austria in 1955 – or more specifically the Soviet withdrawal – was something of a unique event in the otherwise grim history of the Cold War. And something of a surprise, given the previously unscrupulous behaviour of the Soviets in Austria (and elsewhere in Europe).

For nearly ten years negotiations over a peace treaty with Austria were at stalemate, with the Soviets insisting that a German peace treaty be prerequisite to an Austrian treaty. The Soviet threat over the future of Austria was used by them to try and forestall German rearmament. However, with the establishment of the Federal Republic of Germany in 1949, it was clear that this policy had failed. A struggle within the Kremlin then ensued over Soviet policy towards Austria. Following the death of Stalin, this struggle intensified and was eventually won by Krushchev, who decided to use the Austrian State Treaty as a way of initiating a period of détente.

Other factors influenced Soviet policy. Hopes of creating a Communist Austria had died with the failure of the 1950 putsch. The Soviet sector meanwhile had been bled dry and was no longer of any great economic benefit. A neutral Austria, on the other hand, created a convenient buffer that split NATO's northern and southern flanks. And so on May 15, 1955, the Austrian State Treaty or *Staatsvertrag* was signed by the four powers in Vienna's Belvedere (see p.157). The Austrian chancellor, Leopold Figl, waved the treaty triumphantly from the balcony and over half a million Austrians celebrated in the streets of the capital.

1955–83: consensus politics

With the popular vote split between Left and Right, the two main parties of the ÖVP and the

SPÖ formed a succession of coalitions which lasted until 1966. To avoid repeating the mistakes of the past, and to placate the occupying powers, a system of *Proporz* was established, whereby each party shared equally every governmental and state post. In some ways institutionalized political corruption, this process began at the top among the ministries, and continued right down to the local post office. At the same time, various special bodies or chambers representing the various interest groups – the Chamber of Trade, the Chamber of Labour and so on – were established. Like *Proporz*, these new institutions ensured that the country enjoyed an unprecedented period of political and social stability, but left the parliament without an effective opposition and created a system open to widespread abuse. Like the Germans, though, the Austrians enjoyed a period of economic growth and prosperity, and there were few voices of complaint.

In the elections of 1966, the People's Party at last achieved an absolute majority and formed the first one-party government of the postwar era. Many Austrians feared a repeat of the 1920s, but in practice little changed. The system of *Proporz* and the institutions of the corporate state continued to hand out "jobs for the boys", and only at the very top level of government were the Socialists excluded from power. Their turn came, though, in 1970, when a slight economic downturn gave the SPÖ overall victory, followed by an outright majority in elections the following year. Under the chancellorship of Bruno Kreisky, the Socialists enjoyed thirteen years of power, during which Kreisky carried the SPÖ further away from their radical Marxist past than ever before. The end came in the elections of 1983 when the SPÖ lost its overall majority and was forced into a coalition government with, of all people, the far-right Freedom Party (FPÖ).

The Waldheim affair

Having struggled to make the headlines of the international press in the 1960s and 1970s, Austria was catapulted on to the world media stage in 1986 during the campaign for the Austrian presidency. The candidate for the VPÖ was Kurt Waldheim, a figure of some international stature who had been UN Secretary-General for ten years (1972–82). However, during the campaign, Waldheim's war record was called

into question. From the summer of 1942 until the end of the war, he had served as a lieutenant in the Balkans with the German Army. Waldheim was never a member of the Nazi Party (one of the initial charges) and there was never any clear evidence that he was directly involved in the atrocities committed by the army in the Balkans, though he was formally charged with (but never tried for) war crimes by the Yugoslavs after the war. What was more difficult to believe, however, was his claim that he had no knowledge of the deportation of Greek Jews to the death camps, despite being an interpreter for the Italian Army in Greece for much of the war.

To the dismay of many around the world, these charges, albeit unproven, did Waldheim's candidacy no harm at all domestically, and he was duly elected to the Austrian presidency with 54 percent of the vote. The international campaign against Waldheim began with the boycott of his swearing-in ceremony by the US ambassador, and culminated in his being put on the US Department of Justice's "Watch List" of undesirable aliens. Waldheim – and by association Austria – became an international pariah, restricted in his state visits to Arab countries. At Waldheim's suggestion, a commission was set up to investigate the charges against him; however, far from exonerating him, the commission's report found him guilty of "proximity to legally incriminating acts and orders", a somewhat wooly phrase that could be applied to just about any Austrian who'd served in the German Army. The British government, meanwhile, followed up the Yugoslav charge that Waldheim had been involved in war crimes against British commandoes in the Balkans. The British enquiry concluded that Waldheim's rank was too junior to have had any influence over the fate of the commandoes, adding that "knowledge is not itself a crime".

The political present

As if the Waldheim affair were not bad enough, the country has also had to contend with the rise of the far right FPÖ under their charismatic leader Jörg Haider. In his first stab at the polls, in 1986, Haider won nearly ten percent of the vote, frightening the two main parties back into the grand SPÖ-ÖVP coalition of the postwar years under the Socialist Franz Vranitzky. Unfortunately, this has only played into Haider's hands, increasing popular resentment against the system of *Proporz* (from which the FPÖ is excluded) and thus boosting support for the FPÖ.

Haider has also exploited many Austrians' fears over the country's new wave of immigrants, who have arrived from the former eastern bloc and war-torn Yugoslavia in considerable numbers in the 1990s. The final straw, though, for many Austrians has been the country's entry into the European Union in 1994. Although in a referendum sixty percent voted in favour of joining, the austerity measures the country is now having to implement have convinced many that it was the wrong decision.

In the national elections in 1994 and 1995, popular dissatisfaction was publicly registered with Haider's FPÖ taking a staggering 22 percent of the vote, behind the ÖVP, with 28 percent, and

the Socialists on 38 percent. The biggest shock, though, was in Vienna, where the SPÖ lost its overall majority for the first time in the city's history, with the FPÖ receiving 27 percent of the vote and becoming the main opposition in the Rathaus, ahead of the ÖVP.

The postwar Austrian republic appears to have overcome the crisis of national identity that plagued the inter-war republic, although celebrations over the country's spurious millennium (see p.313) in 1996 were decidedly muted. The country has also moved away from the polarized politics First Republic in favour of consensus, but the rise of FPÖ looks set to upset this cosy set-up, with Haider setting his sights on the presidential elections in 1998. It remains to be seen as to whether Vranitzky's successor as chancellor, Viktor Klima, can reverse his party's decline in the polls.

Books

There's a bevy of books in print about the Habsburgs and various aspects of Vienna's glorious past, but precious little written in English about the city in the twentieth century – hence the rather uneven selection below. We've chosen mostly books that are currently in print, plus a few classics that you might pick up in second-hand bookshops.

History, Culture and Journals

Ilsa Barea *Vienna: Legend and Reality* (Pimlico). Magisterial overview, by Vienna-born émigré, concentrating mostly on culture and society from Baroque times until the end of the Habsburgs .

Stephen Brook *The Double Eagle* (Picador). Taking their shared Habsburg tradition as a starting point, Brook explores the three main cities of the former empire – Vienna, Budapest and Prague – in the 1980s and produces a thoroughly readable and very personal travel journal.

Gordon Brook-Shepherd *The Austrians* (Harper Collins). Readable, if a little over-earnest history – the author refers to himself several times in the third person – which attempts to trace the Austrian-ness (or lack of it) in the country's history from the Babenbergs to entry into the EU in 1994. Brook-Shepherd draws on his experience as a *Telegraph* correspondent and as someone who worked in the Allied High Commission in Vienna after World War II.

George Clare *Last Waltz in Vienna; the destruction of a family 1842–1942* (Macmillan). Incredibly moving – and far from bitter – autobi-ographical account of a Jewish upbringing in inter-war Vienna that ended with the Anschluss.

Edward Crankshaw *Vienna: the image of a culture in decline* (Macmillan). Part travel journal, part history, and first published in 1938, this is a nostalgic, but by no means rose-tinted, look at the city from a writer who knew it well.

William M. Johnston *The Austrian Mind. An Intellectual and Social History 1848–1938* (University of California Press). Johnston knows his stuff, and though this is pretty academic stuff, it's a fascinating insight into *fin-de-siècle* Vienna.

Robert A. Kann *History of the Habsburg Empire 1526–1918* (Univeristy of California Press). Weighty and wide-ranging 600-page account of the empire originally written in the 1970s.

Claudio Magris *Danube*, 1989 (Collins Harvill). In this highly readable travel journal from the 1980s, Magris, a wonderfully erudite Trieste-based academic, traces the Danube, passing through Vienna along the way.

Frederic Morton *A Nervous Splendor: Vienna 1888/1889* (Penguin); *Thunder at Twilight: Vienna 1913–1914* (Penguin). Morton has trawled through the newspapers of the time to produce two very readable dramatized accounts of two very critical years in the city's history. The first centres on the Mayerling tragedy; the second revolves around the Sarajevo assassination.

Carl E. Schorske *Fin-de-Siècle Vienna* (CUP). Fascinating scholarly essays on, among other things, the impact of the building of the Ringstrasse, Freud, Klimt, Kokoschka and Schönberg on the city's culture.

A.J.P. Taylor *The Habsburg Monarchy 1809–1918* (Penguin). Readable, forthright and as ever thought-provoking account of the demise of the Habsburgs.

Andrew Wheatcroft, *The Habsburgs* (Penguin). Wheatcroft's intriguing history traces the rise and fall of the Habsburgs from their modest origins in Switzerland to their demise at the head of the Austro-Hungarian empire, concentrating on the family and the way it promoted its dynastic image.

Stefan Zweig *The World of Yesterday* (University of Nebraska Press). Seminal account of *fin-de-siècle* Vienna written just before Zweig was forced into exile in South America by the Nazis where he and his wife committed suicide.

Memoirs and Biography

Richard Appignanesi & Oscar Zarate *Freud for Beginners* (Icon Books). One of the popular entertaining series of cartoon-illustrated beginner's guides to Freud's life and ideas.

Steven Beller *Franz Joseph* (Longman). Shortest and most portable of the books on Franz-Josef; more political than biographical and a bit short on personal history.

Kurt & Herta Blaukopf, *Mahler, his life, work and world* (Thames & Hudson). A selection of letters and quotes by Mahler, plus material by those who knew him.

Jean Paul Bled *Franz Joseph* (Blackwell). Well-rounded account of the old duffer, with a smattering of the sort of scurrilous gossip missing in some other biographies.

Katerina von Burg *Elisabeth of Austria*. Latest biography of the endlessly fascinating empress who was assassinated by an Italian anarchist in 1898.

Edward Crankshaw *Maria Theresa* (Constable). Readable account of the "Virgin Empress", though disappointingly short on light touches.

Peter Gay *Freud* (Papermac). Big tome, a healthy mixture of biography and philosophy, with a bit of spicy drama just for good measure.

Michael Hamburger (ed), *Beethoven, Letters, Journals and Conversations* (Thames & Hudson). Fascinating insight into the great eccentric's brain: a mixture of his correspondence and the notebooks in which he used to get his conversational partners to write.

Joan Haslip *The Emperor and the Actress* (Weidenfeld & Nicolson). Detailed, steamy account of Franz-Josef's relationship with his long-term mistress, the actress Katharina Schratt.

John Heaton & Judy Groves *Wittgenstein for Beginners* (Icon Books). Even this accessible, irreverent series fails to shed much light on the great philosopher's thinking, but it's more fun than the real thing, that's for sure.

Michael Jacobs *Sigmund Freud* (Sage). Brief biography of the bearded one, a quick trot through his ideas and the subsequent criticisms thereof.

Ernest Jones *Life and Work of Sigmund Freud* (Penguin). Abridged version of the definitive three-volume biography that Jones – one of Freud's disciples – published in the 1950s just before he died.

H. C. Robbins Landon *Mozart, the golden years 1781–1791* (Thames & Hudson). Big illustrated romp through the composer's mature Vienna years, a mixture of biography and musicology.

Alan Levy *The Wiesenthal File* (Constable). Thoroughly entertaining account of the controversial Vienna-based Nazi-hunter and the various Nazis he has helped pursue, plus an account of the Waldheim affair.

Ray Monk *Ludwig Wittgenstein: The Duty of Genius* (Vintage). Exhaustive account of the life of Vienna's perplexing philosopher, whose life is a lot more fun than his mathematical formulas.

Alan Palmer *The Twilight of the Habsburgs* and *The Life and Times of the Emperor Francis Joseph* and *Metternich* (both Phoenix). The first is the latest scholarly and somewhat weighty tome on this much-biographied emperor; the latter a solid account of the arch-conservative who ruled the roost in Vienna from 1815 to 1848.

Hella Pick *Wiesenthal*. (Orion) The most recent of the Wiesenthal biographies, its publication coinciding with another controversy over the octogenarian Nazi-hunter.

Alfred Weidinger *Kokoschka and Alma Mahler: testimony to a passionate relationship* (Prestel). Detailed account of the artist's doomed relationship with Mahler's widow, illustrated with lots of Kokoschka's drawings and paintings from the period.

Austrian Fiction

Elfriede Jelinek *The Piano Teacher* and *Wonderful Wonderful Times* (both Serpent's Tail). From one the best writers to come out of Austria for some time, *The Piano Teacher* is an unsentimental look at Vienna from a woman's perspective, while *Wonderful Wonderful Times*, which takes place in the late 1950s, digs up the city's murky past.

Heinrich Mann *Man of Straw* (Penguin). Masterpiece of a now little-read writer, anatomizing the hypocrisies of *fin-de-siècle* Vienna in a manner more direct than the fiction of his famous older brother, Thomas.

Robert Musil *The Man Without Qualities* (Picador). Often compared with Joyce and Proust's great works, Musil's 1000-page unfinished novel takes place at the twilight of the empire, and was newly translated for this Picador edition.

Josef Roth *Radetsky March* (Penguin). The pitifully underrated Roth's finest work – a nostalgic and melancholic portrait of the moribund Vienna of Franz-Josef. Check also the second-hand stores for his masterful brief novels *Job*, *The Emperor's Tomb* and – above all – *Flight Without End*, a heartbreaking tale of dislocation and worldweariness.

Arthur Schnitzler *Hands Around* (Dover Publications). Schnitzler's play features ten seductions each of which shares at least one character with the next one until the circle is complete. A classic portrayal of Viennese decadent *fin-de-siècle* society, it came back to prominence in the 1950s after being filmed as *La Ronde* by Max Ophüls

Harold B. Segel (ed), *The Vienna Coffeehouse Wits 1890–1938* (Purdue University Press). A rare opportunity to read translated snippets of work by *Kaffeehaus* regulars such as Karl Kraus, Peter Altenberg and Felix Salten (the little-known author of *Bambi* and *The Story of a Vienna Whore*, one of which was made into a Disney cartoon).

Literature by Foreign Writers

Richard & John Lehmann Bassett, *Vienna, a travellers' companion* (Constable). Out of print but, if you can get hold of it, it features some interesting travellers' impressions from over the centuries.

John Irving *Setting Free the Bears* (Black Swan). Stream-of-verbiage novel centred (vaguely) on Vienna's zoo after the war.

Philip Kerr *A German Requiem* (Penguin). Last volume of a gripping spy trilogy set in postwar Vienna.

Mary Stewart *Airs Above the Ground* (Coronet). Murder mystery written in the 1960s and set in and around Vienna's Spanish Riding School.

Art and Photography

Gabriele Fahr-Becker *Wiener Werkstätte 1903–1932* (Taschen). The definitive volume on the WW, with lots of colour and black and white illustrations showing the enormous breadth of its output.

Hans Bisanz *Vienna 1900* (Berghaus Verlag). Full of colour reproductions of drawings and paintings from turn-of-the-century Secession artists.

Peter Haiko and Roberto Schezen *Vienna 1850–1930 Architecture* (Rizzoli). The ultimate coffee-table book on Vienna's most important works of architecture, beautifully photographed (by Schezen) and intelligently discussed.

Ingrid Helsing Almaas *Vienna; a guide to recent architecture* (Artemis). Dinky little illustrated pocket guide to Vienna's modern architecture of the last decade or so, with forthright accompanying critiques and interviews.

Robert Lustenberger *Adolf Loos* (Artemis). One of Artemis's Studio Paperback series, cheaper than Schezen's (see below), with more text and black-and-white photos only.

Roberto Schezen *Adolf Loos Architecture 1903–32* (Monacelli Press). Beautiful colour and black-and-white photos of Loos's major works in Vienna and elsewhere.

Patrick Werkner *Austrian Expressionism: the formative years* (SPOSS). Black-and-white illustrations only, but interesting articles on Schönberg, Schiele, Kokoschka, Gerstl and Kubin.

Language

Although a high proportion of Austrians speak some English, any attempts at learning a few phrases of **German** will be heartily appreciated. That said, German is a highly complex language which you can't hope to master quickly. The biggest problem for English-speakers is that German words can be one of three genders: masculine, feminine or neuter. Each has its own ending and corresponding ending for attached adjectives, plus its own definite article. If in doubt, it's safest to use either the neuter or male forms. Pronunciation (and spelling) is less of a problem, as individual syllables are generally pronounced as they're printed – the trick is learning how to place the stresses in the notoriously lengthy German words. Though Austrians speak German with a distinct accent, and the Viennese have their own dialect, when speaking to a foreigner most folk will switch to standard German.

The following is a rundown of the basics you'll need on a city break to Vienna. For more detail, check out the *Rough Guide German phrasebook*, set out dictionary-style for easy access, with English-German and German-English sections, cultural tips for tricky situations and a menu reader.

VOWELS AND UMLAUTS

a as in r**a**ther

e as in g**ay**

i as in f**ee**t

o as in n**o**se

u as in b**oo**t

ä is a combination of a and e, sometimes pronounced like **e** in b**e**t (eg Länder) and sometimes like **ai** in p**ai**d (eg spät).

ö is a combination of o and e, like the French *eu*

ü is a combination of u and e, like bl**ue**

VOWEL COMBINATIONS

ai as in d**ie**

au as in m**ou**se

ie as in tr**ee**

ei as in tr**ia**l

eu as in b**oi**l

CONSONANTS

Consonants are pronounced as they are written, with no silent letters. The differences from English are:

j pronounced similar to an English y

r is given a dry throaty sound, similar to French

s pronounced similar to, but slightly softer than an English z

v pronounced somewhere between f and v

w pronounced same way as English v

z pronounced ts.

The German letter β usually replaces ss in a word: pronunciation is identical.

ch is a strong back-of-the-throat sound as in the Scottish loch

sp (at the start of a word) is pronounced shp

st (at the start of a word) is pronounced sht

GERMAN WORDS AND PHRASES

Basics

Ja, Nein	Yes, No	*Jenes*	That one
Bitte	Please/ You're welcome	*Gross, Klein*	Large, small
Bitte schön	A more polite form of *Bitte*	*Mehr, Weniger*	More, less
		Wenig	A little
Danke, Danke schön	Thank you, Thank you very much	*Viel*	A lot
		Billig, Teuer	Cheap, expensive
Wo, Wann, Warum?	Where, when, why?	*Gut, Schlecht*	Good, bad
Wieviel?	How much?	*Heiss, Kalt*	Hot, cold
Hier, Da	Here, There	*Mit, Ohne*	With, without
Geöffnet, Offen, Auf	All mean "open"	*Rechts*	Right
Geschlossen, Zu	Both mean "closed"	*Links*	Left
Da drüben	Over there	*Gerade aus*	Straight ahead
Dieses	This one		

Greetings and Times

Grüss Got	Good day	*Vorgestern*	The day before yesterday
Guten Morgen	Good morning		
Guten Abend	Good evening	*Übermorgen*	The day after tomorrow
Gute Nacht	Good night	*Tag*	Day
Auf Wiedersehen	Goodbye	*Nacht*	Night
Auf Wiederhören	Goodbye (on the telephone)	*Mittag*	Midday
		Mitternacht	Midnight
Tschüs	Goodbye (informal)	*Woche*	Week
Wie geht es Ihnen?	How are you? (polite)	*Wochenende*	Weekend
Wie geht es dir?	How are you? (informal)	*Monat*	Month
Geh weg	Go away	*Jahr*	Year
Heute	Today	*Am Vormittag/ Vormittags*	In the morning
Gestern	Yesterday		
Morgen	Tomorrow	*Am Nachmittag/ Nachmittags*	In the afternoon
		Am Abend	In the evening

Days, Months and Dates

Montag	Monday	*September*	September
Dienstag	Tuesday	*Oktober*	October
Mittwoch	Wednesday	*November*	November
Donnerstag	Thursday	*Dezember*	December
Freitag	Friday	*Frühling*	Spring
Samstag	Saturday	*Sommer*	Summer
Sonntag	Sunday	*Herbst*	Autumn
Januar	January	*Winter*	Winter
Februar	February	*Ferien*	Holidays
März	March	*Feiertag*	Bank holiday
April	April	*Montag, der erste April*	Monday, the first of April
Mai	May		
Juni	June	*Der zweite April*	The second of April
Juli	July	*Der dritte April*	the third of April
August	August		

continued overleaf

Some Signs

Damen/Frauen	Women's toilets	*Notausgang*	Emergency exit
Herren/Männer	Men's toilets	*Krankenhaus*	Hospital
Eingang	Entrance	*Polizei*	Police
Ausgang	Exit	*Nicht rauchen*	No smoking
Ankunft	Arrival	*Kein Eingang*	No entrance
Abfahrt	Departure	*Drücken*	Push
Ausstellung	Exhibition	*Ziehen*	Pull
Autobahn	Motorway	*Frei*	Vacant
Umleitung	Diversion	*Besetzt*	Occupied
Achtung!	Attention!	*Verboten*	Prohibited
Vorsicht!	Beware!	*Kasse*	Cash desk/ticket office
Not	Emergency		

Questions and Requests

All enquiries should start with the phrase *Entschuldigen Sie bitte* (Excuse me, please). Though strictly you should use *Sie*, the polite form of address, with everyone except close friends, young people often don't bother with it. However, the older generation and anyone official will certainly be offended if you address them with the familiar *Du*.

Sprechen Sie Englisch?	Do you speak English?	*Die Rechnung bitte*	The bill please
		Ist der Tisch frei?	Is that table free?
Ich spreche kein Deutsch	I don't speak German	*Die Speisekarte bitte*	The menu please
Sprechen Sie bitte langsamer	Please speak more slowly	*Fräulein . . .!*	Waitress . . . ! (for attention)
Ich verstehe nicht	I don't understand	*Herr Ober . . .!*	Waiter . . . ! (for attention)
Ich verstehe	I understand		
Wie sagt mann das auf Deutsch?	How do you say that in German?	*Haben Sie etwas billigeres?*	Have you got something cheaper?
Können Sie mir sagen wo . . . ist?	Can you tell me where . . . is?	*Haben Sie Zimmer frei?*	Are there rooms available?
Wo ist . . .?	Where is . . .?	*Wo sind die Toiletten bitte?*	Where are the toilets?
Wieviel kostet das?	How much does that cost?	*Ich hätte gern dieses*	I'd like that one
Wann fährt der nächste Zug?	When does the next train leave?	*Ich hätte gern ein Zimmer für zwei*	I'd like a room for two
Um wieviel Uhr?	At what time?	*Ich hätte gern ein Einzelzimmer*	I'd like a single room
Wieviel Uhr ist es?	What time is it?		
Sind die Plätze noch frei?	Are these seats taken?	*Hat es Dusche, Bad, Toilette . . .?*	Does it have a shower, bath, toilet . . .?

Numbers

0	*null*	10	*zehn*	20	*zwanzig*	90	*neunzig*
1	*eins*	11	*elf*	21	*ein-und-zwanzig*	100	*hundert*
2	*zwei*	12	*zwölf*	22	*zwei-und-zwanzig*	1000	*tausend*
3	*drei*	13	*dreizehn*	30	*dreissig*	1997	*neunzehn-hundert-sieben-und-neunzig*
4	*vier*	14	*vierzehn*	40	*vierzig*		
5	*fünf*	15	*fünfzehn*	50	*fünfzig*		
6	*sechs*	16	*sechszehn*	60	*sechzig*	1998	*neunzehn-hundert-acht-und-neunzig*
7	*sieben*	17	*siebzehn*	70	*siebzig*		
8	*acht*	18	*achtzehn*	80	*achtzig*		
9	*neun*	19	*neunzehn*				

Glossary

German terms

Ausstellung Exhibition.

Bahnhof Station.

Bau Building.

Beisl Pub.

Berg Mountain, hill.

Bezirk City district.

Brücke Bridge.

Brünn Brno, capital of Moravia (Czech Republic).

Brunnen Fountain.

Burg Castle.

Denkmal Memorial.

Donau River Danube.

Dom Cathedral.

Dorf Village.

Durchgang Passageway.

Durchhaus Literally a "through-house" – a house whose ground floor is open, allowing access to a street or courtyard.

Einbahnstrasse One-way street.

Erzherzog Archduke.

Fasching Carnival.

Feiertag Holiday.

Flughafen Airport.

Friedhof Cemetery.

Fussgängerzone Pedestrian zone.

Gasse Alley.

Gemälde Painting.

Gemütlich Snug or cosy.

Grab Grave.

Gürtel The city's outer ring road.

Haltestelle Bus/tram stop.

Haus House.

Herzog Duke.

Heuriger Wine tavern.

Hof Court, courtyard, mansion, housing complex.

Innere Stadt Vienna's first district, the "Inner City".

Jugendherberge Youth hostel.

Kaffeehaus Café.

Kaiser Emperor.

Kapelle Chapel.

Kärnten Carinthia.

Kaserne Barracks.

Kino Cinema.

Kirche Church.

Kloster Monastery, convent.

König King.

Kunst Art.

Kunstkammer Cabinet of curios.

Land (pl Länder) Name given to each of the nine federal provinces of Austria.

Niederösterreich Lower Austria.

Not Emergency.

Oberösterreich Upper Austria.

Palast Palace.

Platz Square.

Prinz Prince.

Pressburg Bratislava, capital of Slovakia.

Rathaus Town hall.

Reich Empire.

Residenz Palace.

Ring The Ringstrasse, built on the old fortifications in 1857.

Ritter Knight.

Saal Hall.

Sammlung Collection.

Säule Column.

Schanigarten Summer terrace/backyard.

Schatzkammer Treasury.

Schloss Castle.

Stadt Town.

Steiermark Styria.

Stift Collegiate church.

Strasse Street.

Tor Gate.

Trakt Wing (of a building).

Turm Tower.

Viertel Quarter, district.

Volk People, folk.

Vororte The outer suburbs which lie beyond the Gürtel: Vienna's tenth to twenty-second districts.

Vorstädte The inner suburbs which lie between the Ring and the Gürtel: Vienna's third to ninth districts.

Wald Forest.

Wien Vienna.

Zimmer Room.

Political terms and acronyms

Anschluss Literally a "joining together" or "union" – the euphemism coined by the Nazis for the invasion and annexation of Austria in March 1938.

Austro-fascism Term to describe the one-party state set up by Engelbert Dollfuss in 1934. Dollfuss headed the Fatherland Front, a non-Nazi clerical-fascist movement which lasted until the Anschluss in 1938.

Austro-Marxism Philosophy expounded by SDAP theorists such as Otto Bauer in the early twentieth century. While still adhering to the language of class war, its programme was essentailly revisionist, arguing that the downfall of capitalism was inevitable, and didn't have to be brought about by violence.

Babenburgs Dynasty who ruled over Austria from 976–1246.

Biedermeier The term (*Bieder* means "upright") derives from the satiric figure of Gottlieb Biedermeier, a Swabian schoolmaster created in 1850 by Ludwig Eichrocht, modelled on Eichrocht's own pious, law-abiding teacher in Baden-Baden, Samuel Sauter. It has come to be applied retrospectively to the period between 1815 and 1848 when Austria was under the sway of Prince Metternich. The era came to symbolize a safe, bourgeois, cosy lifestyle, and was applied to the history, art and culture of the period.

CSP (Christlichsoziale Partei) The Christian Social Party was founded in the 1890s by Karl Lueger, who later became Mayor of Vienna. The Christian Socials' combination of Catholicism, municipal socialism and anti-semitism proved very popular with the Austrians. They were the main party of government in the 1920s and from their ranks rose Engelbert Dollfuss, who later introduced Austro-fascism in 1933.

FPÖ (Freiheitliche Partei Österreichs) The Austrian Freedom Party was the successor to the postwar VdU (see below). A far-right party who rose to prominence in the 1980s and scored spectacular electoral success under the charismatic and controversial leadership of Jörg Haider.

Habsburg Royal dynasty whose powerbase was Vienna from 1273 to 1918. They also held the office of Holy Roman Emperor from 1452 to 1806, and by marriage, war and diplomacy acquired territories all over Europe.

Heimwehr Right-wing militia whose origins lay in the local armed groups formed after the collapse of the empire in 1918. After 1927, these regional militias joined together and created a political wing, the *Heimatblock*, which supported the onset of Austro-fascism in 1933.

Holy Roman Empire Revived title of the Roman Empire first bestowed by the Pope on Charlemagne in 800. The emperor was chosen by the seven electors and passed around between the Hohenstaufen, Luxembourg and Habsburg families until 1438, when the Habsburgs made the title hereditary. It was dissolved on the orders of Napoleon in 1806.

Josephine Of or pertaining to the reign of Emperor Josef II (1780–1790).

KPÖ (Kommunistische Partei Österreichs) Austrian Communist Party.

Kristallnacht Literally "Crystal Night", after the broken glass which was strewn across the streets during the pogrom of November 9–10, 1938. On this one night the majority of Jewish shops and institutions in the Third Reich – and all but one of the synagogues in Vienna – were destroyed by the Nazis.

k.u.k. kaiserlich und königlich; (Imperial and Royal) – a title used after 1867 to refer to everything in the Austro-Hungarian empire. Everything within Hungary was prefaced with a **k** for königlich, everything in the rest of the empire **K. K.** (kaiserlich-königlich; Imperial-Royal). For more details, see p.320.

NSDAP (National Sozialistiche Deutsche Arbeiterpartei) National Socialist German Workers' Party, the official name for the German Nazi Party.

ÖVP (Österreichische Volkspartei) Austrian People's Party, the postwar descendant of the Christian Socials.

Pan-German This adjective covers a whole range of far-right political parties, who advocated

Anschluss with Germany, many of whom came together in the 1920s under the banner of the Greater German People's Party (Grossdeutsche Volkspartei, GDVP).

Red Vienna The period of Socialist municipal government in Vienna which lasted from 1919 to 1934.

Schutzbund SDAP militia founded in 1923.

SDAP (Sozial-Demokratische Arbeiterpartei) Social Democratic Workers' Party, the name given to the Socialist Party, prior to World War II.

SPÖ (Sozialistische Partei Österreichs) The post-war Austrian Socialist Party, later changed to the Sozialdemokratische Partei Österreichs, but keeping the same acronym.

Staatsvertrag The Austrian State Treaty of 1955, which signalled the withdrawal of Allied troops – American, British, French and Soviet – from Austria, in return for Austrian neutrality.

Toleranzpatent The Patent of Tolerance decreed by Josef II in 1782 which allowed freedom of religious observance to Lutherans, Jews and, to a lesser extent, Protestants.

VdU (Verband der Unabhängigen) Union of Independents. Extreme nationalist party formed in 1949 and precursor of the FPÖ.

VF (Vaterländische Front) The Fatherland Front were founded in 1934 by Engelbert Dollfuss, the Christian Social Austrian chancellor who dissolved parliament and introduced Austro-fascism in 1933. The Front was a patriotic, clerico-fascist organization aimed at preventing the Nazis from seizing power.

Architectural terms

Ambulatory Passage round the back of a church altar, in continuation of the aisles.

Art Nouveau Sinuous and stylized form of architecture and decorative arts, known as Secession or Jugendstil in Austria.

Atlantes Pillars in the shape of muscle men, named after the Greek god Atlas whose job it was to hold up the world.

Baldachin A canopy over an altar, tomb, throne or otherwise.

Baroque Expansive, exuberant architectural style of the seventeenth and eighteenth centuries, characterized by ornate decoration, complex spatial arrangement and grand vistas.

Biedermeier Simple, often Neoclassical, style of art and architecture popular from 1815 to 1848 (see also opposite) and in part a reaction against the excesses of the Baroque period.

Caryatid Female version of Atlantes (see above).

Chancel Part of the church where the main altar is placed, usually at the east end.

Diapers Ornamental patterning in brickwork.

Empire Neoclassical style of architecture and decorative arts practised in the first half of the nineteenth century.

Filigree Fanciful delicate ornamental decoration in stone or metal.

Fresco Mural painting applied to wet plaster, so that the colours immediately soak into the wall.

Glacis Sloping ground between walls of Vienna's Innere Stadt and the suburbs prior to 1857.

Gothic Architectural style prevalent from the twelfth to the sixteenth centuries, characterized by pointed arches and ribbed vaulting.

Historicism Style of architecture which apes previous styles – ie neo-Baroque, neo-Renaissance, neo-Gothic – also known as Ringstrasse style.

Jugendstil German/Austrian version of Art Nouveau, literally "youthful style" – see also Secession, below.

Loggia Covered area on the side of a building, usually arcaded.

Lunette An oval or semi-circular opening to admit light into a dome.

Nave Main body of a church, usually the western end.

Neoclassicism Late eighteenth- and early nineteenth-century style of architecture and design returning to classical Greek and Roman models as a reaction against the excess of Baroque and Rococo.

Oriel A bay window, usually projecting from an upper floor.

Quoins External corner stones of a wall.

Ringstrasse Pompous historicist style of architecture which aped Gothic, Renaissance, Baroque and Classical architecture, and which was very popular during the construction of Vienna's Ringstrasse.

Rococo Highly florid style of architecture and design, forming the last phase of Baroque.

Romanesque Solid architectural style of the late tenth to thirteenth centuries, characterized by round-headed arches and geometrical precision.

Secession Movement of artists who split (seceded – hence the term) from the city's Academy of Arts in 1897. Also used more generally as a term synonymous with Art Nouveau and Jugendstil.

Sgraffito Monochrome plaster decoration effected by means of scraping back the first white layer to reveal the black underneath.

Spandrel The surface area between two adjacent arches.

Stucco Plaster used for decorative effects.

Transepts The wings of a cruciform church, placed at right angles to the nave and chancel.

Trompe l'oeil Painting designed to fool the onlooker into thinking that it is three dimensional.

Wiener Werkstätte (Vienna Workshops) A group of Secession artists founded in 1903.

Index

direct orders from

Amsterdam	1-85828-218-7	£8.99	US$14.95	CAN$19.99
Andalucia	1-85828-219-5	9.99	16.95	22.99
Australia	1-85828-141-5	12.99	19.95	25.99
Bali	1-85828-134-2	8.99	14.95	19.99
Barcelona	1-85828-221-7	8.99	14.95	19.99
Berlin	1-85828-129-6	8.99	14.95	19.99
Belgium & Luxembourg	1-85828-222-5	10.99	17.95	23.99
Brazil	1-85828-102-4	9.99	15.95	19.99
Britain	1-85828-208-X	12.99	19.95	25.99
Brittany & Normandy	1-85828-224-1	9.99	16.95	22.99
Bulgaria	1-85828-183-0	9.99	16.95	22.99
California	1-85828-181-4	10.99	16.95	22.99
Canada	1-85828-130-X	10.99	14.95	19.99
China	1-85828-225-X	15.99	24.95	32.99
Corfu	1-85828-226-8	8.99	14.95	19.99
Corsica	1-85828-227-6	9.99	16.95	22.99
Costa Rica	1-85828-136-9	9.99	15.95	21.99
Crete	1-85828-132-6	8.99	14.95	18.99
Cyprus	1-85828-182-2	9.99	16.95	22.99
Czech & Slovak Republics	1-85828-121-0	9.99	16.95	22.99
Egypt	1-85828-188-1	10.99	17.95	23.99
Europe	1-85828-159-8	14.99	19.95	25.99
England	1-85828-160-1	10.99	17.95	23.99
First Time Europe	1-85828-270-5	7.99	9.95	12.99
Florida	1-85828-184-4	10.99	16.95	22.99
France	1-85828-228-4	12.99	19.95	25.99
Germany	1-85828-128-8	11.99	17.95	23.99
Goa	1-85828-156-3	8.99	14.95	19.99
Greece	1-85828-131-8	9.99	16.95	20.99
Greek Islands	1-85828-163-6	8.99	14.95	19.99
Guatemala	1-85828-189-X	10.99	16.95	22.99
Hawaii: Big Island	1-85828-158-X	8.99	12.95	16.99
Hawaii	1-85828-206-3	10.99	16.95	22.99
Holland	1-85828-229-2	10.99	17.95	23.99
Hong Kong	1-85828-187-3	8.99	14.95	19.99
Hungary	1-85828-123-7	8.99	14.95	19.99
India	1-85828-200-4	14.99	23.95	31.99
Ireland	1-85828-179-2	10.99	17.95	23.99
Italy	1-85828-167-9	12.99	19.95	25.99
Kenya	1-85828-192-X	11.99	18.95	24.99
London	1-85828-231-4	9.99	15.95	21.99
Mallorca & Menorca	1-85828-165-2	8.99	14.95	19.99
Malaysia, Singapore & Brunei	1-85828-103-2	9.99	16.95	20.99
Mexico	1-85828-044-3	10.99	16.95	22.99
Morocco	1-85828-040-0	9.99	16.95	21.99
Moscow	1-85828-118-0	8.99	14.95	19.99
Nepal	1-85828-190-3	10.99	17.95	23.99
New York	1-85828-171-7	9.99	15.95	21.99
Norway	1-85828-234-9	10.99	17.95	23.99
Pacific Northwest	1-85828-092-3	9.99	14.95	19.99

In the UK, Rough Guides are available from all good bookstores, but can be obtained from Penguin by contacting: Penguin Direct, Penguin Books Ltd, Bath Road, Harmondsworth, West Drayton, Middlesex UB7 0DA; or telephone the credit line on 0181-899 4036 (9am–5pm) and ask for Penguin Direct. Visa, Access and Amex accepted. Delivery will normally be within 14 working days. Penguin Direct ordering facilities are only available in the UK and the USA. The availability and published prices quoted are correct at the time of going to press but are subject to alteration without prior notice.

around the world

Paris	1-85828-235-7	8.99	14.95	19.99
Poland	1-85828-168-7	10.99	17.95	23.99
Portugal	1-85828-180-6	9.99	16.95	22.99
Prague	1-85828-122-9	8.99	14.95	19.99
Provence	1-85828-127-X	9.99	16.95	22.99
Pyrenees	1-85828-093-1	8.99	15.95	19.99
Rhodes & the Dodecanese	1-85828-120-2	8.99	14.95	19.99
Romania	1-85828-097-4	9.99	15.95	21.99
San Francisco	1-85828-185-7	8.99	14.95	19.99
Scandinavia	1-85828-236-5	12.99	20.95	27.99
Scotland	1-85828-166-0	9.99	16.95	22.99
Sicily	1-85828-178-4	9.99	16.95	22.99
Singapore	1-85828-135-0	8.99	14.95	19.99
Spain	1-85828-240-3	11.99	18.95	24.99
St Petersburg	1-85828-133-4	8.99	14.95	19.99
Sweden	1-85828-241-1	10.99	17.95	23.99
Thailand	1-85828-140-7	10.99	17.95	24.99
Tunisia	1-85828-139-3	10.99	17.95	24.99
Turkey	1-85828-242-X	12.99	19.95	25.99
Tuscany & Umbria	1-85828-243-8	10.99	17.95	23.99
USA	1-85828-161-X	14.99	19.95	25.99
Venice	1-85828-170-9	8.99	14.95	19.99
Vietnam	1-85828-191-1	9.99	15.95	21.99
Wales	1-85828-245-4	10.99	17.95	23.99
Washington DC	1-85828-246-2	8.99	14.95	19.99
West Africa	1-85828-101-6	15.99	24.95	34.99
More Women Travel	1-85828-098-2	10.99	16.95	22.99
Zimbabwe & Botswana	1-85828-186-5	11.99	18.95	24.99

Phrasebooks

Czech	1-85828-148-2	3.50	5.00	7.00
French	1-85828-144-X	3.50	5.00	7.00
German	1-85828-146-6	3.50	5.00	7.00
Greek	1-85828-145-8	3.50	5.00	7.00
Italian	1-85828-143-1	3.50	5.00	7.00
Mexican	1-85828-176-8	3.50	5.00	7.00
Portuguese	1-85828-175-X	3.50	5.00	7.00
Polish	1-85828-174-1	3.50	5.00	7.00
Spanish	1-85828-147-4	3.50	5.00	7.00
Thai	1-85828-177-6	3.50	5.00	7.00
Turkish	1-85828-173-3	3.50	5.00	7.00
Vietnamese	1-85828-172-5	3.50	5.00	7.00

Reference

Classical Music	1-85828-113-X	12.99	19.95	25.99
Internet	1-85828-198-9	5.00	8.00	10.00
Jazz	1-85828-137-7	16.99	24.95	34.99
Opera	1-85828-138-5	16.99	24.95	34.99
Rock	1-85828-201-2	17.99	26.95	35.00
World Music	1-85828-017-6	16.99	22.95	29.99

In the USA, or for international orders, charge your order by Master Card or Visa (US$15.00 minimum order): call 1-800-253-6476; or send orders, with complete name, address and zip code, and list price, plus $2.00 shipping and handling per order to: Consumer Sales, Penguin USA, PO Box 999 – Dept #17109, Bergenfield, NJ 07621. No COD. Prepay foreign orders by international money order, a cheque drawn on a US bank, or US currency. No postage stamps are accepted. All orders are subject to stock availability at the time they are processed. Refunds will be made for books not available at that time. Please allow a minimum of four weeks for delivery.

Good Vibrations!

¿Qué pasa?

WHAT'S HAPPENING?
A NEW ROUGH GUIDES SERIES –
ROUGH GUIDE PHRASEBOOKS

Rough Guide Phrasebooks
represent a complete shakeup of
the phrasebook format.
Handy and pocket sized, they
work like a dictionary to get you
straight to the point. With clear
guidelines on pronunciation,
dialogues for typical situations,
and tips on cultural issues, they'll
have you speaking the language
quicker than any other
phrasebook.

Czech, French, German, Greek,
Hindi, Italian, Indonesian,
Mandarin, Mexican Spanish,
Polish, Portuguese, Russian,
Spanish, Thai, Turkish,
Vietnamese
Further titles coming soon...

Stay in touch with us!

ROUGH*NEWS* is Rough Guides' free newsletter.
In three issues a year we give you news, travel
issues, music reviews, readers' letters and the
latest dispatches from authors on the road.

I would like to receive ROUGH*NEWS*: please put me on your free mailing list.

NAME . . . .

ADDRESS . . . .

Please clip or photocopy and send to: Rough Guides, 1 Mercer Street, London WC2H 9QJ, England
or Rough Guides, 375 Hudson Street, New York, NY 10014, USA.

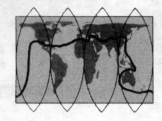

the perfect getaway vehicle

low-price holiday car rental.

rent a car from holiday autos and you'll give yourself real freedom to explore your holiday destination. with great-value, fully-inclusive rates in over 4,000 locations worldwide, wherever you're escaping to, we're there to make sure you get excellent prices and superb service.

what's more, you can book now with complete confidence. our £5 undercut* ensures that you are guaranteed the best value for money in holiday destinations right around the globe.

drive away with a great deal, call holiday autos now on **0990 300 400** and quote ref RG.

holiday autos
miles ahead

*in the unlikely event that you should see a cheaper like for like pre-paid rental rate offered by any other independent uk car rental company before or after booking but prior to departure, holiday autos will undercut that price by a full £5. we truly believe we cannot be beaten on price.